RITUAL MURDER in RUSSIA, EASTERN EUROPE, and BEYOND

RITUAL MURDER
in RUSSIA, EASTERN EUROPE, and BEYOND

*New Histories of
an Old Accusation*

Edited by
EUGENE M. AVRUTIN,
JONATHAN DEKEL-CHEN,
and ROBERT WEINBERG

INDIANA UNIVERSITY PRESS

This book is a publication of

Indiana University Press
Office of Scholarly Publishing
Herman B Wells Library 350
1320 East 10th Street
Bloomington, Indiana 47405 USA

iupress.indiana.edu

© 2017 by Indiana University Press

All rights reserved

No part of this book may be reproduced or utilized in any form or by any means, electronic or mechanical, including photocopying and recording, or by any information storage and retrieval system, without permission in writing from the publisher. The Association of American University Presses' Resolution on Permissions constitutes the only exception to this prohibition.

⊛ The paper used in this publication meets the minimum requirements of the American National Standard for Information Sciences—Permanence of Paper for Printed Library Materials, ANSI Z39.48–1992.

Manufactured in the United States of America

Library of Congress Cataloging-in-Publication Data

Names: Avrutin, Eugene M. editor. | Dekel-Chen, Jonathan L., editor. | Weinberg, Robert, editor.
Title: Ritual murder in Russia, Eastern Europe, and beyond : new histories of an old accusation / edited by Eugene M. Avrutin, Jonathan Dekel-Chen, and Robert Weinberg.
Description: Bloomington ; Indianapolis : Indiana University Press, [2017] | "The collection emerged out of a conference at the University of Illinois in October 2014"—Acknowledgments. | Includes bibliographical references and index.
Identifiers: LCCN 2017002956 (print) | LCCN 2017006559 (ebook) | ISBN 9780253025814 (cloth : alk. paper) | ISBN 9780253026408 (pbk. : alk. paper) | ISBN 9780253026576 (e-book)
Subjects: LCSH: Blood accusation—Russia—History—Congresses. | Blood accusation—Europe, Eastern—History—Congresses. | Jews—Persecutions—Russia—History—Congresses. | Jews—Persecutions—Europe, Eastern—History—Congresses. | Antisemitism—Russia—History—Congresses. | Antisemitism—Europe, Eastern—History—Congresses. | Russia—Ethnic relations—Congresses. | Europe, Eastern—Ethnic relations—Congresses.
Classification: LCC BM585.2 .R58 2017 (print) | LCC BM585.2 (ebook) | DDC 305.892/4047—dc23
LC record available at https://lccn.loc.gov/2017002956

1 2 3 4 5   22 21 20 19 18 17

CONTENTS

Acknowledgments   vii

Introduction: Ritual Murder in Russia, Eastern Europe, and Beyond / EUGENE M. AVRUTIN, JONATHAN DEKEL-CHEN, AND ROBERT WEINBERG   1

1 Imagined Crimes, Real Victims: Hermeneutical Witches and Jews in Early Modern Poland / MICHAEL OSTLING   18

2 The Jewish Blood Libel Legend: A Folkloristic Perspective / HAYA BAR-ITZHAK   39

3 Ritual Murder in a Russian Border Town / EUGENE M. AVRUTIN   56

4 The Saratov Case as a Critical Juncture in Ritual Murder History / ANDREW C. REED   73

5 The Blood Libel in Nineteenth-Century Lithuania: A Comparison of Two Cases / DARIUS STALIŪNAS   95

6 *Yahrzeits*, Condolences, and Other Close Encounters: Neighborly Relations and Ritual Murder Trials in Germany and Austria-Hungary / HILLEL J. KIEVAL   110

7 Human Sacrifice in the Name of a Nation: The Religion of Common Blood / MARINA MOGILNER   130

8 The Predatory Jew and Russian Vitalism: Dostoevsky, Rozanov, and Babel / HARRIET MURAV   151

9 Connecting the Dots: Jewish Mysticism, Ritual Murder, and the Trial of Mendel Beilis / ROBERT WEINBERG   172

10 A Half-Full Cup? Transnational Responses to the Beilis Affair / JONATHAN DEKEL-CHEN   185

11 Simulating Justice: The Blood Libel Case in Moscow, April 1922 /
Gennady Estraikh   204

12 The Blood Libel and Its Wartime Permutations: Cannibalism
in Soviet Lviv / Elissa Bemporad   219

13 Was the Doctors' Plot a Blood Libel? / Jeffrey Veidlinger   238

14 The Sandomierz Paintings of Ritual Murder as *Lieux de mémoire* /
Magda Teter   253

Index   279

ACKNOWLEDGMENTS

THE COLLECTION EMERGED out of a conference at the University of Illinois in October 2014. The editors acknowledge the generous support of the University of Illinois, the Leonid Nevzlin Research Center for Russian and East European Jewry at the Hebrew University of Jerusalem, and Swarthmore College. These institutions also provided funds for the publication of this volume. At the University of Illinois, the Program in Jewish Culture and Society, College of the Liberal Arts and Sciences, and the Russian, East European, and Eurasian Center provided financial and organizational resources. We would like to express our appreciation to Helmut Walser Smith of Vanderbilt University, Nadja Berkovich of the University of Arkansas, and Bruce Rosenstock and Diane Koenker of the University of Illinois for their critical commentary and participation at the conference. At Indiana University Press, the editors are grateful to Robert Sloan, Dee Mortensen, and Paige Rasmussen for their professionalism and enthusiastic interest in the project. The two peer reviewers, Glenn Dynner and Shaul Stampfer, provided insightful critical commentary. Finally, we would like to say a special thank you to Helmut Walser Smith for creating the beautiful map, Carolyn Pouncy for copyediting the entire volume, and Dina Dineva for creating the index.

RITUAL MURDER in RUSSIA, EASTERN EUROPE, and BEYOND

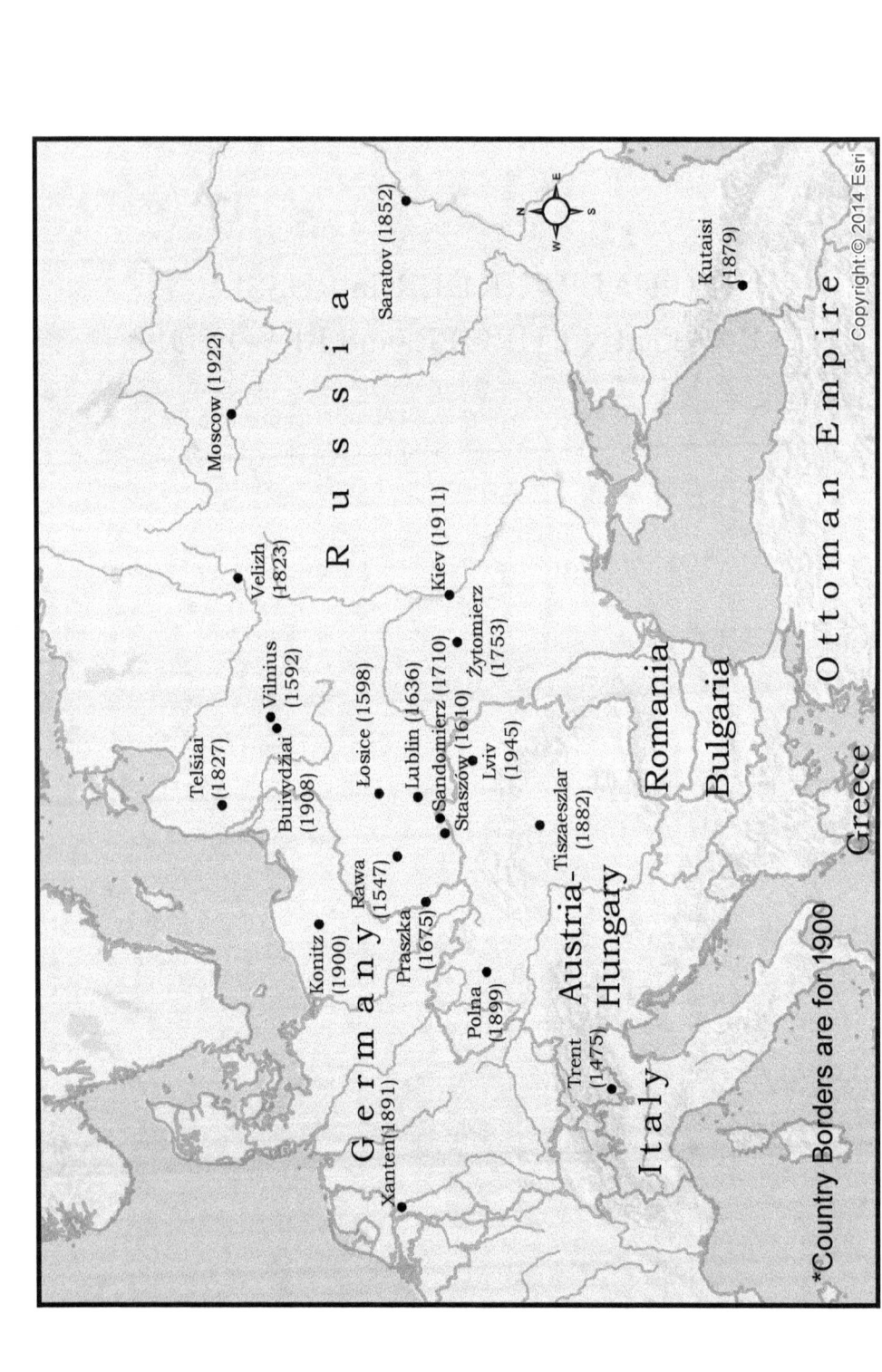

Sites of ritual murder trials. *Credit:* Map drawn by Helmut Walser Smith.

INTRODUCTION

Ritual Murder in Russia, Eastern Europe, and Beyond

Eugene M. Avrutin, Jonathan Dekel-Chen,
and Robert Weinberg

ON JUNE 10, 1636, after the end of the Shavuot celebration and on the eve of Pentecost, the butcher woman Leskowa told her neighbors that her son was missing "and 'no doubt' had been ritually murdered by Jews." Word quickly spread throughout the town of Lublin that the Jews had killed the Christian boy, drawn his blood for religious rituals, and thrown the corpse in the river. Late that evening, a mob of townsfolk broke into the Jewish quarter. As students and journeymen looted Jewish homes and shops, two Jews, Nahman and Baruch, were charged with the crime of ritual murder and locked up in a castle dungeon. Another Jew named Joseph was caught hiding out in a nearby town and was also chained up in the same prison.[1]

In accordance with the inquisitorial process, a criminal code used in early modern Europe to prosecute serious crimes such as witchcraft, heresy, and murder, all three men were brought into the torture chamber for questioning and face-to-face confrontations.[2] The judge was particularly interested as to why the Jews killed the Christian boy and what they wanted to do with the blood. "I don't know why [the boy died]," Baruch answered the judge, "and no Jew, whether [old or young], knows why. We Jews do not need Christian blood, and we do not kill any Christian children." To the question "What do Jews use Christian blood for?" Nahman responded, "They do not need it, and you will hear nothing about this among Jews." He continued, "Jews do not kill children," averring that "This child perhaps drowned, but Jews had nothing to do with it. I don't know, I don't know!"

To the question "Where did you steal the child?" Joseph answered, "I did not do it, never ever! I did not participate in the matter, neither with advice nor with deeds, and I left the city out of fear." To induce a confession, the executioner stretched the Jews on the rack and burned them with candles. But after four days of exhaustive interrogations, agonizing stretches of the body, and severe burns, the men stood their ground. Without a confession—what was regarded as the queen of proofs in the law—the court decided to acquit Jews of the crime.[3]

Many Jews were not as lucky as Nahman, Baruch, and Joseph. In early modern Poland-Lithuania, hundreds of Jewish men and women were tried, tortured, and publicly executed for allegedly murdering Christian children for ritual purposes such as baking matzo for the Passover holiday with the blood of the victim. Originating in England with the 1144 case of William of Norwich, ritual murder trials and accusations enjoyed popular appeal in late medieval and early modern Europe. The earliest case of alleged Jewish consumption of blood took place in the Germanic town of Fulda in 1235. Fueled by an extensive Christian folklore concerning the demonic uses of Jewish magic and a judicial apparatus intent on punishing murderers of children, the belief in the tale was standardized, commercialized, and widely disseminated in chronicles, ballads, and judicial records, especially (but not exclusively) in the politically decentralized lands of the Holy Roman Empire.[4] By the middle of the sixteenth century, as new theological and legal discourses in Reformation Europe helped discredit the concept of ritual murder, the legend spread to the eastern regions of Europe, where a multitude of ethnicities and religions, including the largest communities of Jews in the world, lived side by side.

Nearly four hundred years after the criminal proceedings in Lublin, ritual murder accusations found new life in a radically different cultural, judicial, and political context. The secrecy of the torture chamber gave way to the open courtroom, where judges, lawyers, criminal investigators, medical experts, and interested observers witnessed the unfolding of the drama. Accusations of Jewish ritual murder made for sensational headlines. Journalists from Budapest to St. Petersburg fed a hungry reading public by publishing hundreds of stories of Jewish criminality in newspapers and periodicals. The circulation of the news reinforced fantasies about Jewish conspiracy. Forensic physicians and psychiatrists formally reviewed the evidence and determined the facts of the crime. Supporting their observations with respectable race science, experts played no small role in helping legitimize the accusations against Jews.

Although nowhere near as substantial in output as witchcraft studies, the scholarship on Jewish ritual murder has witnessed a remarkable renaissance since the mid-1990s.[5] Most studies, however, continue to interpret the trials and accusations as a "lethal obsession," an "evil folklore," or an "irrational fantasy."[6] Focusing primarily on Eastern Europe, including Russia, this collection brings together an interdisciplinary group of scholars—working in history, folklore, ethnography, and literature—to summarize the state of what is rapidly emerging as a dynamic area of historical scholarship. Most significantly, the essays in this book, comprising focused case studies and wide-ranging reflections on the history of ritual murder, move away from a monocausal framework in favor of dynamic explanations of the mechanisms, evolution, popular appeal of, and responses to the blood libel. Drawing on court records, unpublished manuscripts, the mass circulation press, archival materials, and literary works, the essays critically reassess a topic that intersects with some of the most important themes in historical studies: popular belief and scientific knowledge; the connections between antisemitism, prejudice, and violence; the rule of law versus the power of rumors; the politics of memory; and humanitarian intervention on a global scale.

Mechanisms and Explanations

At first glance, the large number of documented trials and accusations in the Polish-Lithuanian Commonwealth (around a hundred for ritual murder and more than eight hundred for witchcraft) paints an extraordinarily intense landscape of Jew- and witch-hunting.[7] It is worthwhile, as a number of scholars have done, to reflect on the intersections of the phenomena.[8] Temporally, there was a noticeable chronological overlap between legal prosecutions of witchcraft and ritual murder. Almost always, the accusations took place in small towns and villages, where legends about evil Jews and witches circulated by word of mouth in streets, taverns, marketplaces, and peasant huts. The judicial proceedings shared many common motifs: from the murder of innocent children to the performance of symbolic acts of vengeance against the Christian religion. When all other means of gathering evidence were lacking, authorities relied on a panoply of torture instruments to extract confessions and convict the accused.

Notwithstanding their commonalities, at several critical junctures, as Michael Ostling reminds us in his provocative contribution in this volume, the comparisons break down. Unlike witch trials, ritual murder trials and accusations generated considerable publicity, both locally and internationally. Significantly, the high number of witchcraft cases did not translate into an increase in the publication of demonologies related to witchcraft. In early modern Poland, most of the compendious tracts were direct translations of Western European originals and had little influence in courtroom proceedings against alleged witches.[9] This was not the case for ritual murder. The Catholic Church relied on virulent anti-Jewish propaganda—with lengthy descriptions of past cases—to help spread the blood libel charge against Jews. Centuries later, the imperial Russian government cited these and other similar works as direct evidence of Jewish ritual fanaticism. As Andrew Reed explains in his analysis of the Saratov case, this literature, including the 1844 report purportedly authored by the renowned lexicographer Vladimir Dal', produced a "prepackaged set of assumptions," that could be accessed and applied as needed.

Most fundamentally, Ostling shows that ritual murder trials had "disastrous consequences for whole communities of real people." One of the earliest accusations took place in the Polish town of Rawa in 1547, resulting in the expulsion of the entire community of Jews. In the sixteenth and seventeenth centuries, authorities expelled or threatened to expel the Jewish communities of Staszów, Praszka, and Sandomierz. Well into the first half of the nineteenth century, a criminal investigation could terrorize an entire community, as it did in the Belorussian town of Velizh, when officials imprisoned more than forty Jews, including the wealthiest and most powerful men and women for their alleged role in the blood sacrifice. A witch trial, by contrast, could result in an execution of the alleged witch, which brought shame to families and orphaned children, but, as Ostling points out, "had no wider effect on the community of witches, because there existed no such community except in the minds of magistrates and accusers."

In the late medieval ages, writers created a large body of tales featuring the Jew as a familiar protagonist. Horrifying stories of Jewish ritual murder and host desecration were widely translated and disseminated in pamphlets, chronicles, epic poetry, and folklore, becoming the stuff of local knowledge and lore.[10] In response to the tenacity of the anti-Jewish tale, Jewish communities generated their own oral traditions that were passed from generation to generation. Some of the legends, as Haya Bar-Itzhak explains, were designed to refute the blood libel, rescue the Jewish community from imminent danger, and punish the enemy. Others, usually ending in the tragic death of the hero–generally a man—kept alive the trauma of the event in historical memory.

Ritual murder thus possessed the power to connect disparate phenomena in unexpected ways and across boundaries of time and space. Paintings such as Stefan Żuchowski's sensational depictions of Jews killing Christian children in Sandomierz purported to have represented a local Polish trial, but were in fact influenced by the cult of Simon of Trent and the literary and iconographic works that it generated.[11] The disappearance of a two-year-old boy named Simon on Easter Sunday 1475 in Trent, Italy, led to the arrest of nineteen Jewish men and women. Vigorously promoted by observant Franciscans and humanists, little Simon's cult spread to many communities in Europe, including Poland. In a meticulous reconstruction, Magda Teter argues that the Simonine iconography not only made a strong impression on the Polish painter Żuchowski, but also his artistic works actually represent a "conscious play on both Simon's story and local trials." To twenty-first-century observers, the historical and iconographic legacy of the paintings has been entirely forgotten. But in the eighteenth century, the connections to the events in Trent served to justify and frame the accusations against Jews.

The Catholic clergy spent considerable effort and time writing accusatory works about the veracity of ritual murder. Questions remain as to how significant this literature was in spreading beliefs and instigating trials at the local level. Were the trials organized by forceful state and church officials or from below by vengeful and enraged neighbors? What role did rumor, gossip, and oral traditions play in breeding the accusations? A careful exploration of the cases, from various times and places, demonstrates the inherent difficulty of coming up with an unequivocal explanation of causes and motivations. Historians have shown that in the eighteenth century powerful Polish bishops and clergymen not only spoke out against Jews, but also took an active role in fueling accusations and carrying out trials.[12] Eugene M. Avrutin, studying an exceptionally well-documented nineteenth-century case, explores the social dynamics of prosecution in Velizh. Shifting the focus away from antisemitism, Avrutin shows how an ordinary neighborhood dispute between a Christian beggar woman and her well-to-do neighbor ultimately led to the ritual murder charge. A close reading of the trial records suggests that a well-established oral culture helped legitimize the narrative. In 1827, at the same time the Velizh investigation was taking place, a seven-year-old farm boy disappeared in the Tel'shi district of Kovno province, resulting in the arrest of as many as twenty-eight Jews and a series of protracted criminal investigations at the local level. Darius Staliūnas's analysis of the case confirms that popular prejudices played an important role in the accusations, but he also emphasizes that mixed signals from the highest members of the imperial Russian government, including Tsar Nicholas I himself, played no small role in what turned out to be the inability of the courts to decide the case.

Beginning with the Elisavetgrad pogrom of May 15, 1881, rumors of Jews preparing to kidnap and slaughter Christian babies became a prominent feature of physical violence directed at Jews and Jewish property. Fueled by the strains of Russia's uneven economic development, fierce antisemitic press campaigns, demographic fears, and a rootless, hard-drinking, working-class culture, waves of anti-Jewish violence spread along railroad routes, highways, and rivers.[13] The pogroms intensified in the last years of the old regime. Unruly peasants, townspeople, and workers used the metaphors of blood drinking and cannibalism as a rallying cry to engage in anti-Jewish violence. Focusing on a small Lithuanian town of Šalnaičiai in 1908, Staliūnas illustrates how rumors of ritual murder culminated in a spontaneous attack on Jewish property. Rather than attributing the pogrom purely to antisemitic or nationalist agitation, Staliūnas argues for a more prosaic explanation: a mob of peasants decided to take matters into their own hands when they realized that authorities were unwilling or unable to "defend us or our faith."

RACE, RELIGION, AND SCIENCE

In fin-de-siècle Europe, ritual murder trials and accusations began to acquire new characteristics and assume new forms. The charge became imbued with secular concerns linked to the development of industrial capitalism, the rise of the nation-state, and the gradual emancipation of European Jewry. Political activists used the electoral process and the mass circulation press to further their own agendas. Hillel Kieval's research on modern trials stresses the importance of ritual murder discourse for shaping political agendas such as nation building and economic nationalism.[14] The discourse reflects critical developments in European society and demonstrates how the blood libel in the nineteenth and twentieth centuries differed from earlier accusations, revealing critical social, cultural, and political transformations that Europe underwent. For centuries the blood libel flourished in the countryside and small towns of Central and Eastern Europe, but an uptick in the number of accusations in the last quarter of the nineteenth century shifted the locus to major urban centers without supplanting the continued occurrence of such allegations in rural and small-town Europe.[15]

The authority of jurists and the testimony of expert witnesses in the open courtroom may help explain the resurgence of the accusations. Prosecutions of Jews who allegedly killed gentile youths and used their blood for religious rituals and rites turned to science and forensic medicine to demonstrate the verity of ritual murder. As several essays in this volume demonstrate, prosecutors used the modern court system to accommodate the growing secularization of the ritual murder accusation. Relying on the testimony of "expert" witnesses steeped in forensic medicine, criminology, psychology, and psychiatry to fashion cases, they felt confident of their ability to sway the jurors to accept the prosecution's charges. Such witnesses claimed in-depth knowledge of how certain knife wounds guaranteed the maximum bloodletting and how murderers collected the blood from their victims. Accusers, who formerly relied on religious prejudices and popular superstitions to build their cases, now couched their arguments in the language of science and medicine.

Another new feature of the accusation was the extent to which the Jews' alleged behavior was posited to be the consequence of an ineffable quality of the Jewish people, namely that the supposed racial characteristics of Jews embedded in blood were ineradicable and could be passed down from generation to generation. As Marina Mogilner notes in her contribution to this volume, the blood libel contributed to the conviction that nations were communities of people based on bonds of shared blood or lineage. Moreover, those who accused Jews of ritual murder pointed to Judaism's supposed fixation on blood and bodily mutilation, such as circumcision and dietary laws that forbid the consumption of animal blood, as evidence of why Jews required the sacrifice of gentile youths for religious purposes.

Many historians argue that, by the turn of the twentieth century, the theological underpinnings of antisemitism had yielded to a hatred of Jews that reflected a backlash against the nineteenth-century ideologies of liberalism and Marxism, and the greater integration of Jews into mainstream society.[16] According to this scenario, the nature of antisemitism in general and the blood libel in particular changed as state officials turned to secular modes of inquiry such as science and medicine to persuade jurors. It is important, however, not to lose sight of the religious underpinnings of ritual murder trials and accusations. The high incidence of accusations during Holy Week—a characteristic that has run throughout the entire sordid history of ritual murder from the beginning—indicates the impact of Christian and Jewish religious calendars on people's way of life.[17] Religious prejudice continued to inspire anti-Jewish attitudes and behaviors at the same time that antisemitism began to be used to satisfy social and political purposes. The sensational trial of Mendel Beilis in 1913 for the murder of a gentile youth in Kiev two years earlier reveals the persistence of religious injunctions supposedly found in foundational Jewish texts such as the Talmud to explain ritual murders. In short, the blood libel may have fulfilled different social and political functions than it did in previous centuries, but the religious roots of the accusation were still evident in the decades prior to World War I.

Believers in the blood libel pointed to several phenomena to support the contention that Jews engaged in ritual murder and conspired to world domination. One was the disappearance of a gentile child, particularly at the time of Passover when Jews purportedly required Christian blood for baking matzo. Invariably the mutilated body of the missing child showed up soon after the cry of foul play by Jews became public. A second was the conviction that Jewish religious texts such as the Talmud and Kabbalah commanded Jews to collect the blood of non-Jews for a variety of ritual purposes. The trial of Beilis underscored the power of and reliance on the written word to prove the veracity of the blood libel.[18] This belief that the written word revealed the genuine motivations of Jews was harder to dismiss because it possessed a special quality as the expression of truth. Because Jewish religious texts were written in a language that few non-Jews knew, it was widely believed that Jews hid their true intentions from gentiles in abstruse texts that contained instructions about bloodletting.[19]

Another factor, namely the canard that Jews conspired on a global level to promote Jewish dominance of the world, served a secular function in terms of a response to the greater involvement of Jews in the social, political, and economic life of Europe. Still, the religious roots of this conspiratorial frame of mind should not be discounted. Believers in the worldwide Jewish conspiracy as expressed in the notorious fabrication *Protocols of the Elders of Zion* worried about Jews dominating gentile society through capitalism, liberalism, and socialism. But Jewish marching orders could also be found in religious texts.[20] The trial of Mendel Beilis is an excellent illustration of this kind of thinking. Proponents of the ritual murder accusation in the Russian Empire came from all quarters of society, including educated theologians, philosophers, linguists, and charlatans who argued that the secret of the Jews' efforts to subjugate non-Jews is contained in the major texts of Judaism. Some were well-known personages such as the lexicographer Dal' and the philosopher and writer Vasilii Rozanov, but others were complete fools masquerading as serious intellectuals.

As Robert Weinberg has shown, one of the chief witnesses for the prosecution of Beilis was a shady Catholic priest by the name of Father Justin Bonaventure Pranaitis.[21] In 1893 he published a pamphlet titled *The Christians in the Jewish Talmud, or the Secrets of the Teachings of the Rabbis about Christians*, which proclaimed that Judaism obligated Jews to engage in ritual murder. Government prosecutors in Kiev, who had been unable to find any Russian Orthodox priest or theologian to testify on behalf of the state, turned to Pranaitis to make the case for ritual murder. Notwithstanding Pranaitis's testimony, two of Russia's leading scholars on Judaism—both non-Jews—denied the veracity of the accusation, much to the chagrin of the prosecution. The indictment of Beilis drew on the views of Pranaitis, who claimed that the Talmud commands the killing of non-Jews, which hastens the coming of the Messiah. Moreover, the Zohar (the foundational text of Jewish mystical thought), so argued Pranaitis, provided secret instructions on how to inflict wounds in accordance with Jewish religious prescriptions.[22]

Reliance on the word of scientific authorities also played a role in the trial of Beilis, notwithstanding religious prejudice. In his contribution to the volume, Weinberg argues that government lawyers based their case on contemporary scientific and medical standards precisely to counter the defenders of Beilis who they knew would characterize the trial as a holdover of medieval religious prejudices and hatreds. The ritual murder accusation had to draw sustenance in a manner befitting late imperial Russia's open court system and membership in the world's scientific and intellectual community. No wonder, then, that the prosecution turned to the eminent psychiatrist Ivan Alekseevich Sikorsky, a rabid antisemite who lectured about the religious foundations of the blood libel at St. Vladimir University. At the trial Sikorsky authoritatively claimed that the pattern of wounds on the boy supposedly killed by Beilis and others indicated that Jews were responsible.²³

In a similar vein, several contributors in this volume analyze how forensic-medical experts and social scientists shaped courtroom proceedings. Hillel Kieval's examination of ritual murder trials in Germany and the Habsburg Monarchy at the end of the nineteenth century reveals the reliance of prosecutors on up-to-date forensic science to develop cases against Jews suspected of killing gentiles for ritual purposes. Even accusers who lacked professional credentials understood the essential role played by science and medicine. For example, the former butcher Heinrich Junkermann, who claimed that a Jewish butcher had killed a gentile youth, supported the accusation with the opinion of his son, a medical student. Andrew Reed shows how police investigators examining the murder of two gentile youths in Saratov in the mid-nineteenth century called on local physicians to ascertain whether or not the wounds on the victims indicated a ritual murder. Local officials even asked the medical doctors to compare the botched circumcision of one of the victims with that of two boys, one Jewish, the other Tatar. Authorities assumed that the murderer (or murderers) had subjected the victim to a crude mutilation, but the boy's parents told officials that they had had their son circumcised, thereby deflating the investigators' case that the cuts on the boy's penis had been part of a ritualistic killing.

Shifting the focus to the last decades of the nineteenth century, Marina Mogilner reveals that the emergence of anthropology and its subdiscipline ethnography as a new academic discipline provided proponents of the ritual murder accusation with a veneer of legitimacy and respectability. By positing that "primitive" societies engaged in human sacrifice as a natural and universal practice, ethnographers made it all the more believable that indigenous peoples living among "civilized" Christians in the Russian Empire practiced ritual murder. The purported survival of such savagery well into the modern age reinforced the timeworn stereotype of bloodthirsty Jews and provided a new way of thinking about blood libel. In her contribution Harriet Murav provides the cultural context of this fixation on Jews and blood. She examines the writings of Fyodor Dostoevsky, Vasilli Rozanov, and Isaac Babel, three literary luminaries who drew on the trope of the bloodthirsty Jew in their respective descriptions of Jews and their relationship to Russian society. Dostoevsky and Rozanov relied on the image of the Jewish bloodsucker, at times literally and at other times figuratively, as a way to comment on the vitality of Russian culture, which was purportedly under attack by Jews and Judaism.

Transnational Mobilizations and Echoes

Most of the chapters in this volume deal with the causes, features, frequency, or intensity of threats to local Jews arising from ritual murder accusations in what might be considered the illiberal "East" during the period under discussion. Important in their own right, these localized threats also ignited wider responses in the Jewish world. Consequently, in light of the bubbling up of what can generally be called blood libel accusations in East-Central Europe and in the Ottoman Empire came a series of responses from prominent Jews and Jewish communities in West-Central Europe and the United States. These reactions by leaders and laypeople should be taken into account not only for their mere occurrence at times of peril for the accused, but also for their place in the longer-term history of transnational Jewish philanthropy and advocacy. Why? While the incidence of ritual murder accusations declined steeply from the World War I period onward, the need for transnational Jewish political and humanitarian intercession did not. On the contrary, new types of emergent threats to Jews in Europe, the Middle East, and Africa spurred intercession for many decades after the events examined in this volume. As Jonathan Dekel-Chen concludes in his contribution to this volume, actions taken on behalf of Jews accused of ritual murder were both informed by earlier intercessions and formed precedents for action in subsequent defenses.

Transnational responses to ritual murder accusations first arose from within the local communities. Communal leaders at the municipal, regional, and national levels more often than not did what they could to aid the accused, at times at their own peril. But perhaps more surprisingly for some, responses also intensified across borders as time went on. Why did Jewish leaders in Western Europe and North America choose to mobilize on behalf of co-religionists so far away, even if the blood libel seemed preposterous? Given the stubborn persistence of ritual murder accusations and their changing forms, somewhere in the mid-nineteenth century Jewish communal leaders in the West began to understand the need for some sort of organized, focused response.

The increased frequency and sophistication of ritual murder charges generated more serious, systemic transnational responses for two reasons. First, as an interconnected diasporic people since ancient times, Jews have almost always had support mechanisms that mobilized at times of crisis and could project aid over long distances. This tradition can be seen, for example, in the generations of support that flowed from diasporic communities to the small enclave of Jews living in the Land of Israel from late antiquity until the rise of the Zionist movement.[24] Second, the relatively affluent Jewish communities in the West recognized the potential dangers to themselves arising from unbridled judeophobia spreading from the "East" throughout Europe. Hence, efforts from the West to combat ritual murder accusations accomplished two connected goals: they fell in line with a tradition of transnational intercession for embattled co-religionists and served the interests of diaspora communities who resided far from the sites of the accusations but felt threatened by the potential specter of unchecked anti-Jewish libels proliferating westward.

Increased Jewish responses around the turn of the twentieth century incorporated not just prominent businessmen, politicians, and rabbis, but also widening circles of lay activists.[25] All of this became possible as a result of the times themselves: with the arrival of nearly instant, affordable communication via telegraph networks, the press, and the rapidity of reasonably priced travel made possible by steamships and railroads, mobilization for threatened communities abroad became possible for legions of activists instead of only a privileged few who could afford in previous times such personal mobilization on behalf of faraway brethren. As we learn from Dekel-Chen, these efforts predated the events surrounding the Beilis ritual murder trial in Kiev from 1911 to 1913, but found distinct expressions there. The trial of Beilis became, in fact, an accelerator of trends and techniques already emerging among Jewish transnational intercessors.

Taking a step back from specific cases of ritual murder accusations and the responses they sparked from abroad, let us consider whether these accusations constituted a special challenge for intercessors. After all, negative rumors about Jews had circulated periodically almost wherever Jews lived in Europe or the Muslim lands. Over the generations, rumors cast aspersions on Jews as a group for many supposed misdoings, including but not confined to economic malfeasance, disproportionate political power, collusion with non-Jewish elites against lower classes, or insufficient loyalty to one's homeland.

What then, if anything, made confrontation with the ritual murder libel more or less difficult for transnational intercessors? First, by the end of the nineteenth century ritual murder accusations had become an issue that merged older trends of judeophobia with state-sponsored antisemitism. This enlarged threat in the East generated energetic responses from the West, no matter the apparent absurdity of the charges and the unlikelihood that the accused Jew(s) would be punished by their home states, given an expectation that even the darkest regimes could not approve such convictions lest they incur international scorn and ridicule. Second, unlike almost all other types of anti-Jewish rumors or accusations, the blood libel carried a universal quality. If given legitimacy in one place, there was a real danger that it could be leveled against other Jews anywhere else in the world they resided; this was a highly transportable threat with few national peculiarities that might limit its contagion throughout the Christian world, or even into Muslim lands. And third, the ritual murder accusation seemed to belie a core piece of the narrative of modernization and enlightenment in the Jewish world. According to this political philosophy, which had burned brightly among Jewish leaders for many decades before the turn of the twentieth century, the coming of modernity would bring an end to old-world, theological anti-Jewish hatreds and prejudices. The reappearance of this profoundly old-world libel—when most other signs seemed to point to the progress of Jewish individuals and communities in Europe on the wings of emancipation—caused acute worry throughout the continent and beyond.

With the benefit of hindsight, we can see fascinating parallel developments along the pathways of modernity among judeophobes and the Jewish transnational activists who confronted them. For both the accusers and the defenders in episodes of ritual murder accusations, the tools of modernity took on core functions. The printed press played perhaps the most conspicuous part. Just as judeophobes used the press to disseminate rumors about the supposed evil intentions or actions of local Jews, Jewish transnational intercessors mobilized these same modern tools to mount a defense among the masses on behalf of the rights of the accused Jews. We should also not lose sight of the fact that the modernized rationale and dissemination of ritual murder accusations around the turn of the twentieth century occurred more or less in parallel to—and, to a degree, were a motivation for—the rise of the Zionist movement in Europe. Although sparked by completely opposing perceptions of Jews, both the proponents of ritual murder accusations and Zionism believed that Jews embodied unique traits. So in an odd, somewhat horrifying way when viewed in retrospect, these phenomena fed one another.

The mobilization of modern resources by transnational activists did not end with newspapers. Jewish intercessors in the West, starting at least as early as Moshe Montefiore and Adolphe Crémieux, tried in the mid-nineteenth century to mobilize democratic parliamentary politics at home as a means to combat anti-Jewish actions by repressive regimes in the East.[26] From the standpoint of Jewish activists, the mobilization of Western parliaments—or at least attempts to lobby Western politicians—became necessary once the accusers in ritual murder cases conscripted their own home governments. In effect, once ritual murder trials moved from the realm of church-based inquisitions to the province of open, adversarial courts, effective Jewish transnational responses required intercessors to enlist goodwill and active intervention from government officials in their home states, not just support from liberal-minded churchmen. Added to these efforts, toward the end of the century individual Jewish bankers (and banking families) tried to leverage the force of international loans given to the Russian Empire as a means to deter the worst antisemitic tendencies of the tsarist regime. While it is certainly true that accusers in ritual murder trials increasingly called on modern medical and legal "experts" to prove the verity of charges against the Jewish defendants, it is equally true that the defenders of Jews in these cases called on similar witnesses to counter the charges through "modern" evidence. It should also be noted that the teams devoted to the defense of defendants in ritual murder cases in Europe increasingly featured international components and benefited from funds sent by concerned co-religionists abroad.

Ritual Murder after World War I

The collapse of the autocracy in Russia and the coming to power of a communist regime in 1917 did not spell the end of suspicions that Jews engaged in ritual murder. But it did bring about a concerted effort by the communist government to make sure that accusers of Jews were brought to justice. Gennady Estraikh examines blood libel accusations in Moscow during the early years of the New Economic Policy, making clear that the Beilis Affair still resonated among readers of the Yiddish press: journalists observed that these new accusations were a replay of the persecution of Beilis a decade earlier. In addition, the early Soviet authorities issued a book about the trial of Beilis, and *Izvestiia*, the official organ of the government, had been publishing reports about some of the persons involved in the prosecution of Beilis. Soviet Jews were not the only ones whom the press reminded about the Beilis Affair. An article titled "A Moscow Beilis Case" in the *New York Times* introduced the events in Moscow to the American reading public.

A few decades later, communist officials still had to contend with the persistence of such accusations. Elissa Bemporad explores the proliferation of claims about Jewish cannibalism and ritual murder in areas that had been under German control during most of World War II. Yet unlike in tsarist times, Soviet authorities took a firm stance against public expressions of antisemitism and prosecuted people who sounded the alarm that Jews were killing Christian youths. Her analysis of the arrest and conviction of five Ukrainian and Polish residents of Lviv at the end of the war indicates that interethnic tensions ran high, and the government had to take stern measures against those who believed that Jews were trying to establish their control of gentiles through the spread of communism.

Finally, Jeffrey Veidlinger's examination of the infamous Doctors' Plot at the end of Joseph Stalin's life underscores how tropes of the ritual murder accusation, particularly the Jews' purported lust for blood, persisted and influenced the thoughts and behavior of Russians living in the mid-twentieth century. Jews were no longer suspected of conspiring to murder gentiles for religious purposes, but the Kremlin demonized Jews who were now allegedly targeting non-Jews for political purposes. Many non-Jewish Soviet citizens evidently still believed that Jews were intent on obtaining the blood of gentiles for baking matzo and shunned Jews, particularly medical professionals, out of fear that Jews engaged in ritual cannibalism.[27] The repudiation of the Doctors' Plot in the immediate aftermath of Stalin's death in 1953 reveals that the communist state did not want to stoke the flames of potential social unrest by turning to the timeworn canard of ritual murder.

More than an artifact of the past, ritual murder continues to play a conspicuous role in contemporary culture, politics, and society in Europe, the Middle East, and the United States. In Kyiv the grave of Beilis's purported victim Andrei Iushchinskii has become a site of pilgrimage for nationalists and antisemites, attracting visitors who view the boy as a martyr, the victim of a vast Jewish conspiracy to destroy the fabric of Russian and Ukrainian culture and society. Similarly, television shows, speeches, and books in parts of Europe and the Middle East focus on the blood libel as part of their anti-Israel propaganda.[28] As late as the mid-1990s some clerics in Italy agitated for the return of the relics of a victim of a purported sixteenth-century ritual murder. One church publication in Turin devoted space to articles that urged readers to accept the veracity of the charge.[29] As Magda Teter explains in her contribution, the restoration and uncovering of the controversial ritual murder paintings in the Church of St. Paul in January 2014 has helped Poland confront a complicated, if tragic, historical legacy.

Clearly, the blood libel has ongoing resonance, continuing to survive for so long because of its uncanny ability to adapt to and reflect contemporary needs and problems. Nonetheless, it would be misleading to view the malevolent fantasies as part of a coordinated persecution of Jews dating to medieval and early modern times. What Hans Rogger had written about the Beilis case applies for over four hundred years of intermittent blood accusations and campaigns: "There had been no grand design; there had not been a tactical plan."[30] All villages, towns, and cities are delicate ecosystems in which the inhabitants live in intimate daily contact with their neighbors. As the essays in this volume indicate, rumor and prejudice make for a very combustible situation when the calm of the mundane everyday world is shattered by the unexpected death of a child. Thus, rather than interpreting ritual murder as mass terror inspired by a static, if all pervasive, antisemitism, it is useful, as the contributors in this volume suggest, to pay particular attention to the larger social and cultural worlds that made these phenomena possible.[31]

EUGENE M. AVRUTIN is Associate Professor of History and Tobor Family Scholar in the Program of Jewish Culture and Society at the University of Illinois, Urbana-Champaign. He is the author of *Jews and the Imperial State: Identification Politics in Tsarist Russia* (2010). He is the coeditor of several volumes, including *Photographing the Jewish Nation: Pictures from S. An-sky's Ethnographic Expeditions* (2009) and *Story of a Life: Memoirs of a Young Jewish Woman in the Russian Empire* (2012).

JONATHAN DEKEL-CHEN is a Senior Lecturer in Modern History at the Hebrew University of Jerusalem and academic Chair of its Leonid Nevzlin Research Center for Russian and East European Jewry. His work has been widely published at prestigious university presses and in scholarly journals. During the 2015–2016 academic year, he was an Israel Institute Visiting Professor in the Department of History and the Institute for Israel and Jewish Studies at Columbia University.

ROBERT WEINBERG, the Isaac H. Clothier Professor of International Relations and History at Swarthmore College, is the author of *The Revolution of 1905 in Odessa: Blood on the Steps* (1994); *Stalin's Forgotten Zion: Birobidzhan and the Making of a Soviet Jewish Homeland* (1998); and *Blood Libel in Late Imperial Russia: The Ritual Murder Trial of Mendel Beilis* (2013).

NOTES

1. Meir Bałaban, "Hugo Grotius and the Blood Libel Trials in Lublin, 1636," *Polin* 22 (2010): 47–67, quotation on 52.
2. On the criminal process, see Michael Ostling, *Between the Devil and the Host: Imagining Witchcraft in Early Modern Poland* (Oxford: Oxford University Press, 2011), 91–103; and Nancy Shields Kollmann, *Crime and Punishment in Early Modern Russia* (Cambridge: Cambridge University Press, 2012), 113–32.
3. Bałaban, "Hugo Grotius and the Blood Libel Trials in Lublin," 52–54.
4. On the dissemination of the ritual murder tale, see R. Po-chia Hsia, *The Myth of Ritual Murder: Jews and Magic in Reformation Germany* (New Haven, CT: Yale University Press, 1988). For a treatment of William of Norwich, see E. M. Rose, *The Murder of William of Norwich: The Origins of the Blood Libel in Medieval Europe* (Oxford: Oxford University Press, 2015).
5. For a selection of scholarship, see Helmut Walser Smith, *The Butcher's Tale: Murder and Anti-Semitism in a German Town* (New York: W. W. Norton, 2002); Jonathan Frankel, *The Damascus Affair: "Ritual Murder," Politics, and the Jews in 1840* (Cambridge: Cambridge University Press, 1997); David Biale, *Blood and Belief: The Circulation of a Symbol between Jews and Christians* (Berkeley: University of California Press, 2007); Hsia, *Myth of Ritual Murder*; and Hillel Kieval, *Blood Inscriptions: Science, Modernity, and Ritual Murder in Fin de Siècle Europe* (forthcoming).
6. Robert S. Wistrich, *A Lethal Obsession: Anti-Semitism from Antiquity to the Global Jihad* (New York: Random House, 2010); Alan Dundes, "The Ritual Murder or Blood Libel Legend:

A Study of Anti-Semitic Victimization through Projective Inversion," in *The Blood Libel Legend: A Casebook in Anti-Semitic Folklore*, ed. Alan Dundes (Madison: University of Wisconsin Press, 1991), 337; Gavin I. Langmuir, *Toward a Definition of Antisemitism* (Berkeley: University of California Press, 1990), 195–298.

7. Jacek Wijacka counted a hundred blood libel trials in the Polish-Lithuanian Commonwealth. See his "Ritual Murder Accusations throughout the 16th to 18th Centuries," in *Ritual Murder: Legend in European History*, ed. Susanna Buttaroni and Stanisław Musiał (Krakow: Association for Cultural Initiatives, 2003), 195. Paweł Maciejko and Michael Ostling provide slightly lower estimates. See Ostling's contribution in this volume, and Maciejko's *The Mixed Multitude: Jacob Frank and the Frankist Movement, 1755–1816* (Philadelphia: University of Pennsylvania Press, 2011), 96.

8. For an excellent overview of the scholarship on witchcraft, see Brian P. Levack, ed., *The Oxford Handbook of Witchcraft in Early Modern Europe and Colonial America* (New York: Oxford University Press, 2013).

9. Maciejko, *Mixed Multitude*, 96–97; Magda Teter, *Jews and Heretics in Catholic Poland: A Beleaguered Church in the Post-Reformation Era* (Cambridge: Cambridge University Press, 2006), 118–19.

10. Miri Rubin, *Gentile Tales: The Narrative Assault on Late Medieval Jews* (Philadelphia: University of Pennsylvania Press, 2004). For a classic account, see Joshua Trachtenberg, *The Devil and the Jews: The Medieval Conception of the Jew and Its Relation to Modern Anti-Semitism* (Philadelphia: The Jewish Publication Society, 1983).

11. On the centrality of the Trent blood libel in a long chain of historical events, see R. Po-Chia Hsia, *Trent 1475: Stories of a Ritual Murder Trial* (New Haven, CT: Yale University Press, 1992), 92.

12. This does not mean that all Polish notables, including King Stanisław II, agreed with the involvement of such powerful bishops as Kajetan Sołtyk to demonize and marginalize Jews. See Gershon David Hundert, *Jews in Poland-Lithuania in the Eighteenth Century: A Genealogy of Modernity* (Berkeley: University of California Press, 2004), 72–77; and Zenon Guldon and Jacek Wijacka, "The Accusation of Ritual Murder in Poland, 1500–1800," *Polin* 10 (1997): 139–40.

13. John D. Klier, *Russians, Jews, and the Pogroms of 1881–1882* (Cambridge: Cambridge University Press, 2011), 83. See also Klier's *Imperial Russia's Jewish Question, 1855–1881* (Cambridge: Cambridge University Press, 1995), 433.

14. Hillel Kieval, "Death and the Nation: Ritual Murder as Political Discourse in the Czech Lands," *Jewish History* 10, no. 1 (1996): 75–91.

15. For an overview of ritual murder accusations at the end of the nineteenth century, see Smith, *Butcher's Tale*, 91–133.

16. For general histories of antisemitism, see Jacob Katz, *From Prejudice to Destruction: Anti-Semitism, 1700–1933* (Cambridge, MA: Harvard University Press, 1980); Albert Lindemann, *Esau's Tears: Modern Anti-Semitism and the Rise of the Jews* (Cambridge: Cambridge University Press, 1997); and Albert Lindemann, ed., *Antisemitism: A History* (Oxford: Oxford University Press, 2010).

17. For a brief overview, see Elisheva Carlebach, *Palaces of Time: Jewish Calendar and Culture in Early Modern Europe* (Cambridge, MA: Harvard University Press, 2011), 142–48.

18. See the contribution of Robert Weinberg in this volume and his "The Trial of Mendel Beilis: The Sources of 'Blood Libel' in Late Imperial Russia," in *Russia's Centuries of Revolutions: Parties, People, and Places*, ed. Michael Melancon and Donald Raleigh (Bloomington, IN: Slavica Publishers, 2012), 17–35.

19. Ritual murder accusations during the late medieval period did not point to Judaic texts since that would require knowledge of Hebrew, a phenomenon that did not occur until much later. Early proponents of the blood libel asserted that rabbis decided whom to sacrifice, but they were not explicit regarding where the requirement to do so came from. But as a group of scholars in the early thirteenth century noted, "neither the Old or New Testament states that the Jews lust for human blood." See Trachtenberg, *Devil and the Jews*, 132–33.

20. Ibid.

21. Robert Weinberg, *Blood Libel in Late Imperial Russia: The Ritual Murder Trial of Mendel Beilis* (Bloomington: Indiana University Press, 2014).

22. *Delo Beilisa: Stenograficheskii otchet*, 3 vols. (Kiev: T-vo "Pechatnaia S. P. Iakovleva," 1913), 2:293–440.

23. See Marina Mogilner's essay in this volume. Harriet Murav also notes that public intellectuals such as Vasilii Rozanov "read" the dead body as a text: Murav, "The Beilis Ritual Murder Trial and the Culture of Apocalypse," *Cardozo Studies in Law and Literature* 12 (2002): 243–63.

24. For an enduring overview of early Jewish philanthropic and political intercession, see Ephraim Frisch, *An Historical Survey of Jewish Philanthropy from the Earliest Times to the Nineteenth Century* (New York: Macmillan, 1924). See also Jonathan Dekel-Chen, "Philanthropy, Diplomacy and Jewish Internationalism," in *Cambridge History of Judaism*, 8: *The Modern Period, c. 1815–c. 2000*, ed. Mitchell Hart and Tony Michels (Cambridge: Cambridge University Press, forthcoming 2017).

25. For further discussion of the process of democratization, see Jonathan Dekel-Chen, "Faith Meets Politics and Resources: Reassessing Modern Transnational Jewish Activism," in *Purchasing Power: The Economics of Modern Jewish History*, ed. Rebecca Kobrin and Adam Teller (Philadelphia: University of Pennsylvania Press, 2015), 230–37.

26. For the most comprehensive account, see Frankel, *Damascus Affair*.

27. Alexander Lokshin, "The Doctors' Plot: The Non-Jewish Response," in *Jews and Jewish Life in Russia and the Soviet Union*, ed. Yaacov R'oi (Portland, OR: Frank Cass, 1995), 157–67.

28. For examples of how the blood libel penetrated the Islamic world, see Raphael Israeli, *Blood Libel and Its Derivatives: The Scourge of Anti-Semitism* (New Brunswick, NJ: Transaction Publishers, 2012), 117–208.

29. Tomasso Calio, "The Cult of the Alleged Ritual Murder Victims in the Second Half of the 20th Century in Italy," in Buttaroni and Musiał, *Ritual Murder*, 225–45.

30. Hans Rogger, *Jewish Policies and Right-Wing Politics in Imperial Russia* (Berkeley: University of California Press, 1986), 55.

31. This is an important direction of scholarship on witchcraft. For a judicious critique of panic trials, see H. C. Erik Midelfort, "Witch Craze? Beyond the Legends of Panic," *Magic, Ritual, and Witchcraft* 6, no. 1 (2011): 11–33. For the importance of close reading of trials and a deep sense of context, see Valerie A. Kivelson, "Introduction: Bringing the Slavs Back In," *Russian History* 40 (2013): 281–95. For a classic statement, see Robin Briggs, *Witches and Neighbors: The Social and Cultural Context of European Witchcraft* (London: Penguin, 1996).

❧ 1 ❦

IMAGINED CRIMES, REAL VICTIMS
Hermeneutical Witches and Jews in Early Modern Poland

Michael Ostling

> For the Lele evil is not to be included in the total system of the world, but to be expunged without compromise. All evil is caused by sorcery. They can clearly visualize what reality would be like without sorcery and they continually strive to achieve it by eliminating sorcerers.
>
> Mary Douglas, *Purity and Danger*

> Rachel, Rachel, I've been thinking
> What a queer world this would be
> If the girls were all transported
> Far beyond the Northern Sea!
>
> "Reuben and Rachel," traditional American song

IMAGINED COMMUNITIES

In 1639 *Witch denounced*, an anonymous tract criticizing the growth of witch trials in Poland, began with the suggestion that the burning of supposed witches was on everyone's mind: "In times of war, about war: in times of plague, about death: in times of famine, about bread: in times of conflagration, about fire people choose to converse. And ... in these times our Poland has become extraordinarily dense with the conflagration of Witches, either real or alleged, to such a degree that at table or at ordinary gatherings one hears of no other subject than of Witches."[1] Historians have little access to the "tables and ordinary gatherings" of early modern Poland; we cannot overhear the casual conversations where the burning of alleged witches may have been discussed. So we cannot decisively assert that the author of *Witch denounced* got things wrong. People may well have whispered their anxieties and suspicions about the practice of witchcraft, but if the written record is any guide, they were not talking much about the worrisome growth of witch *trials*. What they did talk about, or at least read and wrote about, was ritual murder: the allegations that "the Jews" regularly kidnapped, murdered, and drained the blood of Christian children. As Adam Teller and others have emphasized, the Christian and Jewish populations of early modern Poland interacted extensively in everyday ways that could not have been tolerable had all Christians believed every Jew to be complicit in the murder of children.[2] And yet public documents, nearly silent about witchcraft, are replete with stories of ritual murder.

Indeed, in the decade before the publication of *Witch denounced* the country was full of news of ritual murder and of its symbolic equivalent: the torture of the innocent Christ child embodied in the consecrated Eucharistic host.[3] Trials for both crimes became matters of high state politics, talked about nationally and even internationally—in 1636 the great Dutch political theorist Hugo Grotius was called upon for his opinion of a case of alleged ritual murder in Lublin.[4] In Bochnia in 1600 allegations against Jews for host desecration resulted in their expulsion from that city in 1605, an event celebrated in verse by city father Jan Achacy Kmita.[5] By contrast, a later trial in the same town (1679) involved two Christian beggar women who had abducted a *niewiniątko*—a "little innocent one" or infant child, "one presumes, to sell to the Jews": this trial received no public memorialization once the motif of Jewish ritual murder was set aside in favor of maleficent witchcraft.[6]

These cases and their public effects repeat a pattern found from the mid-sixteenth century to the last decades of the eighteenth century. The Sochaczew host-desecration trial of 1556 inspired a flurry of pamphlets and even international commentary (partly fueled by its use in interconfessional polemic between Catholics and Protestants).[7] In contrast, a witch trial involving theft of the Eucharist in Lublin in 1644 remained entirely unremarked in print until the twenty-first century.[8] The ritual murder trial at the Crown Tribunal in 1598 inspired the no-longer-extant *Collection of decrees of the tribunal in Lublin against the Jews*,[9] as well as Szymon Hubicki's *Jewish cruelty toward the Most Holy Sacrament and christian children*.[10] Bishops Maciejowski and Szyszkowski also ensured that the story was "sent to the Vatican Library in Rome *ad perpetuam rei memoriam*."[11] The verdicts of the Lublin ritual murder trials of 1636 are well known to us today, despite the loss of the Crown Tribunal records, thanks to their verbatim preservation in two contemporaneous pamphlets and in the later tracts of Stefan Żuchowski.[12] And such pamphlets continued to commemorate ritual murder trials deep into the eighteenth century, as with the *Decree concerning the torture by jews of a catholic child in Żytomierz* (Zhitomir), from 1753.[13] Meanwhile the bloodiest episode of witch-hunting in Poland—a long series of trials before the Kleczew town court between about 1675 and 1710, including numerous accusations of host desecration and magical child murder—went so unremarked at the time that it finds barely an echo even in the Kleczew court record books themselves: with the exception of the special, separately preserved volumes of criminal records, Kleczew appears to have been a sleepy, peaceful provincial town.[14]

Witch trials and ritual murder trials featured similar motifs and narratives—charms hidden about the person to help suspects resist torture; the malicious murder of children; desecration of the consecrated hosts so central to post-Tridentine Polish Catholic devotion. Witches and Jews alike figured in such trials as enemies both of God and of the human race. But witch trials disappear into the court records, while ritual murder and host-desecration trials were celebrated and commemorated in pamphlets, in epic poetry, in frescoes, plaques, and shrines.[15] These differences in cultural attention paid to witch trials and ritual murder trials reflect important differences in the cultural work accomplished (or attempted) by the trial processes themselves and by the textual productions they inspire. The Polish ritual murder trials and the very considerable publicity surrounding them construct, delimit, and demonize "repulsive Jewry" (to borrow the words of the verdict from one such trial) as an "infidel nation living in this Catholic state."[16] In contrast, witchcraft is demonized already, by definition: a witch had a pact with the Devil and used her magic to harm and kill. Nevertheless, the witch trials in Poland were not *about* the demonstration of witches' depravity. The reality of witchcraft was widely accepted: despite a concerted ecclesiastical campaign against witch trials from the 1630s onward, secular court magistrates rarely expressed the slightest doubt that witches existed, were in league with the Devil, and could harm humans and cattle out of their malice and spite. What magistrates did sometimes doubt, and what was constantly at stake in every trial, was whether *this or that specific accused woman* (or occasional man) was in fact a witch. In ritual murder trials, on the contrary, magistrates harbored no doubt at all that the accused were in fact Jews—argument instead centered on whether they (or rather, whether Jews in general) really do kill and bleed Christian babies. Witch trials and ritual murder trials both prosecuted real people for imagined crimes, and magistrates and accusers imagined both crimes in very similar ways. Nevertheless the two sets of trials, and the literature they produced, performed very different cultural work. Although most accused witches were women, the imagined community of witches never comprised all women without exception, and not even the wildest misogynist ever recommended the expulsion or extirpation of women as such. In contrast, anti-Judaic pamphlets did deploy the equally imaginary crime of ritual murder to demonize all Jews and to agitate for their expulsion from the Commonwealth.

It may then be true, as the eminent Polish historian Stanisław Salmonowicz argued some years ago, that "the mechanisms that produced ritual murder trials were analogous—*mutatis mutandis*—to the mechanisms that produced the mass of witch trials."[17] Nevertheless the present chapter warns against the impulse to treat, in Joanna Tokarska-Bakir's provocative but potentially misleading phrase, "the Jew as witch and the witch as Jew."[18] Demonization functions very differently when the persons demonized actually exist as a recognizable group, as the Jews did and the witches did not.

Symbolic Equivalences

Tokarska-Bakir is nevertheless quite justified in making the comparison of witch to Jew and vice versa. Witches and Jews played similar roles in the imaginations of late medieval and early modern European Christians, and the trials prosecuting them—the trials imagining and narrating their diabolical iniquity—correspondingly share many important similarities. While medieval Christian art sometimes depicted Jews quite literally as demons, with horns and fangs, in the early modern period Jews were more commonly grouped with witches and the native peoples of the New World as infanticidal and cannibalistic "children of Saturn," given over to savagery.[19] As Norman Cohn showed long ago, both ritual murder accusation and the image of the diabolical infanticidal witch drew upon a "traditional stock of defamatory clichés" previously applied to Christian heretics, and before that, to early Christians themselves by the pagan Romans, who imagined the Eucharist as a cannibalistic feast.[20] Notably, several fifteenth-century accounts of the alleged witches' infanticidal assembly describe it as a "synagogue";[21] conversely, in Spain, where witch trials remained infrequent, Jews replaced witches as stereotypical servants of the Devil.[22] Moreover, at least in the fifteenth century (and outside Poland), witch trials and trials for ritual murder were often incited by the same people: the Franciscan Bernardino of Siena, whose sermons inspired some of the earliest large witch trials in Italy, was also a notorious Jew-baiter; the Dominican Vincent Ferrer, famed for his coercive conversions of the Jews of Spain, also incited a wave of early witch trials in southern France.[23] Heinrich Institoris, principal author of the notorious witch-hunting manual *Malleus maleficarum* (*Hammer of witches*), is very likely identical to the "Brother Heinrich of Schlettstadt" who played an important role in the seminal trial for the alleged ritual murder of "Little Simon" of Trent, 1475; certainly he emphasized the propensity of witches, like Jews, to injure children and desecrate the Eucharistic host, and he drew extensive comparisons between the wickedness of Jews and witches in the *Malleus* and in his other writings.[24]

The symbolic equivalence of witches to Jews is graphically expressed in a stained glass *Allegory of Good Government* commissioned for the city hall of Nuremburg in 1598: the image shows a young boy, emblematic of both the Christ Child and of Innocence, being attacked by a soldier (the Furies of War), a Witch (Envy), and a Jew (Avarice).[25] Stuart Clark has shown how witches could function as hermeneutical subjects not unlike the "hermeneutical Jews" of medieval Christian theology—imagined others constructed for the exegesis of *Christian* questions and problems.[26] And yet, unlike the abstract, theoretical hermeneutical Jews and witches of theology and demonology, the Jews and Christian women accused of ritual murder and witchcraft were real people, through whose real screams under torture the worldview that demonized them was underwritten and legitimated. In both sorts of trials, confessions coerced through torture provided the materials for what R. Po-chia Hsia has called an "ethnography of blood"—the ostensible exposure of the secret rites and practices of an abominably inversionary counter-society against which Christian rites and practices could be proven and defined.[27] Whether allegedly committed by a witch or a Jew, host desecration and the ritual murder of innocent children helped link Christ's Passion with his Nativity, and both with the miracle of the Eucharist.[28] These connections are made unusually explicit in the hagiographic description of Szymon Kierel, allegedly murdered by the Jews of Vilnius in 1592, "who in such a small body expressed the greatest pains of suffering Christ."[29]

Polish writers on witchcraft or ritual murder often themselves drew explicit attention to the (imagined) similarities between the crimes of witches and Jews. Anti-Judaic tracts equated the Jew to the witch, as when the Kraków astronomer and polemicist Sebastjan Miczyński claimed that Jewish elders and rabbis are experts in black magic: "they have taken the Devil for their father, protector, and custodian, from whom they have received enchantments and witchcraft as inheritance."[30] Reciprocally, the Jesuit encyclopedist Benedykt Chmielowski explained that witches, in desecrating the consecrated host, "imitate the Jews."[31] But despite these imputed associations between Jews and witches, Polish Jews were never accused of witchcraft.[32] Trials for ritual murder very occasionally turned toward witchcraft (as in the Bochnia case of 1679, mentioned above). More often but still rarely, a Christian woman's theft of the Eucharist for magic evolved into an accusation against the local Jewish community for host desecration, as at Przemyśl in 1630 or Sandomierz in 1639.[33] Witchcraft and Jewish host desecration occasionally appear side by side in Polish legal decrees, but very rarely on the ground.[34] They differ from each other in other important ways as well.

Official attention: From the interference of papal nuncio Luigi Lippomano in the Sochaczew host-desecration trial of 1556 to the patronage of Bishop Kajetan Sołtyk in the 1753 Żytomierz ritual murder trial two centuries later, judicial prosecution of Jewish communities often proceeded at the instigation and behest of high church officials (and were just as often opposed by the king or his representatives).[35] In contrast, on the rare occasions when ecclesiastical authorities intervened in Polish witch trials, it was nearly always on the side of the accused witch—as when Bishop Kazimierz Florian Czartoryski circulated a pastoral letter against secular-court witch trials in 1669, or when Bishop Krzysztof Antoni Szembek successfully halted or ameliorated a few such trials in the early eighteenth century.[36] But the same Bishop Czartoryski who came to the defense of accused witches declared before the Sejm (parliament) in 1664 that "we must not tolerate the proven crimes, blasphemies, and sacrilege" of the Jews, and their "evident villainy must not go unpunished."[37]

Treatment of the alleged victims: At least in later retellings and often in fact, the bodies of the child-victims of "Jewish cruelty" were treated with great pomp and reverence: the remains of young Wojciech, allegedly murdered by the Jews of Łosice in 1598, was given "to the Jesuit Fathers in Lublin as a jewel" or "a great treasure," placed on the altar of the Jesuit church by Bishop (later Archbishop) Bernat Maciejewski himself.[38] Another alleged victim of ritual murder was buried before the altar of a Dominican church, and sometimes one can sense a light and a "beautiful odor" emanating from his grave.[39] In contrast, the children allegedly murdered by witches received ordinary burial and no official memorialization of any kind. The young son of the nobleman Jan Breza remained unnamed and hardly discussed in the court records of his alleged maleficent murder in 1688: a murder accomplished through complex rites of witchcraft involving a stolen Eucharistic host stabbed until it transformed into a bloody and crying baby Jesus.[40] Although the confessions of the accused witches in this trial closely parallel motifs found in the famous Sochaczew trial of 1556, the child victim of witchcraft was subject to no hagiography.

Consequences: The equivalence of witch to Jew, of the imagined witches' infanticidal cannibalistic feast to the imagined Jewish rites of murder, is most clear in the tragic consequences of both: the bodies burnt, beheaded, hanged, drawn and quartered; the ashes of the innocent scattered at the crossroads. Yet here too or perhaps especially, we see important differences. Between 1547 and 1787 the Jews of Poland suffered some eighty-two more or less official accusations of ritual murder (not all of which came to trial), for which crime approximately seventy-six people were judicially executed or died under torture.[41] In the same area over approximately the same period (1501–1776), some 867 witch trials resulted in the execution of at least 558 alleged witches.[42] But these numbers are not comparable. A witch trial resulting in the execution of one or two alleged witches brought shame on their families and orphaned their children—but it had no wider effect on the community of witches, because there existed no such community except in the minds of magistrates and accusers. Even the few large-scale witch-panics in Poland, fueled though they were by fantasies of collective witch covens assembling for orgiastic sabbats, even such panics had no effect on the broader Polish community of witches because this community was purely imaginary. Ritual murder and host-desecration trials, by contrast, claimed relatively few victims judicially executed for the crime itself, but the trials frequently had disastrous consequences for whole communities of real people. Alleged host desecration triggered the expulsion of all the Jewish inhabitants of Bochnia in 1605; ritual murder trials led to the expulsion of the Jewish communities of Rawa (1547), Staszów (1610), and Praszka (ca. 1675).[43] This is not to mention ultimately unsuccessful attempts to expel local Jews on the basis of host-desecration or ritual murder accusation (as at Przemyśl in 1630, or Sandomierz in 1712),[44] nor the ritually repeated demands of regional parliaments that Jews be expelled for their "horrible sacrilege of the Most Holy Sacrament,"[45] nor the anti-Jewish riots that so usually accompanied rumors of ritual murder.[46] Whatever their eventual legal outcome, host-desecration and ritual murder trials effectively terrorized the local Jewish community. Sebastjan Miczyński gleefully recounts the wailing, begging, and crying of the Jews not just of Lublin, but also of Poznań, Lwów, Gniezno, and Kraków, as they await anticipated massacre after the 1598 trial in Lublin for the alleged ritual murder near Łosice.[47]

Nevertheless, such massacres and expulsions occurred much less often than one might expect, given the horrific rhetoric of ritual murder accusation. It is to this puzzle, and what it tells us about the differences between witch trials and trials for ritual murder, that I now turn.

Unique Events, Eternal Structures

Halfway through a chronological account of alleged ritual murders in Poland, Sebastjan Miczyński pauses to ask himself, "Why do I busy myself enumerating examples of so obvious a thing?"[48] The anti-Judaic tracts of early modern Poland betray an addiction to such lists and to expressions of the obviousness, the openness, and the clarity of their implications. Ritual murder pamphlets and the trials they reported reinforced each other, creating a web of plausibility, a discourse through which the horrific crimes perpetrated by Jews on Christian children could be represented as common knowledge. When the trial of Katarzyna Kucharzowa in Przemyśl devolved from Eucharistic magic into a generalized attack on the Przemyśl Jewish community for host desecration, the town prosecutor could argue that "it is not new for the Jews to commit such sacrilege and murders of innocent Christian children, to which numerous trials, court decrees, confessions, executions, all brought to light in published volumes, testify."[49] In his *Exposure of the treacheries, the evil Ceremonies, the secret councils, the practices harmful to the Commonwealth, and the horrible intentions of the Jews* (1621), the medical doctor Sebastian Śleszkowski avers that he will not "list out all our Polish children that they have unmercifully murdered": he goes on to do precisely that, at several pages' length.[50] Moreover, these lists tend to highlight the recent and the local. Having recited a few famous international examples of host desecration and ritual murder, Miczyński notes that "we have domestic examples as well, "which he enumerates at length.[51] Stefan Żuchowski alternates chapters demonstrating the universality of Jewish wickedness with local Polish examples:

> Chapter 75. The cruelty and treachery of the Jews against Christians.
> Chapter 79. Similarly in Poland.
> Chapter 87. On the sacrilegious theft of the Most Holy Sacrament.
> Chapter 90. In Poland.
> Chapter 104. Foreign examples of the Jewish murder of children.
> Chapter 105. Examples in Poland of such murder.[52]

Despite this specificity of place and time, of names and dates, the textual memorializations of ritual murder endorse a timeless, universal conclusion. Sebastjan Miczyński, chronicling the alleged ritual murder in Kunia near Vilnius in 1574, displays this double aspect of blood libel, its tendency to demonstrate universal truths through concrete local evidence: we get gory details of the alleged murder, wherein the "Jew Jachym Smerłowicz" "like a cruel wolf," fell upon the Christian girl Elżbieta, threw her in a sack, and, cutting her throat, drained her blood into a pot "as one bleeds a goose."[53] Miczyński recounts this up close and personal anecdote after Piotr Skarga's account from his bestselling *Lives of the saints from the old and the new testament*, where Skarga treats Elżbieta's murder as a local example of the "martyrdom" of little Simon of Trent in 1475.[54] Elżbieta's story underwrote Simon's for Skarga, while Simon's story reciprocally underwrote Elżbieta's for Miczyński, and both reinforce the same message of timeless ubiquity: the general tendency of Jewish cruelty is continually re-proven through this or that particular instance of their "cruel murder of innocent children."[55] Similarly, Miczyński's account of a specific allegation of host desecration in Kraków in 1617 leads on directly to timeless generalizations and similarly universal conclusions: "The cursed Jews can never assuage their inborn wrath; they can never be satisfied or satiated even by the greatest cruelty toward the Lord Christ; they themselves deserve fiery cruelty, to be burnt to ashes."[56] A hundred years after Miczyński, Stefan Żuchowski approached the recent ritual murder trial in Sandomierz in a similar way: as the title of his tract makes clear, it intends to record an extremely specific event—*The Criminal Trial concerning the Innocent Child Jerzy Krasnowski three Years ago, 1710, August 18, in Sandomierz, Cruelly murdered by the Jews*.[57] But Żuchowski presents this single murder in a very specific time and place as token of a type, as a particular moment in an ongoing epic of cruel murders endlessly repeated. As R. Po-chia Hsia has perceptively commented in relation to the famous ritual murder trial in Trent in 1475: "the unique event, Simon's death, and the historicity of past child murders are subsumed in the eternal structure of repeated Jewish rituals."[58] Both the present case and the record of the past serve only to endlessly prove the timeless verity of Jewish cruelty.

Although, as we have seen, the blood-libel pamphleteers are addicted to lists, they rhetorically acknowledge the superfluity of such lists. As Piotr Hyacinth Pruszcz puts the matter:

> But those odoriferous wretches, helpless with desire for the blood of innocent children, often exert and fulfill their cruelty and wrath on innocent children ransomed by the most precious Blood of our Lord and Christ (adding thus not to their own purification but rather to their doom), which blood they themselves first spilt at Christ's cruel death: *let his blood be upon us and upon our children*. Passing over in amnesty by reason of its oldness the excess of their predation on innocent children, I recollect here for examination just a few such attacks, such as elderly people alive today might call to mind.[59]

Of course Pruszcz, like Śleszkowski before him, does not hold to this promise of recollecting "just a few" examples of Jewish perfidy, but his point is clear—examples need not be enumerated, since they are all, always, the same.

The abominable crime of witchcraft, so similar in its details of cruel infanticide and diabolical sacrilege, gains its legitimacy through very different rhetorical strategies. Demonologists tell stories and provide examples, but they rarely provide lists, reproduce court documents verbatim, or enumerate names and dates. To be sure, some writers on witchcraft underwrote their authority by retelling alleged eyewitness anecdotes collected from the magistrates at witch trials: Johannes Nider drew on his "extensive and profound" conversations with the magistrate Peter of Bern.[60] Gianfrancesco Pico della Mirandola insists that his *Strix* relates "unmitigated history, which I gathered partly with my eyes, and partly with my ears, when the transcripts of the interrogations were read to me."[61] Jean Bodin strengthens the verisimilitude of his *Démonomanie des sorciers* with examples prefaced by phrases such as "Aubert de Poitiers, a lawyer of the Parlement, told me ... ," "Master Claude Dessay, the King's Prosecutor at Ribemont, told me ... ," "Bouvin, Bailif of Châteauroux, ... , told me ... ," and so on.[62] But such stories never lose the character of anecdote: similar to the *legenda* of saints lives or the *exempla* of sermons on which demonological accounts were sometimes modeled, these stories were presumed true without requiring extensive corroboration through multiplicity of witness. Institoris, for example, rests his account of witches' desecration of the host on the testimony of an unnamed witch "in a town that it would not be helpful to name, since considerations of charity and reason order and urge this."[63] The demonological literature does not catalog witch trials: it does not name and list the accused witches, their victims and judges, the date and place of trial. No demonological text, in Poland or elsewhere, provides anything similar to the long catalogs of cases collected by Miczyński or Śleszkowski or Żuchowski. Writers on witchcraft argued with great heat about a vast array of contested points, and they often deployed alleged eyewitness accounts drawn from witch trials to support their claims and counterclaims; nevertheless until very late in the witch-trial era, almost none of them doubted the reality of witchcraft itself. As Stuart Clark has influentially argued, so-called skeptical writers on witchcraft shared a discourse with the "credulous" demonologists they critiqued, and their arguments often amounted to matters of detail or emphasis.[64]

It should be noted that the preceding discussion of demonology relies entirely on non-Polish examples. Poland produced no demonology at all, unless one wishes to count Stanisław Ząbkowic's translation of the *Malleus maleficarum*, which enjoyed just one edition in 1614.[65] In Poland, witch trials self-perpetuated without any apparent need for literary texts to fuel the pyres.[66] As Luise White suggests, people tend to "construct and repeat stories that carry the values and meanings" that uphold their general worldview.[67] The accusations against Polish witches display a sufficient coherence of motif to suggest that stories about witches were whispered in peasant huts and noble manors for hundreds of years—perhaps the author of the *Witch denounced* was right after all that "at table or at ordinary gatherings one hears of no other subject than of Witches." Joanna Tokarska-Bakir has demonstrated a similar underground current of ritual murder legend in nineteenth- and twentieth-century Polish folklore, an undercurrent that could surface in violence at any time.[68] Tokarska-Bakir argues that such legends sustain an "open secret" about Jewish perfidy—a secret that could be and sometimes was made explicit, with tragic results.[69] But the early modern Polish tracts on ritual murder demanded, and did not receive, a more total adherence: they strove for but did not succeed in demonstrating the indubitability of ritual murder and of the irredeemably evil Polish Jew.

The blood-libel pamphlets typically insist that at least some cases of ritual murder and host desecration were "openly known throughout the Polish Crown."[70] They are spoken of "not only in Warszawa in Parliament; all of Poland was full of this news."[71] We have seen at the beginning of this chapter that this characterization is probably accurate. Every effort was made to publicize and memorialize such trials: the verdicts of the Crown Tribunal printed in pamphlet form, the body of the "martyred" victim preserved "like a jewel" in a local church, the testimony of accusers and confessions of the accused commemorated in verse. And yet despite the tediously repeated insistence that "these facts are indubitable," many continued to doubt the reality, or at least the generality, of Jewish ritual murder and host desecration.[72] The ritual murder pamphlets wielded court documents as a weapon against *Christian* qualms and quibbles; the findings of the Tribunal and the burnt bodies of the condemned Jews were made to bear witness to the clear and present danger of further ritual murders. Śleszkowski's *Exposure of the treacheries . . . of the Jews* is typical in this regard: it reprints the entire 1598 verdict of the Crown Tribunal in Lublin against the Jews, not for its own sake nor even as a commemoration of the "martyred" boy Wojciech, but rather so that: "having written it out word for word, from this judicial trial everyone can clearly and evidentially come to understand that it is a certain and unmistakable fact, that *everywhere and over the entire world, wheresoever they live amongst us*, the Jews murder and slay Christian children, and drink and eat their innocent blood at Eastertime."[73] Concerning the same trial (the records of which he likewise reproduces), Szymon Hubicki exclaims: "What do those indispensible half-Jews say to this? Those who suppose all Jewish [ritual] murders are just fairytales and idle gossip? This trial took place at the [Crown] Tribunal, almost *in Theatro* of the whole Kingdom, not in some corner, not perfunctorily nor without due consideration, but carefully, nor did just a single judge preside, but many illustrious magistrates."[74]

The Kraków physician Sebastian Petrycy also rests his case on the purportedly indubitable evidence of authoritative legal documents: "They thirst for blood and spill Christian blood, concerning which one finds a great deal in Chronicles, and even in our own time: in Lublin before the Tribunal they were punished for this. Also in Bochnia. The court records bear witness to what they did."[75] Śleszkowski makes the same point more concisely: the details of ritual murder "all may be found in the court record-books of the [Crown] Tribunal. Search under the Year 1598."[76] And yet doubts remained; not everyone was convinced.

Ambiguous Monstrosities

"These matters are no secret," Miczyński insists.[77] Yet he and his many imitators went to great trouble to demonstrate and prove this supposedly common knowledge. And they do so because of what they perceive to be the stubborn persistence of doubts about the reality of ritual murder—doubts engendered, Żuchowski implies, from reading accounts of ritual murder "through Jewish eyeglasses."[78] It would be a mistake to attribute these imputations of incredulity to mere rhetoric. On the contrary, the problem of general unbelief, or at least general doubt, runs through this genre as its central problem. For if it really did seem clear to the entire Christian community that "the Jews without the slightest doubt ... must kill at least one Christian child, if not a few, every Year in every Country"—if this were generally held to be true—then Śleszkowski's recommended solution of expulsion in any town where this was proved at trial would be hopelessly inadequate.[79] If the "Universal Proposition" that "Jews murder Christian Children, and require their blood" were securely established in the minds of the majority of the Polish Christian community, if such a timeless, universal propensity to infanticide were proved, what solution could there possibly be except the immediate expulsion of the entire Jewish community from Poland?[80]

But despite the constant protests that "everybody knows" about Jewish ritual murder, everyone did not know, or did not accept, or did not fully accept as necessarily true of all Jews the claims of these authors. Magda Teter has shown that accusations against the local Jewish community of ritual murder or host desecration "turned into public displays of anti-Jewish sentiments *only when officials did accept anti-Jewish myths*"—and not every official always did so.[81] "The outcome was dependent on the complicity of local authorities and local judges who allowed such religious dramas to happen," and in any number of cases, incipient trials fizzled due to complex factors of local and even national politics.[82] As Miczyński laments, having been driven out of Spain, Hungary, Bohemia, Silesia, Nuremberg, Regensburg, Strasburg, Basel, and "just now from Frankfurt," in Poland "the Jew finds the safest sanctuary, in your land he finds protection; your land is his Asylum."[83] Such political factors that mitigated ritual murder allegations, and such asylum as Jews found in Poland (however tenuous, however conditional, however impermanent) could not have occurred if the myth of ritual murder were widely and securely believed. As Hugo Grotius's student Jerzy Słupecki remarked, "here in our Poland ... Jews are accused of a most atrocious crime, and one that, if it can be proved, can never in my view be expiated by any punishment."[84]

As a number of scholars have stressed, rumors of the ritual abuse, murder, and cannibalistic consumption of children constitute central ingredients in an ancient and global demonization of the other.[85] Whether it is alleged Satanic Ritual Abuse in twentieth-century California daycare centers or the orgiastic infanticidal anthropophagy ascribed to early Christians by their opponents, whether it is the witches of the Pyrenees eating "the heart of some . . . baby stewed in violence" or the Jews of Lithuania slitting open the innocent child Elżbieta "as one bleeds a goose," such rumors of murder contribute, as Michael Lambek suggests, to a sense of "the moral collapse of the world."[86] From one perspective then, both ritual murder and witchcraft accusations appear as more or less equivalent moments in a long, dreary, predictable history of the human propensity for demonizing others. David Frankfurter, while not discussing alleged Jewish ritual murder specifically, traces a long trajectory of Western civilization's propensity to imagine "tableaux of perversity" depicting the early Christian, the medieval heretic or the early modern witch as "a cannibal and pervert who engages in unspeakable and irrational acts; consequently he is not human."[87]

Imagined witchcraft incorporated individual accused witches into such tableaux of perversity, but they were never deployed against a recognizable community of witches—for the simple reason that no such communities existed, in Poland or anywhere else. Nine out of ten Polish witches were female, and there can be little doubt that, as elsewhere in Europe, witchcraft accusation rested on and helped maintain a deep current of misogyny. But nobody ever identified all women with witches or deployed the image of the infanticidal witch to propose the expulsion or eradication of women as such. Even the most rabid demonologist had a mother, and only in fantasy or absurd jest has anyone imagined "what a queer world it would be, if the girls were all transported far beyond the Northern Sea."[88] As the early, influential demonologist Johannes Nider put it, although most witches are women, the female sex per se, created in the image of god, cannot be condemned: women are a "necessary evil."[89] The fears invoked by diabolical witchcraft and the vengeance those fears engender remain chronic and indeterminate: this or that specific witch can be found out and burnt, but there are always others and it was never clear who those others might be: "the fear surrounding the witch lay in the very fact that it was *not* easy to categorically say whether someone was evil or not; the threat did not lie in their 'otherness' but rather in their very sameness."[90] Indeed, as the anthropologist Manning Nash argued long ago, such ambiguity is definitional of witchcraft beliefs worldwide: "Since witches are practitioners of aggressive and deadly magic and are continual threats to the social order, and operate in violation of the moral rules of a society, it is not possible to have a set of cultural beliefs which provides general and immediately verifiable rules for the identification of a witch. If such operational witch theory did exist it would mean that no witches would, for nobody would suffer their presence."[91]

Witchcraft accusation constructs an imagined demonized community, and constructs it ambiguously. Without this ambiguity, fears of witchcraft would lack their typically chronic, long-term character: if membership in the imagined community of witches correlated clearly with a real group of real people, all witches would immediately be identified and eliminated from the world once and for all. Ritual murder accusation, in contrast, lacks this ambiguous reference: it demonized and made monstrous an already stigmatized community of real, recognizable local people.[92] To quote Słupecki again, "this accusation is pinned not merely on a few individuals, but on the whole people, as if they all consented to committing such a heinous act."[93] Suspicions of ritual murder served to reinforce, inflame, and exacerbate an already present prejudice. Despite the concreteness of reference, the names and dates and places so characteristic of accounts of ritual murder, the "ethnography of blood" these accounts uphold remains strangely timeless, placeless, and free-floating: as Miri Rubin says of the related crime of host desecration, its universalizing framework turns "the abusers into offenders against every Christian and all Christians, as far removed as possible from any immediate context."[94] Ritual murder trials are never really about themselves: they point outward from the courtroom or the torture chamber to the local Jewish community and ultimately to (Christian imaginaries of) "the Jews" as such, always and everywhere. The confessions of tortured witches similarly contribute to "an ethnography of blood," but this ethnography has no subject outside the imagination. And thus witch trials, despite the hermeneutic uses to which they are put, tend to be about themselves—about identifying who, in this instance in this time and place, is guilty of witchcraft.

While both myths transform real people into dehumanized monsters worthy only of the stake, witchcraft accusation could never lead to the destruction of the (nonexistent) communities of witches. In contrast, ritual murder accusations could, and often did, spread to the whole local Jewish community, resulting in edicts of expulsion, the granting of *privilegia de non tolerandis Judaeis*, and popular violence directed indiscriminately at all local Jews.[95] As Francesca Matteoni argues, "the fear expressed by monstrous beings finds *a visible, and therefore, a destructible form* in the ethnical and religious difference embodied by the Jews."[96] But the Jews of Poland were not destroyed; they survived through centuries of such accusations and despite the continued ravings of Miczyński and his imitators. It is a peculiar and melancholy reflection that the frustration expressed by the pamphleteers of blood libel pays tribute to the (relative, tentative, ultimately destroyed) *convivencia* of early modern Poland.

MICHAEL OSTLING teaches at Barrett, the Honors College of Arizona State University, and is an Honorary Fellow of the Institute for Advanced Studies in the Humanities, University of Queensland. He is the author of *Between the Devil and the Host: Imagining Witchcraft in Early Modern Poland* (2011) and editor of *Fairies, Demons and Nature Spirits: "Small Gods" at the Margins of Christendom* (2017).

NOTES

1. *Czarownica powołana, abo krotka nauka y prestroga z strony czarownic* (Gdańsk, Poland: Jan Daniel Stoll, 1714 [1639]), 3. Here and elsewhere I preserve the idiosyncratic capitalization of early modern sources.

2. Adam Teller, "In the Land of Their Enemies? The Duality of Jewish Life in Eighteenth-Century Poland," *Polin* 19 (2006): 431–46. See also Gershon Hundert, *The Jews in a Polish Private Town: The Case of Opatów in the Eighteenth Century* (Baltimore, MD: John Hopkins University Press, 1992).

3. Throughout this chapter I make little attempt to distinguish trials for host desecration from trials for ritual murder. For the Polish Catholics who instigated both, they were variations on a theme. As the nobility of Bielsk put the matter in a regional parliamentary decree of 1650, the Jews unleash "their wrath and cruelty against little Christian children and . . . commit sacrilege against the most holy sacrament." See Adam Kaźmierczyk, *Sejmy i sejmiki szlacheckie wobec Żydów w drugiej połowie XVII wieku* (Warsaw: Wydawnictwo Sejmowe, 1994), 152. The best overviews of host-desecration and ritual murder trials in early modern Poland remain Hanna Węgrzynek, *"Czarna legenda" Żydów. Procesy o rzekome mordy rytualne w dawnej Polsce* (Warsaw: Bellona, 1995); and Zenon Guldon and Jacek Wijaczka, *Procesy o mordy rytualne w Polsce w XVI–XVIII w.* (Kielce: DCF, 1995). For a summary of the latter in English, see the same authors' "The Accusation of Ritual Murder in Poland, 1500–1800," *Polin* 10 (1997): 99–140. Magda Teter's *Sinners on Trial: Jews and Sacrilege after the Reformation* (Cambridge, MA: Harvard University Press, 2011) brings close archival research and a rich interpretative framework to this material.

4. Meier Bałaban, "Hugo Grotius and the Blood Libel Trials in Lublin, 1636," *Polin* 22 (2010): 47–67.

5. Jan Achacy Kmita, *Lament żydów Bocheńskich dla wygnania z Bochnie o Sakrament Naświętszy* (Kraków: Drukarnia Jana Szeligi, 1606). See also Teter, *Sinners on Trial*, 166–73.

6. Kazimierz Kaczmarczyk, "Opisy i notatki z starych aktów: Proces o czary w Bochni 1679 roku," *Lud* 16 (1910): 46. The Bochnia witch trial of 1679 is usefully juxtaposed to a trial in Przemyśl in 1630, which runs a similar story in reverse. A case of Christian host theft for fertility magic was heard quietly by the town court, until the accused witch implicated the Jews of Przemyśl. The case, now about Jewish host desecration, engaged the attention of Palatine of Kraków Stanisław Lubomirski and eventually of King Sigismund III himself. See Teter, *Sinners on Trial*, 176–99.

7. Teter, *Sinners on Trial*, 131–41, 150–53.

8. Michael Ostling, "Nieznany proces o czary i świętokradztwo w Lublinie, 1643," *Lud* 89 (2005): 191–204.

9. *Zbiór dekretów trybunału lubelskiego przeciw Żydom* (Kraków, Andrejowczyk, 1598); on which see briefly Stanisław Salmonowicz, "Niemiecki erudyta barokowy W. E. Tenzel a wyrok Trybunału Koronnego z 1598 r.," *Odrodzenie i Reformacja w Polsce* 33 (1988): 256.

10. Szymon Alexander Hubicki, *Zydowskie okrucieństwa nad Naświętszym Sakramentem y dziatkami chrześcianskimi* (Kraków: Mikołaj Szarffenberger, 1602).

11. Sebastjan Miczyński, *Zwierciadło Korony Polskiey* (Kraków: Maciej Jędrzeiowczyk, 1618), 17.

12. *Processus, Causae inter Instigatorem Judicji Tribunalis Regni, et perfidum Marcum Judaeum [etc.]* (Kraków: n.p., 1636), reproduced in Guldon and Wijaczka, *Procesy o mordy*, 118–22; *Decretum Tribunalis Regni Poloniae Anno Domini 1636 [etc.]* (n.p.: n.p., n.d.); Stefan Żuchowski, *Ogłos processow kryminalnych na Zydach o rozne Excessy także morderstwo dźieci [etc.]* (Sandomierz, Poland: n.p., 1700); *Process Kryminalny o Niewinne Dźiećię Jerzego Krasnowskiego . . . Okrutnie od Zydow zamordowane [etc.]* (Kraków: n.p., 1713).

13. *Dekret o zamęczeniu przez żydów dziecięcia katolickiego ferowany w grodzie żytomierskim* (Kraków: n.p., 1753). This and two other eighteenth-century pamphlets preserving the records of contemporaneous ritual murder trials can be found in Guldon and Wijaczka, *Procesy o mordy*, 130–51.

14. Tomasz Wiślicz, "The Township of Kleczew and Its Neighborhood Fighting the Devil (1624–1700)," *Acta Poloniae Historica* 89 (2004): 36.

15. This literary record is so rich that both Węgrzynek and Guldon and Wijaczka have been able to draw upon it to generate long and detailed tables of all known ritual murder trials in Poland (Węgrzynek, "Czarna legenda," 182–92; Guldon and Wijaczka, *Procesy o mordy*, 96–101). A similar table relying primarily on contemporaneous literary records of Polish witch trials would be very short indeed.

16. *Dekret w sprawie o zamordowanie okrutne przez Żydow chrześcianina Antoniego pod Zasławiem [etc.]* (n.p.: n.p., n.d.) in Guldon and Wijaczka, *Procesy o mordy*, 140.

17. Salmonowicz, "Niemiecki erudyta," 253.

18. Joanna Tokarska-Bakir, "Ganz Andere? Żyd jako czarownica i czarownica jako Żyd w Polskich i obcych źródłach etnograficznych, czyli jak czytać protokoły przesłuchań," *Res Publica Nowa* 8 (2001): 3–32. For a similar argument centered on Western Europe, see Carlo Ginzburg, *Ecstasies: Deciphering the Witches' Sabbath* (New York: Pantheon, 1991), 63–86.

19. Debra Higgs Strickland, "Monstrosity and Race in the Late Middle Ages," in *The Ashgate Research Companion to Monsters and the Monstrous*, ed. A. S. Mittman and P. Dendle (Farnham, UK: Ashgate, 2012), 376–80; Sigrid Brauner, "Cannibals, Witches and Shrews in the 'Civilizing Process,'" in *Neue Welt/Dritte Welt*, ed. S. Bauschinger and S. L. Cocalis (Tübingen: A. Franke, 1994), 1–27; Yvonne Owens, "The Saturnine History of Jews and Witches," *Preternature* 3, no. 1 (2014): 56–84.

20. Norman Cohn, *Europe's Inner Demons: The Demonization of Christians in Medieval Christendom*, rev. ed. (Chicago: University of Chicago Press, 2000 [1975]); cf. Andrew McGowan, "Eating People: Accusations of Cannibalism against Christians in the Second Century," *Journal of Early Christian Studies* 2 (1994): 413–42; David Frankfurter, "Ritual as Accusation and Atrocity: Satanic Ritual Abuse, Gnostic Libertinism, and Primal Murders," *History of Religions* 40, no. 4 (2001): 352–80. It was to such slanders that Hugo Grotius referred in his commentary on the Lublin ritual murder allegations of 1636: "What has not been alleged against the early Christians, nor against those almost of our age who had seceded from the Pope, and before then the Waldensians?" (Letter of Hugo Grotius to Jerzy Słupecki, 1636, reproduced in Bałaban, "Hugo Grotius and the Blood Libel Trials," 66).

21. Alan Charles Kors and Edward Peters, eds., *Witchcraft in Europe, 400–1700: A Documentary History*, 2nd ed. (Philadelphia: University of Pennsylvania Press, 2001), 153, 160, 165, 168. This term was gradually replaced by "sabbath" or "sabbat" (which also, if less directly, imply a Jewish connection), but "synagogue" can be found into the sixteenth and seventeenth centuries, e.g., in Francesco Maria Guazzo, *Compendium Maleficarum*, trans. E. Ashwin (New York: Dover, 1988 [1626]), bk. 1, ch. 12. The indispensable history of medieval Christian conflation of Jews with sorcerers remains Joshua Trachtenberg, *The Devil and the Jews: The Medieval Conception of the Jew and Its Relation to Modern Anti-Semitism* (New York: Jewish Publication Society, 2002 [1943]). For an important corrective to Trachtenberg's study that anticipates some of the arguments of the present chapter, see Anna Foa, "The Witch and the Jew: Two Alikes That Were Not the Same," in *From Witness to Witchcraft*, ed. J. Cohen (Wiesbaden: Harrassowitz, 1997), 361–74.

22. Stephen Haliczer, "The Jew as Witch: Displaced Aggression and the Myth of the Santo Niño De La Guardia," in *Cultural Encounters: The Impact of the Inquisition in Spain and the New World*, ed. M. E. Perry and A. J. Cruz (Berkeley: University of California Press, 1991), 146–55.

23. Michael D. Bailey, *Battling Demons: Witchcraft, Heresy, and Reform in the Late Middle Ages* (University Park: Pennsylvania State University Press, 2003), 121; Miri Rubin, *Gentile Tales: The Narrative Assault on Late Medieval Jews* (New Haven, CT: Yale University Press, 1999), 128; Bernadette Paton, "'To the Fire, to the Fire, Let Us Burn a Little Incense to God': Bernardino, Preaching Friars, and Maleficio in Late Medieval Siena," in *No Gods Except Me*, ed. C. Zika (Melbourne: University of Melbourne History Department, 1991), 7–36.

24. R. Po-chia Hsia, "Witchcraft, Magic, and the Jews in Late Medieval and Early Modern Germany," in Cohen, *From Witness to Witchcraft*, 419–33; Tamar Herzig, *Christ Transformed into a Virgin Woman: Lucia Brocadelli, Heinrich Institoris, and the Defense of the Faith* (Rome: Edizioni di Storia e Letteratura, 2013), 8–10, 38–44, 64–65, 136–40; Heinrich Institoris, *Malleus maleficarum* (Speyer, Germany: Peter Drach, 1487), bk. 2, quest. 1, chs. 5, 7, 12; Heinrich Institoris, *The Hammer of Witches: A Complete Translation of the Malleus Maleficarum*, ed. and trans. Christopher S. Mackay (New York: Cambridge University Press, 2009), 315–20, 323–30, 361–66.

25. For the image and analysis, see Charles Zika, *Exorcising Our Demons: Magic, Witchcraft, and Visual Culture in Early Modern Europe* (Leiden: Brill, 2003), 475–79; and Charles Zika, *The Appearance of Witchcraft: Print and Visual Culture in Sixteenth-Century Europe* (New York: Routledge, 2007), 233–35.

26. Stuart Clark, *Thinking with Demons: The Idea of Witchcraft in Early Modern Europe* (New York: Oxford University Press, 1997). On the notion of "hermeneutical Jews," see Jeremy Cohen, *Living Letters of the Law: Ideas of the Jew in Medieval Christianity* (Berkeley: University of California Press, 1999).

27. R. Po-chia Hsia, *Trent 1475: Stories of a Ritual Murder Trial* (New Haven, CT: Yale University Press, 1992), 81.

28. Węgrzynek, "*Czarna legenda*," 27–30; Rubin, *Gentile Tales*, 24–28; Walter Stephens, *Demon Lovers: Witchcraft, Sex, and the Crisis of Belief* (Chicago: University of Chicago Press, 2002); Caroline Walker Bynum, *Wonderful Blood: Theology and Practice in Late Medieval Northern Germany and Beyond* (Philadelphia: University of Pennsylvania Press, 2007); Michael Ostling, *Between the Devil and the Host: Imagining Witchcraft in Early Modern Poland* (Oxford: Oxford University Press, 2011), 165–82; Herzig, *Christ Transformed*, 64–65.

29. Albrycht Stanisław Radziwiłł, *Żywoty Świętych z naukami doktorów kościelnych* (Vilnius, Lithuania: n.p., 1693 [1653]), 520–21, quoted in Jurgita Šiaučiūnaitė-Verbickienė, "Blood Libel in a Multi-Confessional Society: The Case of the Grand Duchy of Lithuania," *East European Jewish Affairs* 38, 2 (2008): 205.

30. Miczyński, *Zwierciadło*, 78. Although other Polish anti-Jewish tracts similarly ascribe witchcraft to the Jews, this "witchcraft" often serves simply as a metaphor for traditional stereotypes about Jewish cleverness with money. See, e.g., Sebastian Śleszkowski, *Odkrycie zdrad, zloslivvych Ceremoniy, . . . y straszliwych zamyslow Zydowskich* (Brunsbergae, Germany: Georgii Schonfels, 1621), ff. 38v.–39v.; Żuchowski, *Proces Kriminalny*, cap. 82.

31. Benedykt Chmielowski, *Nowe Ateny, albo Akademia Wszelkiej Sciencyi pełna*, 4 vols. (Lwów, Poland: Drukarnia JKMci Collegii Societatis Jesu, 1754–1756), 3:244.

32. Already in 1844 an early survey of the Polish witch trials noted "the fact worth pondering, that although our small towns were full of Jews, one finds no trace that any Jew, male or female, was ever summoned before the terrifying Tribunal for the witches" (S.X., "Kilka słów o czarownicach w Polsce," *Przyjaciel Ludu* 11, nos. 22–23 [1844]: 169). This assertion has stood the test of time, with two marginal exceptions: the semijudicial lynching of a Jewish woman in 1681 in Lithuania, and the imprisonment of the Jewish woman Czajka Szmujlicha on suspicion of magical healing in 1718 in Kamieniec Podolski (Kamianets-Podilskyi). See Kaźmierczyk, *Sejmy i sejmiki*, 70–71; Małgorzata Pilaszek, *Procesy o czary w Polsce w wiekach XV–XVIII* (Kraków: Universitas, 2008), 299. On the near absence of Jews from witch trials elsewhere in Europe, see H. C. Erik Midelfort, *Witch Hunting in Southwestern Germany, 1562–1684* (Stanford, CA: Stanford University Press, 1972), 189–90; Foa, "The Witch and the Jew," 362–68; Foa, "Stregoneria ed espulsione degli ebrei: Spunti ed appunti per una ricerca," *Archivio italiano per la storia della pietà* 25 (2012): 35–53. I am indebted to Tamar Herzig for bringing this final reference to my attention.

33. See Węgrzynek, *"Czarna legenda,"* 79–82, 85–89; Teter, *Sinners on Trial*, 176–99.

34. As when in a single decree of 1673 the Royal Assessory Court censured the town counsel of Kłodawa for its tendency to overeagerly "condemn both Christians and Jews to death." However, the high court was here responding to two separate trials, one against a Jewish man for host desecration, the other against five alleged witches. See Józef Rafacz, "Sprawy karne w sądach miejskich w epoce nowożytnej," *Kwartalnik Historyczny* 47 (1933): 562–63.

35. See esp. Teter, *Sinners on Trial*, 148–56, 86–94.

36. Kazimierz Florian Czartoryski, *Mandatum pastorale . . . de cautelis in processu contra sagas adhibendis* (Kraków: Krzysztof Domański, 1705 [1669]); Zenon and Stanisław Chodyński eds., *Monumenta Historica Dioceseos Wladislaviensis*, 25 vols (Włoclawek, Poland: Seminarii Dioecesani, 1881–1910), 5:10–15, 59–68; Michael Ostling, "Konstytucja 1543 r. i początki procesów o czary w Polsce," *Odrodzenie i Reformacja w Polsce* 49 (2005): 93–103.

37. Kaźmierczyk, *Sejmy i sejmiki*, 116.

38. Miczyński, *Zwierciadło*, 16–17.

39. Piotr Hyacinth Pruszcz, *Forteca Duchowna Krolestwa Polskiego [etc.]* 2 vols., (Kraków: Dźiedźicow Stanisława Lenczewskiego Bertut, 1662), 1:184. Concerning the similar honors accorded to Szymon Kierel in Vilnius, see Šiaučiūnaitė-Verbickienė, "Blood Libel in a Multi-Confessional Society," 205.

40. Poznańskie Towarzystwo Przyjaciół Nauk (PTPN), ms. 859 (Kleczew Criminalia 1624–1738) ff. 146–51. See Ostling, *Devil and the Host*, 176–80, for the relationship of this trial to legends of Jewish host desecration.

41. Guldon and Wijaczka, *Procesy o mordy*, 95–101. Guldon and Wijaczka do not calculate the number executed or otherwise killed as a direct consequence of a ritual murder accusation; my rough calculation of seventy-six such victims is estimated from their table of accusations and outcomes. This calculation does not include the forty Jews supposedly executed in Krasnocin at an unspecified date near the end of the seventeenth century—an occurrence known only from its brief, ambiguous mention in Żuchowski, *Proces Kriminalny*, 97. The figure also does not include trials against Jews for host desecration, for which no authoritative numbers are available.

42. Pilaszek, *Procesy*, 266, 292. These are minimal numbers, likely representing something like half the actual trials and executions; see Ostling, *Devil and the Host*, 16–24.
43. Guldon and Wijaczka, *Procesy o mordy*, 96–101; Teter, *Sinners on Trial*, 157–75.
44. Guldon and Wijaczka, *Procesy o mordy*, 18–34; Teter, *Sinners on Trial*, 176–99.
45. Kaźmierczyk, *Sejmy i sejmiki*, 68–69, 74–76, 116–20; Zenon Guldon, "Straty ludności żydowskiej w Koronie w latach potopu," in *Rzeczpospolita w latach Potopu*, ed. J. Muszyńska and J. Wijaczka (Kielce, Poland: Wyższa Szkoła Pedagogiczna, 1996), 302–3.
46. This pattern can be traced forward deep into the present: most postwar antisemitic violence in Poland was sparked by rumors of ritual murder. See Marcin Zaremba, "Mit mordu rytualnego w powojenney Polsce. Archeologia i hipotezy," *Kultura i Społeczeństwo* 51, no. 2 (2007): 91–135.
47. Miczyński, *Zwierciadło*, 15.
48. Ibid., 18.
49. Quoted in Teter, *Sinners on Trial*, 179.
50. Śleszkowski, *Odkrycie zdrad*, f. 23v. contains the promise not to list cases—a promise broken at ff. 82r.–98v. Cf. Miczyński, *Zwierciadło*, 13–19; Pruszcz, *Forteca Duchowna Krolestwa Polskiego*, 1:182–85, 2: 10–12; Żuchowski, *Proces Kriminalny*, 104–5.
51. Miczyński, *Zwierciadło*, 7, cf. similar lists at 10, 13.
52. Żuchowski, *Proces Kriminalny*, unpaginated table of contents.
53. Miczyński, *Zwierciadło*, 14.
54. Piotr Skarga, *Żywoty świętych starego i nowego zakonu [etc.]*, 12 vols. (Kraków: Anczyc i Spółka, 1881–1889 [1579]), 3:343–51.
55. Miczyński, *Zwierciadło*, 13.
56. Ibid., 9. See also the recorded verdicts from ritual murder trials themselves: "Therefore the court, for such a serious crime of the infidel nation in this Catholic state, [perpetrated] on an innocent Christian by means of cruel torture and murder, and Christian blood [extracted] for the superstitious medicaments of repulsive Jewry . . . , sentences each of them as described severally below" (*Dekret w sprawie o zamordowanie okrutne przez Żydów chrześcianina*, in Guldon and Wijaczka, *Procesy o mordy*, 140).
57. Żuchowski, *Proces Kriminalny*.
58. Hsia, *Trent 1475*, 94.
59. Pruszcz, *Forteca Duchowna Krolestwa Polskiego*, 1:183, emphasis in the original.
60. Johannes Nider, *Formicarius* (Vienna, ca. 1437), bk. 5, ch. 3, quoted in Bailey, *Battling Demons*, 28.
61. Stephens, *Demon Lovers*, 91.
62. Jean Bodin, *On the Demon Mania of Witches*, trans. Randy Scott (Toronto: Centre for Renaissance and Reformation Studies, 1995 [1580]), esp. 113, 119.
63. Institoris, *Malleus maleficarum*, bk. 2, quest. 1, ch. 5 (*Hammer of Witches*, 319). Similarly unrooted anecdotes conscerning "a certain witch" or "a certain woman" abound in the demonological literature: see, e.g., Stephens, *Demon Lovers*, 159–61; and *Czarownica powołana*, 26.
64. Clark, *Thinking with Demons*, esp. 195–213.
65. Stanisław Ząbkowic, *Młot na czarownice* (Kraków: Szymon Kempini, 1614). On the very limited literary representation of early modern Polish witchcraft, see Ostling, *Devil and the Host*, 48–53.
66. The same can be said of Western Europe, despite the vast outpouring of demonological literature in this region. After the important intellectual work of constructing the stereotype of a diabolical witch cult—work more or less completed in the *Malleus maleficarum* of 1487—witch trials proceeded largely under their own power and for their own reasons. See Clark, *Thinking with Demons*, vii–viii.

67. Luise White, *Speaking with Vampires: Rumor and History in Colonial Africa* (Berkeley: University of California Press, 2000), 30.
68. Joanna Tokarska-Bakir, "Żydzi u Kolberga," in *Rzeczy mgliste. Eseje i studia* (Warsaw: Fundacja Pogranicze, 2004). See also Tokarska-Bakir, *Legendy o krwi. Antropologia przesądu* (Warsaw: W.A.B., 2008); and Jolanta Żyndul, *Kłamstwo krwi: Legenda mordu rytualnego na ziemiach polskich w XIX i XX wieku* (Warsaw: Cyklady, 2011).
69. Tokarska-Bakir, "Blood Libel in Poland and the Eastern Borderlands at the Beginning of the Twenty-first Century: Politics of Memory" (paper precirculated at the Strange World of Ritual Murder Symposium, University of Illinois, October 16–19, 2014), 4. Compare the insinuative strategy of "contrahistory" deployed by twenty-first-century Polish antisemites (ibid., 12–13) to the explicit declarative claims of their early modern confreres.
70. Śleszkowski, *Odkrycie zdrad*, f. 23v.
71. Miczyński, *Zwierciadło*, 14.
72. Sebastian Petrycy, *Polityka Aristotelesowey* (Kraków: Szymon Kempini, 1605), 74.
73. Śleszkowski, *Odkrycie zdrad*, f. 84r., emphasis added.
74. Hubicki, *Żydowskie okrucieństwa*, quoted in Salmonowicz, "Niemiecki erudyta," 161.
75. Petrycy, *Polityka*, 74.
76. Śleszkowski, *Odkrycie zdrad*, f. 24r. See also Miczyński, *Zwierciadło*, 13.
77. Miczyński, *Zwierciadło*, 13.
78. Żuchowski, *Ogłos Processow*, unpaginated, final page.
79. Śleszkowski, *Odkrycie zdrad*, f. 82r. See also Miczyński, *Zwierciadło*, 13; and Żuchowski, *Proces Kriminalny*, 111–12.
80. Żuchowski, *Proces Kriminalny*, sec. III.
81. Teter, *Sinners on Trial*, 209, emphasis added.
82. Ibid., 8; cf. Kaźmierczyk, *Sejmy i sejmiki*, 154.
83. Miczyński, *Zwierciadło*, 4–5.
84. Letter of Jerzy Słupecki to Hugo Grotius, 1636; reproduced in Bałaban, "Hugo Grotius and the Blood Libel Trials," 64.
85. Richard Kieckhefer, "Avenging the Blood of Children: Anxiety over Child Victims and the Origins of the European Witch Trials," in *Heresy and Witchcraft in the Middle Ages*, ed. A. Ferreiro (Leiden: Brill, 1998), 91–109; Jean S. La Fontaine, *Speak of the Devil: Tales of Satanic Abuse in Contemporary England* (Cambridge: Cambridge University Press, 1998); Frankfurter, "Ritual as Accusation."
86. Pierre de Lancre, *De l'inconstance des mauvais anges et Demons, 1612*, as quoted in *Evil Incarnate*, 74; Miczyński, *Zwierciadło*, 14; Michael Lambek, "Monstrous Desires and Moral Disquiet: Reflections on Jean Comaroff's 'Consuming Passions,'" *Culture* 17, nos. 1–2 (1997): 22.
87. Frankfurter, "Ritual as Accusation," 368.
88. "Reuben and Rachel," in *Arizona 4-H Song Book*, ed. H. R. Baker (Tucson: University of Arizona College of Agriculture Extension Circular no. 87, 1935), 19. Tokarska-Bakir's otherwise perspicacious analysis of the parallels between witch and Jew is vitiated by her failure to recognize this crucial difference between the two communities. See especially Tokarska-Bakir, "Żyd jako czarownica," 8–11.
89. Nider, *Formicarius*, bk. 5, ch. 8, quoted in Bailey, *Battling Demons*, 51. Similarly, Rebecca Lesses notes that the Talmudic dictum that "most women are sorceresses" could never become the basis for a gynocidal persecution of witches, because "'most women' included the rabbis' sisters, mothers, daughters, and wives." See Rebecca Lesses, "'The Most Worthy of Women Is a Mistress of Magic': Women as Witches and Ritual Practitioners in *I Enoch* and Rabbinic Sources," in *Daughters of Hecate: Women and Magic in the Ancient World*, ed. K. B. Stratton and D. S. Kalleres (New York: Oxford University Press, 2014), 89.

90. Laura Kounine, "The Gendering of Witchcraft: Defence Strategies of Men and Women in German Witchcraft Trials," *German History* 31, no. 3 (2013): 296.

91. Manning Nash, "Witchcraft as Social Process in a Tzeltal Community," in *Witchcraft, Magic, and Curing*, ed. John Middleton (Garden City, NJ: Natural History Press, 1967), 128. See also Mary Douglas, *Purity and Danger* (London: Routledge, 2002 [1969]), 172 (quoted as the epigraph to this chapter).

92. For a sensitive account of the interplay between stigmatization and integration of the Jewish community in early modern Poland, see Teller, "Land of Their Enemies."

93. Jerzy Słupecki, letter of 1636, quoted in Bałaban, "Hugo Grotius and the Blood Libel Trials," 64.

94. Rubin, *Gentile Tales*, 155.

95. Joanna Tokarska-Bakir makes a similar point: "In contrast to texts about weather-workers, vampires, or the so-called plague-maiden, 'Jewish motifs' designate real people, and for that very reason one must not limit analysis to their symbolic representation." See Tokarska-Bakir, "Żydzi u Kolberga," 49.

96. Francesca Matteoni, "The Jew, the Blood, and the Body in Late Medieval and Early Modern Europe," *Folklore* 119, no. 2 (2008): 184, emphasis added.

THE JEWISH BLOOD LIBEL LEGEND
A Folkloristic Perspective

Haya Bar-Itzhak

IN THE STUDY of genres in folk literature, "legend" is defined as a story, set in a specific geographic space and in historical time that the narrating society believes to be true.[1] The Jewish blood libel legend is an example of Jewish folklore created as an inner response to the folklore of the Other, the Christian blood libel and its devastating results. This chapter analyzes different types of Jewish blood libel legends, their message and function. To understand the essence of the Jewish legend, I begin with a short description of the Christian blood libel legend and a review of the scholarship about its origin. Whereas the Christian blood libel is an accusation legend, the Jewish tale is a deliverance legend. Golem legends are a special cycle of deliverance legends. I discuss their sources and the genre of *aggadot shevah* (praise legends) about the Maharal that created the golem for the purpose of saving Jews from the blood libel. The last section relates to historical legends that end with the protagonist's death and reflect the connection between folklore and history. I focus on the versions of a blood libel legend with a woman at its center and discuss it in the framework of legends about women set in times of "persecution." By exposing the message, function, and paradigm created by this legend, I show that Jewish blood libel tales that center on women add an additional model to the existing paradigms about women.

THE CHRISTIAN LEGEND

The accounts of blood libels in Jewish folklore are a reaction to the folklore of the Christians among whom Jews lived and its tragic results. Christian legends tell of ritual murders committed by Jews who ostensibly kill a Christian child (usually a boy) and use his blood in their Passover rites. Over the centuries, blood libels led to the torture and killing of many Jews, and, on occasion, to the massacre of entire communities. In a collection of articles on the subject, the folklorist Alan Dundes describes these tales as the "most bizarre and dangerous legend ever created by the human imagination," declaring that the goal of his volume is "to hold an evil legend up to the light of reason."[2] As I wrote in my review of the book, unlike scholars who refrain from value judgments in their research, Dundes takes a clear stand, asserting that there can be an "evil folklore" and that the Christian blood libel is a classic example of this type of folklore. Noting the catastrophic outcome of blood libels, he argues that folklore, which is generally identified with pleasure and aesthetics, can be destructive.[3]

Although this chapter does not deal with the Christian legend and its origins, we need to briefly review a number of hypotheses that scholars have advanced about it. Using a psychoanalytical approach, Dundes sees the Christian blood libel as a "projective inversion" of the central Christian ritual of eating the consecrated host, which represents the body of Christ, and drinking the wine, which represents his blood, that caused guilt feelings. The guilt feelings that this ritual stirred among the faithful, who are eating the flesh and drinking the blood of the Son of God, caused them to project the same action onto the Jews.[4]

The scholar Magdalene Schultz links the blood libel to the frequent abandonment and consequent death of children in medieval Christian society. Accusing the Jews of responsibility for the children's deaths, so that they could celebrate Passover "properly," was one way for Christians to cope with their guilt feelings over how they treated their children.[5] Cecil Roth traces the source of blood libels to a misinterpretation of a Jewish Purim custom, namely, hanging and burning Haman (the Jew hater from the Book of Esther) in effigy, which triggered associations of human sacrifice.[6] The Israeli historian Ora Limor sees the blood libel as using a Jewish ritual to confirm a fundamental Christian paradigm, namely crucifixion—sacrifice—redemption. The blood libels repeat, time and again, the Jews' killing of a Christian, and the Christian victim becomes the redemptive sacrifice.[7] According to Amos Funkenstein, the blood libel helped the Church achieve its goals. The demonization of the Jews, which exploited the fear of the Other, resolved the paradox of its inability to convert the unbelievers.[8]

As noted, Jewish legends about blood libels are a reaction to the Christian narrative and its devastating results. From this perspective, Jewish legends offer us a way to study the reciprocal relations between different types of folklore and the influence of the folklore of the Other on the evolution of Jewish folklore, and point out the manner in which a persecuted minority creates a folklore response to the evil folklore directed against them.

The Jewish Deliverance Legend

This suggests that if the Christian legend accused the Jews of ritual murder and resulted in the persecution and massacre of Jews, the Jewish legends should refute the accusation and tell how a Jewish individual or community was delivered from a blood libel. This is, indeed, the most common paradigm in Jewish folk narratives on the subject.[9]

The Jewish *oikotype* formulated in the Israel Folktale Archives (IFA), AT 730*, "Rescue of a Jewish Community," enumerates a number of possibilities, on the basis of the many such legends in its holdings:[10]

- AT 730d: The resuscitation or resurrection of the "murdered child" leads to the discovery of the truth.
- AT 730e: "He Who guards Israel neither slumbers nor sleeps": The (gentile) ruler cannot sleep. He goes out in the middle of the night and comes on the plotters who are trying to incriminate the Jews by murdering a Christian or exhuming a dead body. He frustrates their scheme.
- AT 730f: The Christian child whom the Jews were accused of murdering turns up safe and sound.
- AT 730g: The Jews, warned in advance (usually by a dream), get rid of the bottle of blood that the plotters planted in the Holy Ark, and thus are saved from the libel.

From a genre perspective, most Jewish stories about blood libels are sacred legends. The community is saved by divine intervention, overt or concealed. For the most part, this involves the appearance of the prophet Elijah, the figure that rescues and saves in times of trouble and crisis in Jewish folklore, and is associated both with Passover and with the final redemption of the Jewish people at the time of the Messiah.[11] These legends, with their happy ending—the individual or community is saved and the wicked enemies are punished—reflect the terror inspired by Christian blood libels and the yearning for God to save his people and rescue them from the threatening outcome of blood libels in the sacred time of Passover.

The Golem Legend

One of most famous cycles of deliverance legends from blood libels consists of the stories about the golem. Many of them are praise legends about Rabbi Judah Leib ben Bezalel, otherwise known as the Maharal of Prague (1520?–1609).[12] In the *shevah* the saintly figure becomes the object of identification, veneration, and emulation and serves to reinforce the world of sacred values. The legends about the Maharal and the golem are unique in the corpus of praise tales. In this cycle, already at his birth, the Maharal is associated with the refutation of a blood libel.

What follows is an analysis of one example of a legend from the IFA:

The Birth of the Maharal[13]

This story happened long ago, just before the Maharal was born. It happened on the eve of Pessah. The Maharal's mother was in labor. In those days the Jews would be charged with the murder of a Christian whose blood they allegedly used to prepare the matzo of Pessah. This is what they would do to the Jews before every holiday.

Now it happened that a Christian who hated Jews wanted to bring false charges against the Jews. He removed the body of a Christian from the churchyard. The body of a man who had died shortly before Pessah. He carried the body from the churchyard in a sack and dropped it at the rabbi's house, Rabbi Bezalel, the Maharal's father, saying: "They are going to find it, and they are going to say 'There! The rabbi has killed the Christian because he wants his blood for the Matzoth.'"[14]

That very night the rabbi's wife went into labor, and there was a great commotion in the house. Several people came to help. The midwife lived far away, and they wanted to go and bring her to the rabbi's house. They rushed out to fetch her. The Christian, who was an enemy of the Jews, saw them run, and he too started running so they should not catch him. They run—he runs, they run—he runs, they run—he runs.

The watchmen saw a man running and other men running in pursuit of him. They said: "Surely this man has stolen something, and they are trying to catch him." The watchmen caught him, opened the sack, and found the corpse. They said: "What is this?"

They took the Christian to the police station and kept him there till morning. Meanwhile, the people who were running to fetch the midwife found her and brought her to the rabbi's house, and this is how the Maharal was born. That is when you say, "There was a miracle."

In the morning they questioned the man, and the man pleaded guilty, saying he had taken the corpse in order to drop it at the rabbi's house so people should say the rabbi had killed a Christian for his blood because he needed it for the Matzoth.

The rabbi knew nothing about it, and the people who had brought the midwife did not know anything about it either. On the following day, which was Pessah, the governor sent for the rabbi. A messenger came to the rabbi's house and said, "The governor wants you." The rabbi replied: "You know today is a Jewish holiday, don't you; I cannot go to the governor's house on a holiday. Perhaps I can come tomorrow." But he said: "No, you have to go right now."

The rabbi went to the governor's house.

The governor said to him: "What did they steal yesterday? Was anything stolen from your house?"—"No, God forbid."

The governor continued: "Then why were there so many people at your house, and why did they all rush out?"

He answered: "They rushed out to bring the midwife because my wife was in labor."

And the rabbi explained all of it to the governor.

The governor said to the rabbi: "I want you to know that a miracle happened to you. I will issue an ordinance prohibiting blood libel as of today."

This is a classic *shevah*, set just before the birth of the saintly figure, which endows that event with a metaphysical dimension.[15] Surely, according to the legend, it was not by chance that the mother's contractions began at that precise moment! In this folk legend, the Maharal saves his people even before his birth—a sign of the future that links up with later legends about how, as an adult, he delivered the Jews from blood libels. In the version of this legend, discussed by the folklorist and ethnographer S. An-sky, it is told at the end of the legend that the father said: "He will save us from blood libel." Therefore, he was named Judah-Lion, as he will defend the Jewish people as the lion defends his offspring.[16]

The legends about the Maharal and blood libels circulated orally in Prague but also among other Jewish communities.[17] They were written down and published in several collections and articles.[18] The legend of the Maharal and the golem is unique among the well-known praise tales about Jewish saintly figures. As noted, the legend turns its hero into a figure who inspires veneration, identification, and emulation. Even if this legend about the Maharal expresses society's veneration for and identification with him, it is hard to say that it attempts to stimulate others to emulate his action, which combines controversial magical practices and ultimately causes the rabbi to destroy the golem he created.

In the ancient traditions the golem is a manlike creature, created by some artificer who employs mystical techniques. We know similar tales from the ancient cultures of Egypt, China, and Greece. In these ancient traditions, the creation of an anthropoid is associated with idol worship. In Jewish culture, too, the history of the golem does not begin with the Maharal and blood libels, and its earlier form has links with idolatry. When Enosh, Adam's grandson, was asked to show how God created Adam, he mixed together water and dirt and fashioned a manlike figure. Satan animated this body and people began worshiping him. This is how idolatry began. A better-known Jewish tradition associates the golem with the stages of the creation of the first man. The word *golem* (unformed substance) appears once in the Bible (Psalms 139:16), where it refers to the first stage in the formation. Later commentaries (B *Sanhedrin* 38b, *Genesis Rabba* 24:2) presented the creation of a golem as one of the stages in the process of God's creation of human beings. This tradition is also widely disseminated in the Middle Ages. Much has been written about the golem's appearance in ancient magical and mystical sources.[19] I do not intend to linger on golem stories in the ancient traditions, but it is important to note that the tradition is associated with *Sefer Yezirah* (The Book of Creation). In this work, which dates to late antiquity, the letters of the Hebrew alphabet are represented as the source of the divine creation of humankind and the world. God created man using the letters of the alphabet; the mystic can imitate his act and create a human being in the same fashion.

Special interest attaches to the story tradition in the Middle Ages, which coalesced around the German Pietists of the twelfth and thirteenth centuries. These legends focus on Rabbi Samuel Hasid and his son, Rabbi Judah Hasid. The legend about Rabbi Elijah of Chelm, the sixteenth-century healer and mystic, also bears mention. The story about his creation of a golem includes the play on the Hebrew words *emet* and *met*—"truth" and "dead"—in the context of its animation and destruction.

When the scholar Moshe Idel discusses the golem in the writings conceived to constitute the mystical literature of Judaism, he claims that in this literature the golem is not a person having any importance in itself: "It has not a particular name, its disappearance does not matter even to its human creator. It is an entity that serves the role of a silent witness of the creativity inherent in the tools which served God and man in their creative endeavours."[20] Idel does not relate to folk legends about the golem, or as he puts it, "the legendary and folkloristic material remains basically beyond the scope of our presentation."[21]

According to the folk legends about the golem created by the Maharal, he is characterized as free of desires. He does not speak, is soulless, and does not perform Jewish commandments. He has a supernatural power and can see below the earth. The golem is never sick, he does not burn or drown in water, and he does exactly what he is told by his creator, the Maharal. Thus, he possesses all the traits needed to guard against blood libels or uncover them. As An-sky puts it, "How much suffering the soul of the Jewish folk accumulated to create such a golem!"[22] In fact, many legends depict the golem sympathetically, and he even has a pet name—Yosseleh Golem.[23]

The ancient literature evinces an ambivalent attitude toward the creation of a golem, ranging from utter condemnation, because, attempting to play God, the perpetrator is guilty of the sin of pride, at one extreme, to wonder at and admire the power possessed by those initiated in the secrets of magic and mysticism.[24] By contrast, the legends about the creation of the golem by the Maharal (assisted by one of his students and his son-in-law) justify his action almost without question, on account of the reason for making it—defending the Jews against a blood libel. Even if in these stories we may detect a hint of criticism, reflected in the very fact that the Maharal must ultimately destroy his creation, this element is negligible. The admiration of and identification with the Maharal's act expresses the Jews' fierce wish to be delivered from the most sinister conspiracy of all, thanks to the saintly figure and his handiwork.

How can a golem, a body without a soul, rescue the Jewish people? In a symbolic manner, we might see this as the Jewish folk tradition's ultimate criticism of the gentile world, as epitomized in the Yiddish expression *oylem goylem*—which might be rendered in English as "the world is an ass" (or, more literal but less idiomatic, "the masses are blockheads"). According to Jewish folk culture, the only one who can overcome the architects of the most nefarious scheme imaginable, who have no heart or soul, is not a Jew, who in fact possesses an extra soul, but a creature who resembles them, a stupid and soulless golem like themselves.

The legends recount that the Maharal destroyed the golem when he was not needed anymore. According to the legends, the substance in a human shape was kept in the attic of the old synagogue. This reflects the storytelling society's anticipation that disaster may occur in the future. One of the stories in the IFA states that the golem will return in the future.[25] Against this background it is interesting to mention the story of the golem that saves the Jewish synagogue from the Nazis. This story, which circulated among the Holocaust survivors in Prague, was transcribed by Shlomo Laba, who heard it from a Holocaust survivor in 1945, when he was a soldier in the Jewish brigade in the British army:

> The Holocaust created legends told by people that were even less religious than myself. When the refugees of the camps became free, they crossed the borders and came to us. We, the soldiers, took care of them and used to meet with them frequently. One of them, a secular Jew from Prague, told me the following story:
> The golem did not disappear and even during the war he came out of his hiding place to protect his synagogue. The Nazis decided to tear down the Altneushul. They came to destroy it and suddenly, from within the silence of the synagogue, they could hear giant footsteps coming from the roof, where the golem was walking, and they saw the shadow of a huge hand fall from the window to the floor. The Germans were terrified. They threw down their tools and ran away as fast as they could.[26]

This tale is an etiological legend to explain the rather astonishing fact that the Nazis did not destroy the synagogue. The story attributes the synagogue's survival to the terror that the golem's huge shadow and echoing footsteps cast on the Germans sent to blow it up. The fact that the "shadow" of the golem of Prague tale, created by the Maharal to save the Jews from a blood libel, turns up in this story is evidence that the survivors perceived the Holocaust as one more link in the long series of blood libels, and indeed the most atrocious in Jewish history. So it is not surprising that the golem, enshrined in the collective memory as a savior of the distant past, should be evoked by the Jews of Prague to save one of the main icons of their culture. The narrating society employs well-known traditional structures associated with traumatic events of the long-ago past and adapts them to the terrible event it experienced recently.

Historical Legends—Martyrdom

Alongside legends of this type, there are also historical legends that end with the hero's death. These keep alive a traumatic historical event in the collective memory of the community. Such legends reflect the link between ethnopoetics and legendary chronicles, a topic I have addressed elsewhere.[27] In these legends the hero is usually a community leader, a rabbi, or Torah scholar who is targeted by the Christian blood libel. The legend associates his death with two key Jewish values—the individual's willingness to give his life to save the community and his willingness to die a martyr's death in sanctification of the divine name (because he turns down a chance to save himself by means of apostasy). The well-known Eastern European Jewish folk narratives in this category include the legends of the Reitzes brothers (Ḥayim and Joshua) and of Rabbi Aryeh Leib of Poznań. These legends played two key roles: first, they gave voice to the terror that the historical incidents branded on the Jewish psyche and preserved it in the community's collective memory. Second, they glorified the protagonist, manifested in his willingness to die a martyr in order to sanctify God's name and sacrifice himself to save the community.

As noted, in most legends of this type the hero is a historical figure, an eminent man. This does seem to be de rigueur. On one hand, the legends recount a confrontation that has a religious basis and in which the leading actors on both sides have roles in the public space: hence, in legends told in Jewish patriarchal society a man acting as a protagonist is obvious. On the other hand, although I am aware that the private space is the arena of action deemed appropriate for women in Jewish folk narratives and that they are excluded from the public sphere, it is obvious that blood libels are a time of crisis and persecution. Having learned from my previous research that in such times legends permit women to go beyond the private sphere and act in the public space as well, I looked for Jewish blood libel legends with a woman at their center.[28] It turns out that Eastern European Jewish legends include several legends about Adil Kikinesh of Drohobycz, the daughter of Moshe Kikinesh, to which I now turn.

There are a number of versions of the story of Adil Kikinesh of Drohobycz, in Hebrew and in Yiddish. Gabriel Suchestow first published the legend in Hebrew in *Matzevet kodesh* (Holy Tombstone), and all the subsequent versions closely resemble this story.[29] The most important difference is that Salomon Buber assigns the historical event to 1718 rather than to 1710.[30] Here is the story, as presented by Suchestow:

> The martyr, Adil (daughter of Rabbi Moshe Kikinesh), made her home in the city of Drohobycz and was caught up in a blood libel along with the entire community. On Seder night, her gentile serving maid had hidden a dead Christian child in her home and said that she had killed him at her mistress' behest for the needs of the community. When this righteous woman saw the distress of the many, she sacrificed herself and said that she alone had given the order and the people were guiltless. After she had been sentenced to death the serving maid regretted her wickedness and made a full confession to the judges that she had perjured herself. But the judges refused to overturn their verdict. The priests, however, said that they would allow her to live if she converted and endeavored to seduce her with this promise. The woman was young and very beautiful, her husband was very wealthy, and her family was renowned in Israel. In her righteousness she refused to turn away from the Lord and died willingly to sanctify His great name.[31]

Suchestow also quotes the inscription on her tombstone: "On Friday, the eve of the Sabbath, 27 Elul 5778, the holy and pure woman Adil, the daughter of the magnate and leader Rabbi Moshe Kikinesh, sanctified [God's name] and gave her life on behalf of all Israel. May the Lord avenge her blood and by this merit may her soul be bound up in the bond of eternal life."[32]

The first sentence of the story already refers to her as a "martyr," thereby alerting readers to her tragic end. The Hebrew adjective *qadosh*, whose primary signification is "holy," also bears the connotation of "martyred," just as many early Christian saints earned that title through martyrdom. The confrontation in the story has a religious background. On one side, we have Adil and the Jewish community as a collective hero; on the other, the judges, priests, and Adil's serving maid. Even though this version does not say that the maid planted the boy's body in Adil's house at the instigation of the priests and judges, members of the upper class, this is implied by the continuation, when the maid recants her story but the judges refuse to vacate their verdict and the priests are willing to save Adil only if she converts.

All the Hebrew versions are short and concise. The Yiddish versions, by contrast, are marked by epic expansion and the typical poetics of oral narrative.[33]

The Story of Adil Kikinesh

They told many stories about the martyr Adil Kikinesh, who lived in Drohobycz at the beginning of the eighteenth century, both during her life and after her death. She was the daughter of the merchant Moses Kikinesh, a magnate from Lemberg, and was renowned for her extraordinary beauty. Her husband was a scholar who sat and learned Torah day and night. After receiving the salt concession from her wealthy father-in-law, she conducted the business with great skill. Her beauty, wisdom, and way with words enflamed the local magnates and priests. In their rabid jealousy the priests looked for a way to destroy the lovely Adil, and with her the whole Jewish community.

They say that they persuaded her Christian serving-woman to murder her own child and blame Adil for it, as if she had done it with her own hands to get Christian blood for the Passover matzo.

Adil was arrested and thrown into prison, where they tried to get her to betray her accomplices. But she took the full blame on herself and said she had done the deed with no help from anyone.

She was convicted in Lemberg and sentenced to death—an extremely cruel and painful death. The verdict was that her long tresses be tied to the tail of a wild stallion and that the beast be whipped along a rock-strewn path; afterwards she would be burned.

When the Christian serving-woman heard this sentence she recanted and told the truth about who had instigated her to kill her child. But they immediately dragged her off to prison and strangled her.

Adil was promised her life if she would convert. But she steadfastly refused the offer.

Adil's execution was conducted with much pageantry in the market square of Lemberg, which was packed with tens of thousands of Christians. Even the roofs and windows were jammed with spectators. The judges sat on the dais in their velvet robes. Next to them stood Adil, bound. The Archbishop of Lemberg asked her if she had a last wish.

She asked that they untie her hands and give her some pins. She forced the pins through the hem of her dress and then deep into the flesh of her calves. Now she was sure that when the wild stallion dragged her through the market square her naked body would not be exposed.

On her tombstone they engraved that she died on Friday, the eve of the holy Sabbath, the seventh day of the month of Elul, in the year 5478 [1718]. She is described there as "the holy and pure woman, who sanctified God's name and gave her life for all Israel. May the Lord avenge her blood."[34]

The Yiddish versions hint at an oral tradition, inasmuch as Yiddish, not Hebrew, was the spoken vernacular of Eastern European Jews in which the stories were told. This is reflected in the use of phrases such as "They *told* many stories about the martyr Adil Kikinesh." Or again, "They *say* that they persuaded her Christian serving-woman." In addition, they are marked by the contrast and dramatization typical of folk legends. In the Hebrew versions the serving maid kills "a boy"; in the Yiddish texts, carrying the matter to an extreme, she "murders her own child." In all the versions she regrets what she has done, but whereas in the Hebrew versions the judges simply refuse to retract their verdict and sentence, in the Yiddish versions "they dragged her off to prison and strangled her."

What all the versions have in common is their depiction of the heroine as raised above the common herd, extremely wealthy, respected, and beautiful.[35] In the Yiddish versions, unlike the Hebrew, these traits are explicitly presented as the reason behind and motivation for the blood libel. There is a covert message here, found in other legends about women who came into contact with non-Jews on account of their status, such as the legends about women who rescued a synagogue—Golden Rose (di gildene Roize) of Lwów and Mirele of Brahilov: exposure to such contacts is extremely perilous for a Jewish woman and should be avoided, unless important matters are in the balance such as saving a synagogue from demolition, in one case, or saving the entire community from death, in the other.[36]

The Yiddish versions say in so many words what can only be inferred from the Hebrew: that the priests were looking for a way to attack Adil and the Jews and that they were the ones who persuaded the serving woman to her action. Whereas the scene of Adil's execution is not found in any of the Hebrew versions included in volumes of historical documentation, it is given wide play in the Yiddish versions, which were published in more popular books, including a description of the mode of death (tied to the tail of a horse and dragged over a rock-strewn path), the description of the throng that turned out to watch, the judges in their velvet robes, and the bound Adil, standing on the other side. Her confrontation with the archbishop, the representative of the Christian faith, and her last wish to be given pins, which she uses to attach the hem of her dress to the flesh of her calves, so that her nakedness will not be exposed, are important elements in the characterization of a woman who became a cultural hero and died to sanctify God's name—as a woman who, even at the last and worst moment of all, guarded the values and behavioral norms consecrated by Judaism. We should recall that the same motif appears in the literary legend by I. L. Peretz, "Three Gifts," in which a pin, smeared with the blood of a female martyr, is the second gift brought by the wandering soul that is seeking redemption.[37]

Men, too, suffer cruel deaths in the wake of blood libels. It is stated explicitly that Rabbi Joshua Reitzes, executed along with his brother, Rabbi Hayim Reitzes (they too are from Lwów, the execution place of Adil), was sentenced to be tied to the tails of horses. But in Jewish culture, when such a fate strikes a woman it arouses associations with the destruction of the Temple and the bitter suffering of noble women at such a time. Echoing in the background is the story of Miriam

(Martha) daughter of Boethus, recounted in the Jerusalem Talmud (*Ketubbot* 5:11 [38b]), in the Babylonian Talmud (*Ketubbot* 67a, *Gittin* 56a), and in Midrash Lamentations Rabbah 1:47, where Rabbi Eleazar b. Zadok says of her, "May I [not] live to behold the consolation [of Zion] if I did not see them tie her hair to the tails of Arabian horses and make her run from Jerusalem to Lydda. I quoted this verse in connection with her, 'She who is most tender and dainty among you . . .'" (Deut. 28:56).[38] The link to the story of Miriam/Martha daughter of Boethus conveys the full force of the terror that the narrating society felt when faced by a blood libel—a terror that can be compared only to the ancient greatest calamity of all—the destruction of the Holy Temple.

The legends about Adil Kikinesh of Drohobycz are legends about women in times of persecution in Eastern Europe. These legends feature two kinds of heroines. The first type are young girls—whom the legends refer to as "virgins"; the best-known of these were published in *Yeven metzulah* (Abyss of Despair), the chronicle of the Chmielnicki pogroms of 1648–1649, first published shortly after the events themselves in 1653.[39] Many of these legends were published in H. J. Gurland's *Annals of the Persecutions of Israel* (1887), including "The Cossack and the Damsel," "The Bride and Groom," and "The Hetman and the Damsel."[40] Legends that circulated orally were an important part of Jews' lives in Eastern Europe, as attested by An-sky, one of the pioneering researchers of Eastern European Jewish folklore, who collected some of them during his ethnographic expeditions.[41] These legends, which can be traced back to 1648–1649, continued to circulate orally in the 1950s; one of them can be found in the IFA, under the title "The Girl and the Cossack."[42]

The second type of legends is about mature women, such as Adil. These relate mainly to the rescue of synagogues and in our case the blood libel. In all these legends the women act in the public space, rather than in the private sphere that is normally deemed to be appropriate for Jewish women. Pogroms, persecutions, and blood libels bring into contact those who never would or should meet in normal times. In these terrifying times, the girls and women in these stories find themselves dealing with murderers, rapists, libelers, and executioners, but they are not helpless. Quite the contrary, each of them, in her own way, takes her destiny in her hands and overcomes the persecutor. Even if the story ends in the heroine's death, she overcomes the villain.

Elsewhere, I have analyzed the existence of several main key paradigms in legends about women in times of persecution, such that every legend of this sort can be assigned to one and sometimes to several patterns:[43]

> 1. The heroine surrenders her innocence, but does so on behalf of her people. She is not depicted in a negative light despite her nonnormative action. In the

folk narratives of Polish Jews, for example, we find Estherke, the beloved of King Casimir the Great. Her character is associated with positive archetypes from ancient Jewish literature, notably the biblical Queen Esther.

2. The heroine fights back and kills her assailant, displaying physical bravery and setting up an association with traditional archetypes such as the apocryphal Judith, who killed Holofernes.

3. The heroine chooses to die rather than surrender her innocence. Here the woman employs the age-old weapon of the weak—deception. Sometimes the woman tricks the villain into killing her against his will; sometimes she kills herself after managing to obtain, by deception, what the community deems to be most important of all; and sometimes she prays to God, who takes her soul.

Although the legend about Adil Kikinesh of Drohobycz, which centers on a blood libel, shares several motifs with the paradigms listed above, it also adds a new paradigm:

4. The heroine chooses death in order to save her community and to avoid apostasy, and she dies a martyr sanctifying God's name.

An analysis of these legends reveals that it is precisely in those that are set in times of persecution that women are allowed a status denied them in other Jewish legends. These legends establish heroines who transcend their normal gender role. The legends legitimize their acting in the public sphere, which is normally reserved to men. Even though the stories highlight the terrible peril that lurks for women in the public sphere, they also recount the strength, ability, and resolve displayed by Adil Kikinesh and her Jewish sisters to safeguard what the narrating society cherishes as most sacred of all.

Although we may assume that these stories were originally told by women, the written texts we have today were set down by men. These legends about women in times of persecution thus received male approval in a patriarchal Jewish society. Cultural heroines such as Adil Kikinesh, who transcend the bounds of gender behavior in times of persecution, are not unique to Jewish culture. At such times, when the social order is overturned by a threatening outside agency, the comprehensive code of values and norms is blurred and the society is forced, whether it wants to or not, to establish a new order, one in which it must concede some of the traditional values in order to preserve those that are most important—the values that Judaism places in the category of those for which one should die rather than transgress.

In times of persecution the men cannot play their traditional gender role of guarding and protecting women, and cultural heroines such as Adil Kikinesh must be created. Adil Kikinesh and other women who are active in times of persecution are set up as revered heroines who are willing to do everything in their power to protect their community and religion. Their actions are presented as worthy of emulation, which ensures that when catastrophe threatens in the future, too, women will stand vigil over the most sacred values of all.

Conclusion

The Jewish legends about blood libels were created in reaction to the folklore of the Other—the Christian legend that accused the Jews of ritual murder and the use of human blood in their religious rites. The Jewish legends refute the Christian narrative, as the plot exposes the falseness of the accusation, and ends with the punishment of the libelers. Jewish culture refashions the Christian blood libel legends, which are accusatory, into tales of rescue and deliverance. This pattern of deliverance, which the society internalizes and preserves in its collective memory, creates a narrative that can also provide consolation in the future, whenever a new enemy arises to plague the suffering minority. This reflects the importance of folk legends, which have the potential to create a unifying and comforting narrative for use in times of distress.

Blood libel legends about specific historical events, like the legends about Adil, reflect the connection between history and folklore. In particular, legends serve as "sites of memory" to keep alive traumatic events of Jewish history and the heroes of these events, in Jewish collective memory.[44] According to Pierre Nora, sites of memory are cultural institutions whose goal is to preserve society's values and pass them on to future generations. The term encompasses monuments, museums, ceremonies, and more, all of which share the purpose of entrenching and reinforcing collective memory. He considered the ways in which a society processes and shapes its collective memory to serve its needs in the present. This links up Maurice Halbwachs's description of collective memory as a heritage of associations, concepts, and values that is shared by a society and creates a sense of belonging to it.[45] The process involves cultural agents and the tradition they pass on to the next generation through ceremonies and hero worship. Epics are created, anthems sung, and commemorative albums written precisely for this purpose.

My contention is that the historical legends about blood libels, like that about Adil Kikinesh of Drohobycz, respond to the community's need to produce texts that buttress its collective memory. They create an awareness of a shared past and thereby constitute the community's identity. The stories that are transmitted orally, as well as those written down, create myths that pass on the heritage and the community's history and values to the generations to come. In the case of blood libels, they preserve those traumatic moments of Jewish history and their protagonists in the collective memory and define the appropriate patterns of behavior for Jewish society to follow when such tragedies recur. When a woman is at the center of the event, patriarchal Jewish society is willing to create a cultural heroine and to compromise on the values and norms that apply to women in less turbulent times. This produces a model for how women should behave when men cannot protect and defend them. The creation of a heroine worthy of emulation can induce women to behave in similar fashion in the future.

HAYA BAR-ITZHAK is Professor Emerita of Literature and Folklore at the University of Haifa, where she served as Head of Folklore Studies and Director of the Israel Folktale Archives. She has published extensively on settlement, immigration, and ethnicity in Israel and on Jewish folk literature in Eastern Europe. She has published eleven books, is editor of the *Encyclopedia of Jewish Folklore and Traditions*, and is the recipient of several awards, among them the American National Jewish Book Award and the Lerner Foundation for Yiddish Culture Award. Since 2016 she has served as Chair of the Department of Communication at the Yezreel Valley College.

NOTES

1. Robert Georges, "The General Concept of Legend," and Alan Dundes, "On Psychology of Legend," both in *American Folk Legend: A Symposium*, ed. W. D. Hand (Berkeley: University of California Press, 1971), 1–13 and 21–36.
2. Alan Dundes, ed., *The Blood Libel Legend: A Casebook in Anti-Semitic Folklore* (Madison: University of Wisconsin Press, 1991), vii, viii.
3. Haya Bar-Itzhak, "Review of Alan Dundes's *The Blood Libel Legend*," *American Anthropologist* 95, no. 1 (1993): 176–77.
4. Alan Dundes, "The Ritual Murder or Blood Libel Legend," in Dundes, *Blood Libel Legend*, 336–76.
5. Magdalene Schultz, "The Blood Libel: A Motif in the History of Childhood," in Dundes, *Blood Libel Legend*, 273–303.
6. Cecil Roth, "The Feast of Purim and the Origins of the Blood Accusation," in Dundes, *Blood Libel Legend*, 261–72.
7. Ora Limor, *Jews and Christians in Western Europe: Encounter between Cultures in the Middle Ages and the Renaissance* [Hebrew], vol. 9 (Tel Aviv: Open University of Israel, 1995).
8. Amos Funkenstein, "Pagan, Christian, and Modern Anti-Jewish Propaganda [Hebrew]," *Zmanim* 10 (1982): 4–15.
9. Dov Noy, "Stories of Blood Libels in Jewish Communities [Hebrew]," *Mahanayim* 110 (1967): 32–51.
10. *Oikotype* is an ethnic tale type based on the international index of folktales. See Antti A. Aarne and Stith Thompson, *The Types of the Folktale: A Classification and Bibliography* (Helsinki: Suomalainen Tiedeakatemia, 1961). The Israel Folktale Archives (hereafter IFA), named in Honor of Dov Noy at the University of Haifa, stores more than twenty-four thousand folk narratives recorded from narrators of different ethnic groups.

11. At the Passover seder, it is customary to fill a goblet with wine for Elijah the Prophet and to open the door to admit him. According to Jewish tradition, Elijah will appear to herald the coming of the Messiah.

12. The Maharal was born in Poznań and died in Prague. He was a rabbi in Nicolsburg, Moravia, until 1598 when he became a rabbi of Prague.

13. IFA 16605. I recorded this tale in 1981 from Ḥananya Portal. Thirteen more versions of this story are stored in the IFA.

14. This is what he intended to do. As we learn from the plot of this story and other versions, he did not do it because the people rushed out to fetch the midwife.

15. Many legends about the birth of saintly figures in the Jewish *shevah* follow the pattern of the birth of the mythical hero. See Lord Raglan, *The Hero: A Study in Tradition, Myth, and Drama* (London: Methuen, 1936); Otto Rank, *The Myth of the Birth of the Hero, and Other Writings*, ed. Philip Freund (New York: Vintage, 1959). For a discussion of this subject, see Haya Bar-Itzhak, "'Saints' Legend' as Genre in Jewish Folk-Literature" (PhD diss., Hebrew University of Jerusalem, 1987).

16. S. An-sky, "Blot bilbulim in yidish folkshafung," *Gezamelte shriften*, 15 vols. (Vilno, Lithuania: Shreberk, 1925), 15:106. Although not stated by An-sky, it is clear that he also uses the tales from Yudel Rosenberg, *Wonders of Maharal* [Hebrew] (Pietrkov, Poland: n.p., 1909).

17. All the stories in the IFA are from oral tradition as told since 1955. In addition to the thirteen versions mentioned, there are six tales about the Golem saving Jews from blood libels (IFA 3168, IFA 3171, IFA 3173, IFA 6554, IFA 7381, IFA 11383).

18. See Eliezer Kartużynski, *Der Berimter Rebe fun Prag* (Warsaw: Kartużynski, 1882); Wolf Paschedes, ed., *Sippurim: Eine Sammlung juedischer Volkssagen, Erzaehlungen, Mythen, Chroniken Denkwuerdigkeiten und Biographien beruehmter Juden* (Hildesheim: G. Olms; Jacob Brandeis, 1976); Jacob B. Brandeis, *Sippurim: Ghettosagen, Jüdische Mythen und Legenden* (Prague: n.p., 1909); An-sky, "Blot bilbulim in yidish folkshafung"; Chajim Bloch, *Der Prager Golem* (Berlin: B. Harz, 1920); Yehuda Yudel Rosenberg, *Wonders of Maharal*; Yehuda Yudel Rosenberg, *The Golem of Prague and Other Tales of Wonder* [Hebrew], ed. Eli Yassif (Jerusalem: Bialik Institute, 1991).

19. See, e.g., Moshe Idel, *Golem: Jewish Magical and Mystical Traditions on the Artificial Anthropoid* (Albany: State University of New York Press, 1990); Gershom G. Sholem, "The Idea of the Golem," in Sholem's *On Kabbalah and Its Symbolism* (New York: Schocken, 1965); Byron L. Sherwin, *The Legend of the Golem: Origins and Implications* (Lanham, MD: University Press of America, 1985).

20. Idel, *Golem*, 265.

21. Ibid., xxix.

22. An-sky, "Blot bilbulim in yidish folkshafung," 105.

23. Ibid., 98–152.

24. Idel suggested another interesting explanation of the mystical literature, namely that golem practices can be described as an attempt of man to know God by the art he used in order to create man (*Golem*, xxvii).

25. IFA 6554.

26. IFA 11383.

27. Haya Bar-Itzhak, *Jewish Poland: Legends of Origin*, trans. Lenn Schramm (Detroit: Wayne State University Press, 2001).

28. See, e.g., ibid., 149–54.

29. Gabriel Suchestow, *Holy Tombstones* [Hebrew] (Lemberg: Lemtpes, 1860), part 2, 46.

30. Even though the legend no longer circulates orally among Jews of Eastern European ancestry, the multiple versions are evidence of a multiple existence that is typical of folk narra-

tives. See Alan Dundes, *Analytic Essays in Folklore* (The Hague: Mouton, 1975), xii–xiii. For a comparative analysis of Hebrew and Yiddish versions, see Bar-Itzhak, "Women and Blood Libel," *Western Folklore* 71, nos. 3–4 (2012): 279–90. For Salomon Buber's version, see *Famous People* [Hebrew] (Krakow: J. Fischer, 1995), 19.

31. Suchestow, *Holy Tombstones*, part 2, 46.

32. Ibid.

33. Gershom Bader, *Draysig doyres iden in Poyln* (New York: Ariam Press, 1927), 212–15; and Leo Finkelstein, *Megiles Poyln* (Buenos Aires: Central Union of Polish Jews in Argentina, 1947), 230–31.

34. Finkelstein, *Megiles Poyln*, 230–31.

35. We can see here an expression of a literary trope according to which men were to dedicate their time to the study of Torah and women were breadwinners. For the historical discussion on wealthy women merchants in Poland, see, e.g., Moshe Rosman, "The History of Jewish Women in Early Modern Poland: An Assessment," *Polin* 18 (2005): 52–55.

36. On Golden Rose, see Majer Bałaban, *Żydzi lwowscy na przełomie XVI i XVII wieku* (Lwów, 1906), 178–86. Bałaban cites three versions of the legend. See also Bader, *Draysig doyres iden in Poyln*, 119–22; David Kahana, *In the Vise of Hatred: Jewish-Polish Relations over the Generation* [Hebrew] (Israel: Union of Jews from Lwów and Its Environs, 1992), 79; and Finkelstein, *Megiles Poyln*, 229. For a detailed discussion of the Mirele of Brahilov legend in the context of stories about synagogues, see Bar-Itzhak, *Jewish Poland: Legends of Origin*, 133–58.

37. I. L. Peretz. *All Works* [Hebrew], 10 vols. (Tel-Aviv: Dvir, 1961), 1:26–36. For a discussion of the origins of "Three Gifts," see Y. D. Abramsky, "On the Source of I. L. Peretz's Story 'Three Gifts' [Hebrew]," *Hado'ar* 26 (1948): 1277.

38. On the story of Miriam the daughter of Boethus, see Galit Hasan-Rokem, *Web of Life: Folklore and Midrash in Rabbinic Literature* [Hebrew] (Tel-Aviv: Am Oved, 1996), 133–34.

39. The years 1648–1649 were the period of the Cossack revolt against the Polish overlords under the leadership of Bogdan Chmielnicki. At first the Cossacks routed the Polish armies and overran many cities and towns in Ukraine. Hundreds of Jewish communities were destroyed during the course of the revolt. The number of Jews killed is still in question. Shaul Stampfer scales down the amount of casualties. See his "What Actually Happened to the Jews of Ukraine in 1648?," *Jewish History* 17, no. 2 (2003): 207–27. For *The Abyss of Despair*, see Nathan Note Hannover, *Abyss of Despair* [Hebrew], ed. Yisrael Halperin (Tel Aviv: Hakibbutz Ha'Me'uhad, 1968), 38.

40. H. J. Gurland, *Annals of the Persecutions of Israel* [Hebrew] (Jerusalem: Kedem, 1887 [1972]), 33–36.

41. S. An-sky, "Folk Legends about the Pogroms of 1648–49 [Hebrew]," *Ha'Olam* 27, no. 5 (1920): 12–14.

42. IFA 1935. For a discussion of this legend, see my "A Study of the 'Cossack and the Damsel,'" in *The Power of a Tale: The IFA Jubilee Book*, ed. Haya Bar-Itzhak and Idit Pintel-Ginsberg (Haifa: University of Haifa, 2008), 59–65. On the heroism of women, see also Dov Noy, "Jewish Valor in the Underground [Hebrew]," *Mahanayim* 52 (1960): 2–8.

43. Bar-Itzhak, *Jewish Poland*, 149–54; and Bar-Itzhak, "Study of the 'Cossack and the Damsel,'" 59–65.

44. Pierre Nora, "Legendary Memory and History: Les Lieux de Mémoire," *Representations* 26 (1989): 7–24.

45. Maurice Halbwachs, *On Collective Memory* (Chicago: University of Chicago Press), 1992.

3

RITUAL MURDER IN A RUSSIAN BORDER TOWN

Eugene M. Avrutin

AT FIRST, THERE did not seem to be anything highly unusual about the murder. The idea that Jews killed Christian children to mix their blood with matzo for the Passover service had circulated in oral and written traditions since the Middle Ages, and the case resembled that of dozens of similar investigations from around the world. From the trial records, we learn that on April 22, 1823, in the Russian border town of Velizh, two small children finished their lunch and went to play outside. Fedor—a three-year-old boy with short blond hair, gray eyes, and a middling nose—and his four-year-old cousin, Avdot'ia, left their home and walked down a dusty path in an easterly direction. When the children reached the Konevtse Creek, Avdot'ia invited her cousin to cross a small bridge and continue on a walk to the forest. But Fedor refused and remained there alone, gazing at the construction site of a new home on the embankment.

It was Easter Sunday when the children went on their walk. Avdot'ia's mother, Kharitina Prokof'eva, did not supervise them. Instead, she used the time to go beg for alms from her neighbor. Kharitina lived at the very edge of town with her sister, Agaf'ia Prokof'eva, and her brother-in-law, Emel'ian Ivanov. After receiving alms, Kharitina gossiped with her neighbor for nearly two hours until Avdot'ia came looking for her. To Kharitina's surprise, Avdot'ia was without her cousin. "Where is Fedor?" Kharitina inquired immediately. Avdot'ia replied that she had left Fedor standing alone on the bridge and had not seen him since. Wasting little time, Kharitina took Avdot'ia to look for the little boy, but the search proved unsuccessful. That afternoon, Emel'ian and Agaf'ia searched the town for their son, but they too were unable to locate him.

Two days later, on April 24, Agaf'ia was chatting with her neighbors when a stranger knocked on the door. From the testimony of several witnesses in the case, we know that the caller was a beggar woman named Maria Terenteeva. As soon as Agaf'ia opened the door, Terenteeva declared that she would be able to locate the missing boy. She asked for a burning candle and, after placing the candle flame in a cold pot of water, revealed that Fedor was still alive, locked inside the cellar of Mirka Aronson's large brick house. Although there was lots of food and drink there, Fedor was not given anything to eat or drink. Terenteeva went on to say that she intended to rescue the boy that night, but she was afraid that evil might have struck already and that he would die the moment she came to rescue him. Frightened and unsure of what to make of the stranger's revelations, Agaf'ia decided to go with her sister to a neighboring village, Sentiury, to talk with Anna Eremeeva, a twelve-year-old girl who, rumor had it, possessed psychic powers. On the way, the sisters passed by Mirka Aronson's home, located in the marketplace in the very center of town. Agaf'ia walked inside the courtyard to look for her son, but she left shortly thereafter, fearing that someone might mistake her for a thief. When the sisters finally reached Sentiury late in the evening, Agaf'ia begged the young girl to tell her about her son. After much prodding, Anna relented: "I've been inside the house where they're keeping your son; he's extremely weak. If you want to see him, then beware, he will die this very night."

By the time Agaf'ia had come home and shared the news with her husband, three police officers were busy conducting a formal criminal investigation. Earlier that day, Emel'ian had informed the Velizh police that his son had disappeared without a trace. Numerous witnesses were questioned in the case while the officers searched for little Fedor. But long before they completed the investigation, rumors began to circulate all over town that Jews had killed the missing boy.[1]

The drama in Velizh was one of more than a dozen ritual murder investigations in the first half of the nineteenth century in the Russian Empire.[2] As a result of the three partitions of the Polish-Lithuanian Commonwealth (1772, 1793, 1795), Russia not only acquired the largest Jewish population in the world, it also inherited an established cultural tradition of ritual murder.[3] By the end of the eighteenth century, the myth began to wane for many of the same reasons that saw the decline of witchcraft prosecution in Western and Central Europe: the elimination of torture techniques in criminal investigations; the promulgation of laws restricting the prosecution of ritual murder to those accusations where conclusive evidence was found; and a new mental outlook that questioned its very existence.[4]

But as was the case with witchcraft allegations, individual cases of ritual murder did not decline entirely in the nineteenth century, and the popular belief in Jews' sacrifice of young Christian children for religious ritual practices continued to persist long after Russia had acquired its Jews.[5]

The disappearance of little Fedor was a long and drawn-out affair that ended officially in 1835, only after the most powerful court in the Russian Empire intervened and acquitted all the Jews of the ritual murder charge. Those twelve years generated an astonishing number of documents—nearly fifty thousand in total. The Velizh archive includes hundreds of depositions from all segments of the population, petitions penned by and about Jews, official correspondence (from provincial administrators to some of the most powerful politicians in the empire), and an extensive summary of the case, as well as memos, reports, denunciations, and scores of letters.[6] In their scope and attention to detail, these archival records offer the historian a rare opportunity to penetrate the mental universe of a small town and reconstruct realms of human experience that have been written out of the historical record.[7] The "imperial turn" in Russian historical studies has done much to illuminate the multiethnic dimensions of the empire as well as the complex encounters between the state and the population.[8] Yet in spite of all the scholarly production over the past fifteen years, we know very little about the day-to-day relations between neighbors and even less about how people of diverse ethnic and religious origins made sense of the world around them.[9]

The Velizh case opens a window onto a time, place, and people that seldom appear in studies of either the Russian Empire or Eastern European Jewry. While it was a truly exceptional event (even in comparison to other scandalous cases of the time), the drama occurred in a town like any other town in the empire, where people's lives were intimately connected, where neighbors were forced to interact with one another in a variety of social settings, and where tensions, rivalries, and confrontations were part of daily life. In this chapter I examine the first act of that drama, exploring in microscopic detail the social dynamics of the case as it unfolded between April 22, 1823, when Fedor first disappeared, and November 22, 1824, when a provincial court reached its verdict. In conclusion, I consider why almost the entire Christian community of Velizh had come to accept the charge that Jews were capable of committing ritual murder.

For four straight days the police conducted an exhaustive search of the town and its environs. Finally, on April 28, unable to uncover a single lead, they suspended the investigation and declared the boy missing. All across the empire, child desertion, infanticide, and infant mortality were common occurrences, and in Vitebsk province in particular, hundreds of young children died each year. The most common explanations for infant mortality were neglect, pregnancy complications, and lack of proper medical attention. Other reasons were more traumatic and violent: mothers suffocated, drowned, or strangled infants; or on more than infrequent occasions the babies were eaten alive by pigs and various wild animals. Each year the corpses of small children were found routinely in animal sheds, barnyards, warehouses, woods, swamps, cemeteries, fields, courtyards, forests, homes, creeks, and rivers. The disappearance of a little boy was not an unusual event.[10]

Even in this context, however, the sudden loss of Fedor must have dealt a severe emotional blow to his parents. Although the judicial records offer no hint of Agaf'ia Prokof'eva's state of mind, emotions must have been running high when Maria Terenteeva appeared once again on the doorstep. "Why did [the officers] stop the search?" Terenteeva asked abruptly. Then, to Agaf'ia's amazement, Terenteeva related just how little Fedor had disappeared. She claimed that a Jewish woman had walked up to the little boy while he stood on the bridge. After giving the boy a piece of sugar, the woman escorted him directly to Evzik Tsetlin's courtyard, where he remained until someone transferred him to Mirka Aronson's home under the cover of darkness. Terenteeva was confident that she would be able to locate the boy's body and invited Agaf'ia to accompany her to the cemetery. But no sooner than she uttered those fateful words, Terenteeva ran out the door, not to be seen again that night. When her husband returned home, Agaf'ia recounted the day's events, but Emel'ian refused to believe that the Jews had abducted his son.[11]

Just as the rumors were gathering steam, a most unexpected discovery added fuel to the fire. On May 2, the day after Terenteeva invited Agaf'ia to the cemetery, Vasilii Kokhanskii's horse broke free. Kokhanskii took his dog to search for the missing horse. They had walked five hundred meters to the thick marsh at the edge of town when the dog suddenly ran ahead, barking loudly and uncontrollably. Initially Kokhanskii thought they had found the horse, but he quickly realized that the dog was barking at a dead boy who was lying on his back with his "body punctured in numerous places." Kokhanskii remembered that Emel'ian Ivanov's son had been missing for several days and went to share the unfortunate news with his neighbor.[12]

Early the next morning, a delegation of four officials inspected the scene of the crime and produced a detailed report. First, they observed, the body was found in overgrown shrubby grass in a swampy forest less than one kilometer from the center of town and no more than one kilometer from the parents' home. Second, the body lay around sixty-four meters from Shchetinskaia Road, a dirt road that could be taken to the center of town by way of three cross streets. Finally, and most importantly, they detected fresh footprints on the right side of the dirt road leading inside the forest and directly to the boy's body. Based on all this evidence, the officials hypothesized that as many as five people had transported the boy in a spring britska with forged metal wheels. In fact, they were certain that the perpetrators had parked the carriage on the side of the road and then dumped the body in the shrubby grass. They were not able to determine the exact route the carriage had taken, for its tracks had been smeared by the traffic traveling back and forth on the dirt road over the course of several days. But since none of the people who lived nearby had witnessed suspicious persons (i.e., Jews) leaving the forest in a spring britska, they concluded that the perpetrators had returned to town. Unable to uncover any other evidence, they set themselves the tasks of questioning two of the most important witnesses in the case, Maria Terenteeva and Anna Eremeeva, and inspecting Mirka Aronson's home for clues that might help them solve the murder.[13]

The boy died a slow and painful death. When Inspector Lukashevich began the investigation, the autopsy report, prepared by the resident physician Levin, had already revealed that little Fedor was stabbed numerous times with blunt nails. The entire body was punctured with little round holes that were no more than one centimeter in depth: five on the right hand, positioned evenly from the elbow to the tip of the hand; three on the left hand; four on the very top of the head and around the left ear; one directly above the right knee; and another on the back. The skin on Fedor's feet, arms, stomach, and head had hardened and turned a burnt yellow or red color, as though someone had vigorously scrubbed the boy's body with a coarse cloth or brush. A piece of cloth was used to restrict the circulation of the blood to the feet and knees, both of which had turned dark blue, perhaps even black, from the trauma. The lips were pressed firmly against the teeth, while the nose appeared to have been smashed in violently. The dark crimson bruise on the back of the neck signified that cloth or rope was used to tie the boy's mouth. The internal organs, both the stomach and the intestines, were completely empty, filled only with air. Whoever punctured the boy fourteen times, the report concluded, did so to draw blood that was hidden within the very recesses of the skin.[14]

On May 5 Inspector Lukashevich made a thorough search of Mirka Aronson's house, paying particular attention to the kitchen, tool shed, and stable, and was not able to uncover any evidence that linked Mirka or any other members of the household (her daughter Slavka, son-in-law Shmerka Berlin, grandson Hirsh, and granddaughter-in-law Shifra) with the murder. He then asked to take a look at the cellar, but Berlin replied that the house had none. Lukashevich later learned that the house was equipped with two cellars—the first one located in the foyer, the other in the *lavka* (trade shop) where goods and spirits were sold. When asked why he had concealed the truth, Berlin replied that he did not see the point of showing them to the inspector: "Both cellars are in the most decrepit shape, and there is absolutely nothing in them." Clearly, Berlin felt that he had much to lose if the authorities uncovered anything remotely suspicious.[15]

Registered officially as a merchant of the third guild, Shmerka Berlin occupied a respected place in the social hierarchy of the town. Not only did Berlin make quite a bit of money selling lumber and spirits while managing a glass factory, but he also married into an affluent family that lived in the most magnificent two-story brick house in Velizh. At the time of the investigation, Velizh was divided along economic, geographic, and confessional lines. Jews made up slightly less than one-third of the population (somewhere around 2,000 out of 6,700 inhabitants), but they owned almost all the homes in the center of town, managed the most lucrative estates in the provincial district, enjoyed a monopoly on the marketplace, and controlled lumber sales, small-scale trade, and the liquor industry.[16] As a result of their economic success, Jews clustered on the right side of the Western Dvina, in the most prosperous part of town, while the Belorussian population, composed mostly of Uniates and a small number of Catholics, lived on the left side, in what was considered to be the poorest section.[17]

Thanks to Miron Ryvkin's historical-ethnographic recollections (one of the earliest and most penetrating accounts of the case), it is possible to get a glimpse of details that are strikingly absent from the official judicial records.[18] On any weekday this imposing structure was the site of much activity and commotion. Customers from various parts of the town as well as the surrounding villages would come to drink beer or vodka at the tavern or purchase foodstuffs from what was considered to be the town's best-stocked grocery store. Besides alcohol, they could acquire buns, cottage-cheese cakes, pickled herring, fruits, coffee, tea, tobacco, matches, candles, and much more.[19] The individuals who came to town on business would walk up the wooden staircase to the *traktir* (tavern), where they could get a bite to eat at the diner and retire for the night in one of the guest rooms. The poor and needy showed up from time to time on the doorstep, as well: Mirka Aronson, it seems, was well known for her exceptional generosity. Aronson's two sons lived quite comfortably only a few doors away on Il'inskaia Street, while Shmerka Berlin's brother lived right around the corner on Petersburg Street, next to two of Velizh's most prominent personalities, the town councilor Evzik Tsetlin and his wife Khanna. On Saturdays and on holidays, the entire extended family—around forty people in all—would gather for a meal on the second story of the house.

Under the Polish-Lithuanian regime, Jews faced numerous restrictions on their residence. Some cities, such as Warsaw and Lublin, did not tolerate Jewish residence within their city limits at all, while others, such as Vilna and Kovna, restricted where Jews could reside. Partly as a result of the extensive restrictions outlined in the town charters, Jews in pre-partition Poland were forced to congregate in easily identifiable neighborhoods, districts, or streets.[20] At the turn of the nineteenth century, tsarist authorities dropped most of the burdensome restrictions from the law books, and permitted Jews to live, engage in trade, and build synagogues and schools wherever they wished in the Pale of Settlement, provided they observed the general laws on movement and residence.[21] But long after the partitions of Poland-Lithuania, Jews continued to live in easily identifiable streets or neighborhoods, most of which were centrally located. In the eastern borderlands, a large territory that extended from the Baltic region to the Black Sea, ethnic groups usually chose to live among their own types. Segregation did not, however, mean that populations lived in isolation from everyone else. Since early modern times, residents routinely met and socialized in courtyards, streets, homes, taverns, and grocery stores. The cultural boundaries between ethnic groups were highly permeable. While neighbors did not always exhibit esteem or affection toward one another, people's lives intersected on a daily basis.[22]

Without the support of their Catholic and Uniate neighbors, neither Shmerka Berlin nor Khanna Tsetlina would have been able to operate successful taverns. According to Ryvkin, all the respected residents of the town—from the wealthiest Polish landowners to the most powerful bureaucrats—could be spotted, from time to time, at either Berlin's or Tsetlina's tavern.[23] We should, however, be careful not to paint Velizh as a multicultural idyll. The day-to-day exchange of goods and services not only brought people together but also produced many of the conflicts between town residents—conflicts over issues such as the management of land and homes, contractual obligations, taxes, inheritance rights, and property—most of which were litigated and settled in courts of law.[24] This was a world that was consumed by petty conflicts, disputes, jealousy, and gossip.

Given the intimacy of small-town relations, it is tempting to make the argument, as so many scholars do, that ritual murder accusations were the product of intense economic rivalries and antisemitism.[25] No doubt, these reasons help explain why certain individuals denounced Jews for engaging in blood sacrifice. Yet they do not offer a satisfactory explanation for the vitality of the blood libel tale in the popular psyche—for why almost the entire Christian community in Velizh asserted that Jews were capable of committing ritual murder. Was this some sort of conspiracy? Did the townspeople harbor resentment that was brought out in the open at the time of the investigation? Or were other more powerful forces at work? To answer these questions, we must first return to the case itself and reconstruct the events as they transpired that spring.

If Mirka Aronson and Shmerka Berlin were regarded as two upstanding members of the community, Anna Eremeeva and Maria Terenteeva were considered to be some of the town's most marginal characters. Anna had lived a hand-to-mouth existence in and around Velizh for over a year when the murder took place. On March 25, about a month before Fedor disappeared, Anna found herself in the village Sentiury. While out walking, Anna suddenly felt weak and fell asleep on the side of the road. The townsman Larion Pestun noticed Anna and brought her to his warm bathhouse, where she continued to sleep for two days and nights without waking up. Anna dreamed of the Archangel Michael, who took her by the arm and whispered in her ear that the Jews would murder a Christian soul on Easter Day. This was not the only time that Anna dreamed of Michael: on Easter Saturday, he appeared to her one more time, revealing that the Jews would seize a Christian soul and bring him to Mirka Aronson's home. So when Agaf'ia Prokof'eva came to Sentiury on the third day of Easter Week to inquire about little Fedor's whereabouts, Anna told her: "On the way here you walked into the very home where they're keeping your son. If you have the strength to rescue the boy, then do so. But if you don't make it on time, then stay vigilant and watch over [the house]."[26]

Like Anna, Maria Terenteeva had lived in Velizh for a year or two at the time of the investigation (it is impossible to determine for sure from the archival records) and survived on whatever food and money she could find. She married a man who spent most of his adult life serving in the army. Several residents testified that Terenteeva had led a "debauched" lifestyle ever since she came to town—giving birth to a son out of wedlock, stealing food every chance she could, walking in the streets at all hours of the night screaming, "God help me, they're trying to suffocate me."[27] Abram Kisin first encountered Terenteeva during broad daylight, when he caught her stealing carrots and beets from his yard. No sooner had he confronted her than Terenteeva hit him so hard that he barely made it back home that day. On other occasions, as well, Terenteeva would come by Kisin's house in a fit of rage to steal fresh vegetables or throw clean linens on the ground and stomp on them with her bare feet in wild rage.[28]

Terenteeva testified that on Easter Day she begged for alms in front of a church and chatted briefly with a woman who was passing by. Afterward, she made her way to the outskirts of town, seeking charitable handouts along the way. It was already nightfall when she made her way to the Konevtse Creek, at which time she saw two small children standing on the bridge. One was a boy with white blond hair, wearing a cap and dressed in a coat and boots. At that precise moment, Terenteeva recalled, Khanna Tsetlina walked up to the boy and took him away by the arm. Although Terenteeva did not say anything about the whereabouts of the other child, she claimed that Tsetlina took the boy back to her own home, where four Jewish women were waiting for her. Terenteeva was not certain if the women had come from Shmerka Berlin's home, but she was confident that she would be able to identify at least two of them. She then described her encounters with Emel'ian Ivanov and Agaf'ia Prokof'eva and concluded the deposition by saying that Emel'ian had refused to believe a word she had said.[29]

Maria Terenteeva's testimony proved absolutely devastating for the Jewish community. Over the course of several weeks, authorities questioned dozens of Jews and Christians, focusing their attention on four primary suspects—Evzik and Khanna Tsetlin, Mirka Aronson, and Shmerka Berlin—and on the missing spring britska. Emel'ian Ivanov's sister-in-law, Kharitina Prokof'eva, was convinced by all the talk that "the Jews had murdered her nephew." Another town resident, Efim'ia Fedorova, heard from one of her neighbors that the Jews took the little boy inside their school, where they proceeded to torture and kill him. Avdot'ia Maksimova, who worked as a housekeeper for Khanna Tsetlina (and would play an important role in the case at a later date), testified that she had not seen a Christian boy at the house and had not seen Tsetlina walk outside that day. Eleven other witnesses—representing a broad cross-section of the population—declared that they, too, had not seen Jews with the young boy and had no knowledge of who had committed the crime. They acknowledged, however, that the Jews must have been involved in the murder. The investigators then proceeded to question twelve more people. Two testified that Shmerka Berlin's and Khanna Tsetlina's behavior had always been excellent; eight said they did not suspect either Berlin or Tsetlina of doing anything malicious; but all twelve were convinced beyond a shadow of a doubt that the Jews had killed the little boy.[30]

The court records demonstrate how influential tales of blood sacrifice were in the mindset of the town residents. Witness after witness asserted that Jews had ritually murdered the boy, even though no one had actually seen them with him. The only person other than Maria Terenteeva who claimed to have observed Khanna Tsetlina with a Christian boy was Daria Kasachevskaia. On Easter Day, at either one or two o'clock in the afternoon, Kasachevskaia went to Shmerka Berlin's store to purchase beer. On the way, she saw Khanna Tsetlina with a blond-haired boy who was dressed in either a blue or green caftan. Kasachevskaia surmised that Tsetlina and the little boy were walking to town from either the embankment or the creek, but she had no idea where they were going. After purchasing the beer, Kasachevskaia returned home immediately and did not see either Tsetlina or the boy again that afternoon. It seems likely that Kasachevskaia based her narrative on the many tales that were circulating around town, for when authorities pressed her to provide additional testimony, she could not remember any other details.[31]

Over the course of the investigation, tsarist officials attempted to obey the letter of the law by not casting blame on any suspects until they had interviewed all possible witnesses, exhausted all possible lines of inquiry, and reviewed all the forensic evidence. And as they questioned more and more people, gathered more and more evidence, communal tensions began to rise. How could they not? The Jews, it seems, thought that it was just a matter of time before the most respected and wealthiest members of their community would be formally charged with ritual murder. When on May 17 Inspector Lukashevich interviewed Father Kazimir Serafinovich, who had come to town to visit his friend the land surveyor Kottov, over one hundred Jews encircled Kottov's house, climbed on the fence, and began to shout to the inspector, "You don't have the right to treat the town councilor Tsetlin in this manner; he's our leader!" This unexpected turn of events put the authorities on high alert. Fearing that the heated emotions could easily escalate into unrestrained hostility, the magistrate issued an immediate injunction: none of the suspects or witnesses would be allowed to travel beyond the town's boundaries, and everyone would be kept under strict surveillance until all the sordid details of the case were sorted out. The last thing the magistrate needed to deal with was a full-blown riot.[32]

The Jews of Velizh, meanwhile, vehemently denied their role in the murder. Khanna Tsetlina testified that she was at home on Easter Day taking care of her ailing son. Furthermore, she insisted that she had not brought a Christian boy inside the house and did not know who had committed the crime. Several days after the deposition, Tsetlina submitted a formal appeal to the town council proclaiming her innocence. She added that most likely Maria Terenteeva invented the "awful slander" to settle an old score, for each time Terenteeva had come around looking for charity, Tsetlina had immediately "run her out of the house." Tsetlina's husband, Evzik, did not deny the possibility that his wife ventured out on Easter Day, but he was convinced that no Christian boy had set foot inside the home. Mirka Aronson had no idea who killed the little boy, but she was certain that her son-in-law Shmerka and her grandson Hirsh could not have been involved in the murder because she knew for a fact that they did not go out that day. Shmerka Berlin even made the outlandish conjecture that someone had "run over the boy accidently and then proceeded to puncture the body" to mask the death as a ritual murder.[33]

As far as the fate of the spring britska, several witnesses saw two mysterious Jews riding around town in such a carriage on Friday, April 27. No one in Velizh had ever seen them before, but as it turned out they were Shmerka Berlin's distant relatives: a middle-aged man by the name of Iosel' Glikman and his fifteen-year-old son, who had come to Velizh for the very first time that day from the *mestechka* Uly to purchase hay. They had parked the britska in a neighboring courtyard and then walked around the fence to Berlin's home, where they stayed until May 1. Authorities immediately suspected that Shmerka and Hirsh Berlin had used Glikman's spring britska to transfer the boy's body to the forest, so they proceeded to question Glikman, Berlin's neighbor Itska Nakhimovskii, and numerous other town residents for clues that would help them solve the murder. But Glikman refuted accusations that he was involved with the murder, testifying that his britska did not have forged metal wheels and that he borrowed the horses from the nobleman he was working for at the time. None of the other witnesses' testimony did anything to cast doubt on Glikman's self-proclaimed innocence.[34]

From the late medieval ages to early modern times, religious and civic authorities began to discredit the intellectual and popular foundations of the ritual murder charge. Their ideas, rooted in new theological and legal discourses, did not gain immediate currency. But by the end of the seventeenth century, official attitudes, especially in the German-speaking territories of Europe, had changed to such an extent that it became extremely difficult to convict Jews of blood sacrifice in a court of law.[35] In 1247, in one of the earliest pronouncements against the charge, Pope Innocent IV pleaded for popular restraint "if the body of a dead man is by chance found anywhere." "Duly redress all that has been wrought against the Jews in the aforesaid matter by the said prelates, nobles, and potentates," the pope concluded, "and do not allow them in the future to be unjustly molested by anybody on this or any other similar charge."[36] Over five hundred years later, in a widely circulated memorandum on the subject, the Russian poet and senator Gavriil Derzhavin did not go so far as to refute the veracity of ritual murder. Instead, without implicating the entire Jewish community in the crime, he accused the fanatical sects (i.e., the Hasidim) of engaging in blood sacrifice.[37] Some of Derzhavin's ideas were eventually codified into law. In 1817, shortly after the blood libel charge in Grodno, Count Aleksandr Golitsyn instructed provincial governors not to charge Jews with blood sacrifice without incriminating evidence. And if such cases did arise, Jews would have the same right to a fair trial as any other subject of the Russian Empire who was accused of murder.[38] At the beginning of the nineteenth century, the Russian government may not have discredited the blood libel directly, but it did institute a series of legal measures that made it extremely difficult to condemn Jews of ritual murder in a court of law.

The investigation of Fedor's death lasted for over a year, and on June 22, 1824, the Velizh Appellate Court handed down its verdicts. Khanna Tsetlina was formally acquitted, but at the same time, the court instructed the police to closely supervise her actions and behavior. Thus, while it did not discount the possibility that Daria Kasachevskaia and especially Maria Terenteeva had invented the sensational tale to mask their own role in the murder, it did not dismiss their testimony either. Shmerka Berlin was reprimanded for "spreading false rumors about the boy's death." Nevertheless, Mirka Aronson and her household were cleared of any wrongdoing, as a thorough search of the home had failed to uncover anything remotely suspicious. In fact, the only person severely punished in the case was Maria Terenteeva: to atone for her licentious ways of life, she was instructed to appear before the Catholico-Uniate Spiritual Consistory.[39]

In the final analysis, we will never know what exactly happened to Fedor—whether he drowned accidently, was ruthlessly murdered, or died from some other cause. On November 22, 1824, the most powerful court in Vitebsk province reviewed all the materials in the case and wrote off Fedor's tragic death to the "will of God."[40] Whatever the reason may have been, the documentary evidence suggests that a small town quarrel ultimately led to the ritual murder accusation. Most likely, the beggar-woman Maria Terenteeva took advantage of the boy's death (or killed him herself) to get back at Khanna Tsetlina for her refusal of charity. The culture of giving—the teachings and popular beliefs about offering support to those in need—played an important role in both Jewish and Russian communal traditions.[41] In imperial Russia, as in the early modern world, where mutual aid provided a safety net for the misfortunate and needy, refusing charity signified a breach of neighborly duty. The act of denying food, drink, money, or other charity typically caused the individual who had been turned away to feel angry and resentful. When a personal misfortune subsequently happened to the person who had acted selfishly, the latter would often suspect that the beggar had cast a magic spell against them for their callous behavior. Across most of Western and Central Europe, the overwhelming majority of documented witch cases conformed to the simple pattern that took place in Velizh—involving one neighbor's refusal to give a handout to another neighbor—although in our case the internal logic was reversed and the end result was a charge of ritual murder against a neighbor who refused to offer charity. To put it in slightly different terms, it was usually the very person who failed to perform a social duty who would accuse the person they had turned away of witchcraft. In contrast to the typical witch case scenario, then, Terenteeva represents the "victim" who took matters into her own hands to get back at her well-to-do neighbor Tsetlina for failing to fulfill a social obligation.[42]

If an ordinary neighborhood dispute does indeed explain why one neighbor accused another neighbor of murdering a little boy, we are still left with a puzzle. Why did so many other people support the charge that Jews had killed little Fedor? The answer has less to do with what is often referred to as "antisemitism" in the scholarly literature or economic rivalries (although we should be careful not to dismiss those twin factors altogether) than with popular cosmologies of the time. Much like early modern witchcraft charges, ritual murder accusations proved profoundly durable because of their capacity to mobilize fears and express popular worldviews. In the Russian Empire, ritual murder allegations never materialized in a full-blown panic along the likes of the early modern witch hunts in France or Germany, but their appearance and reappearance in the small towns of Minsk, Vil'na, Vitebsk, and Mogilev provinces, where Jews constituted a highly visible part of the population, suggests that a well-established oral culture—fueled by the circulation of stories, rumors, and gossip—helped legitimize the narrative.[43] Over the course of the eighteenth and nineteenth centuries, the imperial Russian state attempted to reshape "superstition"—the belief in the supernatural, magical powers, and miracle-working icons and relics—without much success.[44] Well into the twentieth century, the supernatural continued to offer convenient explanations for the basic needs of the community, while at the same time offering protection against numerous worldly dangers, and the boundaries between religious and magical beliefs were difficult to distinguish with any certainty. That folk medicine and the supernatural played an important role in Jewish daily life (especially among Hasidic communities known for their internalization of mysticism) only heightened the fantastical charge made during a ritually charged time of the year for both Jews and Christians. Thus, at a time when spoken spells brought illnesses to enemies or warded off evil spirits, when gathering ceremonies enhanced the healing properties of herbs, and when churches, cemeteries, barns, and bathhouses were associated with popular magic and divination, there was nothing strikingly peculiar about the idea that Jews required Christian blood for religious ritual services. If, according to popular White Russian folk traditions, witches preyed on unsuspecting children, why could Jews not kill little children for their blood?[45]

The provincial court's decision concluded the first act of the ritual murder drama. In only a few months' time authorities reopened the case, this time at the request of Tsar Alexander I himself. Shortly before his death, while passing through Velizh on his way to the port town of Taganrog on the Azov Sea, Alexander received a sensational petition from none other than Maria Terenteeva. In the petition, Terenteeva revealed that a terrible tragedy had occurred to her son [sic] Fedor in the town of Velizh: Khanna Tsetlina, with the help of her husband, had pierced Fedor to death, and they committed the crime for the boy's blood.[46] Alexander immediately instructed Governor-General Nikolai Nikolaevich Khovanskii to begin a full-blown investigation of the case. Khovanskii sent his most trusted and experienced man, Inspector-Councilor Vasilii Ivanovich Strakhov, to direct the inquiry. For the next five years Strakhov interrogated dozens of residents and produced hundreds of detailed depositions, reports, and memos. The result of all this work would be the longest and one of the most comprehensive investigations of ritual murder in the modern world.

EUGENE M. AVRUTIN is Associate Professor of History and Tobor Family Scholar in the Program of Jewish Culture and Society at the University of Illinois, Urbana-Champaign. He is the author of *Jews and the Imperial State: Identification Politics in Tsarist Russia* (2010). He is the coeditor of several volumes, including *Photographing the Jewish Nation: Pictures from S. An-sky's Ethnographic Expeditions* (2009) and *Story of a Life: Memoirs of a Young Jewish Woman in the Russian Empire* (2012).

NOTES

This is a revised essay that first appeared in Jewish History 26, nos. 3–4 (2012): 309–26.

1. Russkii gosudarstvennyi istoricheskii arkhiv (hereafter RGIA), f. 1345, op. 235, d. 65, ch. 25, ll. 3–5.

2. For the most authoritative study of the Velizh Affair, based mostly on the official summary of the case prepared by the Senate, see Iulii Gessen, *Velizhskaia drama: Iz istorii obvineniia evreev v ritual'nykh prestupleniiakh* (St. Petersburg: Tipografiia A. G. Rozena, 1904). See also M. D. Ryvkin, "Velizhskoe delo v osveshchenii mestnykh predanii i pamiatnikov," *Perezhitoe* 3 (1911): 60–102; Robert Lippert, *Anklagen der Juden in Russland wegen Kindermords, Gebrauchs von Christenblut und Gotteslaesterung: Ein Beitrag zur Geschichte der Juden in Russland im letzten Jahrzehend und frueherer Zeit* (Leipzig: W. Engelmann, 1846). For a recent treatment that relies heavily on Gessen's original research, see I. M. Shkliazh, *Velizhskoe delo: Iz istorii antisemitizma v Rossii* (Odessa, Ukraine: n.p., 1998).

3. John D. Klier, "The Origins of the 'Blood Libel' in Russia," *Newsletter of the Study Group on Eighteenth Century Russia* 14 (1986): 12–22; Klier, "Krovavyi navet v russkoi pravoslavnyi traditsii," in *Evrei i khristiane v pravoslavnykh obshchestvakh Vostochnoi Evropy*, ed. M. V. Dmitrieva (Moscow: Indrik, 2011), 181–205; Marcin Wodzinski, "Blood and the Hasidim: On the History of Ritual Murder Accusations in Nineteenth-Century Poland," *Polin* 22 (2010): 273–90.

4. Brian P. Levack, *The Witch-Hunt in Early Modern Europe*, 2nd ed. (New York: Longman, 1995), 233–50.

5. The number of recorded ritual murder cases should not be used to gauge the popularity of belief in blood sacrifice. As with the witch case, the ritual murder case reflects the preoccupations

of the educated classes rather than of those people who left no written records. For witchcraft, see Keith Thomas, *Religion and the Decline of Magic* (London: Penguin, 1971), 538–39. Most likely, the belief in ritual murder did not enjoy a modern "revival," as David Biale has argued. Although print (and to a lesser extent visual) culture played an important role in the dissemination of the discourse, in the small towns and villages of Central and Eastern Europe, the tale continued to enjoy popular appeal since early modern times, largely as a result of popular oral culture. On the modern revival argument, see Biale's *Blood and Belief: The Circulation of a Symbol between Jews and Christians* (Berkeley: University of California Press, 2007), 126–29. According to R. Po-chia Hsia, even after the suppression of ritual murder trials, the tale "retained much of its cohesion and force of persuasion" in popular culture (R. Po-chia Hsia, *The Myth of Ritual Murder: Jews and Magic in Reformation Germany* [New Haven, CT: Yale University Press, 1988], 228).

6. The Velizh Affair archive is preserved at RGIA, f. 1345, op. 235, d. 65, ch. 1–25; and at the Natsional'nyi istoricheskii arkhiv Belarusi (hereafter NIAB), f. 1297, op. 1.

7. For a good introduction to crime and the microhistorical genre, see Edward Muir and Guido Ruggiero, eds., *History from Crime* (Baltimore, MD: Johns Hopkins University Press, 1994).

8. See, e.g., Jane Burbank, Mark von Hagen, and Anatolyi Remnev, eds., *Russian Empire: Space, People, Power, 1700–1930* (Bloomington: Indiana University Press, 2007); Robert D. Crews, *For Prophet and Tsar: Islam and Empire in Russia and Central Asia* (Cambridge, MA: Harvard University Press, 2006); Benjamin Nathans, *Beyond the Pale: The Jewish Encounter with Late Imperial Russia* (Berkeley: University of California Press, 2002); Eugene M. Avrutin, *Jews and the Imperial State: Identification Politics in Tsarist Russia* (Ithaca, NY: Cornell University Press, 2010); and Willard Sunderland, *Taming the Wild Field: Colonization and Empire on the Russian Steppe* (Ithaca, NY: Cornell University Press, 2004).

9. For some of the most innovative work on interethnic relations, see, e.g., David Frick, "Jews and Others in Seventeenth-Century Wilno: Life in the Neighborhood," *Jewish Studies Quarterly* 12 (2005): 8–42; and the essays collected in *Polin* 22 (2010), on the problem of crossing and maintaining social and cultural boundaries in premodern Poland. Less sophisticated are the essays on the theme of "neighbor" in *Ab Imperio* 3 (2010) and *Polin* 24 (2012).

10. On Vitebsk province for a slightly later period, see Viktor Lindenberg, "Materialy k voprosu detoubiistve i plodoizgnanii v Vitebskoi gubernii" (PhD diss., Iur'ev University, 1910). See also ChaeRan Y. Freeze, "Lilith's Midwives: Jewish Newborn Child Murder in Nineteenth-Century Vilna," *Jewish Social Studies* 16, no. 2 (2010): 1–27. For a richly documented study of abandonment and peasant life, see David L. Ransel, *Mothers of Misery: Child Abandonment in Russia* (Princeton, NJ: Princeton University Press, 1988).

11. RGIA, f. 1345, op. 235, d. 65, ch. 25, l. 4.

12. NIAB, f. 1297, op. 1, d. 190, l. 9; RGIA, f. 1345, op. 235, d. 65, ch. 25, l. 4.

13. NIAB, f. 1297, op. 1, d. 190, ll. 13–15 ob.; RGIA, f. 1345, op. 235, d. 65, ch. 25, l. 6.

14. NIAB, f. 1297, op. 1, d. 190, ll. 20–22 ob.; RGIA, f. 1345, op. 235, d. 65, ch. 25, l. 7.

15. NIAB, f. 1297, op. 1, d. 190, ll. 23–23 ob., 58–59; RGIA, f. 1345, op. 235, d. 65, ch. 25, l. 7.

16. Until the second half of the nineteenth century, population statistics in the Russian Empire were notoriously inexact. For Velizh and the province of Vitebsk, see RGIA, f. 1290, op. 1, d. 16, l. 4 ob. (1828). For histories of Velizh, see Ryvkin, "Velizhskoe delo," 77–81; *Iz istorii Velizha i raiona* (Smolensk, Russia: Smolenskaia gosudarstvennaia tipografiia, 2000); and S. M. Kiselev, comp., *Velizh* (Vitebsk, Russia: Gubernskaia tipografiia, 1895).

17. During the reign of Nicholas I, the Uniate Church came under attack for, among other things, destabilizing the boundaries of religious identity. Tsars Nicholas I and Alexander II succeeded in their efforts to thoroughly suppress the Uniate Church, to forcibly convert the Uniates to Russian Orthodoxy. For a thorough and penetrating analysis of the Uniate problem,

see Mikhail Dolbilov, *Russkii krai, chuzhaia vera: Etnokonfessional'naia politika imperii v Litve i Belorussii pri Aleksandre II* (Moscow: Novoe literaturnoe obozrenie, 2010), 68–108; and Barbara Skinner, *The Western Front of the Eastern Church: Uniate and Orthodox Conflict in Eighteenth-Century Poland, Ukraine, Belarus, and Russia* (DeKalb: Northern Illinois University Press, 2009).

18. Miron Ryvkin, "Velizhskoe delo v osveshchenii mestnykh predanii i pamiatnikov," *Perezhitoe* 3 (1911): 69–81.

19. Glenn Dynner, *Yankel's Tavern: Jews, Liquor, and Life in the Kingdom of Poland* (Oxford: Oxford University Press, 2014), 17–20; Yohanan Petrovsky-Shtern, *The Golden Age Shtetl: A New History of Jewish Life in Eastern Europe* (Princeton, NJ: Princeton University Press, 2014), 129–35.

20. Antony Polonsky, *The Jews in Poland and Russia* (Oxford: Littman Library of Jewish Civilization, 2010), 1:68–90; Gershon David Hundert, *The Jews in a Polish Private Town: The Case of Opatów in the Eighteenth Century* (Baltimore, MD: John Hopkins University Press, 1992), 3–10.

21. In the second half of the nineteenth century, Jews continued to face restrictions on their residence in cities such as Vil'na, Kovno, and Zhitomir. See Nathans, *Beyond the Pale*, 113–14.

22. See, e.g., Adam Teller and Magda Teter, "Introduction: Borders and Boundaries in the Historiography of the Jews in the Polish-Lithuanian Commonwealth," *Polin* 22 (2010): 3–46; and David Frick, "Jews in Public Places: Further Chapters in the Jewish-Christian Encounter in Seventeenth-Century Vilna," *Polin* 22 (2010): 215–48. See also Dynner, *Yankel's Tavern*.

23. Ryvkin, "Velizhskoe delo," 79.

24. Eugene M. Avrutin, "Jewish Neighbourly Relations and Imperial Russian Legal Culture," *Journal of Modern Jewish Studies* 9, no. 1 (2010): 1–16.

25. See, e.g., Marvin Perry and Frederick M. Schweitzer, *Antisemitism: Myth and Hate from Antiquity to the Present* (New York: Palgrave Macmillian, 2002), 43–72; Biale, *Blood and Belief*, 126–38; and Robert S. Wistrich, *A Lethal Obsession: Anti-Semitism from Antiquity to the Global Jihad* (New York: Random House, 2010), 79, 88–90.

26. NIAB, f. 1297, op. 1, d. 190, ll. 18–19, 29–30; RGIA, f. 1345, op. 235, d. 65, ch. 25, ll. 6–7, 9.

27. NIAB, f. 1297, op. 1, d. 190, ll. 62–65 ob.; RGIA, f. 1345, op. 235, d. 65, ch. 25, l. 12.

28. RGIA, f. 1345, op. 235, d. 65, ch. 25, l. 116.

29. NIAB, f. 1297, op. 1, d. 190, l. 234.

30. NIAB, f. 1297, op. 1, d. 190, ll. 24 ob.–33, 46, 51, 74–81, 112–13 ob.; RGIA, f. 1345, op. 235, d. 65, ch. 25, ll. 5, 11, 13, 18, 23.

31. RGIA, f. 1345, op. 235, d. 65, ch. 25, l. 20.

32. NIAB, f. 1297, op. 1, d. 190, ll. 100–102; RGIA, f. 1345, op. 235, d. 65, ch. 25, ll. 15–16.

33. RGIA, f. 1345, op. 235, d. 65, ch. 25, l. 21.

34. RGIA, f. 1345, op. 235, d. 65, ch. 25, ll. 17, 19.

35. Hsia, *Myth of Ritual Murder*, 227–28.

36. As quoted in Cecil Roth, ed., *The Ritual Murder Libel and the Jew: The Report by Cardinal Lorenzo Ganganelli (Pope Clement XIV)* (London: Woburn Press, 1934), 97–98. Pope Innocent IV issued the pronouncement to the archbishops and bishops of Germany and France on July 5, 1247.

37. For a good explanation of the connection between Hasidic Jews and blood sacrifice, see Wodzinski, "Blood and Hasidim," 273–90. See also John D. Klier, *Russia Gathers Her Jews: The Origins of the "Jewish Question" in Russia, 1772–1825* (DeKalb: Northern Illinois University Press, 1986), 104.

38. Iulii Gessen, "Obvineniia evreev v ritual'nykh prestupleniiakh v Rossii," *Evreiskaia entsiklopediia: Svod znanii o evreistve i ego kul'ture v proshlom i nastoiashchem*, 16 vols. (Moscow: Terra, 1991), 11:871.

39. RGIA, f. 1345, op. 235, d. 65, ch. 25, ll. 24–26.

40. RGIA, f. 1345, op. 235, d. 65, ch. 25, l. 27.

41. On charity and mutual aid, see Adele Lindenmeyr, *Poverty Is Not a Vice: Charity, Society, and the State in Imperial Russia* (Princeton, NJ: Princeton University Press, 1996); and Mordechai Zalkin, "Charity," in *The YIVO Encyclopedia of Jews in Eastern Europe*, 2 vols. (New Haven, CT: Yale University Press, 2008), 1:306–9.

42. Thomas, *Religion and the Decline of Magic*, 660–69; Robin Briggs, *Witches and Neighbors: The Social and Cultural Context of European Witchcraft* (New York: Penguin, 1996), 137–46.

43. On popular cosmologies and witchcraft, see Briggs, *Witches and Neighbors*, 99–133. On the witch hunt in early modern Europe, see Bengt Ankarloo and Stuart Clark, eds., *Witchcraft and Magic in Europe: The Period of the Witch Trials* (Philadelphia: University of Pennsylvania Press, 2002).

44. Historians working on a wide range of geographic regions and across vast chronological timeframes have had heated debates over the popular beliefs of populations who left few written records of their everyday prejudices, fears, and preoccupations. For the Russian Empire, see, e.g., Simon Dixon, "Superstition in Imperial Russia," *Past and Present*, supplement 3 (2008): 207–28. See also Christine D. Worobec, *Possessed: Women, Witches, and Demons in Imperial Russia* (DeKalb: Northern Illinois University Press, 2003), 20–63; and Robert H. Greene, *Bodies like Bright Stars: Saints and Relics in Orthodox Russia* (DeKalb: Northern Illinois University Press, 2010), 17–102.

45. W. F. Ryan, *The Bathhouse at Midnight: Magic in Russia* (University Park: Pennsylvania State University Press, 1999), 79.

46. RGIA, f. 1345, op. 235, d. 65, ch. 1, ll. 5–5 ob. (Maria Terenteeva's petition to Tsar Alexander I, July 25, 1825).

4

THE SARATOV CASE AS A CRITICAL JUNCTURE IN RITUAL MURDER HISTORY

Andrew C. Reed

THE CHARGE OF Jewish ritual murder obtained newfound public interest in the Russian Empire in the 1850s and 1860s, in connection with events in Saratov. Between 1852 and 1860, a small group of Saratov Jews were imprisoned while investigators carried out a protracted inquiry into the possibility that they murdered two Christian boys for religious purposes.[1] The investigation attracted the attention of leading officials from various ministerial organs within the imperial government and gradually fell under the auspices of the Ministry of Internal Affairs. Ritual murder cases in Velizh (1823–1835) and Saratov became early battlefields where religious loyalties were challenged within the empire.[2] The Saratov ritual murder case was unique because it was the first investigation to occur outside the Pale of Settlement.[3] Significantly, the individuals who entered into the debates surrounding the Saratov investigation later spent their lives arguing for the veracity or fallaciousness of such charges and left indelible marks on Russian and Jewish communities in its aftermath.

The emergence of a case against Jews in Saratov was remarkable in part because it represented the presence of the myth of Jewish ritual murder in a relatively "safe" locale within the central regions of the empire but sufficiently far away from the imperial capital of St. Petersburg. The growing presence of Jews in Saratov—mostly due to military presence along the Volga River—made the possibility that such a case might arise all the more possible. Saratov was once an outpost located nearly 1,600 versts (approximately 1,564 miles) southeast of St. Petersburg. The city became a provincial capital under Catherine the Great in 1780, and during the nineteenth century the once small town experienced remarkable growth. By 1850 the city became a commercial center for trade and served as a link between cities north and diverse lands south.⁴ The population in Saratov province in 1862 was 69,660.⁵ Saratov grew rapidly, and by mid-century boasted twenty-three Orthodox church structures, one Roman Catholic church, and one Protestant chapel. Non-Christians could worship in the city's synagogue or mosque. According to imperial records, there were sixty-five factories and fifteen mills in the city.⁶ During this same period, a small number of Jews from the Pale found their way to Saratov to benefit from the economic activity within the interior of the empire. Among the Jews in the region, some were enlisted men in the imperial army while others used conversion to legally cross the Pale.

The events in Saratov garner relatively little coverage in accounts of Russian-Jewish history and therefore the case appears only as a marginal event that occurred on the Volga frontier with little impact on the empire at large.⁷ However, when viewed from within the historiography of Russian exposure to the ritual murder accusation, it should be viewed as a significant turning point within the larger development of anti-Jewish sentiment.⁸ The Saratov case brought the pernicious charges squarely into the interior of the empire and allowed the myth to perpetuate anti-Jewish fears among populations where few Jews lived. Between December 1852 and March 1853 there were several dozen Jews in the city.⁹ Most Jews in Saratov were enlistees assigned to the region with their battalion, but a handful of them were semipermanent residents of the city who remained there thanks to local government permission. During the period of interest to this chapter, some locals in Saratov and the surrounding region viewed Jews in the city as economic pariahs who benefited from illegitimate economic ventures and relations—an argument that gained some ground during the investigation. The first aim of this chapter is to outline the basic narrative of the Saratov case. Second, the case is contextualized through an examination of reports connected to the accusations that were composed at the behest of government officials seeking to validate the blood libel and thereby condemn Jews collectively. This examination of the events and emerging discussions about ritual murder during the 1840s and 1850s serves to place Saratov more firmly within the spectrum of similar cases ranging from Velizh to Beilis. In doing so, this chapter responds to Jonathan Frankel's assertion that "open discussion of the ritual-murder accusation did not gain momentum until late in the reign of Alexander II" and locates the backdrop that led to the proliferation of ritual murder debates in the 1870s and 1880s.¹⁰

The Saratov Ritual Murder Case

On December 3, 1852, Feofan Sherstobitov, a ten-year-old boy from Saratov, did not arrive home from school. Young Sherstobitov lived in the city with his parents. His father, Efim Grigor'ev Sherstobitov, was a local shopkeeper. His parents, desperate to find their son, began searching the neighborhood and placed announcements in prominent locations around the city. The young boy's father described the missing boy as having blond hair, grayish eyes, and a fair complexion. On the day he disappeared, Sherstobitov was dressed in a lambskin coat, a Crimean winter hat, nankeen trousers, and winter boots.[11] It was not until December 8, 1852, that Efim Sherstobitov filed a report with the local police and insisted that they assist in finding his young son. According to city police reports, officials searched the city from one end to the other.[12] There was no sighting of the young boy and there was very little, if any, available evidence as to his whereabouts.

Although the initial investigation into Sherstobitov's disappearance lasted only a few days, it began anew at the end of January when another young man, eleven-year-old Mikhail Maslov, disappeared from Saratov.[13] On January 27, 1853, Maslov disappeared after playing in the street with his close friend, Stepan Kanin. According to Kanin's story, the two boys were playing and running in the streets when a dark-haired, bearded man approached them. The man asked the boys if they wanted to earn money by helping carry small slate slabs (*aspidnye doski*) to the banks of the Volga River. Excited by the possibility of earning money, the two boys readily agreed to help the man and followed him away. After a short while, Kanin, fearing that he might get into trouble if his parents found out, headed home to warm himself from the winter cold. According to later testimonies by Kanin, Maslov continued on in hopes of obtaining the promised wages.

When Maslov, whose family hailed from Kerenskaia in neighboring Penza province, failed to return home, his parents immediately initiated a search for the missing child. Their inquiries to neighbors and others on the street yielded little, if any, reliable information. Unlike Sherstobitov's disappearance, however, Maslov's parents initiated the investigation immediately. The police were notified, and local officers were told to exercise vigilance in their search for the boy—an indication that some in the city had begun to make connections between the two mysterious disappearances. On January 29, someone notified police that a local man named Ivan Nikolaev Moskvin, who hailed from the village of Liubavtsov (located about fifty versts, approximately thirty-three miles) traveled to Saratov on or about December 10, 1852, and remained there until about December 20, 1852.[14] This same Moskvin was also in the city on January 26, 1853, "to collect money from some individual" in the city.[15] According to neighbors' reports, Moskvin matched the description given to police by Kanin. Police rounded up Moskvin and asked Stepan Kanin to identify him. Kanin reported to police that Moskvin was not the man that approached him in the streets. According to Kanin's initial report, the boys separated before lunch, near the Moscow Tavern, while the church bells were ringing. Authorities determined that Moskvin was not involved in the case because he did not arrive in Saratov until sometime after six o'clock that evening, and subsequently released him to return home.

In a letter from the Saratov provincial vice-governor to the local authorities, the governor insisted on searching "with all thoroughness to find the young boy, and to discover who this reported kidnapper was that led the two young boys (Maslov and Kanin) away from their homes."[16] At the request of the governor's office in Saratov, the chief of police Vestman submitted a report on February 3, 1853, about the progress of the investigation. By that point, the similarities between the cases seemed to have influenced the opinions of investigators to the point that the two cases were being handled by the same individual or possibly a small group of officers. The early investigations identified commonalities between the cases and caused police to seek for corroborative evidence that might link the two cases together. The police and provincial authorities conducted an initial search that scoured the city looking for clues of the boys' whereabouts but shortly thereafter became frustrated by the shortage of leads. In the report Vestman argued that the investigation had worn out his police force and they were unable to make any substantial progress during the past month.[17]

Almost immediately after Vestman submitted his report calling off the search for the missing boy, the case shifted from kidnapping to murder. Around midday on March 4, 1853, a Saratov police officer named Volokhov reported that the body of a young boy was spotted under the stern side of a boat on the river. The body was identified as that of Mikhail Maslov. Police found the corpse face up with the head pointed downstream. The boy's head and arms were exposed to the harsh winter cold and covered in blood. The head of the boy was partially severed on the right side, his mouth open, both ears were filled with snow and ice, and eyes closed.[18] The boy was covered with a blanket and dressed in a very old coat that was torn at the sleeves. Maslov was adorned in the boots he was wearing when he left home.

The police requested that the local medical inspector immediately begin a complete autopsy, though, at the doctor's request, this did not happen until March 7 due to the fact that the body was frozen and took several days for the tissues to thaw. The doctor's report is both horrific and finely focused in detail and method. The exactitude of the doctor's evaluation reveals the importance of science and medicine in understanding the case. The doctor outlined the results of his examination and showed how there were two major factors that contributed to Maslov's death: strangulation and a sharp, crushing blow to the head.[19] The young boy's temporal bones (located on the lower sides of the skull near the ears) were cracked, and his occipital protuberance (back of the skull) was shattered. According to the doctor, the blow that struck the back of the skull did so with such force that the boy sustained serious injury to the brain and could not have survived more than a few minutes after the strike. At some point after his skull was crushed, but while he was still alive, the boy was strangled using a sash that was found on the ice with his body. In addition, the examiner noted that he was just recently circumcised in a crude and inexact manner.

If the news of two boys disappearing from the area failed to spark public interest and concern, the discovery of one of their mangled bodies most assuredly drew the attention of the local population toward the unfolding events. Local police received a number of letters from members of the community indicating their concern over the boys' disappearances and the startling discovery of Maslov's body.[20] The fact that local police failed to quickly apprehend a guilty party only exacerbated those concerns. Shortly after the investigation began anew, regional government officials pressured local police authorities to send relevant information to their superiors, especially when new leads arose. Even before provincial authorities pushed investigators to press forward unceasingly, and not rest until the whereabouts of the boys was determined, the local community was on high alert for details about the case. After finding the body of one boy, the search for the second shifted from rescue to recovery. Thus, the brutality of Maslov's murder evaporated hope that Sherstobitov might be found unharmed—the realization of which necessitated that the government respond in a way that would reassert its role as a protector of peace, people, and order.

The search for Maslov's killer or killers continued through March and into April. As the investigation broadened to include a wide array of potential suspects, nearly a month and a half after the discovery of Maslov's body police stumbled on yet another gruesome scene. On April 12, police uncovered the body of Feofan Sherstobitov who had disappeared from Saratov on December 3, 1852. The body was discovered behind a building near the river. When originally discovered, the boy's body showed clear signs of severe dehydration, severe tissue deterioration, and blackening by the elements.

Soon after the boys were discovered, the local population began hearing and passing along rumors that the murders were the sinister acts of local Jews who, as legend had it, needed to murder Christian children for ritual purposes. As soon as the focus turned to Jews, the investigative team pushed all their efforts in that direction. When young Maslov's crude circumcision was discovered, investigators assumed this was connected to some Jewish religious rites. To prove that Jews were responsible, local authorities brought together a Jewish boy and a Tatar boy from the local population to evaluate the various methods of performing circumcision and identifying the methods specific to each procedure. The examination of the Tatar boy was not necessarily performed out of concern that local Tatars may have committed the crimes, but rather to reinforce Jewish guilt by ruling out all other parties. The local medical doctors who performed the circumcision for each boy were brought in to ask about the procedure. Following this examination, the parents of Mikhail Maslov were asked whether the peasant boy had undergone circumcision to fulfill some kind of religious rite when he was young. They indicated that he had not.

The corpses revealed that the boys' bodies were inflicted with numerous wounds, but only after they were circumcised in a very crude manner. Local police and medical experts were immediately assigned to the investigation. Shortly after the discovery of the bodies, the case attracted the attention of officials in St. Petersburg. Almost immediately, local and state officials began circulating information that indicated the cases were being investigated as sadistic, cult-like ritual murders and Jews were the primary suspects.

The first suspect in the case was a local peasant named Lokotkov, who was arrested on March 10, 1853.[21] Lokotkov, who was originally suspected of being associated with the case because of early rumors about his proximity to the area of the boy's disappearance, remained a possible suspect for the remainder of the decade, but seemed to garner very little serious interest from investigators or the public once claims of ritual murder became prevalent. The first arrest of a Jew in Saratov in connection with the murders was a military private, Mikhel Shlifferman. Even before the body of the young Sherstobitov was discovered, the investigation moved forward at a steady, though often meandering pace. On March 31, 1853, Saratov police arrested Shlifferman and commenced a long series of interrogations about the young boy and his death. Weeks earlier, on March 10, Shlifferman's home was searched by local investigators, who found nothing that could incriminate him in the murders. A number of articles of clothing were examined and six letters written *na evreiskom iazyke* (in Yiddish) were discovered, although a translation of the letters yielded no useful evidence. Shlifferman was a barber in the army and occasionally performed the circumcisions of young Jewish boys when asked to do so. During questioning on March 11, he claimed that he did not know anything about the boys, including their whereabouts, and that he did not perform the circumcision on young Maslov. When asked for details about the process of circumcision, including the possibility of performing it on older boys (ten or eleven years old), he simply claimed that it could be done but would be much more difficult and painful. When the young boy Stepan Kanin was asked if Shlifferman was the one who had "enticed" him, he said that the man looked similar, but that his voice was different; Shlifferman had a slight lisp, and his Russian was not as clear as the perpetrator's speech.[22]

Other arrests of Jews and Christians soon followed Shlifferman's apprehension. In May of the same year, Private Anton Bogdanov (Roman Catholic) was arrested and interrogated in connection with the case, as were Private Fedor Iurlov (Orthodox), Private Itska Berlinskii (Jewish), Private Ezdra Zaidman (Jewish), city resident Iankel Iushkevicher (Jewish), and state peasant Mar'ia Ivanovna (Orthodox). One more arrest (a peasant named Akirlina) occurred in September 1853. All told, thirteen arrests were made in connection with the Saratov case over a three-year period. The timeline of the arrests helps explain as well the shift from one isolated individual to the Jewish community, or at least a group of local Jews believed to have connections to the case. By mid-May 1853 local authorities had made the connection between the two boys, based on evidence that both boys had undergone recent and crude circumcisions. As these two cases were positioned alongside each other, rumors began circulating that Jews had participated in the events. Those who spread such rumors did not need to look very far to find a plausible scenario that connected Saratov Jews to the historical legacy of Jewish ritual murder charges. The evidence against the Jews arrested came from Private Bogdanov, a local member of the garrison whose character was disreputable at best, but who immediately pointed the investigation toward local Jews.

After Shlifferman's arrest, police built a circle of suspects who might have assisted in the circumcision of the young boys and, ultimately, in their deaths. On May 13, Iankel Iushkevicher, a Jewish resident in the city for more than twenty-five years, was arrested after Bogdanov presented a story that brought Iushkevicher directly into the case. Iushkevicher, a local furrier and father of one of the city's most prominent corset makers who serviced many of the wealthy elite in the region, was accused of coordinating the entire process, from kidnapping to religious ceremonies, and ultimately it was he who local police believed killed the young boys. The day before, Iushkevicher's son, Fedor Iurlov, was arrested and interrogated. Iurlov, formerly Iushkevicher, changed his name when he converted to Russian Orthodoxy, but he maintained close relations with his father's family. Iurlov was a private in the Saratov battalion, and therefore was frequently able to visit his father's home in the city.

Iushkevicher was fifty-four years old at the time of his arrest and appears to have been a familiar face to many Saratov residents. The various testimonies offered to the police during the investigation varied greatly in both content and tone. For example, his daughter, Minareiza Guglina, offered frequent testimonies in her father's defense, and each one suggested that Iushkevicher never housed any young boys at their home and that he most certainly did not perform any circumcisions there.[23] Bogdanov and other witnesses claimed that Saratov's Jews planned to sell (or simply send) the blood of the Christian children to Jews in other provinces of the empire, and most often they cited Mogilev province as the intended destination. This story gained prominence because Bogdanov and others claimed that Iankel Iushkevicher was from the Mogilev region and maintained connections with Jews there. Iankel's father, Faibish Leib Iushkevicher, died in 1819 and had never lived in the interior provinces. Those who supported Iushkevicher's denial of the accusation went so far as to have officials in Mogilev submit an affidavit indicating that his father had died in 1819 and that no remaining relations to Iushkevicher remained in the region.[24]

In the first weeks of the investigation after the discovery of the bodies, the Ministry of Internal Affairs sent one of its own, N. S. Durnovo, to carry out the investigation. Durnovo dutifully carried out the investigation, eliciting from locals all manner of outlandish accusations and testimonies about the case and more generally about Jews and their penchant for Christian blood. Durnovo's management of the investigation led him to conclude that Jews were the perpetrators and that they acted out of religious conviction. The investigator's first effort was to involve local police to conduct a thorough surveillance of all Jews in the area, including a small number of converts to Christianity. As the investigation dragged on, more Jews were brought into police custody for questioning. The archival record suggests a long fascination among some Ministry of Internal Affairs officials with connecting Jews to ritual murders in the Russian Empire. Further, the existence of an already formulated narrative about Jewish blood libel, albeit a limited one that circulated among a small group of government officials, fostered a prepackaged set of assumptions for Durnovo that were readily applied to Jews in Saratov.

Report of the Ministry of Internal Affairs, 1844

An earlier 1844 Ministry of Internal Affairs investigation into Jewish ritual murder heavily influenced Durnovo's perspective on the killings.[25] The 1844 report was possibly written in large part by the scholar Vladimir Dal' (1801–1872). Even today this report remains a contentious subset of blood libel historiography for a number of reasons, particularly the question of authorship and the prolonged dependence on it by later officials who considered it an authoritative text. One of the reasons that the 1844 report became, as John Klier indicated, an "instant bibliographical rarity" was because it was limited in publication and was hardly systematic or comprehensive, tending more toward a "cut and paste job" than anything else.[26] The work is truly a collection of curiosities rather than any kind of coherent report. In the report are a collection of letters between ministry officials and others and summaries of a book *Obriady zhidovskie* (Jewish Rites), reportedly published in St. Petersburg in 1787, with details of Jews and their need for Christian blood.[27] Also included in the 1844 report were two rather striking images that depicted popular Christian understandings of Jewish ritual murder. The first is a woodcut of a young Christian boy being crucified on a cross by three Jews. The first Jew is tying the boy's outstretched arms to the cross, while a second puts nails through the palms, and a third is working on the boy's feet. The second image depicts a deceased boy on a table (possibly in a coffin) with stab marks all over his body—thus hinting at the possibility of bloodletting.[28] Also tacked onto the end of the report is a handwritten selection of verses from Numbers 23 and a ruling attributed to the Polish King Casimer III about Jews and their use of blood in 1264 and 1334.[29] Furthermore, the 1844 report became a major contribution to Russian antisemitic literature and was used at two critical moments in connection with subsequent ritual murder charges.

The authorship of the 1844 report on Jewish ritual murder needs to be considered in light of other such reports produced during the same year and within the same ministerial context. Between 1841 and 1852, the Ministry of Internal Affairs was under the direction of Lev Alekseevich Perovskii, a technocrat with deep connections to Russian scholars in the capital. Between March 4 and May 31, 1844, Perovskii sought out sources and evidence of Jewish murder, kidnapped children, and other devious acts that corroborated his belief that Jews engaged in criminal acts. In a series of letters to other ministers and police officials, Perovskii asked repeatedly for case files from police reports regarding specific events involving criminal acts by Jews. On March 4, 1844, Perovskii sent a request to Matvei Mikhailovich Karniolin-Pinskii, then procurator of the Fifth Department of the State Senate, to supply copies of the Senate reports. He specifically asked for details related to "charges against Jews with regard to the murder of Christian children for their blood," as well as those related to the Jews of Velizh (compiled in 1832).[30] Karniolin-Pinskii responded by including two reports, the first related to a Jew accused of killing a twelve-year-old girl, the second in connection with the Velizh case from 1823 and 1835.[31] Perovskii sent similar requests on March 19, 1844, to St. Petersburg Governor-General of the Military A. A. Kavelin, in which he made specific mention of events between 1819 and 1824 involving a kidnapping from Haymarket Square near the Jewish synagogue and the disappearance of a young Christian child from a local bathhouse.[32] In his letter to Kavelin, Perovskii stressed the urgency of obtaining the records of these two cases, and asked Kavelin to "find them as soon as possible" and forward them to Perovskii.[33] In another letter (April 17) to Deputy Procurator of the First Division of the Fifth Department of the Senate Vasilii Mikhailovich Bychkov, Perovskii requested records pertaining to Jews accused of cutting out a peasant's mouth in Kazan (1837).[34] It is clear that the issue of Jewish ritual murder was at the forefront of Perovskii's professional and personal agenda in 1844.The 1844 report on Jews and ritual murder initially circulated internally within the Ministry of Internal Affairs among a limited group. Most likely, the report was the result of several individuals who compiled available information and opinions about blood libel, even though a single, unidentified individual completed the final compilation. The anonymity of the report's author in 1844 meant that later publication of it for public consumption could attribute responsibility to various individuals. The first and most likely candidate was Dal', which makes the most sense given the nature of his work on many of the Ministry of Internal Affairs reports during this period and the later attribution of him as author of the *Rozyskanie ob ubienii evreiami khristianskikh mladentsev i upotreblenii krovi ikh* (Investigations of murders by Jews of Christian children and the use of their blood), published in 1913.[35]

On May 30, 1844, Dal' sent a letter to Archpriest Ioakim Semenovich Kochetov requesting further information about the abduction of children in Haymarket Square and Perovskii's earlier request for information. Dal' made clear that Perovskii brought him into the investigation and requested a full report on the progress of the research.[36] Several months later, the archpriest responded with the following summary of the story of the St. Petersburg kidnapping near a Jewish prayer house:

> It was said to have occurred in St. Petersburg at Sennaia ploshchad' [Haymarket] near the Jewish synagogue and for this the Jews were blamed.[37] The Minister wishes for some reason more information about the incidents, and although no such records were found in the local police archives . . . but as a result of the order of His Excellency, I am required to tell you, for the report to the Minister, everything I know about it. Regarding this matter I have the honor to inform Your Excellency that I do not know many details of the events spoken of, but only that I remember around 1820, near my place of residence at the Haymarket, which was once a bathhouse, I heard talk among the people there that there was a large commotion in the women's bath, a woman kidnapped a baby . . . she having been asked to watch the child who was set on the bench while the mother bathed herself . . . when she [the mother] came out of the bath, she could not find her child, and when she asked around, she was told that two Jewish women left the bathhouse with him.[38]

Kochetov continued that he was unsure if this was a new story or an old recycled one that he heard while walking out of the bath one day (a woman behind him was telling the story). As this letter makes clear, Dal' assumed a leading role in procuring material and following up on previous requests by the minister and his secretary. Given his literary ability, Dal' may well be responsible for the compilation of the various evidence and reports supplied to the ministry during this investigation.

The Perovskii Report, 1853

A second report commented more directly on the events in Saratov and aggressively laid out the ritual murder charges against Jews with specific reference to evidence from the Saratov investigation. The report is dated 1853 and initially looks like a continuation of the more widely disseminated 1844 report on ritual murder in imperial Russia. The 1853 report, similar to the report from a decade earlier, does not indicate the author or the exact date of writing.[39] While fascinating as an account of the accusations and the story behind them, the Perovskii report also reflects the culture of Russian officials. The story of how the Jews carried out the murders is given in detail (according to the author's perspective), which suggests that Perovskii probably had access to many details included in the investigative reports of 1853, and it was from these that he drew his allegations against Jews. It is also quite possible that the author of the report was Durnovo, the official from the Ministry of Internal Affairs. While this report was not written as a letter to Perovskii, and thus, its authorship is disputable, it might well have served as an update on the events by Durnovo for his former boss.[40]

In the early months of the investigation, the possibility existed for Durnovo and others to leverage imaginative, damaging claims against local Jews. Once the initial claims were levied against Saratov Jews, the rumors of Jewish ritual murder quickly spread throughout the city and forced local authorities to look more closely at the entire Jewish community rather than one or two potential suspects. The Perovskii report built on claims of Russian identity and fears of Jewish efforts to undermine that identity through assimilation and conversion. The report suggests that Jews found ways to enter into the greater Russian milieu by becoming pseudo-Russians, who were so uncommitted to their own religious heritage that they would simply choose conversion as a way of escaping residency restrictions and other juridical means intended to limit Jewish influence within the interior provinces of the empire.[41] The Perovskii report built on these fears of Jewish exploitation and highlighted individuals (Christians) who were corrupted by Jews in Saratov. According to the 1853 report, the town of Saratov had become a haven for Jews who sought to live closer to the interior of the empire and gain access to the economic benefits available there. The author of the report felt compelled to explain that the Jews who came to Saratov often converted out of "malicious intent."[42] The author argued: "It was generally noted that Jews baptize for the sole purpose of being able to live freely in the Greater Russian provinces, but in this matter they retain their Jewish convictions, and secretly perform the rituals of their fathers, as evident in Saratov province, where very many baptized Jews—more or less all of them, knew about the Saratov child-murderers."[43]

Here the blame for the two boys' murders is placed squarely on the dangerous Jewish convert, who, out of greedy desire to obtain greater wealth, prominence, or business, sought conversion as a way to escape the Pale of Settlement. The shift in emphasis from Jews as Jews to Jews as ambitious assimilationist Christians highlights one of the major fears of "Great Russian" chauvinists. According to some estimates, the Russian population in Saratov reached as high as 76 percent.[44] This was not merely a matter of classification of peoples, but rather served as a microcosm of the larger processes of identity politics at work in the empire. Jews who professed adherence to Judaism could be dealt with differently from Jews who forged new identities as Christians through conversion. Furthermore, many of the actors in this Saratov case were Jews who either had lived in the city for decades (Iankel Iushkevicher and his family) or were converts (or, in the case of Kriuger, children of converts) allegedly with an uncertain identity—and therefore questionable allegiances to the state and its official religion, Russian Orthodoxy.

The author of the Perovskii report brought together the details of the Saratov murders and the individuals involved. However, in order for the report to function effectively as a diatribe against Jews, the author extended the accusations to Jews outside the city and to other locales in the Russian Empire, thereby leading the reader to assume some Jewish conspiracy involving economic networks that Jews operated. Saratov Jews were connected in various ways to Jews in Mogilev province and to other regions in the empire through their interactions and visits. This also was connected to the blood that Saratov Jews aimed to acquire from young Christian boys. Among the men who allegedly participated in the ritual circumcision of the Christian boys in the Jewish synagogue were some of the Jewish members of the battalion—Shlifferman, Fogel'feld, Berman, and Zaidman. Within the circle of participants were Christians as well, including Iankel Iushkevicher's son, Private Iurlov (Russian Orthodox), and Private Bogdanov (Roman Catholic). Furthermore, the author aimed to exploit the figure of Kriuger, the retired provincial secretary (*Gubernskii sekretar*), to further damage the public image of Jews by showing how Jews tied him to the local crime ring. Kriuger's involvement in the circle is particularly interesting as it revealed the author's belief that Jews actively sought recruits, and did so by exploiting (or enticing) them through economic means. In a footnote to the report, the author included the following: "Regional Secretary Kriuger, the son of a Jewish convert, was educated as a young man—he studied at Kazan University. He was in good standing in the service and was engaged . . . but eventually fell into poverty and despair. The Jews took advantage of this and persuaded him to return to Judaism [*zhidovstvo*] for 500 rubles. Kriuger, fearing the circumcision operation [as the son of a convert he was uncircumcised], first wanted to see the operation on a grown boy and because of this he was present at the circumcision [of Sherstobitov]."[45] The author of the report was persistent in the connection between Jewish rituals and the Saratov case. In every instance, the author set forth specifics of the murders and then tied the details back to the religious requirements. Thus, in the description of Maslov's circumcision and murder, included among the details was the amount of blood removed from the boy at the time of circumcision (three large cups obtained from small cuts to the arms and legs), as well as the comparative amount of screaming and crying between Sherstobitov and Maslov.[46] As each action was described during the circumcision process, the author included phrases about how it was done according to Jewish law or family tradition.

Further, the spatial relations between Jews and the locations of the murders were outlined by the author of the Perovskii report. The spurious report further suggested that on December 3, 1852, Sherstobitov was taken in the middle of the day straight to the Iushkevicher home where he remained until December 13, when he was taken to the synagogue and the circumcision was performed. The author's insistence that the boy was taken at midday to Iushkevicher's home, when it is doubtful the act would have gone unseen, is but one of many similar claims that raises questions about its credibility. According to the Perovskii report, Sherstobitov's circumcision was incomplete (*ne polnoe*) because, while Iushkevicher held the boy down, Shlifferman was supposed to complete the cut but was scared and left the operation unfinished. After forcing Shlifferman to hold the boy down, Iushkevicher took the knife and attempted to finish the procedure. According to the Perovskii report, on January 26 Maslov was taken to the home of Iankel Iushkevicher, at about noon, where he remained until mid-February. During his time at the Iushkevicher home, Maslov "was fed gourmet food, cared for, and given money."[47] On February 16 Maslov was taken to the synagogue, where he was placed in charge of the caretaker, a Jewish man named Berman. Further, the report indicated, that on February 18, 1853, Maslov was stretched out on a table in the synagogue and circumcised according to Jewish practices, in the same manner as Sherstobitov. Already in the early reports, there was evidence that local authorities were attempting to find earlier precedent for the Jewish need for Christian blood. For example, included in the summary of the Maslov circumcision is mention of the Jewish holiday Purim.[48] Purim symbolized for some nineteenth-century Christians another Jewish practice that sought to desecrate an effigy that was often confused by Christians as being Jesus Christ rather than the evil Haman.[49] In addition to the mistaken assumption that Jews burned the effigy of Christ, Purim was also incorporated by proponents of the ritual murder accusation in Damascus in 1840. The blending of the seemingly raucous celebrations of Purim with the traditional Passover celebration lent greater creative space within which Christians could perpetuate erroneous accusations about Jews and their celebratory rituals.

Kriuger reported that during the ceremony, Iushkevicher read prayers from a "secret book" (the Talmud) and carefully followed instructions contained in the book as well.[50] Three days following the circumcision and bloodletting of Maslov, the young boy was returned to the home of Iankel Iushkevicher, where, according to the Perovskii report, Iushkevicher killed him. Further in the report, the author noted that the boy had been tortured—according to the testimony of his parents—as evinced by the wounds to his back and chest and the scrapes on his hands and face. Iushkevicher apparently needed to kill the young boy because he tried to run away from the apartment.[51] On March 4, 1853, Private Bogdanov took the body and placed it along the Volga. In the days that followed, Bogdanov, tormented by his conscience (*vpal v terzaniia sovesti*) reported that he had confessed (*soznalsia na ispovedi*) to a Roman Catholic priest about his involvement in the crime, to which the cleric advised him to immediately report the crime.[52] Shortly after his confession to the priest, Bogdanov turned himself in to the local police.

The author of the report appealed to the emotional side of his potential readers as well, noting that Maslov's mother could not talk about the events for over six months without crying.[53] The report placed the boys in a position of ongoing torture and abuse—and situated the blame squarely on the shoulders of Jewish religious fanatics. However, the report does not make it clear whether those fanatics were part of the mainstream Jewish community in Saratov or whether they were specifically part of the Hasidic movement or an aberrant movement. The author also attempted to tie the biblical Abraham to the religious and historical foundations of the ritual murder charges: "A look at the history of infanticide among the Jews, from Abraham to the present time, gives one the right, with the appearance of such atrocities, to immediately draw attention to the Jews, for we do not know of any other faith in which there would be dogmas like infanticide, and although only some Jews preserve the concept of human sacrifice during our times, across the centuries these people were often found guilty of such crimes generated by their religious beliefs."[54]

The Perovskii report placed the specific events (or at least a version of them) in the context of the long history of ritual murder and appealed to notions of irrefutable evidence and logic to convict Jews. The author referred specifically to the story from the St. Petersburg bathhouse featured in the 1844 investigation. This focus on an event for which there was little or no concrete evidence available places the authorship of the 1853 report squarely in the hands of Perovskii himself or someone who was familiar to a fault with the earlier Ministry of Internal Affairs work on the subject.[55] In the final paragraph of the report, the author noted: "Common sense makes it clear and evident that the Saratov infanticide was produced by Jews and those now suspected, as concluded by the local authorities."[56]

THE UNANSWERED QUESTION, 1854–1860

Unable to find sufficient evidence against the imprisoned Jews, and with no clear suspects, Durnovo was finally asked by superiors to end his investigation. Although the preliminary investigation concluded in the late fall of 1853, it nevertheless carried on more informally through the winter and spring of 1854, while at least five Jews in Saratov were still imprisoned. In midsummer 1854, Nicholas I created a *sudebnaia komissiia* (judicial commission) to carry out a formal investigation of Durnovo's findings and other information that had surfaced in the preceding months. At the head of the commission was a high-ranking Ministry of Internal Affairs official, Aleksandr Karlovich Giers. The judicial commission was charged with three specific tasks related to the Saratov case: (1) summarize the available evidence and facts related to the murder of the two young boys in Saratov, (2) examine the existence of any evidence that might link Private Bogdanov and local authorities to the killings, and (3) conduct a thorough investigation into Jewish texts to determine whether they contained evidence of rituals that could explain the use of Christian blood by Jews.[57] While the first two objectives were rather straightforward and uncontroversial, the third aim, namely the investigation into Jewish ritual use of Christian blood, perpetuated a long-standing story about Jews and their need for Christian blood—made popular by the prolonged Velizh case just years earlier. Giers chose to convene a special internal commission (*osobaia komissiia*) to investigate the third component of the judicial commission's charge.[58] The special commission brought together three particularly impressive Hebraic scholars, who represented three distinct generations of prolific scholarship. Joining Giers were Gerasim Petrovich Pavskii, Fedor Fedorovich Sidonskii, Vasilii Andreevich Levison, and Daniil Avraamovich Khvol'son. The three scholars on the committee represented a quite remarkable effort on the part of Giers to bring together the very best minds of the age that could with competence and erudition comment on the case and the particular question about Jewish textual evidence.[59]

Following a lengthy investigation into the three areas dictated by the judicial commission, the individual members of the internal special commission readied and submitted reports that were to be forwarded to the Sixth Department of the State Senate in Moscow. The individual reports uniformly confirmed that there was no evidence within Hebrew texts that could lend any credibility to the charge of ritual murder. The council approved Giers's (and the commission's) recommendation that there was no conclusive evidence against Saratov's Jews, and they recommended that the Jews who remained imprisoned (Iushkevicher, Iurlov, and Shlifferman) be set free.[60] The three other suspects—Kriuger, Lokotkov, and Bogdanov—they argued, were guilty of murdering the two boys. The State Senate in Moscow submitted its recommendation to the State Council in St. Petersburg, where it underwent yet another review, this time with Tsar Alexander II included in the small audience. A full eight years after Sherstobitov and Maslov disappeared, the jury, so to speak, was still undecided about who killed the boys and what motivation lay behind the dastardly deed. To resolve this, the matter was passed to the State Council in 1860.

The State Council's report, included in full in the Ministry of Internal Affairs documents, shows a systematic reexamination of the various individuals, their stories, and the relations between them.[61] The three ministers assigned to the case reviewed the files submitted to the Ministry of Internal Affairs and divided the two sets of suspects and attempted to place their roles in the murders alongside each other and in connection to the blood libel charge. Curiously, in the opening pages of the summary, the claim was made that the accusations about Jews carried with them centuries of history. To understand the many twists and frequent appearances of such accusations, a full examination of theology and dogmas was required. Without such a study, the council argued, "the question is still clearly unresolved, which is why it cannot be taken into consideration when determining the judgment."[62] Such a statement is fairly shocking when the work of the Ministry of Internal Affairs special commission and judicial commission are considered. How is it that the emperor's closest advisers did not understand the report that Pavskii, Levison, Sidonskii, and Khvol'son—perhaps the greatest nineteenth-century Russian Hebraists—generated? It was unthinkable to those who knew of the special commission and its work that the issue of ritual murder was so easily dismissed as unsolvable.

The focus of the State Council shifted to the question of murder and the perpetrators. However, rather than dismissing the possibility of ritual murder, the basis of the arguments focused on the suspected Jews who co-opted their non-Jewish cosuspects into carrying out the crime along with them. Bogdanov, the "drunkard" and criminal, who was "so easily put up to doing the crimes" (*legko mog byt' podgovoren k prestupleniiu*), was the victim of Jewish exploitation. Further, the charge was that because he spent so much time around Jews (or converted Jews), he was "like a kike" (*kak zhid*).⁶³ By following this line of thinking, it is fairly clear that notions of Jewish infiltration into the greater Russian interior were based on fears that Russian morality was deteriorating as a result. Kriuger, as the 1853 report suggested, was enticed back to Judaism and, through that process, was turned from a former position of prominence in the province to collaborating in two vicious murders carried out because of Jewish convictions. The State Council rejected the Moscow Senate's recommendation, and the charge of ritual murder remained a viable explanation for the deaths of Sherstobitov and Maslov. Minister of Justice Zamiatin defended the Jews before this council and urged the ministers to free them. In the end, however, even Alexander II joined in and added his own "i ia" (and I) to the council's resolution, and voted overwhelmingly against Jews. Thus, the diligent work by the scholars and members of the judicial commission and their conclusions were invalidated by vote (including the vote of Tsar Alexander II) in 1860.⁶⁴ While the few Jews being held for further investigation were eventually released, the council's conclusions raised the possibility of a ritual aspect to the murders and the suspicion that a certain sect of Jews could quite reasonably be responsible.

The failure of the council to provide a definitive statement about ritual murder in 1860 allowed the seeds planted early on through the 1835 Velizh case and perpetuated through the 1844 report to fester and expand into a full-fledged narrative that required nearly eight years to resolve. Although the general premises of the story were familiar strands passed through oral traditions and literary venues since the thirteenth century, they gradually adopted geographical and cultural moorings within Russia that firmly attached the narrative to its nineteenth-century context. By the end of the Saratov investigation and special commission report in 1860, the ritual murder narrative was more firmly fixed within Russian culture than before. The Velizh case allowed the myth to be perpetuated within the Pale of Settlement while the Saratov case moved it into a peripheral local within the Russian empire proper. Thus, the durability of the myth between 1823 and 1860 proved that the basic tenets of the accusations could be applied as needed to a broad set of geographic and societal settings. Moreover, the events in Saratov helped solidify for a small group of writers an interest in the ritual murder charge that led to lengthy publications on all sides of the matter.⁶⁵ The subsequent discussions that took place through literary journals and newspapers fostered a growing public interest in the history of the charges as well as a more accessible set of "experiences" and purported "evidence" that anti-Jewish polemicists later drew on to suggest to their readers that Jews did indeed kill Christian children. Although both major cases (Velizh and Saratov) eventually resulted in acquittals of Jews accused of ritual murder, they opened up a space for literary exploration of social and national issues through the lens created by modern ritual murder charges. Furthermore, it was the students (e.g., Professor Ivan Gavrilovich Troitskii) of some of those "expert Jews" who came to the defense of Beilis and others accused of ritual murder in the late nineteenth and early twentieth centuries. The result of the government's indecision in the Saratov case was that the question remained in play for public discussion for the decades leading up to the Beilis trial in 1913.

ANDREW C. REED is Assistant Professor of Church History at Brigham Young University. He recently completed a book manuscript titled *Contested Identity: Daniil Avraamovich Khvol'son, between Jew and Christian in 19th-Century Russia*. He has published in the fields of Jewish studies and Russian history. Reed holds a doctorate from Arizona State University and master of arts degrees from the University of Oxford and the University of Cambridge, and a bachelor of arts from Brigham Young University.

NOTES

1. At least thirteen individuals (the majority of whom were Jews) were incarcerated in connection with the Saratov murders between March 31, 1853, and June 15, 1856. Simon Dubnow includes details about the prison terms for the several Jews convicted in the case in his *History of the Jews in Russia and Poland*, 3 vols. (Philadelphia: Jewish Publication Society of America, 1918), 2:153. Iulii Gessen noted in his summary of the events in Saratov that the "Saratov prisons and police department did not have sufficient room to hold all those who were arrested and for this reason, they had to rent private homes." See Iulii Gessen, "Saratovskoe delo," in *Evreiskaia entsiklopediia*, 16 vols. (St. Petersburg: Izdatel'stvo Brokgauza i Efron, 1914), 14:4. The government record of the investigation is preserved in Rossiiskii gosudarstvennyi istoricheskii arkhiv (hereafter RGIA), f. 1151, op. 5-1860, d. 49 (Delo gosudarstvennogo soveta grazhdanskogo departamenta "Ob ubiustve v. g. Saratov dvukh kristianskikh mal'chikov" [March 26, 1860–June 12, 1860]). The surviving documentary evidence for a study of the case is contained in the Ministry of Internal Affairs collection of over twelve hundred pages of reports, summaries of letters, and official bureaucratic communication from Saratov to St. Petersburg and Moscow.

2. On the Velizh case, see Eugene M. Avrutin's chapter in this volume. As early as 1817 the Russian government created a set of legal requirements that made it increasingly difficult to prosecute Jews without very solid evidence against them.

3. John D. Klier, *Imperial Russia's Jewish Question 1855–1881* (Cambridge: Cambridge University Press, 1995), 419.

4. James G. Hart, "From Frontier Outpost to Provincial Capital: Saratov, 1590–1860," in *Politics and Society in Provincial Russia: Saratov, 1590–1917*, ed. Rex A. Wade and Scott J. Seregny (Columbus: Ohio State University Press, 1989), 10.

5. *Spiski naselennykh mest rossiiskoi imperii, sostavlennye i izdavaemye tsentral'nym statisticheskim komitetom ministerstva vnutrennikh del*, "Saratovskaia guberniia" (St. Petersburg, n.p., 1862), 38:1.

6. Ibid.

7. The most striking example of this lacunae might be the absence of any mention of the case in Wade and Seregny, *Politics and Society in Provincial Russia*.

8. For relevant literature on the Saratov case, see Daniil Avraamovich Khvol'son, *O nekotorykh srednevekovykh obvineniiakh protiv evreev: Istoricheskoe issledovanie po istochnikam* (St. Petersburg: Tsederbaum i Gol'denblium, 1880), vii–vxi; P. Ia. Levenson, "Eshche o saratovskom delo," *Voskhod* 4 (1881): 163–78; Gessen, "Saratovskoe delo," 2–8; and Dubnow, *History of the Jews in Russia and Poland*, 2:150–53. For discussions about the significance of the Saratov case during subsequent decades, see Klier, *Imperial Russia's Jewish Question*, 418–36; Stephen K. Batalden, "Nineteenth-Century Russian Old Testament Translation and the Jewish Question," in *Kirchen im Kontext unterschiedlicher Kulturen: Auf dem Weg ins dritte Jahrtausend*, ed. Karl Christian Felmy et al. (Göttingen: Vandenhoeck & Ruprecht, 1991), 577–87.

9. Dubnow, *History of the Jews in Russia and Poland*, 150–53.

10. Jonathan Frankel, *The Damascus Affair: "Ritual Murder," Politics, and the Jews in 1840* (Cambridge: Cambridge University Press, 1997), 424. While Frankel correctly pointed to the ongoing debates between Daniil Avraamovich Khvol'son and Ippolit Liutostanskii as the central figures in the later debates, he does not mention the important role that Khvol'son played in the Saratov case as an *uchenyi evrei* (expert Jew), thereby leading to his later public arguments in the literary and scholarly journals. For more on this role as an "expert Jew," see Eli Lederhendler, *The Road to Modern Jewish Politics: Political Tradition and Political Reconstruction in the Jewish Community of Tsarist Russia* (Oxford: Oxford University Press, 1989), 84–110.

11. RGIA, f. 1151, op. 5, d. 49, od. 1, ch. 1, l. 1 (1860 g.) (Rozyska politsii). Nankeen is a type of cotton cloth produced throughout Europe in the nineteenth century that was most often a light yellow or beige color, although it could be dyed other colors (most often black) as well. See *Oxford English Dictionary*, 2nd ed., s.v. "nankeen." Most likely, the "Crimean winter hat" resembled a fur hat or a tightly woven sheepskin *kalpak*.

12. RGIA, f. 1151, op. 5, d. 49, od. 1, ch. 1, l. 1 (1860 g.).

13. RGIA, f. 1151, op. 5, d. 49, od. 1, ch. 1, l. 38 (1860 g.).

14. It is unclear why the local villagers notified the police, especially given the distance between the village and Saratov.

15. RGIA, f. 1151, op. 5, d. 49, od. 1, ch. 1, l. 3 (1860 g.).

16. RGIA, f. 1151, op. 5, d. 49, od. 1, ch. 1, l. 3 (1860 g.). This memorandum is dated January 29, 1853.

17. RGIA, f. 1151, op. 5, d. 49, od. 1, ch. 1, l. 3 (1860 g.).

18. RGIA, f. 1151, op. 5, d. 49, od. 1, ch. 1, l. 6 (1860 g.). Report of Private Vand'ishev, the local officer who first saw and reported on the condition of the body.

19. RGIA, f. 1151, op. 5, d. 49, od. 1, ch. 1, ll. 8–11 (1860 g.).

20. RGIA, f. 1151, op. 5, d. 49, od. 1, ch. 1, l. 31 (1860 g.).

21. The government record does not provide a given name for the peasant Lokotkov.

22. RGIA, f. 1151, op. 5, d. 49, od. 1, ch. 1, l. 12 (1860 g.).

23. RGIA, f. 1151, op. 5, d. 49, od. 1, ch. 1, ll. 58–58 ob.; 78, 155; ch. 2, l. 339, 346; ch. 3, l. 667 (1860 g.).

24. RGIA, f. 1151, op. 5, d. 49, od. 1, ch. 4, ll. 822–23 (1860). This report was requested by Aleksandr Karlovich Giers, the Ministry of Internal Affairs official who replaced N. S. Durnovo on the case.

25. RGIA, f. 1282, op. 2, d. 2138, ch. 1 (March 4–September 9, 1844), Kantseliariia ministra vnutrennykh del "Delo ob obvinenii evreev v ritual'nykh ubiistvakh." See also Aleksandr Panchenko, "Vladimir Dal' i krovavyi navet," *Novoe literaturnoe obozrenie*, 111 (2011): 288–315. A

second set of archival documents related to the Velizh case and the 1844 report is in RGIA, f. 821, op. 8, d. 296.

26. Klier, *Imperial Russia's Jewish Question*, 416.

27. RGIA, f. 1282, op. 2, d. 2139, ch. 2, ll. 1 ob., 2. The original thirty-page book was published as *Obriady zhidovskie, proizvadimye v kazhdom miesiatsie u siapvstsietsiukhov* (St. Petersburg: V tipografii Bogdanovicha, 1787). John Klier wrote about this book and its entrance into Russian society in "The Origins of the 'Blood Libel' in Russia," *Newsletter for the Study Group on Eighteenth Century Russia* 14 (1986): 18. Klier argued that the 1787 publication was a version of the Frankist (anti-Talmudist) book by a Catholic priest. See Gaudenty Pikulski, *Błędy talmudowe od samych żydow uznane i przez nową sektę saipwscieciuchów czyli Contra-Talmudystów wyjawione* (1760). See also a broad contextualization of this text within the larger Central and Eastern European history in Paweł Maciejko, *The Mixed Multitude: Jacob Frank and the Frankist Movement, 1755–1816* (Philadelphia: University of Pennsylvania Press, 2011), 92–126.

28. RGIA, f. 1282, op. 2, d. 2139, ch. 2, ll. 47–48.

29. For the reference to Numbers in the Hebrew Scriptures, see RGIA, f. 1282, op. 2, d. 2139, ch. 2, l. 163. Within the report, the opinion is made quite clear that *all* Jews are required to use Christian blood because it is decreed in their law (upotrebliaiut' chelovecheskuiu krov', potomu chto vse zhidy, po predpisanno [ikh'] zakona). See RGIA, f. 1282, op. 2, d. 2139, ch. 2, l. 162.

30. RGIA, f. 1282, op. 2, d. 2139, l. 50 (Kopiia otnosheniia 5 departamenta Senata M. M. Karniolinu-Pinskomu ot 4 marta 1844 g.).

31. RGIA, f. 1282, op. 2, d. 2139, l. 51, "Otnoshenie ober-prokurora 1-ogo otdeleniia 5-ogo departamenta Senata M. M. Karniolina-Pinskogo ministru vnutrennykh del L. A. Perovskomu ot 8 marta 1844 g."

32. This point is critical for reasons explained below in connection with the Saratov Affair and Perovskii after he finished his term of service in the Ministry of Internal Affairs in 1852. See RGIA, f. 1282, op. 2, d. 2139, l. 54, "Otpusk pis'ma ministra vnutrennikh del L. A. Perovskogo moskovskomu grazhdanskomu gubernatoru I. G. Seniavinu ot 20 aprelia 1844". See also RGIA, f. 1282, op. 2, d. 2139, l. 61, "Pis'mo Moskovskogo grazhdanskogo gubernatora I. G. Seniavina ministru vnutrennikh del L. A. Perovskomu ot 7 maia 1844 g."

33. This urgency is stressed in RGIA, f. 1282, op. 2, d. 2139, l. 52, "Kopiia otnosheniia ministra vnutrennikh del L. A. Perovskogo sankt-peterburgskomu voennomu general-gubernatoru A. A. Kavelinu ot 19 marta 1844 g."; and RGIA, f. 1282, op. 2, d. 2139, l. 58 "Kopiia otnosheniia ministra vnutrennikh del L. A. Perovskogo sankt-peterburgskomu voennomu general-gubernatoru A. A. Kavelinu ot 15 maia 1844 g."

34. RGIA, f. 1282, op. 2, d. 2139, l. 53, "Kopiia otnosheniia ministra vnutrennikh del L. A. Perovskogo zamestiteliu ober-prokurora 1 otdeleniia 5 department Senata V. M. Bykovu ot 17 aprelia 1844 g."

35. Vladimir Dal', *Rozyskanie ob ubienii evreiami khristianskikh mladentsev i upotreblenii krovi ikh* (St. Petersburg: Suvorin, 1913). The Dal' authorship question remains contentious today among some scholars. See Ivan O. Kuzmin, *Materialy k voprosu ob obvineniiakh evreev v ritual'nykh prestupleniiakh* (St. Petersburg, 1913); Iulii Gessen, *Zapiska o ritual'nykh ubiistvakh (pripisyvaimia V. I. Daliu) i ee istochniki* (St. Petersburg: L. Ia. Ganzburg, 1914); Panchenko, "Vladimir Dal' i krovavyi navet"; Semen E. Reznik, "Zachem zhe snova piatnat' V. I. Dalia?," *Novoe literaturnoe obozrenie* 107 (2011): 435–41; and Semen E. Reznik, *Vmeste ili vroz'? Sud'ba evreev v Rossii*, 2nd ed. (Moscow: Zakharov, 2005), 60–71.

36. RGIA, f. 1282, op. 2, d. 2139, l. 62, "Kopiia pis'ma V. I. Dalia prot[oieriia] I. S. Kochetovu ot 30 maia 1844 goda."

37. A large synagogue was built on the Haymarket in the 1880s. Although almost no information has been found to suggest that earlier there was anything on the site other than perhaps

a prayer house, Dal' and Perovskii's letters consistently claimed that during the 1820s there was a synagogue on the square.

38. RGIA, f. 1282, op. 2, d. 2139, l. 161, "Pis'mo protoieriia I. S. Kochetova V. I. Daliu ot 8 September 1844 g."

39. RGIA, f. 1021, op. 1, d. 52, Perovskii, Lev Alekseevich, "Zapiska neustanovlennogo litsa ob ubiistve evreiami dvukh mal'chikov v Saratove dlia soversheniia religiozniv obriiazov." No author is listed for the twenty-four-page report and the date is 1853. The 1853 report does not bear the notations common among other Ministry of Internal Affairs reports and letters. For more on the Seniavin and Perovskii communications, see RGIA, f. 1282, op. 2, d. 2139, l. 54.

40. Durnovo is not mentioned by name in the report, thus making his role as author more plausible.

41. RGIA, f. 1021, op. 1, d. 52, l. 7.

42. RGIA, f. 1021, op. 1, d. 52, l. 7.

43. RGIA, f. 1021, op. 1, d. 52, l. 5.

44. Wade and Seregny, Politics and Society in Provincial Russia, 1–2.

45. RGIA, f. 1021, op. 1, d. 52, l. 11. He was also allegedly present later at the circumcision of Maslov.

46. While the report contains exact measurements about how much blood was drawn from the victim, it does not specify how the author obtained such knowledge.

47. RGIA, f. 1021, op. 1, d. 52, l. 12.

48. RGIA, f. 1021, op. 1, d. 52, l. 14.

49. Elliot Horowitz, *Reckless Rites: Purim and the Legacy of Jewish Violence* (Princeton, NJ: Princeton University Press, 2006), 28–29. A growing number of nineteenth-century Jews sensed the Christian animosity toward Purim and attempted to reform, or in some cases end, the Purim celebrations. Among those who attempted to lessen the impact of the celebration was Claude Montefiore, who went so far as to write an article titled "Purim Difficulties" in the *Jewish Chronicle* (March 2, 1888), 8. Daniil Khvol'son wrote extensively about the Purim connection to the ritual murder charge in his *O nekotorykh srednevekovykh obvineniiakh protiv evreev*.

50. RGIA, f. 1021, op. 1, d. 52, l. 11, Kriuger argued that "Iankel' chital po kakim to osobym sekretnym knigam' molitvy."

51. RGIA, f. 1021, op. 1, d. 52, l. 14.

52. RGIA, f. 1021, op. 1, d. 52, l. 16.

53. This is one of the internal references that helps place the dating of this report sometime in the final months of 1853, or even after, if the date was applied by a second hand. See RGIA, f. 1021, op. 1, d. 52, l. 3.

54. RGIA, f. 1021, op. 1, d. 52, l. 16.

55. The 1844 report was distributed within the Ministry of Internal Affairs, although the search for earlier occurrences of Jewish infanticide and ritual use of blood seems to have been the result of Perovskii's personal interest in the myth.

56. RGIA, f. 1021, op. 1, d. 52, l. 24.

57. See D. A. Khvol'son, *Upotrebliaiut-li evrei khristianskuiu krov'?: Razsuzhdeniie* (St. Petersburg: M. A. Khana, 1879), 1.

58. This special commission convened under the guidance of the MVD's Departament dukhovnykh del i inostrannykh ispovedanii (Department of Spiritual Matters and Foreign Faiths).

59. After high government officials disregarded his work on the special commission, Khvol'son committed much of his scholarly life to the refutation of the ritual murder charge. For a more developed analysis of his work on the subject, see Andrew C. Reed, "For One's

Brothers: Daniil Avraamovich Khvol'son and the 'Jewish Question' in Russia, 1819–1911" (PhD diss., Arizona State University, 2014), 143–223.

60. RGIA, f. 1151, op. 5, d. 49, ot. 4, ll. 948–1032 (1860 g.), "Rezoliutsiia Pravitel'stvuiushchego Senata po 1-mu Otdeleniiu 6-go Departamenta po delu ob' deistve v gorode Saratove dvukh mal'chikov."

61. RGIA, f. 1151, op. 5, d. 49, ot. 5, ll. 1–18 (1860 g.).
62. RGIA, f. 1151, op. 5, d. 49, ot. 5, l. 1 (1860 g.).
63. RGIA, f. 1151, op. 5, d. 49, ot. 5, l. 2 (1860 g.).
64. Gessen, "Saratovskoe delo," 7.
65. For more on the literary debates in the aftermath of Saratov until 1881, see Klier, *Imperial Russia's Jewish Question*, 417–19.

… 5 …

THE BLOOD LIBEL IN NINETEENTH-CENTURY LITHUANIA

A Comparison of Two Cases

Darius Staliūnas

THIS CHAPTER ANALYZES two blood libel cases that occurred in two different locations in the Lithuanian countryside: in Zdoniškė Manor (Kovno province) in 1827 and in Šalnaičiai (Vil'na province) in 1908.[1] By "Lithuania," I refer to the ethnic Lithuanian lands, which in the nineteenth century and early years of the twentieth were part of the Russian Empire. Some parts belonged to the Pale of Jewish Settlement, others to the Kingdom of Poland (Augustów and later Suwałki province). Although both accusations produced ethnic tensions, the 1827 case involved only minor skirmishes, Christians throwing rocks at Jews, while the events in 1908 turned into a full-fledged pogrom. In the first part of the chapter I describe the events, and in the second half I consider why a ritual murder accusation resulted in mass anti-Jewish violence. This question has broader implications for understanding the changing dynamics of Christian-Jewish relations in the long nineteenth century.

A comparison of two cases separated by eighty years not only reveals the persistence of beliefs in Jewish ritual murder, but also highlights the larger social, cultural, and political changes that took place in the Russian Empire. Beginning in the 1880s, blood libel accusations turned into pogroms both in Lithuania and in other parts of the Pale of Settlement. The emergence and development of nationalist ideologies and modern antisemitism indirectly influenced mass anti-Jewish violence. However, other factors were more important, namely the wave of pogroms that broke out in the Pale of Settlement beginning in the 1880s and the changing attitudes of local officials toward blood libel accusations. By analyzing the different reactions of various actors involved in the two cases, I illustrate how Christian-Jewish relations changed over time.

Apart from the superstition itself there were some other commonalities between the two events. Like many other blood libel accusations that occurred in Lithuania (investigations also took place in 1801, 1861, 1892, and 1900), these two were related to Easter. Certainly one of the reasons why this happened in this period was a belief widespread among Christians in Europe that during Passover or Easter, Jews reenacted Christ's Passion by choosing a Christian child as their victim.[2] Beyond that, the Easter festival in Lithuania was a period when special efforts were made by clergy to stress the difference between Christians and Jews. The reenactment of the Passion underlined hostility toward Jews. For example, in the town of Samogitia parishioners would dress up as Roman soldiers and Jews to create mischief in church and shoot guns. Those dressed up as Jews would attempt to steal the cross, guarded by those playing Roman soldiers. The weapons of the "Jews"—wooden pliers, whips, and nails—symbolized the implements used during Christ's Passion. On Easter morning the play-acting was somewhat different: the "Jews" would head in the opposite direction as the official procession and make a commotion.[3] Christians were thus reminded of their belief that the Jews inflicted suffering on Christ. Thus, during the Easter festivities, anti-Jewish sentiment intensified markedly. Second, in both cases, the version about the "Jewish footprint" was raised *by minors*. However, in these cases there was evidence that their elders had coached the young people to blame the Jews. Even so, it is likely that children in Lithuanian villages were frightened from birth with the story that if they behaved badly, they would be taken by Jews and used in baking matzo.

Tel'shi, 1827

The view of Jews in the sources produced by Polish-speaking gentry society in the first half of the nineteenth century in the former lands of the Grand Duchy of Lithuania is negative in almost every way. This literature in Polish at the time depicted Jews as an "other" group that did not wish to integrate into the local society and were different from those around them in appearance, language, religion, customs, and behavior. In an agricultural society, which valued work on the land, Jewish economic activity in trade or finance was invariably regarded with contempt. The majority of the gentry was particularly irked by Jewish innkeepers, whom they accused of intoxicating peasants. Furthermore, this literature depicted Jews as politically suspect. As the 1830–1831 uprising showed, they did not support the gentry's attempts to reestablish the Commonwealth of the

Two Nations and were inclined to support the Russian government not only because it was the stronger side but also due to the very weak integration of Jews. More generally, the authors who wrote in Polish depicted Jews as those who spread amorality, crime, and other related activities. That literature regarded Talmudic Judaism as the primary source of these "sins," as it not only kept Jews apart from the rest of society but also allegedly encouraged them to despise Christians. On occasion, stories about the blood libel appeared in the first half of the nineteenth century, but usually Polish authors depicted it as an outdated superstition the public no longer believed.[4]

At the same time, belief in blood libel was one of the essential elements that shaped the perception of Jews in the worldview of peasants who spoke one of the Lithuanian dialects. As one Russian military officer who made a very comprehensive overview of Vil'na province noted in the mid-nineteenth century: "Increasing Christian hatred blamed the Jews for various misdemeanors; most commonly they were accused of the theft of Christian children, whom they would allegedly murder and then use their blood in matzo. . . . This belief has become ingrained in the common people to such an extent that to this day in Vil'na province, one comes across tales of the kidnapping of Christian children by Jews with similar descriptions of a barrel lined with nails, where they place the youth and shake him until he dies."[5] From time to time this superstition resulted in concrete accusations against Jews. Exactly that happened in Tel'shi in 1827.

On April 8, 1827, the Friday after Easter, a seven-year-old farm boy, Juozapas Petravičius, disappeared from Zdoniškė Manor in Tel'shi (Kovno province).[6] A youth named Augustinas Žukovskis, who herded pigs with the boy, reported that two Jews had grabbed Petravičius and carried him off to the forest. The local landowner, Petras Dimša, instructed others to search for the boy, but that day no one was able to locate him. Local officials then started an official investigation. The archival records indicate that the local community forgot about the child until April 26, when his body was found near a lake. At first, Žukovskis stood by his original account. He even described the two Jews in detail, recognizing one of them as Hirsh Katz from a police lineup. Soon other alleged evidence appeared that indirectly corroborated Žukovskis's version of events. One girl, Karolina Kumzovna, testified that Jews had chased her that day. Another boy claimed he had seen two Jews driving three horses and that one of them had apparently attempted to disguise himself. Still another peasant family said that their son Jonas had also disappeared. The Jews' guilt was allegedly proven by their suspicious behavior. One Jew refused to allow animals to be herded near the storeroom, where, according to rumors, the child was hidden. Another Jew claimed that Petravičius was kidnapped by his own father. Furthermore, peasants believed that, by spreading this version of the events, Jews were trying to cover up their crime. They even found a Jewish child who claimed to have heard that Jews played a role in the disappearance. One Jewish convict alleged that he heard Katz say that the Jews had bribed local policemen not to report the incident to their superiors. The allegation was corroborated by several converts from Judaism who claimed that Jews needed Christian blood and that they bought off their guilt with money.[7]

No sooner than the Jews filed a complaint, the governor-general sent a man named Kermenskii to investigate. At this point, Augustinas Žukovskis and several others who had originally testified against the Jews changed their story. Žukovskis said that the farm boy Petravičius had drowned accidentally and that, fearing that blame would fall on his shoulders, Žukovskis made up the story. Together with his older brother, Žukovskis said that he dragged the corpse out of the water and stabbed it to make the story appear more convincing. Apparently, the idea of blaming Jews occurred spontaneously, since "he had heard talk in the area previously about how Jews torment Christian children because they need their blood."[8] Witnesses appeared who claimed that they had seen Žukovskis visit his older brother that day, and that they had seen the two of them go off somewhere early the next morning. Juozapas testified that his "brother had done something stupid but put it right." Other witnesses such as the peasant girl Kumzovna admitted to making up the story about Jews chasing her. The members of the peasant family who claimed that their son had disappeared confessed that they had made up the story so that the estate manager would not bother them.

Using a carrot-and-stick tactic, the investigating officer, Kermenskii, played an important role in getting the peasants to change their initial story. But the new developments in the case did not satisfy local Christians, and so they submitted a complaint to the governor-general. As a result, a new investigator was dispatched to Tel'shi. Witnesses reverted to their earlier versions of events about the two Jews who allegedly kidnapped the child. The peasants most likely would not have maintained their version of the events without the support of the local elite. The landowner Dimša, for example, was mentioned several times in Jewish complaints for supposedly encouraging the peasants to provide evidence against the Jews.[9] Kermenskii testified that Dimša had boasted to him of having an old Polish book proving that Jews needed Christian blood.[10]

The variety of witness testimony and the changes of investigators show that the investigation depended to a great extent on the views of officials of varying ranks. Those such as Kermenskii, who were convinced from the outset that the murder accusations against Jews could not be substantiated, were in the minority. However, there were also officials who believed that Jews had murdered Petravičius because they needed Christian blood. Thus, when investigating this case, the

Tel'shi Castle Court attempted to gather information about similar events from other areas that helped prove the veracity of the allegation. The court used the book *Jewish Malice* as evidence.[11] According to testimony provided by local Jews, one of the Jews was asked by an official during the investigation whether he had killed the boy "to obtain Christian blood, which Jews need for matzo during Passover."[12] In the end, as many as twenty-eight Jews were arrested on the basis of Christian allegations of suspicious behavior at the time of the boy's disappearance.[13] Even more interestingly, the Castle Court ruled that the Žukovskis's brothers–one of whom, as noted earlier, was allegedly involved in the crime—was deemed to be unworthy of suspicion.

The behavior of officials toward Jewish suspects speaks volumes in itself. Officials bound their hands and feet and left them outside all day without food. They also forced the prisoners to march to interrogation so quickly that they fell. They cut their beards or some of their sidelocks. Although interrogators later denied having treated the Jews unfairly, much of the evidence suggests that at least some of the humiliations mentioned in the Jewish complaints did take place. They were indeed shackled outside all day without food, and preparations for beard cutting did take place (one soldier was given a pair of scissors for this).[14]

Discrepancies in witness testimony, the changing versions presented by Jews and Christians alike, and the large number of complaints that investigators acted unlawfully, all helped complicate the case. The death of a child, which local Christians interpreted as ritual murder, or perhaps even the tardy nature of the investigation into the crime, especially the repeated interrogations, increased interethnic tensions. Thus, "nowhere in Tel'shi did Jews feel safe because of the rumor that Jews harmed Christians." Gentiles yelled "murderer" and threw stones at Jews on the street, and officials feared that even worse consequences could be expected.[15] It should be stressed that no official directly encouraged these acts of violence in any way. Information did indeed spread around the region by word of mouth.[16]

The case eventually made it to the highest court in Vil'na province, which conducted its own investigation.[17] This was, however, not the last time imperial officials decided to look into the matter. According to one gendarme officer, who observed that the whole business was designed to "ruin" (*razorit'*) the Jews, the seventh investigation of the case began at the end of 1827.[18] The inability of the various courts to decide this case may be explained not only by local circumstances but also by the ambiguous signals being sent from the highest imperial authorities. Tsar Nicholas I was suspicious of Jews and associated the Tel'shi case with the Velizh case, which was being investigated at the same time.[19] Although the Velizh Jews were acquitted, the case nevertheless confirmed for Nicholas that secret Jewish sects used Christian blood in their religious rituals.[20] With regard to the Tel'shi case, Nicholas instructed that "attention be paid to this case for its similarity with the Velizh case, which, alas, confirmed that not one but seven children were tormented."[21] Such ambiguous signals from the capital may have added to delays in resolving the matter. In 1838, after reviewing the file, the Senate did not find enough evidence to convict Jews of the crime of ritual murder. The highest court in the empire thus released all the accused Jews and punished their accusers.[22]

ŠALNAIČIAI, 1908

The events in Šalnaičiai (Vil'na province) took place under very different circumstances. After lunch on Saturday, March 29, 1908, a two-year-old child named Nikodemas Rinkevičius was murdered. The boy's neighbors encountered a dreadful scene: the boy lay in his cot, with his throat slit and his "head hanging from the cot with considerable blood both in the cradle and on the ground."[23] The boy's eight-year-old sister Marija, who was left in charge while the parents went off to the nearby village of Buivydžiai to work for a certain Jew, explained that two people had entered the house. One was a Jewish cobbler named Josel Gelbert, who came by to look for a rake he had left behind. Marija did not know the second person, but described him as "tall, with a long russet beard, and a long black coat and hat." As he approached the cot with a raised knife, Marija ran out to call her neighbors.[24]

Rumor of the murder spread swiftly.[25] According to one version, a "large crowd" gathered near the Rinkevičius home. The crowd "was very excited and blamed what had happened at the Rinkevičius house on the Jews, who were using Christian blood to bake matzo because the 'Jewish Easter' was nigh."[26] Others claimed that Jews needed blood for "Easter."[27] "The mob's feelings rose and rose." At the same time, plans were made for all different kinds of vigilante justice: some suggested drowning all the Jews, while others recommended burning them or stoning them.[28] The official version held that disaster was narrowly averted by one official who was able to calm the mob by promising that he would go immediately to Vil'na and ask the governor to investigate the crime.[29]

The local community divided into two camps along confessional lines. Some Catholics blamed the Jews, while the Jews thought the victim's sister was guilty. Some sources mention that the girl initially alleged that the unknown visitor was a Russian and that only later did her neighbors and the priest coerce her into blaming the Jews.[30] This version seemed worthy of investigation by the officials, because there was blood on Marija's clothing and a knife had disappeared from the house. The third explanation to gain credence held that some madman had committed the crime.[31]

That same evening peasants near Buivydžiai detained seven Jews, including Josel Gelbert, and took them to the local policeman's house to "beat the names of the murderers out of them." Despite peasant discontent, the Jews were released and extra policemen were stationed in the town. The next morning local authorities arrived in town, and a day later officials arrived from Vil'na. The excitable peasants were not afraid to tell the governor himself what they thought: they demanded the expulsion of all Jews from the town and threatened Gelbert with vigilante justice. The governor took Gelbert into custody for his own safety.[32]

Peasant wrath regarding the Jews was further inflamed by news that Marija apparently identified the killer as Khon Viker, whom the police had already arrested.[33] In Christian minds this incident seemed to confirm suspicions that Jews were indeed responsible. Only a few days after the murder, market day arrived in the nearby small town Bistritsa, when many people gathered in the town. "Agitators" appeared in the crowd, shouting that Jews had killed a child and needed to be beaten. Many local Jews had taken refuge after hearing the rumors, which spread before market day, of a possible pogrom.[34] A stick-waving mob chased two Jews who had recently come to town. Shortly thereafter the mob attacked Jewish houses and shops near the market square, smashing windows and causing other damage. Later they headed to the area known as the "Colony," where Jewish laborers lived. Here they also smashed windows. Two Jewish witnesses said that one peasant woman threw a Torah out of the synagogue and trampled on it, while several other rioters tore up Jewish books. All the victims asserted that the mob "only smashed windows but did not attack people or steal property."[35]

Based on the material at hand, it seems that peasant reaction to news of the alleged murder of a boy by Jews was spontaneous, and there is no information that it was incited, for example, by educated society. Admittedly, on March 31, after the governor arrived in Buivydžiai, the local priest was among the crowd, but there is no evidence of any clerical involvement.[36] The press in various languages usually reported events neutrally, and some newspapers reprinted accounts from other similar publications.[37] The press reports of certain events even suggest that publishers made special efforts not to fan the flames of judeophobic sentiment and behavior. Thus, the account of the boy's murder and the girl's version in *Vilniaus žinios* (Vilnius news) did not mention that the suspect was a Jew.[38] The press in this case did not contribute to the spread of anti-Jewish feeling.[39]

Although the governor of Vil'na asserted that the police halted the mob's frenzy, all evidence suggests that no one stopped the mob from rampaging in the market square and smashing windows in the "Colony."[40] Unquestionably, the local authorities' main concern was to prevent possible mass outbreaks of violence.

The 1905 Revolution forced officials to be more careful in situations where mass disturbances might erupt. Thus, during these incidents, not only were police units increased but also the governor himself paid two visits to talk to peasants and attempt to calm them down.[41] Jews suspected of having committed a crime had to be taken into custody for their own safety. Eventually, both Gelbert and Viker were released, and seven of the seventeen Christians arrested for violating public order were given short jail sentences.[42] Local authorities wanted to maintain law and order and follow legal procedure. At the same time, the attempt to halt peasant vigilante justice and maintain public order does not necessarily mean that the local officials involved in the case doubted that Jews had committed ritual murder. During the investigation, the prosecutor of the Vil'na Chamber of Justice approached the Justice Ministry to ask Professor Troitskii of the St. Petersburg Orthodox Spiritual Academy, in his capacity as an expert witness, whether fanatical and savage (*izuvercheskie*) Jewish sects used Christian blood in their rituals.[43]

EXPLANATIONS AND CONCLUSIONS

Why did the blood accusation in Tel'shi in 1827 end without mass anti-Jewish violence, while a similar accusation in 1908 turned into a pogrom? It is difficult to come up with a simple explanation, and the question about the causes of eruptions of mass violence presents a huge challenge for the researcher. In such situations one cannot rule out the accidental or coincidental nature of events as a factor. The two blood libel cases discussed in this chapter took place in different locations, and under quite different circumstances. One of the factors that likely drove peasants to violence in 1908 was the appearance of the dead child. The slit throat and "head hanging out of the cot" may have excited even completely jaded imaginations and led people to vigilante actions. In Tel'shi, some time had passed between the child's disappearance and the discovery of the body. One can imagine that in this case the scene of the corpse was perceived by peasants as not very brutal. But this or any other coincidence cannot be the most important one. None of the blood libel cases that occurred in Lithuania (and elsewhere in the Russian Empire) in the first half of the nineteenth century turned into a pogrom, while some (but not all) that took place in late imperial Russia did. Thus, we need to look for some more general changes in society that affected the behavior of the Christian population.

One important factor was the 1905 Revolution. We should, however, be cautious about associating the peasant movement in 1905 with any kind of nationalism. The influence of nationalistic ideology on Christian-Jewish relations in this region was ambiguous. Nationalisms of nondominant ethnic groups (Poles,

Lithuanians, Belarusians) were starting to take shape in the late nineteenth century, drawing new lines between "us" and "them." These nationalisms were ethnocultural, or to be more specific—ethnolinguistic, which means that only those who spoke the same language were perceived as belonging to "our" nation. Since Jewish acculturation into Polish culture was very weak, and nonexistent when it came to Lithuanian or Belarusian cultures, Jews were perceived as the "other." Some of these nationalisms, especially the Lithuanian variant, became mass movements by 1905. At the end of that year Lithuanians were taking control over the local government in many places of ethnic Lithuanian residence, making Russian officials and teachers leave. That movement was, above all, directed against the imperial government but the feeling of insecurity also grew on "the Jewish street," and some incidents even reached the scale of pogroms.[44] It does not mean, however, that the impact of new nationalistic ideologies was always detrimental to Christian-Jewish relations. Lithuanian nationalism needed allies in its struggle against its main enemies—Poles and Russians—and that led to the formation of a pragmatic alliance between the Jewish and the Lithuanian intelligentsia in some situations at the turn of the twentieth century. However, it can be assumed that the genuine or circumstantial benevolence of some Lithuanian nationalist leaders toward Jews was not transmitted to the masses.[45] Thus, Lithuanian and Polish nationalist ideologies stressed Jewish otherness, but one cannot find any direct link between these types of nationalism and the events of 1908 discussed in this chapter.

At the same time, modern political antisemitism began to penetrate Lithuania. Some Lithuanian and Polish activists had become acquainted with modern antisemitic theories and even attempted to spread them in Lithuania.[46] Economic arguments were most often mentioned in antisemitic texts. Yet religious condemnation of Jews continued to play a role in antisemitic pronouncements; probably the most radical and undoubtedly the best-known example of Lithuanian religious judeophobia in the late imperial period was Justinas Bonaventūra Pranaitis and his *The Talmud Unmasked: The Secret Rabbinical Teachings concerning Christians*, first published in Latin in 1892, and later translated into many other languages (German, Russian, Italian, and Polish), as well as Lithuanian.[47] Pranaitis accused the Jews of all manner of wrongdoing and a contempt for Christianity; for this he blamed the Talmud, which he said permitted Jews to kill Christians. The accusation that Jews morally corrupted gentile neighbors, primarily the peasantry, was closely related to anti-Judaism. In late nineteenth-century publications of all ideological currents there were often articles claiming to report actual events that illustrated just how Jews were seeking to morally corrupt the peasantry. Catholic-oriented publications featured another claim typical of the antisemitic discourse then popular in Europe: that Jews aimed to control the world, or nearly did already. Serafinas Laurynas Kušeliauskas saw the roots of this supposed Jewish aim in the teachings of the Talmud.[48] The clerical periodicals had no doubt that Jews controlled the world via banks, other financial institutions, trade, and the press. Articles also appeared that highlighted Jewish solidarity in a specific location or region. Of course, there was only one step between similar discussions and claims of worldwide Jewish control.[49] But racialist theories were generally not part of modern antisemitic ideology in Lithuania. Unlike in Western Europe, racialist theories were not required in the eastern part of the continent for the generation of antisemitism. In Eastern Europe, as Rudolf Jaworski noted, Jews were readily recognizable because of their large numbers and weak degree of assimilation or acculturation.[50]

It is much more difficult to uncover the peasants' attitudes toward Jews. This is how one of the Lithuanian politicians most positively inclined toward Jews, Andrius Bulota, characterized the attitude of Lithuanians toward Jews in the late imperial period:

> I would not conceal from you that among Lithuanians, especially in the uneducated and unenlightened strata of our peasantry, antisemitism is sprouted with all its ulcers. But this is not the *political* antisemitism that Mr. Purishkevich and Mr. Krushevan profess; it is also not similar to the diplomatic antisemitism of Polish chauvinists. The roots of this hostility to Jews, which is seen among us, should be sought in religion in the medieval survivals [*perezhitki*]. The Lithuanian people, notwithstanding its revolutionary mood, remains deeply a religious people; and a good Catholic, who is in addition an ignorant man, naturally does not like Jews because they "crucified Christ."[51]

Although antisemitic agitation declined due to the "pragmatic alliance" in the liberal press at the turn of the twentieth century, the Catholic Lithuanian press continued to propagate a whole spectrum of antisemitic stereotypes (about a world Jewish plot, harm done to Christians, Jews morally corrupting gentiles, the slovenliness of Jews, and so on) around 1900. It would be difficult to find a direct link between antisemitic agitation in some Lithuanian periodicals and the events of 1908 discussed in this chapter. But it is reasonable to assume that such publications heightened anti-Jewish sentiments.

The events of 1908 (like those of 1886, 1892, and 1900) differed from the earlier cases of blood libel because, starting in the 1880s, antipathy toward Jews developed into pogroms. Some physical force was used in earlier cases, too. In 1861 Jewish complaints even referred to casualties, even though there probably were none. However, none of these incidents from the first half of the nineteenth century escalated into mass violence. In seeking to explain this change, one also must note that these incidents took place in an era that began in 1881, when pogroms became a widespread phenomenon that was known about not only from rumor but also from a wealth of press reports. These pogroms in other places in the Russian Empire created a kind of a "pogrom atmosphere"—that is, the conviction of some Christians that the tsar allowed them to beat up Jews and ransack their property, and that it is an appropriate way to punish Jews. Waves of pogroms that started in the 1880s in other parts of the Jewish Pale of Settlement set a model for how one could punish Jews for their alleged crimes.

At the same time, an important role in this story was played by the authorities, including members of the local social elite who held various positions within the local government in the first half of the nineteenth century. Although in both cases officials tried to follow formal legal procedures, the local populace had changed its attitudes toward ritual murder. During the incidents in the first half of the nineteenth century, many local officials were perceived as siding with the accusers. No doubt exists regarding these officials' antipathy toward Jews. Let us remember that in 1827 Jews were humiliated by being locked up for an entire day in the manor house yard, waiting to be questioned, and even if their hair and sidelocks were not in fact cut, threats to shave them were made. Similar stories survive from other incidents in the first half of the nineteenth century.

However, officials did not express clear support for the accusations made against Jews in 1886, 1892, 1900, and 1908. While in earlier cases some part of the Christian population could hope that the authorities would carry out justice as the peasants saw it, after the 1880s, they most likely no longer entertained such illusions. Peasants thought they had no choice but to take action themselves. When, for example, priests in 1900 attempted to hold back the mob, they were told: "How can we not beat up Jews when in the town of Konstantinovo they murdered a Christian girl, when Jews have desecrated our church and our faith, when they are starting to beat us up here, burn us with vitriol and shoot us! And the police do not defend us or our faith, so we must defend ourselves and our faith by ourselves!"

Thus, in the early nineteenth century at least some imperial authorities abetted the functioning of the blood libel in Lithuanian Christian society in one way or another, although they were in no way the driving force behind this superstition. The authorities' position gave ordinary people the hope that their version of justice would be done and that there was no need for mob rule. In the late imperial period, when the authorities began to treat blood libel cases as a kind of medieval superstition, part of Christian society in Lithuania, which still believed in blood libel, saw itself as having been hurt by Jews and believed that the authorities would do nothing about it. They therefore had to take action themselves. The German sociologist Werner Bergmann accurately describes the pogrom as "a one-sided and non-governmental form of social control, as 'self-help by a group' that occurs when no remedy from the state against the threat which another ethnic group poses can be expected."[52]

DARIUS STALIŪNAS is the author of *Making Russians. Meaning and Practice of Russification in Lithuania and Belarus after 1863* (2007), *Enemies for a Day: Antisemitism and Anti-Jewish Violence in Lithuania under the Tsars* (2015), and with Dangiras Mačiulis, *Lithuanian Nationalism and the Vilnius Question, 1883–1940* (2015). Since 2000, Staliūnas has been a Deputy Director at the Lithuanian Institute of History. He teaches at Vilnius University and Klaipėda University.

NOTES

1. This article is based on my book *Enemies for a Day: Antisemitism and Anti-Jewish Violence in Lithuania under the Tsars* (Budapest: Central European University Press, 2015).

2. John D. Klier, "The Pogrom Paradigm in Russian History," in *Pogroms: Anti-Jewish Violence in Modern Russian History*, ed. John D. Klier and Schlomo Lambroza (Cambridge: Cambridge University Press, 1992), 33.

3. Laima Anglickienė, *Kitataučių įvaizdis lietuvių folklore* [The Image of Others in Lithuanian Folklore] (Vilnius, Lithuania: Versus aureus, 2006), 94–96; and Stasys Skrodenis, *Folkloras ir gyvenimas* [Folklore and Life] (Vilnius, Lithuania: Vilniaus pedagoginio universiteto leidykla, 2010), 345.

4. Zita Medišauskienė has discussed in some detail the image of Jews in Lithuanian Polish-language literature during the first half of the nineteenth century. See Zita Medišauskienė, "'Ottalkivaiushchii, no bez nego ne oboitis': Evrei kak alter ego litovskogo dvorianina serediny XIX v.," *Ab Imperio* 4 (2003): 93–114. The blood libel was known already in the Grand Duchy of Lithuania: Jurgita Verbickienė, "Blood Libel Accusation in a Multi-Confessional Society: The Case of the Grand Duchy of Lithuania," *East European Jewish Affairs* 38, no. 2 (2008): 201–9.

5. Anton Koreva, "Evrei," *Pamiatnaia knizhka vilenskoi gubernii na 1860 god* (Vilnius, 1860), 39.

6. Passover was on March 31 that year. All dates are given in the Old Style (according to the Julian calendar), which was used in the Russian Empire in the nineteenth century. The Julian calendar was twelve days behind the Gregorian calendar (thirteen days, starting in 1900). See Lietuvos valstybės istorijos archyvas (Lithuanian State Historical Archives, hereafter LVIA), f. 378 (Vilniaus generalgubernatoriaus kanceliarija [Chancellery of the Governor-General of Vil'na]), bs., 1827 m., b. 826 ("O smerti 7-mi letnego mal'chika naidennogo mertvym na Zemle Pomeshchika Dymshi.—Petrovicha"); LVIA, f. 443 (Vyriausias Lietuvos teismas [Lithuanian Supreme Tribunal]) ap. 6, b. 1071, 1086, 1110 ("Ob ubiistve semiletnego Petrovicha Iosifa"); Central Archives for the History of the Jewish People (hereafter CAHJP), Jerusalem, HMF/764, HMF/898; Jolanta Żyndul, *Kłamstwo krwi. Legenda mordu rytualnego na ziemiach polskich w XIX i XX wieku* (Warsaw: Wydawnictwo Cyklady, 2011), 98–99. An infamous nineteenth-century antisemite, Ippolit Liutostanskii, described this story: Ipolit Liutostanskii, *Ob upotre-*

blenii evreiami Talmudicheskimi sektatorami) khristianskoi krovi dlia religioznykh tselei, v sviazi s voprosom ob otnosheniiakh evreistva k khristianstvu voobshche, 2nd ed., vol. 2 (St. Petersburg, 1880), 136–58. Clearly, Liutostanskii told this story in such a way that the reader would believe what he said about the blood libel.

7. Material collected by the Tel'shi Castle Court, July 26, 1828 (LVIA, f. 443, ap. 6, b. 1086, ll. 482–83). The accusation was maintained by one Jew, who was later murdered. See Liutostanskii, *Ob upotreblenii evreiami*, 146–47.

8. Report by Kermenskii to the governor-general of Lithuania, July 18, 1827 (LVIA, f. 378, bs., 1827 m., b. 826, l. 39).

9. Jewish complaints (LVIA, f. 378, bs., 1827 m., b. 826, ll. 51–52, 274).

10. Report by Kermenskii to the governor-general of Lithuania, July 18, 1827 (LVIA, f. 378, bs., 1827 m., b. 826, l. 41).

11. Report of the Tel'shi Castle Court to the Lithuanian Supreme Tribunal, May 8, 1828 (LVIA, f. 443, ap. 6, b. 1071, ll. 339–42). This book (*Złość żydowska przeciwko Bogu i bliźniemu prawdzie y sumnieniu na obiaśnienie Talmudystów: Na dowod ich zaślepienia, y religii dalekiey od prawa boskiego przez Moyżesza danego*, 1760) by Gaudenty Pikulski claimed that Jews, especially Orthodox Jews, tried to harm Christians in general. On the authorship of this book, see Paweł Macejko, "The Mixed Multitude," *Jacob Frank and the Frankist Movement, 1755–1816* (Philadelphia: University of the Pennsylvania Press, 2011), 105–6. That book also reappeared during the Velizh trial.

12. Interrogation of David Glos (LVIA, f. 443, ap. 6, b. 1071, l. 94).

13. Request from Favel' Katsen, May 27, 1827 (LVIA, f. 443, ap. 6, b. 1071, l. 62).

14. File "Ob ubiistve semiletnego Petrovicha Iosifa" (LVIA, f. 443, ap. 6, b. 1071). Much of this case is devoted to examining this episode in the interrogation of the accused Jews. This manner of humiliating and mocking the appearance (and identity) of Jews was quite widespread in similar situations. For example, Ekhezkel Kotik, known as a local maskil who advocated progressive views, asserted that Polish rebels at Kamenets-Litovskii mocked Jews in this way in 1863. See Ekhezkel Kotik, *Moi vospominaniia* (St. Petersburg: Mosty Kul'tury, 2009), 218–19.

15. Jewish complaint (LVIA, f. 378, bs., 1827 m., b. 826, l. 274).

16. Minutes of interrogation, report of the victim, and reconciliation agreement (LVIA, f. 443, ap. 6, b. 1071, ll. 269, 278, and 281).

17. Report from the prosecutor of Vil'na province to the governor-general, April 13, 1829 (LVIA, f. 378, bs., 1827 m., b. 826, ll. 218–24).

18. Secret report of the head of the First Section of the Fourth Corps of Gendarmes to the chief of Gendarmes, November 16, 1829 (CAHJP, HMF/764, l. 46).

19. For more on Velizh and other case of that year, see Avrutin's chapter in this volume.

20. Semen Reznik, "Zachem zhe snova piatnat' V. I. Dalia? Pis'mo v redaktsiiu," *Novoe literaturnoe obozrenie* 107 (2011): 441. On the Velizh case, see Eugene Avrutin, "The Ritual Murder in a Russian Border Town," *Jewish History* 26, nos. 3–4 (2012): 309–26.

21. Report to the First Department of the Lithuanian Supreme Court, December 17, 1827 (LVIA, f. 443, ap. 6, b. 1086, l. 1); Iulii Gessen, *Velizhskaia drama: Iz istorii obvineniia evreev v ritual'nykh prestupleniiakh* (St. Petersburg: Tipografiia A. G. Rozena, 1904), 97.

22. Request sent by Jewish merchants to the tsar (Rossiiskii gosudarstvennyi istoricheskii arkhiv [Russian State Historical Archive]), f. 1269 (Evreiskii komitet), op. 1, d. 53a, l. 3.

23. Top secret report by the governor of Vil'na to the governor-general of Vil'na, April 1, 1908 (LVIA, f. 378, ps., 1908 m., b. 4, l. 10).

24. Ibid.

25. Officials asserted that the information later reached Vil'na, forty versts away.

26. Top secret report by the governor of Vil'na to the governor-general of Vil'na, April 1, 1908 (LVIA, f. 378, ps., 1908 m., b. 4, l. 10). Since Passover was more or less at the same time as

Easter, it was a quite widespread practice among the Christians to apply their own name of the holiday to the Jewish one.

27. Report by the Vil'na district prosecutor to the prosecutor, Vil'na Chamber of Justice, April 16, 1908 (LVIA, f. 446, ap. 6, b. 839, l. 2).

28. Report by the Vil'na district prosecutor to the prosecutor, Vil'na Chamber of Justice, April 2, 1908 (LVIA, f. 446, ap. 6, b. 905, l. 4).

29. Ibid.

30. Apparently the girl got tired of looking after her brother and decided to do away with him. See the letters from the rabbi of Novo-vileika (Vil'na district), Meir Levin to Daniil Khvol'son and Baron David Gintsburg, the day before the beginning of Iyar 1908 (CAHJP, Ru. 142.5 [pages unnumbered]). *Vilniaus žinios* also mentions a *burlak* (Russian for boatman). See "Šalnaičiai (Viln.gub.). Užmušimas vaiko Šalnaičiuose [Šalnaičiai (Vilnius Province). The Killing of a Child in Šalnaičiai]," *Vilniaus žinios* 88 (1908): 1.

31. Report by the Vil'na district prosecutor to the prosecutor, Vil'na Chamber of Justice, April 2, 1908 (LVIA, f. 446, ap. 6, b. 905, l. 4); "Z Belarusi i Litvy," *Nasha niva* 8 (1908): 6.

32. Top-secret report by the governor of Vil'na to the governor-general of Vil'na, April 1, 1908 (LVIA, f. 378, ps., 1908 m., b. 4, ll. 10–11).

33. Ibid., l. 14. The rabbi of Novo-vileika asserted that Viker had thirty witnesses to confirm that he did not leave home that day. See the letters from the rabbi of Novo-vileika (Vil'na district), Meir Levin to Daniil Khvol'son and Baron David Gintsburg, the day before the beginning of Iyar 1908 (CAHJP, Ru. 142.5 [pages unnumbered]).

34. The rabbi of Novo-vileika noted the fear among Jews in surrounding villages (ibid.).

35. Report by the Vil'na district prosecutor to the prosecutor of the Vil'na Chamber of Justice, April 16, 1908 (LVIA, f. 446, ap. 6, b. 839, l. 2).

36. Top secret report by the governor of Vil'na to the governor-general of Vil'na, April 1, 1908 (LVIA, f. 378, ps., 1908 m., b. 4, l. 10).

37. "Vilniaus gubernijos kalėjiman [To the Prison of Vil'na Province]" *Vilniaus žinios* 80 (1908): 2; "Šalnaičiai (Viln.gub.). Užmušimas vaiko [Šalnaičiai in Vilnius Province: Killing a Child]," *Vilniaus žinios* 88 (1908): 1–2; "Buivydžiai (Vilniaus pav.)," *Vilniaus žinios* 97 (1908): 2; "Kūdikio papiovimas [Slaughtering a Baby]" *Viltis* 41 (1908): 4; "Iš Lietuvos [From Lithuania]" *Lietuvos ūkininkas* 5 (1909): 46; "Z Belarusi i Litvy." For more on how the press reported the Buivydžiai case, see Vladas Sirutavičius, "Kai prietarai tampa prievarta: Kaltinimai žydams vartojant krikščionių kraują. Kelių atvejų Lietuvoje analizė" [From Prejudice to Violence: Accusations that the Jews Were Using the Blood of Christians. An Analysis of Three Cases in Lithuania]," in *Kai ksenofobija virsta prievarta. Lietuvių ir žydų santykių dinamika XIX a.–XX a. pirmoje pusėje* [When Xenophobia Turns to Violence: The Dynamics of Lithuanian-Jewish Relations during the Nineteenth and First Half of the Twentieth Centuries], ed. Vladas Sirutavičius and Darius Staliūnas (Vilnius, Lithuania: LII leidykla, 2005), 111–15.

38. "Kūdikio papiovimas."

39. It would be very difficult to find clear evidence that the clergy or the press were fomenting anti-Jewish violence. Usually even Lithuanian periodicals that were to some degree antisemitic tried to persuade their readership that violence was not the right way to solve problems.

40. Top secret report by the governor of Vil'na to the governor-general of Vil'na, April 5, 1908 (LVIA, f. 378, ps., 1908 m., b. 4, l. 14).

41. On another occasion the governor visited Vorniany and Ostrovets on market day (ibid.).

42. Copy of the resolution of the Vil'na Chamber of Justice, January 23, 1909 (LVIA, f. 446, ap. 6, b. 905, l. 19). Report by the Vil'na district prosecutor to the prosecutor, Vil'na Chamber of Justice, January 12, 1910 (LVIA, f. 446, ap. 6, b. 839, l. 4).

43. Report by the prosecutor of the Vil'na Chamber of Justice to the minister of justice, August 26, 1908 (LVIA, f. 446, ap. 6, b. 905, l. 10). On *izuvercheskie sekty* and blood libel, see Marina Mogilner's chapter in this volume.

44. Darius Staliūnas, "Antisemitic Tension during the 1905 Revolution in Lithuania," *Jahrbuch für Antisemitismusforschung* 21 (2012): 54–88.

45. For more on this topic, see Vladas Sirutavičius and Darius Staliūnas, eds., *A Pragmatic Alliance: Jewish-Lithuanian Political Cooperation at the Beginning of the Twentieth Century* (Budapest: Central European University Press, 2011).

46. Most of the Polish-speaking gentry identified with the modern Polish nation in the late imperial period.

47. Justinas Bonaventūra Pranaitis, *Krikščionis žydų talmude, arba, Slaptingas rabinų mokslas apie krikščionybę* [Jewish Talmud Concerning Christians, or Secret Rabinical Teaching on Christianity] (Seiniai, Lithuania: Laukaičio, Dvaranausko, Narjausko ir b-vės sp., 1912).

48. Serafinas Laurynas Kušeliauskas, *Talmudas žydų* [Jewish Talmud] (Tilsit: Otto v. Mauderodės spaustuvė, 1906), 7.

49. For more on Lithuanian antisemitism, see Linas Venclauskas, "Moderniojo lietuviško antisemitizmo genezė ir raida (1883–1940 m.) [Genesis and Development of Modern Lithuanian Antisemitism (1883–1940)]" (PhD diss., Vytautas Magnus University, Kaunas, 2008); Klaus Richter, "Antisemitism, 'Economic Emancipation,' and the Lithuanian Co-operative Movement before World War I," *Quest: Issues in Contemporary Jewish History. Journal of Fondazione CDEC*, July 3, 2012, http://www.quest-cdecjournal.it/focus.php?id=300; Richter, "Antisemitismus und die litauische Intelligenzija (1900–1914)," *Jahrbuch für Antisemitismusfoschung* 21 (2012): 89–114; and Darius Staliūnas, "Lithuanian Antisemitism in the Late Nineteenth and Early Twentieth Centuries," *Polin* 25 (2013): 135–49.

50. Rudolf Jaworski, "Voraussetzungen und Funktionsweisen des modernen Antisemitismus in Ostmitteleuropa," in *Jüdische Welten in Osteuropa*, ed. Annelore Engel-Braunschmidt and Eckhard Hübner (Frankfurt am Main, Germany: Peter Lang, 2005), 35–36.

51. Quoted in Vladimir Levin, "Lithuanians in the Jewish Politics of the Late Imperial Period," in Sirutavičius and Staliūnas, *Pragmatic Alliance*, 98.

52. Werner Bergmann, "Ethnic Riots in Situations of Loss of Control: Revolution, Civil War, and Regime Change as Opportunity Structures for Anti-Jewish Violence in Nineteenth- and Twentieth-Century Europe," in *Control of Violence: Historical and International Perspectives on Violence in Modern Societies*, ed. Wilhelm Heitmeyer, Heinz-Gerhard Haupt, Stefan Malthaner, and Andrea Kirschner (New York: Springer, 2011), 488.

❧ 6 ❧

YAHRZEITS, CONDOLENCES, AND OTHER CLOSE ENCOUNTERS

Neighborly Relations and Ritual Murder Trials in Germany and Austria-Hungary

Hillel J. Kieval

ON THE MORNING of June 29, 1891, in the Rhineland town of Xanten, the mother of Johann Hegmann, aged five, sent her son outside to play so that she could attend mass in commemoration of the Feast of Saints Peter and Paul. As one might guess, the little boy never returned home, and the discovery that evening of his stabbed and bloodied body set in motion a series of events, which culminated in Germany's first formal trial on the charge of ritual murder since the sixteenth century.[1] Adolf Buschhoff, aged fifty, a native of Xanten and one of the town's eighty-five Jewish inhabitants, stood accused of the crime. A former ritual slaughterer for the Jewish community who more recently had been working as a stonecutter, Buschhoff had enjoyed an impeccable reputation as a friendly and mild-mannered citizen almost up to the moment of his becoming the target of suspicion.[2] The obvious question is why? Why does an apparently well-adjusted, sociable, and esteemed member of a small urban community become the prime target of a murder investigation? Why was this murder so quickly and easily understood as a crime committed by Jews acting under religious compulsion? And what is the process by which this discursive transformation happened?

Clearly cultural inheritance plays an important role in the form of received wisdom, popular beliefs, and collective understandings (what I have referred to in other work as "social knowledge").[3] But categories such as "belief" or "knowledge" must not be taken to suggest some kind of ancient, unchanging cultural paradigm. To the contrary: social knowledge is mutable; and popular conceptions of Jewish "ritual murder" have changed over time and varied from place to place.[4] Moreover, most Central European states had proved to be strongly resistant to popular accusations of Jewish ritual murder since the sixteenth century, choosing more often to suppress such questionable knowledge than to act on it. This state/society dynamic alters significantly during the last decades of the nineteenth century, leading up to World War I. Not only does one find an almost unrelenting discussion of Jewish ritual murder during these decades but also, remarkably, a handful of formal—and sensational—murder trials.

Local accusations of ritual murder were reported on with much fanfare in newspapers, pamphlets, and political commentary at the time. They even provided the subject of speeches and interpellations on the floor of parliament in Berlin, Vienna, and Budapest. Friedrich Frank, a German Catholic priest and politician who came to oppose the popular belief in the blood libel, claimed to have discovered no fewer than 128 public accusations of this nature that had been made against Jews between 1881 and 1900. (For the preceding six hundred years, in contrast, he was able to locate only forty-four accusations of Jewish ritual murder!)[5] Writing around the same time, but focusing specifically on the last decade of the nineteenth century, the Berlin-based Verein zur Abwehr des Antisemitismus exposed seventy-nine "bona fide ritual murder charges" that had been leveled at Jews in various European countries, including Austria-Hungary, Germany, Bulgaria, Russia, Romania, Serbia, and France.[6]

Not surprisingly, perhaps, in a climate of growing fascination with this form of Jewish deviance and criminality, some of the allegations of ritual murder managed to break through the legal, political, and institutional constraints of the modern, bureaucratic state to become full-fledged criminal proceedings. The number of formal criminal trials, in which Jewish defendants stood accused of having committed murder for ritual purposes, was fairly small: roughly six between 1879 and 1913. The first and the last of these proceedings took place in the Russian Empire: Kutaisi (Russian Georgia) in 1879, and the well-known Beilis Affair, which transpired in Kiev (Ukraine) between 1911 and 1913. The intervening four trials took place in Central Europe: two in imperial Germany (Xanten, 1891–1892, and Konitz, 1900–1901) and two in Austria-Hungary, the Habsburg Monarchy (Tiszaeszlár, 1882–1883, and Polná, 1899–1900).[7] In my view, the five trials that spanned the years 1883 to 1913 represent a new phenomenon in the long history of the blood libel, as well as in Jewish-state relations during the era of emancipation. These were *modern* proceedings, all of which shared three important criteria distinguishing them from premodern ritual murder trials: (1) the inadmissibility of confessions extracted through torture, (2) the role of modern criminal codes and rules of procedure, under which the trials were organized, and (3) the implicit requirement that the cases be argued in the language of modern science, together with the disciplinary role played by forensic scientists in the presentation and evaluation of evidence. On the basis of these criteria, the famous Damascus Affair of 1840, for example, though falling within what might otherwise be considered a modern time frame, is phenomenologically premodern.

In the Tiszaeszlár case, the first truly modern trial against Jews for ritual murder, the fifteen Jewish defendants represented a large swath of the local Jewish population, but included visitors to the village as well as raftsmen who had been traveling on the Tisza River on logs harvested in the Carpathian Mountains. The Konitz trials (which, technically, prosecuted charges of perjury and libel) featured a defendant who, though younger than Adolf Buschhoff, had a similar occupational and social profile. Mendel Beilis was the Jewish manager of a brick factory in Kiev (Ukr., Kyiv), a city from which Jews had been barred until 1855. As with Adolf Buschhoff, there is no indication that Beilis enjoyed anything but friendly relations with his neighbors up until his arrest. It is only with the Polná case in eastern Bohemia that we are confronted with a Jewish defendant—Leopold Hilsner—who was socially marginalized and had a questionable reputation. Hilsner was an unemployed shoemaker, who lived with his widowed mother on the ground floor of a building belonging to the Jewish community—possibly on charity—and who was known to hang out with friends of unsavory character.[8]

It is to three of the trials that I turn for the remainder of this essay: Xanten, in particular, with comparisons to Tiszaeszlár and Polná. What is the relationship between the accused and his or her local environment? How is the everyday nexus of social relationships disrupted and broken asunder? And what does it take for a viable accusation of ritual murder—compelling enough to lead to formal prosecution—to emerge?

Circumnavigating the Known Universe

Xanten was a small market town nestled in the Lower Rhine Plain, a region consisting largely of isolated farmsteads and towns dating back to the thirteenth century. Towns of similar size served as the setting for other serious accusations of Jewish ritual murder during the last decades of the nineteenth century as well as for the criminal investigations and trials that in some cases ensued. In the view of some, places such as these amounted to little more than glorified villages. Their level of economic and administrative activity might have required the presence of a police barracks and a town hall, a few bank branches and a local doctor (not to mention the ubiquitous inns). But social life in the market towns was structured largely along rural lines. Even as late as the 1930s, a high proportion of town inhabitants was made up of landowners, many of whom led an almost peasant-like existence, going out into the fields during the day; others were owners of estates in the country on which they spent much of their time.[9]

Xanten appears to have been just such an "oversized village." Located in imperial Germany's Lower Rhine Plain in the state of Prussia (the Rheinprovinz), the town was once a Roman river crossing along the main road that ran from Cologne to Cleves and Nijmegen. But Xanten lost much of its economic importance with the subsequent shifting of the course of the river.[10] Between 1875 and 1910 its population grew modestly from 3,292 to just under 4,300; its Jewish population in 1875 stood at 85, roughly 2.6 percent of the whole. Düsseldorf, in contrast, the seat of the main administrative subdivision (*Regierungsbezirk*) to which Xanten belonged, had almost 360,000 inhabitants, while Cologne, the capital of the neighboring *Regierungsbezirk*, had a population of 600,000.[11] A post-1945 geographic guide to Germany commented that the only towns in the region that managed to flourish were those that enjoyed both rail transport and direct contact with the Rhine. Xanten was not one of these. With no industry of its own, and no direct link to the river's traffic, it remained a local market center and appeared to have preserved much of its medieval flavor.[12]

It was this sense of a town resting in suspended animation that Paul Nathan, sent by the Berlin newspaper *Die Nation* to cover the Xanten trial, tried to convey for his readers back home. The reporter paused on his approach to the town to capture the visual impact of the place as it hovered in the distance, contrasting so starkly from the cityscape of the modern metropolis. The town that lay before him seemed to evoke the German past, entangled in bucolic serenity and stern, medieval, Catholic grandeur:

> Xanten—it lies so beautiful. Lost in greenery, the small, neat houses surround the mighty cathedral, the gothic St. Victor's Church, a towering presence, one of the most serious and memorable medieval constructions on the Lower Rhine. As one stands on the gently rising Fürstenberg and looks over the landscape at the clusters of green trees, the small patches of forest, the farms and villages, the gentle hills and the wide, flat plains, through which the Rhine flows wide and steel gray; and as one's eye is drawn again and again to the powerful mass of the cathedral, it seems as though the ruling power of the Middle Ages stands there as a bodily presence.[13]

Johann Hegmann did not show up when the family sat down to morning coffee at 10:30 AM, nor was he seen the rest of the day; sometime in the afternoon, Johann's mother sent family members and friends to look for the child. The boy's body was found around 6:30 PM, in the barn of the local innkeeper and town councilor Wilhelm Küppers, by a maid who had gone in to milk and feed the cows.[14] On the same day, one of the town's other 3,300 residents, Adolf Buschhoff, left his home in the early morning hours and proceeded to walk. Over the course of that day, he would circumnavigate his neighborhood several times. His first stop was the synagogue. June 29 of that year corresponded not only to the Roman Catholic Feast of Saints Peter and Paul—a fact of which Buschhoff and the other Jewish residents of the town were well aware—but also was the anniversary of the death of Buschhoff's father—his *Yahrzeit*—as marked in the Jewish calendar, and Buschhoff wanted to be sure that he said the kaddish, the traditional memorial prayer, for his father at morning and afternoon services.

From the synagogue he moved on to a pub in the market, where he may or may not have joined friends and acquaintances for a morning drink, but where he does at least seem to have had a brief conversation with one of the men present concerning a possible business transaction. On his way home, around 10:00 AM, Buschhoff met a farmer, from whom he had once bought a cow and who now invited Buschhoff to join him for a drink. Along the way they met a third party, and the three proceeded to Buschhoff's house where they sat and talked for a while in the living room. After this bit of sociability, Buschhoff left the house again and went to see a man named Evers, a Catholic butcher, with whom he had worked for more than a decade. He encountered more acquaintances on this excursion—a farmer and a merchant, made another stop in a pub, and spoke there with several people. Setting off for home again a little before 1:00 PM, he met a neighbor named Ullenboom, who accompanied Buschhoff to his house in order to read the *Berliner Abendpost*—to which Buschhoff subscribed—while Buschhoff himself sat down for lunch. At 3:00 PM he left his house once more to attend a local folk festival known as Pumpenkirmes—held every Saints Peter and Paul day—together with two other neighbors. The three men could be found drinking together and playing skittles (*Kegeln*) when news came in the early evening of the discovery of the dead child, a jolting breach in the day's otherwise restful harmony.[15]

Born and raised in Xanten, Adolf Buschhoff knew his neighbors well and seems to have been a modest, friendly, yet gregarious person who felt at home in his native surroundings. Though he owned a small business as a stonecutter at the time of the events in question, his former occupation as butcher and ritual slaughterer had given him the opportunity to work alongside—and sometimes in competition with—Christian butchers and farmers. He may also have sold meat to a non-Jewish clientele, though this is difficult to ascertain. What does seem clear is that Buschhoff socialized on a daily basis with both his Jewish and his

Christian neighbors and felt at home in his small town universe. Numerous individuals testified to Buschhoff's social and psychological integration during the criminal trial, which took place in the nearby city of Kleve—the district capital—in July 1892. Long after much of public opinion in Xanten had turned against Buschhoff, person after person—including witnesses for the prosecution—came forward to testify to the upstanding character of the accused, his good nature, and his affability.[16] The mayor of Xanten referred to Buschhoff as "neither hot-tempered nor vindictive, but rather a good-natured man." Wilhelm van de Handt, a Franciscan monk from the nearby monastery in Dorsten, who had been in Xanten on the morning of the murder and who had interacted with Buschhoff on a few occasions, testified that, as far as he knew, Buschhoff was a "good, orderly person."[17] And one can find in the city archive of Xanten a tape-recorded oral history interview, conducted by Westdeutsche Rundfunk, with an eighty-nine-year-old woman named Frau Thyssen, whose father had had business dealings with numerous Xanten Jews, and who claims to have had very clear memories of Adolf Buschhoff. "Buschhoff never took advantage of us," she remembered, "was always very nice to us." Frau Thyssen went on to say that, following the discovery of the dead body, she—still a young girl—and her aunt went to the Buschhoff home to see what "had happened" there. "This is where it happened," her aunt whispered to her sotto voce. More than a half-century later, Frau Thyssen seems not to have been convinced of Buschhof's guilt. "I don't think so," she told the interviewer. "He was so fond of children."[18]

Asked by the presiding judge at his trial to characterize his relations with his neighbors, Buschhoff replied that they had always been good. As someone who knew from personal experience what it was like to lose a child, he explained—he and his wife had lost three of their original six children—Buschhoff had made it a point to visit the house of the bereaved family on the very evening that he heard the news. Nor was this his first visit to the Hegmann home. During the previous winter, Heinrich Hegmann, the boy's father, had been ill, and members of the Buschhoff family came by to pay their respects. "I thought it was the duty of a neighbor to go there," Buschhoff told the judge concerning his recent condolence call. "I said to Hegmann, 'Heinrich, try to be calm for the sake of your wife. I have gone through two tragedies with my wife.' Then we had something to eat, and I left to go to the synagogue."[19]

Buschhoff's sense of ease in his surroundings, his relaxed relations with the town's Christian inhabitants, seems to have been shared by most Jews in Xanten. In fact, nothing in the historical record indicates that the Christian population of this particular locale was any more (or less) antisemitic than that of other German small towns.[20] Outside observers of the proceedings in Xanten and Kleve at times suggested otherwise, however, imagining that they saw in the faces and outward behavior of local residents evidence of cultural backwardness, fanaticism, and superstition. One such characterization, made by the correspondent for a big city publication who had received credentials to cover the Kleve trial, managed to irk the presiding judge to such a degree that he opened the seventh day of the proceedings with an extended criticism of the unnamed journalist's remarks.

Judge Kluth announced to the courtroom on July 11, 1892, that he had been made aware of a report filed by a reporter at the trial and published in a "much-read newspaper," which had characterized the population of Kleve as uneducated, fanatical, and superstitious. The writer of the article went on to claim that when Adolf Buschhoff's son Siegmund entered the courtroom days earlier as a witness—a moving scene in which father and son saw each other again for the first time in a long while—that "fanaticism and hatred against the Jews" could be read in the eyes of the assembled public.[21] The judge, however, was quick to come to the defense of the people of Kleve, whom he had served in the district and criminal courts for the past three years, remarking that in that time he had gotten to know the local population very well and had come to value and respect them. Regarding their supposed "lack of education," he observed that the populations of many larger cities did not have much more. As to whether or not one could read in the eyes of the people in the courtroom hatred and fanaticism against the Jews, Kluth wondered whether one could really read such sentiments in the eyes of courtroom spectators. He, for one—the judge interjected—did not have sufficiently good eyesight to determine such things in other people. In any event, he noted, the courtroom could seat about a hundred people; whatever expressions they may have had on their faces, they could hardly be said to be representative of Kleve, which had a population of some twenty to thirty thousand.[22] The judge finished with a nice rhetorical flourish:

> I have gotten to know the entire population of the Kleve district within the radius of an hour and would venture the risk of going with Buschhoff from house to house up to the last peasant hut. And I am convinced that no one would disturb a hair on our heads, though I have no desire to give up my life for Buschhoff—or to have my hair ruffled. I would not dare to do this in many large cities without the protection of the police, while here I would go to up to the last peasant hut and am convinced that I would emerge healthy and unscathed.[23]

Arrest and Trial Nevertheless

Despite his reputation as an honest and well-meaning person, despite his apparently seamless integration into Xanten's social life, Adolf Buschhoff's name had surfaced as a likely suspect in the murder of Johann Hegmann early in the investigation. It took very little time for the crime itself to be understood—locally, and in newspapers from around Germany—as a Jewish ritual murder. Nor was the generally favorable impression that Buschhoff's neighbors had of him enough to prevent at least some of the town's residents from rioting against him and other Jews in the town, setting fire to his home, and writing on its walls the word *Mördergrube* (murderer's cell).[24] Things got so bad that at one point in the investigation, Buschhoff approached the town's mayor and requested that he be placed in jail for his own safety.[25] It was some consolation, perhaps, that when Xanten residents did riot against Jews and their property in the immediate aftermath of Buschhoff's arrest, the mayor, the district magistrate, and the provincial governor responded forcefully, threatening swift punishment of the rioters.[26]

All this suggests that the question as to why Adolf Buschhoff should have become the prime suspect in Xanten cannot easily be separated from the question why this particular crime should have been construed in the popular imagination as a ritual murder. Bernd Kölling addresses this intertwining in another way: What does it mean in concrete terms when one reads descriptions such as "immediately after the discovery of the corpse, the rumor arose" that the Jews had killed the child for ritual purposes (as one scholar has suggested)? How does a rumor *arise*? (Out of thin air?) And what does it mean when one says (as still another scholar has written) that the "idea of ritual murder" was brought into circulation in a given society? What are the actual means by which these phenomena take shape?[27]

Kölling argues that ritual murder accusations do not just "take shape"; they are *given* shape by purposeful individuals. In Xanten such purposeful construction was provided in part by a local resident named Heinrich Junkermann—a Christian cattle dealer and former butcher, who arrived quickly on the scene at the barn where Johann Hegmann's body was discovered and who, frankly, made himself conspicuous by his presence. Intuiting the need to link his assumptions to the authority of scientific discourse, Junkermann managed to involve himself in an early examination of the corpse and to issue commentary on the preliminary findings, which he wished to be taken as expert and authoritative. One of these had to do with the nature of the wound on the boy's neck. It was, he assured his audience, a Jewish butcher's cut (*Schächtschnitt*). Calling on his own experience as a butcher, Junkermann was also quick to claim that the boy could not have been killed in the barn. There was simply not enough blood on hand, he explained, to accept the theory of an exsanguination on the spot.[28] (The implication here is that the boy was slaughtered somewhere else, in private.) And he appealed—with unintended irony—to an unimpeachable scientific authority: his own son, who was a medical student in Berlin! Newspapers covering the 1892 trial in Kleve quoted Junkermann as having announced to the assembled townspeople in the barn, "the Jews make use of the blood of Christian children for their Passover bread; I know this from my son, who is a medical student."[29]

Sometimes, then, if other factors are in place, all it takes is a push—in the form of suggestion, authoritative surmise, quickly spreading rumor, or eyewitnesses late to come forward with their testimony—for neighbors to become accused of unsettling crimes, crimes that tear at the social fabric. Close and even good neighborly relations, in and of themselves, do not protect a person from becoming the target of a ritual murder prosecution. While social and political conflicts were endemic to Central and Eastern Europe in the late nineteenth and early twentieth centuries, on the local level, genuinely friendly and peaceful coexistence between Jews and Christians was not unusual—not even in those settings that produced ritual murder trials. In both the Xanten and the Konitz trials, we recall, the individuals who found themselves in the dock were solid, middle-class citizens and long-term residents of their towns. In the Tiszaeszlár case, the fifteen Jewish defendants included the sexton of the small Jewish community, three individuals who had been staying in Tiszaeszlár to interview for the vacant position of cantor/ritual slaughterer, several local householders, and some rugged Carpathian traders who had been floating down the Tisza River on rafts made of logs that they were bringing to market. Recall, too, the Xanten resident who was interviewed in her old age, able to articulate in one breath mutually contradictory opinions regarding Adolf Buschhoff: on one hand, that he was an honest person who was probably innocent of the crime of which he was accused; and on the other, that it was exciting to be led by the hand by her aunt to see for themselves "where it happened." Only in Leopold Hilsner, the defendant in two trials for the murder of Anežka Hrůzová of Polná, can we find a socially marginal, somewhat disreputable character. And it is only in Polná (Eastern Bohemia) that social and political tensions between Jews and Christians—associated to a large extent with growing nationalist strife between Czechs and Germans—had been evident *before* the production of a ritual murder narrative and not only in its *aftermath*.

Neighborly Relations and Self-Incrimination

The investigation into the disappearance of Eszter Solymosi in Tiszaeszlár, Hungary, in 1882 produced testimony regarding a peculiar interaction that apparently took place between some Jewish residents of the village and close relatives of the missing girl. For Tiszaeszlár's small Jewish community, April 1 that year was *shabbat ha-gadol*—the Sabbath preceding the holiday of Passover. It was also special in another sense, as the community was hosting three visitors, candidates for the position of ritual slaughterer (*shoḥet*) who also were expected to chant from the Torah and lead the congregation in prayer. During their stay in Tiszaeszlár, the three men (Ábrahám Bukszbaum, Lipót Braun, and Salamon Schwarcz) were housed with local families, two with the outgoing *shoḥet*, and one with the tavern keeper (and assistant sexton), Emánuel Taub. Saturday morning prayers ended around 11:00 AM, after which the candidates went to their hosts' homes for the midday meal. Four indigent Jews (a family of three and a single woman) also found shelter in Tiszaeszlár on that Sabbath in the home of József Scharf—caretaker of the synagogue, cobbler, and part-time laborer—who lived in a modest house adjacent to the synagogue and the ritual bath (*mikvah*).[30] Scharf, who grew up in the nearby town of Hajdunánás (some thirty kilometers south), was forty-three years old and had lived in Tiszaeszlár with his wife and three children for four years when his Christian neighbor disappeared.[31] Though native to Hungary, and intimately tied to the region around Tiszaeszlár, Scharf was relatively new to the village itself and did not personally know all of its residents. While he could not recall if he had ever met the young Eszter Solymosi, he was acquainted with her mother, and when the latter approached his house that Saturday night in search of news about her daughter, Scharf was eager to greet her with words of comfort.

According to Scharf, the encounter with Mrs. Solymosi took place on the evening of April 1 outside his house.[32] It was Scharf's wife who first went out to speak with Eszter's mother. When she went back inside, she announced that she had heard some news, that someone had sent a child to Ófalu who had not yet returned. Scharf then went out of the house himself, accompanied by his wife, at which point the grieving mother tearfully repeated her complaint.[33] Scharf now proceeded to do something that he would come deeply to regret, and to which would be attributed major significance by both the Solymosi family and, eventually, the investigating magistrate in the case, József Bary. In an effort to allay their worries, he related to the women the story of a similar situation that had taken place in his home town of Hajdunánás, the gist of which he recalled hearing from his mother. Eszter's aunt, Mrs. Gabriel Solymosi, testified to what she heard him say during her trial testimony:

> The sun did not go down until after I had gone with my sister to the village, after we had looked for Eszter without finding her, and after we had set out in the direction of Ujfalu. And as we reached the edge of the graves of the old cemetery, the woman Scharf, the wife of the sexton, approached us. "What's the problem," she asked? "Is Eszter lost?" "Yes," I said. She said: "She's not lost. Perhaps she had a fever and is lying down somewhere." "That cannot be," I said, "She is not that type of child." Her husband also approached us and started up, saying: "When I was

still a child, I heard from my mother that in Nánás a child had gone missing, and people also said that the Jews had killed the child. They even searched the ovens of the Jews, and finally the child was found in the meadow."[34]

Two days earlier, Mária Solymosi had related in court more or less the same version of events: "He came up to me on the street and asked me what the matter was. I didn't say anything, but my sister told him that the Huri woman had sent the girl to the village and that since then she can't be found. Thereupon he said that one mustn't be upset, that a similar case happened in Nánás when he was still a boy: then, too, the Jews were suspected; even their ovens were searched; and in the end the missing child was found in the meadow."[35]

It is possible to view Jakub Scharf's interaction with Mrs. Solymosi simply as the retrieval and recounting of a childhood memory. But it might also be instructive to read this intervention in light of folklore studies, that is, as an example of a Jewish legend concerning ritual murder accusations. As Haya Bar-Itzhak has argued, legends of this type functioned as responses to—and refutations of—Christian narratives and their often devastating effects. It is also worth noting that the recourse to such tales on the part of Jews indicates the extent to which the ritual murder accusation penetrated Jewish culture and informed Jewish conceptions of the world in which they lived.[36] Whatever Scharf's intentions, the tactic of engaging with Eszter's mother and consoling her with memories from his childhood certainly backfired. The encounter became one of the pieces of information that Mrs. Solymosi brought with her two days later when she approached Gábor Farkás, the village head (*bíró*), to request that he initiate a formal search for her daughter.

One wonders what else might have transpired between Saturday evening and Monday morning to make Mária Solymosi resolute in her conviction that Eszter had been the victim of a Jewish conspiracy to kidnap and murder her. Contemporary observers, such as the British churchman and scholar Charles H. H. Wright or the American editors of the trial proceedings *The Tiszaeszlár Ritual Murder Trial*, assigned much of the blame to the production and spread of rumor at the village level. The introduction to *The Ritual Murder Trial* carried the title "The Origins of the Rumor" and informed the reader early on that "before the arrest and investigation of Josef Scharf, his wife, his fourteen-year-old-son, and the thirteen others accused ..., the wildest rumors concerning the disappearance of the girl began to surface in Tisza-Eszlár and in all of Szabolcs county."[37] Wright, who covered the trial for the journal the *Nineteenth Century*, suggested that what had set the rumor of a ritual murder in motion were the interpersonal communications that Mrs. Solymosi had had with her neighbors. He surmised that she had repeated Scharf's remarks to her friends, "who regarded it at once as the utterance of a man with a guilty conscience. Thus Widow Solymosi became fully persuaded that Esther must have been kidnapped by the Jews." As Wright also noted, "The suspicion that the Jews had a hand in the affair, when once ventilated, rapidly gained a footing among a people imbued with prejudices against their Jewish neighbors. Every circumstance was now looked upon with suspicion."[38]

Andrew Handler, writing only a few decades ago, placed similar weight on the importance of speech itself (or, what people in an earlier age might have called "wagging tongues") in the production of local knowledge: "Mrs. Solymosi repeated Scharf's story and conveyed her own fears to a steadily growing audience of neighbors and friends. The hidden meaning of the words uttered in the spirit of compassion and commiseration gradually took on the ring of reality. The willingness of her sympathetic listeners to give ready credence to the possibility of the Jews having something to do with Eszter's disappearance prompted Mrs. Solymosi to turn to the local authorities for help."[39]

According to these views, then, local knowledge of a crime of ritual murder was produced not all at once but in the course of verbal interactions between Mária Solymosi and her Christian neighbors as well as among the neighbors themselves. It was socially constructed knowledge, informed by conventional wisdom and resting on solid communal foundations.

Since Mária Solymosi and her sister claimed that József Scharf had unintentionally blurted out what amounted to an indirect confession of wrongdoing (or, at least, knowledge of a crime), efforts were made in the course of the trial to establish Scharf's ostensible motives in recounting his mother's memory of a ritual murder accusation in Hajdunánás. "How did it occur to you to tell the story in the first place," Szeyffert, the deputy state's attorney, wanted to know. Scharf responded—perhaps testily—that he was moved to tell the story of Hajdunánás for the same reason that Szeyffert himself had brought up the case of a false accusation of Jewish ritual murder from the town of Tisza-St. Imre in his opening statement to the court: presumably, though Scharf never articulates this, to demonstrate how easy it is for dangerous, unfounded rumors to spread.[40]

When the presiding judge stepped in to ask the defendant virtually the same question that had been put to him shortly before, Scharf replied in a different manner: "It may have been rash on my part, but it just came to me. Would that I had never allowed such foolishness to pass through my lips."[41] In fact, Mrs. Solymosi's appearance outside his house, her emotional state, and her frantic searching for her daughter had made him uneasy. His action, while certainly unplanned, was as much an unconscious expression of fear as it was an effort to console a grieving mother. When Scharf went back into the house after speaking with the Solymosi sisters, he turned to the charity recipient who had been staying with him over the Sabbath and said, "Nothing good will come out of this.... Someone will concoct an accusation against the Jews." During the trial, Szeyffert claimed to be surprised at Scharf's expression of foreboding. Why should he have reacted so pessimistically? Certainly it was natural for a mother to look for her child. "She looked for it [the child]," Scharf responded, "but where it would lead, God only knew."[42]

Concluding Thoughts

The proposition that upstanding members of small-town communities could become vulnerable to accusations of ritual murder, or that an atmosphere of strained social relations was *not* a prerequisite in the eruption of such cases, should not come as a surprise. Traditional, premodern understandings of Jewish ritual murder held by Christians, after all, did not attribute this kind of criminality to aberrant personalities or social types but to religious compulsion. And it is not clear, really, how much free will the traditional theory of Jewish ritual murder ascribed to the supposed perpetrators of this offense. In any event one would suspect that only a person truly knowledgeable in Jewish religious teachings would "know what to do," how to do it, and why. In the minds of more than a few, just because one's Jewish neighbors were friendly and polite did not necessarily mean that they would never commit a crime of this sort. It is really only with the growing secularization of Central European culture in the nineteenth century that narratives of Jewish ritual murder began to look for perpetrators among disreputable and potentially dangerous elements of society. Finally, I think it is useful to read the major ritual murder affairs of the turn of the twentieth century as incidents of systemic violence—traumatic disruptions of more or less stable social relations and long-term social patterns. What these accusations, police investigations, trials, and riots disrupted were, if not genuine peace and social harmony, then at least long periods of accommodation and civility.

Rather than simply asking what it takes to produce an accusation of Jewish ritual murder, it might be more productive to inquire into the fateful decision made by state's attorneys and ministries of justice actually to try cases of murder in which the prosecution's theory of the crime incorporated a (rehabilitated) narrative of murder produced by ritual compulsion. It was this intervention of the state into an area of criminal prosecution that had been shunned for several centuries that cries out for explanation. By way of a tentative answer, let me suggest that one crucial step in this process involved the tacit acknowledgment of the need to conform to contemporary legal procedures and rhetorical appeals to scientific method. As I have argued in other contexts, modern ritual murder trials rested on fundamentally different rhetorical structures and cultural authorities than the premodern libel. Procedural legal reforms of the mid- to late nineteenth century and recognized scientific expertise functioned as necessary, if not sufficient, preconditions for the revival of ritual murder trials in this period. Ritual murder discourse, moreover, needed to be expressed in a new idiom, based on a scientific vocabulary employing secular motifs and imagery, if it hoped to have "its day in court."[43]

We have seen in the Xanten case how suspicion against Adolf Buschhoff was advanced through the active intervention of his neighbor Heinrich Junkermann, together with the latter's appeal to expert knowledge in both medicine and Jewish ritual slaughter. One should add the fact that Buschhoff had the misfortune of residing directly in back of the barn (belonging to the non-Jewish Küppers family) where young Johann Hegmann's body was found. But it was the years that Buschhoff had spent as a butcher that appeared to weigh most heavily against him. In the overheated atmosphere that followed the discovery of the body, investigators, prosecutors, and newspapers focused on this particular point, because it appeared to corroborate the theory that had already gained traction in the minds of local residents and officials, not only that the crime had been carried out with anatomical expertise, but that it had incorporated a characteristic feature of Jewish ritual slaughtering, the so-called butcher's cut.

The twin images of Jewish butchering and Jewish ritual murder had begun to be deployed at least as far back as the first Congress of Antisemites, held in the Saxon city of Dresden in 1882. During the Tiszaeszlár affair, the rhetoric of Jewish butchering took on a more nuanced tone, since it took ten weeks for the body of Eszter Solymosi to float up to the surface of the Tisza River, and even then it could not be established for certain whether Eszter Solymosi had in fact come to a violent end. Yet here, too, Jewish butchers featured prominently in the eventual prosecution since three of the individuals eventually charged with her murder had the misfortune to be present in Tiszaeszlár on that fateful Sabbath on which Eszter had disappeared. Indeed in three of the four Central European trials Jewish butchers and ritual slaughterers unwillingly played central, dramatic roles, while in the popular media the image of the "murdering butcher" came almost to dominate discourses of Jewish danger.[44]

The outlier—on a number of counts—remains the troubling Polná case (1899–1900), in which the unemployed shoemaker, Leopold Hilsner, was tried not once, but twice, for the murder of Anežka Hrůzová; found guilty; and sentenced to death on both occasions. Even in this case, however, the trope of the ritual slaughter of animals clung stubbornly to popular representations and understandings of the crime. In the serialized daily newspaper coverage of the local criminal investigation, much heat and space was devoted to a minute description of the various wounds found on the victim's body, the most serious of which (and potentially the cause of death) was a long and deep cut to the throat—so deep in fact that the Polná correspondent for the antiliberal paper *Katolické listy* (Catholic pages) described the victim as having been *zakošerovaná* (koshered)![45] Eyewitnesses eventually came forward during the police investigation to report having seen Hilsner in the vicinity of the German-Jewish school in town, in the company of two identifiably "Jewish" and "foreign" men, shortly before the murder occurred.[46] (Presumably it would have taken at least two or three individuals to immobilize a healthy peasant girl long enough both to perform the "shochet's cut" and to draw off the victim's blood.) By the third week in May, *Katolické listy* had sent its legal correspondent to Polná for on-the-spot reporting. In subsequent dispatches to Prague he described how he sought out the expertise and opinions of local residents and was given guided tours through the topical landmarks of the crime.

In the paper's May 19, 1899, issue, the reporter offered its readers a step-by-step reconstruction of Anežka's murder, which its correspondent claimed to have heard from one of the members of the local judicial commission:

> When Anežka got to the top [of the hill], she began to walk slowly. The murderer grabbed her by the arm or by the throat, threw her down to the overgrowth, where a rope was tossed over her neck to prevent her from crying out. Her clothing was stripped down to her knickers, stockings, and shoes, and there in the thicket—six steps from the path—the act of cutting took place. The wound went from one ear to the other, straight and even above the Adam's apple to the vertebrae: precisely the way in which cattle are (kosher-)slaughtered. Whoever cut the throat of Anežka Hrůzová was not performing the act for the first time; he knew what he was doing. The position of the body pointed downhill, the legs, bent at the knees, tumbled uphill. All of the blood, therefore, must have poured out of Anežka Hrůzová. The body when it was found looked like a white scarf, the head resting on the arms. Her face was to the ground. At a quarter to seven people already saw Hilsner in the town below, but the two foreign Yids did not return from Březina.[47]

This dispatch may represent the first relatively complete, imaginative reconstruction of the Polná murder that exists in print. What is remarkable about it is the virtual absence of religious symbolism: there is no stand-in for Jesus, no crucifixion, no mocking of God, no martyrdom. In its place stand raw brutality and an anatomically precise knowledge of animal slaughter. As a meditation on blood, this text—from a Catholic newspaper—has lost all connection to Calvary;

sacrifice has been transmuted into slaughter, the altar into the cutting block. Similarly what characterizes the crime as "Jewish" has little or nothing to do with the religious rivalry between Judaism and Christianity. If the telltale "signs of crucifixion" had identified the medieval murders as "Jewish" affairs, what defines the Polná case as "Jewish" can be reduced to blood and brutality, to the imagined "butcher's cut" of kosher slaughter. The Jews, themselves, finally, are not religious adversaries; they are Yids.

Cases such as Tiszaeszlár, Xanten, and Polná challenge some of the most cherished assumptions of the historical profession: our confidence that local context matters, that concrete factors produce historical change, that deeply rooted social, cultural, and political structures are more reliable indicators of causation than contingency and chance. In Tiszaeszlár the candidates for the vacant position of ritual slaughterer and a small flotilla of raftsmen from the Carpathian Mountains—who, bizarrely, also faced serious charges in the trial—offer eloquent testimony to the problem of being in the wrong place at the wrong time. In Leopold Hilsner's case, it may well have been only a matter of time before he was arrested and tried for some kind of criminal activity. And for Adolf Buschhoff— who circumnavigated his small universe with ease and good cheer, but who had the double misfortune of living close to the scene of a gruesome murder and having practiced a trade that had become emblematic for some people of frightening cruelty and danger—the nightmare of arrest, imprisonment, trial, and eventual exile from his home town underscored just how thin the line could be separating belonging and marginality. In the final analysis, however, contingency and chance did not really trump context and structure. Rather, purposeful mischief, popular belief, and contingent events had somehow to align with fundamental structural requirements—ranging from parliamentary politics to reformed criminal procedure, from forensic techniques to the grammar of science and medicine—before a trial on the theory of ritual murder could even proceed. On those disturbing, if relatively rare, occasions some exceedingly ordinary lives were thrust, quite unwittingly, into historical significance.

HILLEL J. KIEVAL is the Gloria M. Goldstein Professor of Jewish History and Thought at Washington University in St. Louis. A historian of Jewish culture and society in Central and Eastern Europe in the nineteenth and twentieth centuries, his research interests range widely: from pathways of Jewish acculturation and integration to the impact of nationalism and ethnic conflict on modern Jewish identities; from cross-cultural conflicts and misunderstandings to the discursive practices of modern antisemitism; and from theories of Jewish citizenship to the phenomenology of "ritual murder" trials at the turn of the twentieth century. Among his numerous books and articles are *The Making of Czech Jewry: National Conflict and Jewish Society in Bohemia, 1870–1918* (1988); and *Languages of Community: The Jewish Experience in the Czech Lands* (2000).

NOTES

1. On the late medieval and early modern ritual murder trial in the Holy Roman Empire, see R. Po-chia Hsia, *The Myth of Ritual Murder: Jews and Magic in Reformation Germany* (New Haven, CT: Yale University Press, 1988); Hsia, *Trent 1475: Stories of a Ritual Murder* (New Haven, CT: Yale University Press, 1992); and Wolfgang Treue, *Der Trienter Judenprozeß: Voraussetzungen—Abläufe—Auswirkungen (1475-1588)* (Hanover, Germany: Hahnsche Buchhandlung, 1996).

2. Adolf Buschhoff (1840–1912). On the Xanten ritual murder affair and the Kleve trial, see *Der Fall Buschhoff: Aktenmäßige Darstellung des Xantener Knabenmord-Prozesses* (Frankfurt am Main, Germany: C. Koenitz, 1892); *Der Xantener Knabenmord vor dem Schwurgericht zu Cleve 4.-14. Juli 1892: Vollständiger stenographischer Bericht* (Berlin: Cronbach, 1893); Johannes T. Groß, *Ritualmordbeschuldigungen gegen Juden im deutschen Kaiserreich (1871–1914)* (Berlin: Metropol, 2002); Bernd Kölling, "Blutige Illusionen: Ritualmorddiskurse und Antisemitismus im Niederrheinischen Xanten," in *Agrarische Verfassung und politische Struktur,* ed. René Schiller (Berlin: Arno Spitz, 1998), 349–82; Paul Nathan, *Xanten-Cleve: Betrachtungen zum Prozeß Buschhoff* (Berlin: H. S. Hermann, 1892); and Julius H. Schoeps, "Ritualmordbeschuldigung und Blutaberglaube: Die Affäre Buschhoff im niederrheinischen Xanten," in *Köln und das Rheinische Judentum: Festschrift Germania Judaica 1959–1984* (Cologne, Germany: J. P. Bachem, 1984), 286–99.

3. Hillel J. Kieval, "Representation and Knowledge in Medieval and Modern Accounts of Jewish Ritual Murder," *Jewish Social Studies,* n. s. 1 (1994–95): 52–72; and Kieval, "Antisémitisme ou Savoir Social? Sur la genèse du procès moderne pour meurtre rituel," *Annales: Histoire, Sciences Sociales* 49 (1994): 1091–1105.

4. I enclose the term "ritual murder" here in quotation marks to indicate that it is a cultural and psychological construct. From this point on, I dispense with the quotation marks.

5. Friedrich Frank, *Der Ritualmord vor den Gerichtshöfen der Wahrheit und der Gerechtigkeit* (Regensburg, Germany: G. J. Manz, 1901), 181–302. Frank's efforts to tabulate and describe ritual murder accusations against Jews, though serious, were somewhat arbitrary. For contemporary cases, he relied heavily on German and Austrian newspaper accounts. On occasion he appears to have hewn closely to Leopold Auerbach, *Das Judenthum und seine Bekenner in Preußen und in den anderen deutschen Bundesstaaten* (Berlin: Sigmar Mehring, 1890). Frank seems not to have made use of Slavic sources and shows little awareness of the scores of accusations that transpired in Poland-Lithuania or the Russian Empire.

Frank's own position with regard to Jews was complicated. A conservative Catholic, he voiced his church's traditional theological teachings concerning the Jews—that they had been chosen by God to teach the belief in the one God and to give expression to the hope for a messianic redeemer, but that they betrayed this mission, turning their backs on and, ultimately, crucifying the son of God. The metahistorical status of the Jews then switched from chosenness to abandonment and from blessing to curse. As late as 1892, Frank could write that Jews historically had committed crimes against their Christian neighbors but not, he argued, for religious purposes. (See Frank, *Die Kirche und die Juden: Eine Studie,* 2nd ed. [Regensburg, Germany: G. J. Manz, 1892].) It may well have been his own religious conservatism, his allegiance to official papal teaching, that caused Frank publicly to oppose the blood libel.

6. This assessment comes from Helmut Walser Smith, *The Butcher's Tale: Murder and Anti-Semitism in a German Town* (New York: W. W. Norton, 2002), 123, based on the bimonthly newsletter of the *Verein zur Abwehr des Antisemitismus*. Smith adds: "Of the seventy-nine accusations, fourteen escalated into some level of violence against Jews. In more than half the cases, specific charges were made against individual Jews, as opposed to the more general claim that 'the Jews did it.'"

7. There is a growing literature on individual ritual murder trials from the turn of the twentieth century. On Tiszaeszlár (Hungary), see Andrew Handler, *Blood Libel at Tiszaeslar* (Boulder, CO: East European Monographs, 1980); and György Kövér, *A Tiszaeszlári drama: Társadalomtörténeti látoszögek* [The Tiszaeszlár Drama: Social-historical Angles] (Budapest: Osiris, 2011). On Xanten, see Groß, *Ritualmordbeschuldigungen*; Kölling, "Blutige Illusionen"; and Schoeps, "Ritualmordbeschuldigung und Blutaberglaube." On Polná, see Jiří Kovtun, *Tajuplná vražda: Případ Leopolda Hilsnera* [Mysterious Murder: The Case of Leopold Hilsner] (Prague: Sefer, 1994). On Konitz (Chojnice), see Smith, *The Butcher's Tale*; and Christoph Nonn, *Eine Stadt sucht einen Mörder: Gerücht, Gewalt und Antisemitismus im Kaiserreich* (Göttingen, Germany: Vandenhoeck and Ruprecht, 2002). On Kiev (the Beilis Affair), see Edmund Levin, *A Child of Christian Blood: Murder and Conspiracy in Tsarist Russia: The Beilis Blood Libel* (New York: Schocken Books, 2014); and Robert Weinberg, *Blood Libel in Late Imperial Russia: The Ritual Murder Trial of Mendel Beilis* (Bloomington: Indiana University Press, 2014). I am currently finishing a social and cultural history of the reemergence of ritual murder trials in late-nineteenth- and early twentieth-century Europe titled *Blood Inscriptions: Science, Modernity, and Ritual Murder in Fin de Siècle Europe*.

8. See Kovtun, *Tajuplná vražda*, 18–22; Arthur Nussbaum, *Der Polnaer Ritualmordprozess: Eine kriminalpsychologische Untersuchung auf aktenmässiger Grundlage* (Berlin: A. W. Hayn, 1906), 90–92.

9. C. A. Macartney, *Hungary* (London: Ernest Benn, 1934), 199–200.

10. Robert E. Dickinson, *Germany: A General and Regional Geography* (New York: E. P. Dutton, 1953), 466.

11. Holger Schmenk, *Xanten im 19. Jahrhundert: Eine rheinische Stadt zwischen Tradition und Moderne* (Cologne, Germany: Böhlau, 2008), 312. See also *Die Gemeinden mit 2000 und mehr Einwohnern im Deutschen Reich nach der Volkszählung vom 16. Juni 1925. Sonderhefte zu Wirtschaft und Statistik* (Berlin: Berlin Statistisches Reichsamt, 1926), 6: 48–49. The latter publication compares data from the 1925 census to that of 1910.

12. Dickinson, *Germany*, 464–65.

13. Paul Nathan, *Xanten-Cleve*, 1.

14. Schoeps, "Ritualmordbeschuldigung und Blutaberglaube," 286–87.

15. *Der Xantener Knabenmord*, 5–7. See the discussion of this itinerary in Kölling, "Blutige Illusionen," 372.

16. Kölling, "Blutige Illusionen," 372–73; *Der Xantener Knabenmord*, 144, 205.

17. *Der Fall Buschhoff*, 23, 35. On the challenge of pinpointing the attitudes of everyday townspeople, see Kölling, "Blutige Illusionen," 371–72.

18. Quoted in Holger Schmenk, *Xanten im 19. Jahrhundert: Eine rheinische Stadt zwischen Tradition und Moderne* (Cologne, Germany: Böhlau, 2008), 316. The City Archive of Xanten has an uncatalogued copy of the recording.

19. *Der Xantener Knabenmord*, 3, 77.

20. Kölling, "Blutige Illusionen," 371. Xanten had been the site of anti-Jewish disturbances in 1834 along with other cities and towns in the Rhineland. Stretching further back in time, it also witnessed an attack on its small Jewish community during the 1096 Crusade.

21. *Der Xantener Knabenmord*, 307.

22. Ibid., 307–8. In fact, the 1890 census listed Kleve's population at fifteen thousand (Kölling, "Blutige Illusionen," 374).

23. *Der Xantener Knabenmord*, 308. As to exactly against whom the presiding judge may have directed his attack, it is hard to know. He made it a point of beginning more than a few daily sessions questioning or correcting reports of the previous day's proceedings that had appeared in local or national newspapers. These interventions were faithfully recorded by one writer, Hugo Friedländer, a Berlin correspondent who reported for the *Clever Kreisblatt* among other publications. See his account of the trial proceedings, *Der Knabenmord in Xanten vor dem Schwurgericht zu Cleve vom 4. bis 14. Juli 1892* (Cleve, Germany: W. Startz, 1892).

It is possible that the "big city reporter" was Paul Nathan, who attended the trial on behalf of the Berlin publication *Die Nation*. On Paul Nathan (1857–1927), see his reportage in *Xanten-Cleve*; and Ernst Feder, "Paul Nathan, the Man and His Work," *Leo Baeck Institute Yearbook* 3 (1958): 60–80.

24. *Jewish Chronicle*, July 22, 1892, 9.

25. *Der Fall Buschhoff*, 23.

26. See Schoeps, "Ritualmordbeschuldigung," 287, 297–98 (where he quotes from the file of the district magistrate's office in Moers [Nordrhein-Westfälisches Hauptstaatsarchiv, Düsseldorf (HStAD), LA Moers, Nr. 547]).

27. Kölling, "Blutige Illusionen," 360. The first quotation is taken from Schoeps, "Ritualmordbeschuldigung," 287; the second question paraphrases Dominick La Capra, *Geschichte und Kritik* (Frankfurt am Main, Germany: Fischer, 1987), 14. Concerning the phenomenon of rumors, I am influenced by the writing of Jean-Noël Kapferer, *Rumors: Uses, Interpretations, and Images* (New Brunswick, NJ: Transaction Publishers, 1990). Rumors, he argues, do not arise out of a "reality," which, in their transmission, they proceed to distort. Rather, they spring from "raw, confused facts." The purpose of rumors is not to describe reality but to explain troubling or mysterious facts, to posit a reality in the form of a particular narrative. Rumors also work parallel to, or in the absence of, official investigations and explanations; they "seek out a reality that does not await the verdict of official investigations" (Kapferer, *Rumors*, 30).

28. Kölling, "Blutige Illusionen," 361.

29. *Berliner Tageblatt*, July 15, 1892, quoted in Kölling, "Blutige Illusionen," 361; *Jewish Chronicle*, July 22, 1892, 11. See also Friedländer, *Der Knabenmord in Xanten*, 10–12. Junkermann was not alone in issuing "expert" pronouncements on the murder of Johann Hegmann; the Xanten physician Joseph Steiner seems to have had a hand in promoting a theory of ritual murder as well.

30. Handler, *Blood Libel*, 37–39.

31. See Scharf's trial testimony, day two: *Der Blutprozeß von Tisza Eszlár* (New York: Schnitzer Bros., 1883), 22.

32. Handler's assertion that the meeting took place on the afternoon of April 2 (*Blood Libel*, 41) is contradicted by the trial testimony.

33. *Der Blutprozeß*, 24.

34. Testimony of Mrs. Gabriel Solymosi, day four of trial proceedings. See *Der Blutprozeß*, 73; *Egyenlőség*, June 23, 1883, 4; also quoted in Paul Nathan, *Der Prozess von Tisza-Eszlár: Ein antisemitisches Culturbild* (Berlin: F. Fontane & Co., 1892), 100.

35. *Der Blutprozeß*, 25; Nathan, *Der Prozess von Tisza-Eszlár* (in almost identical language), 101.

36. See Haya Bar-Itzhak's contribution in this volume; also Dov Noy, "Stories of Blood Libels in Jewish Communities [Hebrew]," *Mahanayim* 110 (1967): 32–51. According to the classification scheme put forward by Bar-Itzhak, Scharf's tale corresponds most closely to AT 730f: The Christian child, whom the Jews were accused of murdering, turns up safe and sound.

37. *Der Blutprozeß*, iii.
38. Charles H. H. Wright, "The Jews and the Malicious Charge of Human Sacrifice," *Nineteenth Century* (November 1883): 753–78; quote is from 757. Unaccountably, Wright insists that the fateful encounter between the Scharfs and the Solymosi sisters took place on April 10.
39. Handler, *Blood Libel*, 42.
40. *Der Blutprozeß*, 24–25. Szeyffert's opening statement is recorded on 3–9; the reference to Tisza-St. Imre is on 8. Szeyffert made it in the context of a highly critical overview of the recent surge in ritual murder accusations in Central Europe, including Hungary. Apparently, the Tisza-St. Imre accusation had claimed that the victim was a Christian boy.
41. *Der Blutprozeß*, 25.
42. Ibid.
43. See esp. Hillel J. Kieval, "The Rules of the Game: Forensic Medicine and the Language of Science in the Structuring of Modern Ritual Murder Trials," *Jewish History* 26 (2012): 287–307.
44. This theme is developed more fully in my forthcoming *Blood Inscriptions*. For a discussion of the place of Kosher butchering in German political discourse about Jews, see Robin Judd, *Contested Rituals: Circumcision, Kosher Butchering, and Jewish Political Life in Germany, 1843–1933* (Ithaca, NY: Cornell University Press, 2007).
45. *Katolické listy*, April 16, 1899, 6. On May 26 the paper offered its readers "intimate details" about the family of "the unfortunate Anežka Hrůzová, murdered by means of kosher slaughter (*košeráckým způsobem zavražděné*)" (4).
46. *Katolické listy*, May 20, 1899, 5.
47. *Katolické listy*, May 19, 1899, 5.

7

HUMAN SACRIFICE IN THE NAME OF A NATION

The Religion of Common Blood

Marina Mogilner

THE GREAT REFORMS of the 1860s initiated changes that had led to the formation of mass society in Russia, the proliferation of public discourses, and the gradual crystallization of mass politics. These changing social and intellectual contexts radically altered attitudes toward the archaic blood libel, or even cast it in a new light, making it scientifically grounded and politically charged. The latter factor gradually became more important as the imperial regime embarked on the path of self-nationalization. Rather than encompassing all socially integrated subjects of the empire, loyal to the dynasty, Russians were increasingly perceived as an ethnoconfessional category, distinguished by linguistic, religious, and even racial borders from other groups in the ever more dynamic and fluid imperial society.[1]

In this chapter I explore these developments by focusing on the rise in the 1890s of a scientifically sanctioned public hype over alleged human ritual sacrifices as a living practice among some peoples of the empire. This was the period when members of the broadly defined "general public" grew anxious over the unsettling and unsettled quality of modernity, hoping to stabilize and objectify their own status as moderns by juxtaposing themselves to the figure of some ultimately archaic Other. Reflecting these anxieties and the growing fixation on the archaic, by the late nineteenth century, forensic medicine ceased to be the only modern scientific language of discussion of "ritual murder" in courts. Now it was supplemented with the language of ethnography and physical anthropology and with major civilizational expert narratives. Dozens of Russian anthropologists and ethnographers were dragged into the debates about the reality of human sacrifices as a "survival" of bygone epochs. As I show, in some cases the very construction of a blood libel accusation depended on the shared ethnographic discourse and scientifically informed vision of civilizational development to such a degree that criminal accusations could not present a viable legal case outside the framework of these discourses. In general, such key categories of anthropology as primitivism, survivals, or traditional society found their way into the language of public discussions of culture and modernity, while the trope of "blood" (as in the formula "blood and soil" or as a concept of biological race) became firmly embedded in the discourses of nationalism. This helps explain the paradox of the seemingly obsolete blood libel emerging in the fore of the newest academic and popular debates about imperial modernization and nationalism. I revisit these debates by examining two paradigmatic cases of blood libel trials at the turn of the twentieth century (the Multan case and the Beilis case), and the ethnographic academic discussions that informed them. I then trace these debates in connection with the emergence of the racialized reading of the Jewish nation in Russian Zionism and in the medicalized Jewish social movement. Ultimately, I examine the implications of the new understanding of human sacrifice as closely connected to an ethnographic notion of "survival" that had important political consequences for the modernizing society and its different individual and collective actors.

The Archetypal Case

How can we account for this fascination with the horrifying archaic practice of ritual murder? One obvious explanation is the spread of scientific ethnography and the broad popularity of ideas of such scholars as Charles Darwin, Edward Tylor, or James Frazer, who formed a new social imagination and a new language of discussion of the relationship between archaic and modern. It was the dean of modern social anthropologists, E. B. Tylor, who, in his *Primitive Culture* (1871), outlined the vision of a uniform "prehistoric" society as a necessary stage in the development of all human collectives. Tylor's *Primitive Culture* became an archetypal text of evolutionism. Classifying different forms of beliefs as stages of the linear progression from "animism" to religion and then to science, Tylor also formulated the concept of "survivals" that later informed the reading of human sacrifices as a living practice. Survivals, according to Tylor, were "processes, customs, and opinions, and so forth, which have been carried on by force of habit into a new state of society different from that in which they had their original home, and they thus remain as proofs and examples of an older condition of culture out of which a newer has been evolved."[2]

The Russian translation of *Primitive Culture* was ready in 1872, just one year after its original publication, and the book quickly became an intellectual blockbuster.[3] Its universalism and evolutionism attracted progressive-minded scholars and political activists, while the concept of "survivals" helped explain the heterogeneity of Russian imperial society and the asynchronous social and cultural dynamics of its different peoples, classes, and regions.

An unprecedented success of academic ethnography with the public inspired Tylor's famous disciple, the social anthropologist James George Frazer of Cambridge University, to address a much broader nonacademic readership in 1890, when he published two volumes of his seminal *The Golden Bough: A Study in Comparative Religion*.[4] The book stirred readers' minds not only in Frazer's native Britain. A student of belief systems in primitive societies, Frazer hypothesized that all of them had at some point gone through a stage of human sacrifice to their most worshiped gods. Moreover, this practice was instrumental in moving a primitive culture from the stage of "magic" to the stage of "religion," with the development of human civilization culminating with the stage of scientific thought.

As British readers were greedily consuming Frazer's vivid depictions of animist rituals (including human sacrifices), Russians showed a similarly intense interest in human sacrifice. It is unlikely that they had been inspired directly by Frazer's study.[5] Rather, it seems that Russian evolutionist scholars influenced by Tylor had made the same intellectual journey as did Frazer, but independently of him and over approximately the same span of two decades. It took time for Frazer to realize the fundamental nature of what he initially perceived as an elitist phenomenon limited to sacrificing kings and chiefs (consequently expanding the book from two volumes of the first edition to three volumes of the second, and then to twelve volumes of the third edition). In the extended third edition published on the eve of World War I, he included the words that read as an emotional indictment of the "savage" practice of murderous scapegoating:

> The notion that we can transfer our guilt and sufferings to some other being who will bear them for us is familiar to the savage mind.... In short, the principle of vicarious suffering is commonly understood and practiced by races who stand on a low level of social and intellectual culture. In the following pages I shall illustrate the theory and the practice as they are found among savages in all their naked simplicity, undisguised by the refinements of metaphysics and the subtleties of theology. The devices to which the cunning and selfish savage resorts for the sake of easing himself at the expense of his neighbour are manifold.[6]

As we shall see, Russian scholars also groped their way toward the metaphor of scapegoating. Moreover, from the very beginning they were prepared to treat ritual human sacrifices as a mundane, rather than elitist, practice. However it would be erroneous to assume that—unlike Tylor and Frazer, who were armchair theoretical anthropologists—their Russian disciples and contemporaries relied on practical observations of ritual murders. Their "discoveries" equally had not been prompted by any empirical research. Instead, they resulted from the growing ethnographic theoretical awareness and the need to respond to the challenges of the historical moment.

This was vividly demonstrated by the so-called Multan case. In May 1892 a dismembered male body was found not far from the village of Old Multan, inhabited by a Finno-Ugric people, the Votiaks (today known as Udmurts), in the taiga-covered triangle between the Volga and Kama Rivers, some 150 miles northeast of Kazan. With amazing readiness, local authorities and educated society assumed that the body lying openly across a trail in the forest belonged to the victim of a ritual carried out by Votiaks from Old Multan. Ten of them were accused of the ritual murder of a Russian and put on trial, in what became known as the Multan case. The case dragged on for four years and was heard three times by a jury. Two different juries convicted seven Votiak men to hard labor for sacrificing a Russian to their "pagan gods." Both convictions had been annulled by the Senate before the Votiaks were finally acquitted in the third trial, largely because of the publicity brought to the case by Vladimir Korolenko and Russian journalists. This was the first blood libel trial where both the prosecution and the defense relied on the expertise of ethnographers in framing their arguments. In addition, generalizations about the "common practices" of a whole ethnoconfessional group were deemed relevant for determining an individual's liability. In this regard, the trial differed from previous trials of Jews accused of ritual murder—the only precedent of a blood libel trial in the past.[7] Jews could be suspected of practicing human sacrifices, but their trials would be based on a regular criminal investigation and medical expertise rather than on any specialized scientific ethnographic theory.[8]

It is far from obvious how the version of a ritual murder appeared as natural to the educated public in the Malmyzh district of Viatka province, as well as to many observers in neighboring Kazan province. Just several decades earlier nobody had heard about this "well-known ancient ritual" of the Votiaks, and even in the course of the trial itself those contemporaries who remained ignorant of it but actually knew Votiak culture did not necessarily recognize "the ancient ritual." Thus, the medical student Boris Agafonov—son of the well-known Kazan historian of local antiquities and editor of the *Kamsko-Volzhskaia gazeta*, Nikolai Iakovlevich Agafonov—in 1893 found himself in a remote village of the Birsk district of Ufa province. He worked as a district physician's assistant, was overwhelmed with the amount and complexity of practice, and rarely got a chance to read or even see fresh newspapers. The majority of peasants in the area were Votiaks. In a letter to his father sent on June 16, 1893, Boris described them as "quite a strange people. Their type, clothes, and even language strongly resemble that of Tatars; they follow Mohammedan law, but at the same time perform all pagan rites and from time to time offer prayers to trees, specially fenced for this purpose near each village. Here you cannot find a single Orthodox missionary, which explains why there are no Orthodox Votiaks. They live quite peacefully and honestly, although drunkenness is widely spread among them."[9] Having been unaware of the Multan case, Boris continued to share with his father his observations about the Birsk Votiaks and their pagan traditions, but the theme of human sacrifice never appeared in his correspondence.

James Frazer, who also mentioned Votiaks in his survey of primitive cultures and rituals, read a very similar account. He noted that according to local beliefs, a Russian would die the next day if he "ventured to hew a tree" in one of their sacred groves. However, his source of information, an 1882 ethnographic study authored by a district physician with experience similar to that of Boris Agafonov, did not mention even a rumor about the possibility of human sacrifice by Votiaks.[10] And one century earlier, when this isolated and most underdeveloped and primitive group (as they were described by contemporary visitors and observers) of all peoples of the region was subjected to the first systematic ethnographic survey, the enlightened European author did not even think to ascribe to Votiaks an attribute so savage as human sacrifices. Listing quite a number of actual or imagined superstitions shared by Votiaks, he mentioned only "horses, horned stock, sheep, goats, geese, ducks, woodpeckers, raw and cooked honey, beer and different pies" as their sacrificial objects.[11] Christian missionaries who actively worked among the Votiaks and were prone to stress the need for their baptism never referred to human sacrifice as a Votiak custom. A report to the annual meeting of the St. Guria Brotherhood in Kazan (the leading missionary organization in the region) composed as late as 1873, did not mention human sacrifices when depicting in minute detail Votiak animist rituals.[12]

An ardent critic of the missionary activities in the region and one of the most influential Russian intellectuals, Alexander Herzen, observed Votiaks on the way to and during his stay in internal exile in Viatka (1835–1837). He described them as "miserable, shy, and dull," and their songs, language, and religion as "purely materialistic"—that is, devoid of any sophistication and abstraction. Herzen even reported on a specific type of abuse of the simple Votiaks by local police officials that retrospectively explains quite a bit about the Multan case: "If the chief officer of a district, and the chief of police, find a dead human body, they carry it, for some weeks, all about the Votiak villages, thanks to the cold which renders this possible. In every village, they say that they have just found the corpse, and that a trial will be held in that place. Then the Votiakes prefer giving a ransom."[13] In Herzen's *My Past and Thoughts* this story is immediately followed by another one, in which the same officials tried to pull a similar trick on a Russian village, but were severely punished by the smart and evidently better organized and cultured Russian peasants.[14] In general, in his narrative Herzen employed all the standard clichés of underdevelopment, from dullness and "materialistic" culture to paganism and unsanitary customs. However it never occurred to him to suspect the possibility of human ritual sacrifice as a live practice among the "miserable" victims of the Russian imperial regime. So, how did the idea of the Votiaks practicing human sacrifices acquire the status of a "fact?"

The first mention of ritual human sacrifices by Votiaks dates back only to the middle of the nineteenth century. Alexandra Andreevna Fuchs—the wife of Karl Friedrich Fuchs, a professor of natural history, botany, and medicine at Kazan University and a renowned amateur Orientalist—pioneered the topic in a series of essays for a local newspaper. She was one of the most educated women in the region and hosted an exclusive literary salon, wrote poetry and prose, and, not unlike her husband, enthusiastically studied local ethnography. In 1844 this interest extended to the Votiaks when she traveled to the remote area of the Volga-Kama interfluve. Alexandra Fuchs claimed that Votiaks sacrificed their old people to the spirits of ancestors (senicide). She did not find any firsthand evidence of this practice, but was told "stories" that looked credible to someone knowledgeable in modern archaeology and folklore of the "primitives."[15] Given the fact that senicide was a rare form of sacrifice and never mentioned in other sources, it is possible that Fuchs and her informants were influenced by the stories of senicide in the writings of Herodotus or, closer to home, of Nikolai Mikhailovich Karamzin. In the first volume of his celebrated *History of the Russian State*, published in 1818, Karamzin wrote about the ancient Slavic custom of "the right of children to murder parents overburdened by senium and illnesses, onerous to the family and useless to fellow citizens."[16]

Ten years after Alexandra Fuchs published her observations on the Votiaks, another self-fashioned ethnographer and writer much more visible and influential than the provincial female author, Sergei Vasilyevich Maksimov, promoted the hearsay legend about human sacrifices among Votiaks in a popular magazine catering to the broad educated public empire-wide.[17] Maksimov was not a romantic writer of the earlier epoch: he received medical training first at Moscow University and then at the St. Petersburg Medical-Surgical Academy, and he was highly receptive to a biological understanding of human differences.[18] He wandered on foot in the most remote areas of Russia (including those populated by Votiaks) and published literary sketches of his impressions. Later, Maksimov became quite critical of his qualification as an ethnographer at this earlier stage of his career, but this did not compromise the wide appeal of his ethnographies with the public, which culminated in an invitation from the Naval Ministry to join an ambitious ethnographic expedition (1856–1857).[19] The expedition endowed Maksimov with the status of a real scholar, and added authority to his writings, which spoke to the Naval Ministry, the Academy of Sciences, and the popular press. Still, it took another twenty years before the idea of Votiaks practicing human sacrifices was articulated in a proper academic context. During the Fourth Archaeological Congress in Kazan in 1877, Evpl Titovich Soloviev, an active local scholar and zemstvo activist, mentioned in passing (and apparently referring to common knowledge) that the Votiaks procured sacrificial human blood every thirty years. This allegation was then challenged by another local congress participant, the author of a Chuvash-Russian dictionary, Nikolai Ivanovich Zolotnitskii, who actually studied Finno-Ugric peoples of the region and denied the validity of these stories "at the present time."[20] On October 4, 1884, many participants in this discussion gathered at the Society for Archeology, History, and Ethnography of the Imperial Kazan University to listen to their colleague's presentation, "Pagan Priestly [zhrecheskaia] Hierarchy among the Pagan Votiaks."[21] The presenter, S. K. Kuznetsov, discussed two strata in the hierarchy: healers/sorcerers and pagan priests/sacrificers. But neither of them was believed to practice human sacrifice.

Thus, with a few characteristic exceptions, until the late 1880s we do not find any sustained or even noticeable discourse on Votiak sacrificial rituals. This presents a striking contrast to the tradition of the antisemitic blood libel canard, which had a well-documented history throughout the nineteenth century and earlier epochs, or even the intensifying obsession with "inhuman rituals" of various Christian sects that also left a steady paper trail during the nineteenth century.[22] While both Jewish blood libel accusations and antisectarian propaganda could be responsible for the growing popularity of rumors about human sacrifices among the residents of the Volga-Kama region, the case of the Votiaks proves that there is no need for a long prehistory of such accusations to connect them with a particular group. What is required is an authoritative scholarly worldview that embraces the possibility of such acts and convincing explanatory models.

It seems that in the second half of the 1880s, abstract anthropological knowledge was localized by the educated public of the Volga-Kama region (through efforts by local zemstvo functionaries, physicians, and teachers, such as Soloviev or Zolotnitskii), and "unspecified rumors" became incorporated into a new worldview. This is the moment when information about Votiak sacrificial rituals began to appear regularly in the local press: every case was duly dismissed as counterfactual or a misunderstanding, but the very possibility of human sacrifices remained beyond the sphere of critical inquiry. This possibility was recognized as a legitimate research topic by ethnographers affiliated with Kazan University—at the time, the major educational center of the Volga region. This happened not because of any new empirical evidence, but in response to the request of the local educated public (which, it should be added, also demonstrated a rather high degree of ethnographic theoretical awareness).

The following passage documents this process of converting general theoretical interest into a practical research agenda, and the discontent of empiricist researchers of the earlier generation with this discursive intervention. The author of the passage, Vasilii Konstantinovich Magnitskii, was a local amateur scholar and former criminal investigator who worked at the time as an inspector of public schools. He angrily quoted from a study of the leading expert on Votiak rituals, the Kazan University professor Ivan Nikolaevich Smirnov, peppering his citation with comments in parentheses and italicized words: "In the Birsk district we were directly asked (by whom? by Russians or Votiaks?) *whether it is true* that Viatka Votiaks sacrifice humans to their gods, and then they (who?) told us that Birsk Votiaks firmly believe in this, and that they (Votiaks?) know or, *maybe*, used to know such people who had been designated for sacrifice but managed to escape from the Votiaks with only insignificant injuries."[23]

Magnitskii, who was born in 1839 and graduated from the Faculty of Law of Kazan University in 1862, implied that this line of reasoning was unscientific. But Ivan Smirnov belonged to a different generation of scholars: born in 1856, he graduated with a degree in history from the same university as Magnitskii in 1878, and turned to the study of ethnography, being profoundly influenced by Tylor. To him, it was only logical to discover in the 1880s that the folklore of the Votiaks preserved many remnants (understood as "survivals") of the practice of human sacrifice.[24]

Although the Multan case has been routinely compared to Jewish blood libel trials, and the prosecutor began his speech by referring to the accusation of ritual murder against Jews as a way to frame the case against the Votiaks, this was not a hate-driven trial.[25] The forensic expertise was inconclusive and witness testimonies were contradictory, and the two court convictions were mostly based on the expert testimony of Professor Smirnov, who had never before exhibited any personal or ideological bias against the Votiaks. A true Tylorian, he believed in the universal path of human progress toward civilized cultural and social forms (religion, science, and modern political formations) that, in the case of the Russian Empire, were Russian cultural and social forms influenced by Christianity's moral and ethics. In the 1880s Smirnov was known as a proponent of the imperial civilizing mission and one of the most consistent evolutionists among Russian humanities professors.[26] His papers preserved in the university archive contain multiple letters to him from colleagues, educated readers, representatives of Russian academic societies, and editors of professional periodicals. They sought Smirnov's expert advice and solicited contributions to various collections and journals such as *Etnograficheskoe obozrenie*, recently established in Moscow (1889).[27] Provincial intellectuals in their letters often asked this popular professor to personally mail them his publications at a discounted rate. One such correspondent from Yaroslavl, who characterized himself as "a man of modest means" for whom the price "did matter" and who was not a scholar himself, attached to his letter (1891) an almost complete list of Smirnov's academic works that he wanted to purchase. The list included titles that in the late 1880s and early 1890s bore a clearly sensational appeal, such as "Traces of Human Sacrifices in the Poetry and Religious Rites of Volga Finns" or "The Votiaks."[28] The latter work by Smirnov was completed and published before the trial. It concluded with the optimistic assertion that "it should not take another hundred years before the last Votiak becomes Russian."[29] In "The Votiaks," as in all other Smirnov's ethnographic studies, the inquiry was structured by the accepted pattern of evolutionist analysis. As a rule, his books featured special chapters on the development of family forms, religion (from fetishism and animism to the highest—monotheist—stage), and oral traditions.[30] Hence, for Smirnov, these were not the ten Votiaks being prosecuted, but some of their archaic ethnographic "survivals."

As the case progressed and the political pressure grew, Smirnov's optimistic evolutionist belief in the Votiaks' advancement toward becoming civilized Russians evaporated. By the time of the last trial, he was already talking about the fixed racial border between the "half-savage" Votiaks and their civilizing Russian guardians. Fresh from the courtroom battles, Smirnov took part in debates about the desirable focus for the new ethnographic museum planned in St. Petersburg (the Russian Museum). He now assumed the language of race, and in his strategic planning stopped short of positing the existence of a Russian race as endowed with superior qualities.[31] Thus, Ivan Smirnov proceeded from positing civilizational (historical and temporal) borders between the stages of the universal historical process and ended up rendering them as racial (fixed and unchanging) ones. This was the conceptual evolution of someone who wholeheartedly embraced the possibility that Votiaks engaged in ritual human sacrifices, even though he was not motivated by personal biases, the inertia of a tradition of similar accusations, or newly discovered facts. Essentially, the whole affair was not so much about the Votiaks, but about the new imagination of the cultural and political communities in the empire.

Edward Tylor provided educated Russians with a general map of the historical process as a universally applicable and unilinear succession of stages. Essentially built on the classical liberal episteme, this worldview envisioned a fairly stable and segregated commonwealth, where individual human groups were divided by oceans, centuries, or class status. But what happens if these solid boundaries collapse and everyone comes together, contaminating pure types and discarding clear distinctions, as was the case in the modernizing Russian Empire of the 1890s? This was a turbulent decade that witnessed a large-scale public famine relief campaign in 1892 trigger an unprecedented mobilization of civil society, the formation of modern social parties such as the Dashnaktsutyun in 1890 and the Polish Socialist Party in 1892, and the engagement of increasing number of people with modern ideas and public discourses.[32] The fact that the actual perpetrators of the crime—Russian peasants from a village near Multan who wanted to implicate their neighbors because of a mundane conflict over land—disguised the murder as a blood libel and told police that Votiaks "sacrificed human beings to their gods in times of great need" suggests that they had well mastered the intellectuals' discourse of ritual murder, and knew how to use modern legal procedures and the influential language of human difference to their advantage.[33]

The entire episode with the sudden discovery of "traditional" human sacrifices among the Votiaks thus appears as a metaphor (with ugly practical implications) for the meaning of "otherness" in modern Russian imperial society. Indeed, the prehistoric "savage" was found in the heartland region of the Russian Empire colonized in the sixteenth century, and not in the recently integrated Polish-Lithuanian lands forming the Pale of Jewish Settlement. As a journalist of one Kazan newspaper wrote in 1894, "It's hard to [accept the fact] that this incident occurred not somewhere in central Africa, India, or Polynesia, but just [two hundred miles] from a university city which is the center of missionary work."[34] Thus, the real issue at stake behind the trial was the question: who should belong to the Russian nation, and on what grounds? Given the ambiguity of the concept of Russianness in the late imperial period, and the absence of a developed analytical vocabulary for discussing the problem of cultural categorization, the growing intellectual anxiety expressed itself through the vivid imagery of internal aliens as prehistoric savages mutilating the body of a modern Russian and sacrificing him to their archaic idols.

Perhaps the fascination with one exotic ancient ritual that compelled James Frazer to expand his original study sixfold over the course of the twenty years was akin to the reaction of Russian educated society to the discovery that "savagery" was not a stage of historical development but rather an omnipresent condition.[35] Whether defined as religious, linguistic, economic, or political otherness, "savagery" could be eliminated, contained, or incorporated. That was the spectrum of options still to be elaborated into ideologies of modern mass politics.

The Beilis Case

Two decades divided the Multan case and the most infamous "Russian" blood libel trial—the Beilis case (1911–1913). Jewish human sacrifice had emerged as a popular stereotype well before Tylor and Frazer and, as the nineteenth-century blood libel trials confirmed, the medieval superstition had adapted well to the new scholarly language of modern ethnography and medicine, and to the new political context of a nationalizing society.[36] However, the Multan case throws new light on the Beilis case by showing how minor the role of "tradition" and traditional hatred in particular could be, and how critical a new fascination with savagery as a persistent defect of modernity was. The Beilis case structurally resembled the Multan case: the same competitive legal procedure; the same contradictory evidence and witness testimonies, and even greater publicity; the same far-reaching ideological implications for the accused (as a special group of *inorodtsy*); and for the Russian imperial order, the same pronounced role of scientific expertise. In this case, too, references to the archaic ritual concealed the invention of a new tradition.

The most prominent expert for the prosecution at the Beilis trial was Kiev University's psychiatry professor Ivan Alekseevich Sikorsky, while his no less famous opponents included St. Petersburg Military-Medical Academy professor and neurologist Vladimir Mikhailovich Bekhterev, professor at the same academy and surgeon Evgenii Vasil'evich Pavlov, and a few other reputable scientists.[37] They were not just regular forensic physicians, but highly acclaimed scholars who were expected to uncover the hidden truth by reading the corpse as a text—not by interpreting sacred Jewish texts. The body of the victim and the psychological examination of the perpetrator, who for experts such as Sikorsky stood for the collective Jewish body and psyche, could reveal—but only to a specialist!—all that the superficial disguise of mass culture, political liberalism, and urban civility presumably hid from mundane observers. The blood libel as presented in court was a barbaric crime of a particular Jew against one defenseless Christian boy, and at the same time the crime of the entire Jewish race against modern civilization itself.[38] Sikorsky claimed that to explain the murder of Iushchinskii, "one has to confine himself to considerations of an historical and anthropological character" and treat the murderer as a "criminal anthropological type." "One must admit, with the anthropological criminologists," continued Sikorsky, "that the psychological basis of crimes of that type is sought in racial revenge."[39]

This was a radical post-Tylorian position acknowledging the dangerous omnipresence of savages in an age where they did not belong, and the mortal hold of their "survivals" on progress. Social Darwinism helped make sense of this macabre worldview by reframing the progressive, unilinear vision of history as the eternal competition of races. This social imagination was determined by a radically modernist understanding of groupness as based on a biological race. Using the disturbing imagery of "blood libel," scientists like Sikorsky were no longer concerned with the Christian blood sacrificed for ritual purposes by infidels. Now it was all about Jewish blood—meaning the Jewish race. In the context of the turn of the century discussions about Jewishness, such a transformation was rather predictable, for racialized interpretations of Jewish identity dominated not only what is known in historiography as a new antisemitism, but contemporary scientific, especially medical and anthropological, discourses.[40]

If Tylor inspired a liberal and humanist philosophy of history in which "savagery" was immanent to any culture during a certain period of its development and individual "survivals" could be cured or eliminated without affecting society in general, the new philosophy of history exhibited by Sikorsky reconsidered differences as a synchronous phenomenon of incompatible cultures, civilizations, and races. The ethnographic savage was no longer relegated to the prehistoric epoch; it was perceived as someone living amid civilized society as lower classes or inferior races. Now the entire "savage group" was thought of as a collective "survival," and to get rid of that survival of the primitive epoch, modern society needed to isolate or purge completely the whole group compromised by its embedded savageness. The Beilis case was about the ultimate dehumanization of the Jewish race and its extermination (at least on the symbolic level).

As such, this case, just like Sikorsky's academic and popular writings about Russian race/nation and postimperial Russian nationalism, were literally implementations of Frazer's metaphor of ritual human sacrifice as scapegoating. Jews in this discourse had to compensate for all the inadequacies of Russians as moderns. Early twentieth-century Russian nationalism in general was radically divided into several incompatible interpretations of Russianness based on territorial, political, ethnic, religious, and racial characteristics. To make matters worse, in neither of these versions of Russianness did the Russian nation look more developed, cultured, or politically better organized—in short, more modern—than other groups of the empire. The venerated Slavophile philosophical tradition insisted that the Russian peasant and the peasant commune (reportedly a living survival of the prehistoric period) were the embodiment of the Russian nation. The dominant narrative of Russian history essentially supported this trope in the authoritative language of positivist historiography. So how could a group defined by its "survival" institutions and practices be recognized as a vanguard modern nation? To resolve this dilemma, Russian nationalists followed in the footsteps of their peers in other countries such as Germany or the United States and projected all the elements of archaic otherness on a minority group branded as the ultimate Other. They were inspired by science and believed in the idea of the nation defined by the commonality of historical experience, traditions, language, racial makeup, and national territory. In the post-Tylorian understanding of historical progress, this group of eternal savages could not be changed and integrated, only contained or eliminated. The inferior race was nominated as a sacrificial scapegoat that should take on itself all of society's "sins," which were previously rendered as archaisms, wherever that group was destined to be relocated, symbolically or physically. This was an amazingly archaic logic—in fact, the logic of a ritual human sacrifice—but this is what actually happened in the first decades of the twentieth century. The Beilis case in Russia was a vivid manifestation of this new logic of social imagination, and it was indeed about human sacrifice—the sacrifice of Russian Jewry for the sake of symbolically salvaging the modernity of the Russian nation—illiterate and socially formless, economically backward, and politically passive.

It is a telling coincidence that James Frazer published the ninth volume of the third edition of his *Golden Bough, The Scapegoat* in the year of the Beilis trial (1913). The volume was devoted entirely to the phenomenon of ritually transferring one's own faults to a chosen victim. Unlike the first edition, here Frazer explicitly spoke about the persistence of the archaic ritual in the present, about a "survival" proving to be a living phenomenon.

Jewish Blood as a Path to Jewish Modernity

What complicates scapegoating as a metaphor and a historical reality is the fact that many turn-of-the-century Jewish intellectuals in Europe, North America, and Russia partook of the same racialized discourse. Many of them found in "race" a new conceptual framework allowing the reintegration of a fragmented Jewry that seemed to be losing any common denominator in the age of secularization, nation-states, linguistically based social identities, and increasing class polarization. Regardless of the ideological positions of various participants in this truly international debate, all of them shared the perception of Jews as a race that was fundamentally different from European races, exhibiting clear signs of degeneration. Only the Jewish experts—physicians, demographers, anthropologists, psychiatrists—stressed the role of environmental and cultural conditions that were responsible for the "degeneration" of the Jewish body. Their opponents, on the contrary, stressed the biological and irreversible nature of Jewish "savageness."

Since the second half of the nineteenth century, Jewish public discussions had evolved around the problem of nationality, deliberated in connection with such issues as acculturation, integration, assimilation, language policy, the struggle for general/individual versus collective/national rights, the choice between cultural autonomy, and the slogan of nation-state. Treatments of the main problem of Jewish nationality could vary significantly; however, they coincided in one point—the recognition of the need to address "survivals" in the life of contemporary Jews. Often these survivals were understood as reflected in Jewish bodily constitution. The more acutely the need for the cure was felt by modern intellectuals, the greater the role of the idiom of blood and bodily metaphors became in these debates. "Dear brothers! Our nation is sick," wrote Dr. Leib Gelbak in a conspicuously medicalized language in the journal *Rassvet* as early as 1860. "I invite you to a consultation; we will check its pulse, in which flows pure Jerusalem blood, and rationally we will treat its wounds, on which was formed so much scarred fabric."[41] Or consider the following statement by a certain M.O. in the Russian-Jewish journal *Voskhod*: "The Russian-Jewish body looks like something very far from a unified whole that is full of life juices, youthful freshness, and might; it does not resemble a body on which deep wounds heal quickly and various losses recoup easily."[42] One can provide numerous examples in this vein. Even though the Jews, just like the Votiaks in the Multan case, knew that the medieval blood libel was pure fantasy, they could not be so sure about the hidden internal power of their "ancient" blood that was making them Jewish even when culturally and subjectively they felt otherwise. As a cofounder of the World Zionist Organization together with Theodor Herzl, a physician, and the author of the work *Degeneration* (1892), emblematic of the medicalized approach to social reality, Max Nordau declared in 1901:

> We must know more. We must know with greater precision about the national material with which we have to work. We need exact anthropological, biological, economic, and intellectual statistics of the Jewish People. We must have quantitative answers to the following questions: how is the Jewish People physiologically constituted? What is the average size? What are the anatomical characteristics? What are the numbers of diseased Jews? . . . As long as this remains unknown, whatever one seeks to do for the nation will be a fumbling in the dark; and whatever one says about this nation will be, at best, poetry.[43]

"The sense of national specificity lies in the man's 'blood,' in his physical-racial type, and only there," wrote one of Max Nordau's admirers and the best known leader of Russian Zionism, Vladimir (Zeev) Jabotinsky, in 1904.[44] Jabotinsky consistently spoke about "blood" and "pure-blooded" Jews not only in metaphoric terms but also in a neopositivistic mode outlined by Nordau:

> That is why we do not believe in spiritual [i.e., cultural] assimilation. For a Jew who is born without any admixtures into generations of Jewish blood to adopt the psyche of a German or a Frenchman is physically as inconceivable as for a Negro to cease being a Negro. It is even more inconceivable, because the nucleus of one's psyche is a much more inseparable and irremovable race feature than the color of skin, facial index, or shape of the skull. A Jew reared among Germans may adopt German traditions, words, and habits, [he can] be soaked to the bone with German fluid [*nemetskoi zhidkostiu*]—but the nucleus of his psyche would remain Jewish, because his blood, his body, and his physical-racial type are Jewish.[45]
>
> It is not within the power of a human being to assimilate with people of a different blood. For true assimilation, one has to change the body: to become kin by blood, that is, through a sequence of mixed marriages over the course of many dozens of years, to produce a great-grandson who would have only a negligible admixture of Jewish blood. . . . There is no other way. As long as we remain Jews by blood, the children of a Jew and a Jewess, we may be subject to threats of persecutions, disdain, or degradation, but assimilation in the proper sense of the word, assimilation as a complete disappearance of our psychological specificity—is of no danger to us.[46]

"Do not call yourselves nationalists," Jabotinsky cautioned his Jewish political opponents, "for nationalists are those who aspire to preserve their tribal specificity forever and by all means."[47]

It is not accidental, therefore, that the main ideologist of Jews as a race survival, Sikorsky, was Jabotinsky's ideal interlocutor. They spoke the same scientific language and believed in "tribal specificity" and the power of blood, and they were both aggressive modernists who despised "survivals." In 1911 Jabotinsky literally played out his dialogue with someone like Sikorsky in the feuilleton *Exchange of Compliments: A Conversation* in which a Jew and gentile discuss the role of race in understanding human relations.[48] The Jewish protagonist started with a statement that humanity was divided into races, but they were all equal and ranking them hierarchically had no scientific grounds. To a skeptical remark from the Russian, "How come? Chukchis and Hellenes are equals?" he replied that if put in conditions similar to those of ancient Hellenes, Chukchis would have produced values equal to those that the Hellenes gave to the world.[49]

The very opposition of Chukchis and Hellenes in this context reminds us of the peculiar coexistence of Chukchis and Jews in a Russian-Jewish populist discourse where both stood for idealized communal and traditional peoples, unspoiled by capitalism and colonial interventionism.[50] The well-known Russian

Jewish ethnographers and political activists such as S. An-sky and Lev Shternberg embraced this understanding of primitivism that some scholars today describe as "an unspoken paradox": "Jews were at once civilized and semi-savage, ethnographers and potential objects of ethnography. . . . By the beginning of the twentieth century, the Pale of Settlement had produced numerous intellectuals, artists, political activists, and ethnographers, but An-sky suggested that its Jewish residents were still somehow akin to 'Buryats, Yakagirs, Giliaks, Chukchis, and others.'"[51]

The Jew from Jabotinsky's feuilleton and his Russian interlocutor articulated this "unspoken paradox," but did not really see it as such. They both understood primitivism in light of race science. For Sikorsky this was the diagnosis of a "savage" group. Repeating his writings on the topic almost verbatim, the Russian from *Exchange of Compliments* classified Jews as an "obviously defective" race with "big organic spiritual deficiencies." For Jabotinsky this was a curable condition of a group, but the only cure that he offered was the reconnection of the Jewish racial body with its primordial soil. Thus, the approach influenced by modern scientific discourse objectified the romantic "blood and soil" principle by connecting the formation of "race" to a particular primordial territory. Jews were destined to degenerate and indeed become a "survival" everywhere except in Palestine. Unlike in real life, in his feuilleton Jabotinsky controlled the discourse, and he allowed the Jew to have the last word: "We are an indomitable race forever and ever. I do not know a higher aristocratism than this one."[52] Aristocratism—a favorite word in Jabotinsky's writings on nationalism—connoted dignity, but like any aristocratism it had to be based on the exclusivity of origins, on "blue" and old aristocratic blood.

This fixation on "Jewish blood" as a material carrier of Jewishness in modern culture made many Jewish intellectuals hostages of the "savage" discourse. While stimulating radical constructivist nation-building initiatives, it also bequeathed ambiguity, implicit in the different readings of living survivals. One can certainly trace this ambiguity in political Zionism. It is even more evident in politically all-inclusive Jewish mass social initiatives such as the Society for the Preservation of the Health of the Jewish Population (Obshchestvo okhraneniia zdorov'ia evreiskogo naseleniia), founded in Petersburg in 1912 and especially active after the 1917 Revolution in the former Western borderlands of the Russian Empire and in interwar Eastern Europe.[53] Anthropology, demography, and eugenics rooted in the post-Tylorian ethnographic paradigm played a visible role in Jewish scholarship and education in interwar Eastern Europe.[54] The same ambiguous legacy informed the studies of blood groups, and especially Jewish blood group data in the Soviet Union of the 1920s and early 1930s, which in turn anticipated the blood group population genetics in Israel during the 1950s.[55] The discourse of Jewish regeneration in many ways mirrored the discourse of Jewish degeneration, amalgamating such concepts as living "savages" and "survivals."

Blood libel as it had been constructed in turn-of-the-century legal, scholarly, and public discourses meant that Jewish identity now "resided in very real physical and mental attributes" and did not require external validation to be established as such.[56] The invention of the modern blood libel generated the mode of national imagination that had dramatically ended in the Holocaust, but also the mode of Jewish nationalism that had triumphantly reemerged in the Jewish state after World War II. As Nadia Abu El-Haj writes about population genetics based on the study of blood groups in Israel in the 1950s and 1960s, this was a practice "wedded to the work of *imagining* the nation" on ancient Palestine's soil.[57]

Looking back at theories advanced by Tylor, Frazer, and their Russian counterparts, it seems that anthropologists and ethnologists were acute observers of their societies, writing a self-fulfilling prophecy rather than discovering the ultimate truth about the mores of "savage" cultures of other epochs and regions. In the evolutionist scheme of history constructed by Tylor and Frazer, science occupied the third and highest stage of progressive human development. When science was put into the service of the modern nationalist episteme to sanction a large-scale ritual sacrifice of "savage" groups in the name of progress (through the modern-day blood libel concept), it fell short of its intended high idealist mission. Science became Holy Scripture for the national "religion of common blood."

> MARINA MOGILNER, an Associate Professor at University of Illinois at Chicago, holds the Edward and Marianna Thaden Chair in Russian and East European Intellectual History. Since 1999, she is the cofounder and co-editor of the *Ab Imperio Quarterly,* dedicated to studies in new imperial history and interdisciplinary and comparative study of nationalism and nationalities in the post-Soviet space. Her last book discusses the development of race science and racialized discourses in the Russian Empire: *Homo Imperii: A History of Physical Anthropology in Russia* (2013). Her current research project focuses on Russian-Jewish engagements with the concept of "race" in science, politics, and beyond.

NOTES

1. Richard S. Wortman, Scenarios of Power: *Myth and Ceremony in Russian Monarchy from Peter the Great to the Abdication of Nicholas II* (Princeton, NJ: Princeton University Press, 2006).

2. Edward Tylor, *Primitive Culture: Researches into the Development of Mythology, Philosophy, Religion, Art, and Custom,* 2 vols. (London: John Murray, 1871), 1:15.

3. Eduard B. Teilor [Edward Tylor], *Pervobytnaia kul'tura*, trans. D. A. Koropchevskii, vols. 1–2 (St. Petersburg: Znanie, 1872, 1873). The Russian translation of *Primitive Culture* appeared before the book came out in any other language. The Russian edition of Tylor's fundamental *Anthropology* (1881) followed in 1882. See Margaret Hodgen, *The Doctrine of Survivals: A Chapter in the History of Scientific Method in the Study of Man* (London: Allenson, 1936), 67.

4. Robert Angus Downie, *James George Frazer: The Portrait of a Scholar* (London: Watts and Co., 1940), 9; James George Frazer, *The Golden Bough: A Study in Comparative Religion* (New York: MacMillan, 1894), 1:vii.

5. The first translation of *The Golden Bough* into Russian from the abridged French edition appeared only in 1928. See Dzh. Frezer, *Zolotaia vetv'*, trans. P. F. Preobrazhenskii (Moscow: Ateist, 1928).

6. James George Frazer, *The Golden Bough: A Study in Magic and Religion*, 3rd ed. (New York: MacMillan, 1913), 9:1–2.

7. For a detailed analysis of the trial, see Robert Geraci, *Window on the East: National and Imperial Identities in Late Tsarist Russia* (Ithaca, NY: Cornell University Press, 2001). He also was among the first researchers to notice the structural similarity between the Multan and Beilis cases. See Geraci, "Ethnic Minorities, Anthropology, and Russian National Identity on Trial: The Multan Case, 1892–96," *Russian Review* 52, no. 4 (2000): 530–54. Robert Weinberg also mentions in passing the connection between the Beilis case and the Multan trial (*Blood Libel in Late Imperial Russia: The Ritual Murder Trial of Mendel Beilis* [Bloomington: Indiana University Press, 2014], 9). Harriet Murav has brought the two cases together to reflect on the intersection of law, culture, and power in "The Beilis Ritual Murder Trial and the Culture of Apocalypse," *Cardozo Studies in Law and Literature* 12, no. 2 (2000): 243–63.

8. An excellent example of historical analysis of one such criminal file as a microhistory of local moral economy and customs is Eugene Avrutin, "Ritual Murder in a Russian Border Town," *Jewish History* 26, nos. 3–4 (2012): 309–26.

9. A letter from Boris Agafonov to Nikolai Agafonov, July 16, 1893, Otdel rukopisei i redkikh knig Nauchnoi biblioteki imeni N.I. Lobachevskogo (hereafter ORB, KFU Library), Collection "Agafonov Nikolai Iakovlevich (1842–1908)," d. 213 (Correspondence), vol. 1, ll. 13–14.

10. Frazer, *The Golden Bough: A Study in Comparative Religion*, 65. Frazer relied on the study by a former zemstvo district physician in the region: Max Buch, *Die Wotjäken, eine Ethnologische Studie: Unter Wogulen und Ostjaken* (Helsinki: Druckerei der Finnischen litteraturgesellschaft, 1882).

11. Johann Gottlieb Georgi, *Opisanie vsekh obitaiushchikh v Rossiiskom gosudarstve narodov. Ikh zhiteiiskikh obriadov, obyknovenii, odezhd, zhilishch, uprazhnenii, zabav, veroispovedanii i drugikh dostopamiatnostei* (St. Petersburg: Imperial Academy of Sciences, 1799), 54.

12. See *Godichnoe sobranie bratstva sv. Guriia 30 oktiabria 1873 g.* (Kazan, Russia: Tipografiia universiteta, 1874), 24.

13. Aleksandr Herzen, *My Exile*, 2 vols. (London: Hurst and Blackett, 1855), 1:241.

14. Ibid., 1:241–42.

15. A. A. Fuks, "Poezdka k kazanskim Votiakam," *Kazanskie gubernskie vedomosti*, no. 14–29 (1844). For a complete collection, see Aleksandra Fuks, "Poezdka k votiakam Kazanskoi gubernii," in *Pis'ma A. A. Fuks k suprugu ee K. F. Fuksu* (Kazan, Russia: n.p., 1844).

16. N. M. Karamzin, *Istoriia gosudarstva Rossiiskogo* (Moscow: Olma, 2003), 1:28.

17. S. Maksimov, "Votiaki," *Biblioteka dlia chteniia* 134, no. 12 (1855): 53–89.

18. Aleksei Vdovin, "Russkaia etnografiia 1850-kh godov i etos tsivilizatorskoi missii: Sluchai 'literaturnoi ekspeditsii' morskogo ministerstva," *Ab Imperio* 1 (2014): 91–126.

19. S. V. Maksimov, *Na vostoke: Poezdka na Amur (v 1860–1861 godakh). Dorozhnye zametki i vospominaniia* (St. Petersburg: Obshchestvennaia polza, 1864), 3. On Maksimov's ethnography,

see Catherine Black Clay, "Russian Ethnographers in the Service of Empire," *Slavic Review* 54, no. 1 (1995): 45–51; and Vdovin, "Russkaia etnografiia 1850-kh godov."

20. *Trudy IV arkheologicheskogo s"ezda v Rossii* 1 (Kazan, Russia: Tipografiia universiteta, 1884): cviii.

21. "Minutes of the XLI General Meeting of the Members of the Imperial Kazan University's Society for Archeology, History and Ethnography, October 4, 1884 (Saturday)" at ORB, KFU Library, Collection Obshchestvo arkheologii, istorii i etnografii (hereafter OAIE), d. 7.585-1 (Arkhiv OAIE), l. 135.

22. On the blood libel, see, e.g., Alan Dundes, ed., *The Blood Libel Legend: A Case-book in Anti-Semitic Folklore* (Madison: University of Wisconsin, Press, 1991); R. Po-chia Hsia, *The Myth of Ritual Murder: Jews and Magic in Reformation Germany* (New Haven, CT: Yale University Press, 1998); and Joshua Trachtenberg, *The Devil and the Jews: The Medieval Conception of the Jew and Its Relation to Modern Anti-Semitism* (Philadelphia: Jewish Publication Society, 1983). On sectarian movements, see Laura Engelstein, *Castration and the Heavenly Kingdom: A Russian Folktale* (Ithaca, NY: Cornell University Press, 2003); Nicholas B. Breyfogle, *Heretics and Colonizers: Forging Russia's Empire in the South Caucasus* (Ithaca, NY: Cornell University Press, 2005); Irina Paert, *Old Believers, Religious Dissent, and Gender in Russia 1760–1850* (Manchester: Manchester University Press, 2003); Vadim Menzhulin, *Drugoi Sikorskii: Neudobnye stranitsy istorii psikhiatrii* (Kiev: Sfera, 2004), on Professor Ivan Sikorsky's psychiatric studies of Orthodox religious sects; and Sergei Zhuk, *Russia's Lost Reformation: Peasants, Millennialism, and Radical Sects in Southern Russia and Ukraine, 1830–1917* (Baltimore, MD: Johns Hopkins University Press, 2004).

23. V. K. Magnitskii, "Iz byta kazanskikh inorodtsev (K voprosu o chelovecheskikh zhertvoprinosheniiakh)," *Etnograficheskoe obozrenie* (July–September 1894): 139. In another work Magnitskii denounced "stories" and misinterpretations in the ethnographic reports of Alexandra Fuchs. See Magnitskii, *Materialy k ob"iasneniiu staroi chuvashskoi very* (Kazan, 1881), 123–26.

24. I. N. Smirnov, "Votiaki: Istoriko-etnograficheskii ocherk," *Izvestiia Obshchestva arkheologii i etnografii pri Imperatorskom kazanskom universitete* 7, nos. 2–3 (1890): 1–292.

25. V. G. Korolenko, "Multanskoe zhertvoprinoshenie," in his *Polnoe sobranie sochinenii* (St. Petersburg: A. E. Marks, 1914), 4:361–464.

26. Smirnov's reading of Tylor and his understanding of evolution are analyzed in Geraci, *Window on the East*, ch. 6.

27. See Smirnov's papers in ORB, KFU Library, Collection OAIE, d. 9740 (Letters from different people, 1890s–1900s).

28. A letter to Smirnov from Illarion Aleksandrovich Tikhomirov from Yaroslavl, September 6, 1891, in ibid., ll. 24–25.

29. Smirnov, "Votiaki," 308.

30. Smirnov, "Votiaki"; I. N. Smirnov, *Zadachi i znachenie mestnoi etnografii* (Kazan: IKU, 1891); Smirnov, "Permiaki: Istoriko-etnograficheskii ocherk," *Izvestiia OAIE pri IKU* 9, no. 2 (1891): 1–289; Smirnov, "Mordva: Istoriko-etnograficheskii ocherk," *Izvestiia OAIE pri IKU* 10, no. 1 (1892): 1–309.

31. I. N. Smirnov, "Neskol'ko slov po voprosu ob organizatsii etnograficheskogo otdela Russkogo muzeia Imperatora Aleksandra III," *Izvestiia Imperatorskoi akademii nauk* 15, no. 2 (1901): 229–30; Sergei Kan, *Lev Shternberg: Anthropologist, Russian Socialist, Jewish Activist* (Lincoln: University of Nebraska Press, 2009).

32. See Richard G. Robbins Jr., *Famine in Russia 1891–1892: The Imperial Government Responds to a Crisis* (New York: Columbia University Press, 1975), 176–83; W. Bruce Lincoln, *In War's Dark Shadow: The Russians before the Great War* (New York: Dial, 1983), 26; Ben Eklof,

Russian Peasant Schools: Officialdom, Village Culture, and Popular Pedagogy, 1861–1914 (Berkeley: University of California Press, 1986), 97; and David Kerans, "Agricultural Evolution and the Peasantry in Russia, Tambov Province, 1880–1915" (PhD diss., University of Pennsylvania, 1994), 432.

33. Geraci, "Multan Case," 533. On the engagement with the law, see Jane Burbank, *Russian Peasants Go to Court: Legal Culture in the Countryside, 1905–1917* (Bloomington: Indiana University Press, 2004).

34. As quoted in Geraci, "Multan Case," 535.

35. The booming interest of scholars, artists, and educated members of the public in shamanism and sacrifice as a part of different shamanistic cults that began in the 1880s, in my view, should also be revisited from the perspective of the discovery of "savagery." On ethnographic studies of shamanism in this period, see, e.g., M. A. Devlet, "A.V. Andrianov kak etnograf," *Repressirovannye etnografy*, ed. D. D. Tumarkin (Moscow: Vostochnaia literatura, 2002), 1:9–56; Andrei Znamenski, *Shamanism in Siberia: Russian Records of Indigenous Spirituality* (Norwell, MA: Kluwer Academic Publishers, 2003); Yuri Slezkine, *Arctic Mirrors: Russia and the Small Peoples of the North* (Ithaca, NY: Cornell University Press, 1994); and Peg Weiss, *Kandinsky and Old Russia: The Artist as Ethnographer and Shaman* (New Haven, CT: Yale University Press, 1986).

36. Hillel J. Kieval, "The Rules of the Game: Forensic Medicine and the Language of Science in the Structuring of Modern Ritual Murder Trials," *Jewish History* 26, no. 3 (2012): 287–307.

37. Sikorsky was quite successful in his academic and public pursuits. In Kiev he founded and edited the journal *Voprosy nervno-psikhiatricheskoi meditsiny i psikhologii* (1886–1910) and was among the founders of modern experimental child psychology; he set up the Kiev University Clinic for Nervous Disorders and the Medical-Pedagogical Institute for Mentally Challenged Children. In 1912 Sikorsky opened the world's first Institute for Child Psychopathology. He published extensively in the fields of pathological anatomy, clinical psychiatry and pedagogy, ethnic psychology, and anthropology. Sikorsky was the father of the famous airplane constructor, Igor Sikorsky, and hence I transliterate his family name according to the accepted spelling of Sikorsky (and not Sikorskii). On Sikorsky as an anthropologist and political activist, see Marina Mogilner, *Homo Imperii: A History of Physical Anthropology in Russia* (Lincoln: University of Nebraska Press, 2013), 69–77, 167–200. The best critical biography of Sikorsky as a psychiatrist is Vadim Menzhulin, *Drugoi Sikorskii*.

38. One of the most original writers of the Russian fin de siècle, Vasilii Rozanov, wrote under the influence of Sikorsky's testimony that "just as the body requires the circulation of blood, so the collective body of Israel requires sacrifice in order to sustain itself as such." Quoted in Murav, "The Beilis Ritual Murder Trial," 249.

39. Sikorsky's expert testimony is published in translation as "Document 22" in Weinberg, *Blood Libel in Late Imperial Russia*, 99–100.

40. On race in the European turn-of-the-century context, see, e.g., Neil MacMaster, *Racism in Europe, 1870–2000* (New York: Macmillan, 2001); George W. Stocking, *Race, Culture, and Evolution: Essays in the History of Anthropology* (New York: Free Press, 1968); Stocking, *Victorian Anthropology* (New York: Free Press, 1987); Stocking, ed., *Bones, Bodies, Behavior: Essays on Biological Anthropology* (Madison: University of Wisconsin Press, 1988), 180–205; Stocking, ed., *Colonial Situations: Essay on the Contextualization of Ethnographic Knowledge* (Madison: University of Wisconsin Press, 1991); Henricka Kuklick, *The Savage Within: The Social History of British Anthropology, 1885–1945* (Cambridge: Cambridge University Press, 1991); Nancy Stepan, *The Idea of Race in Science: Great Britain, 1800–1960* (Oxford: Macmillan, 1982); and George Mosse, *Toward the Final Solution: A History of European Racism* (Madison: University of Wisconsin Press, 1985). On racial discourses and race science in the Russian empire, see

Mogilner, *Homo Imperii*; and Vera Tolz, "Discourse of Race in Imperial Russia (1830–1914)," in *The Invention of Race: Scientific and Popular Representations*, ed. Nicholas Bancel, Thomas David, and Dominic Thomas (London: Routledge, 2014), 130–44.

41. L. Gelbak, "Fiziologicheskii vzgliad na zhizn' Russkikh evreev," *Rassvet* 19 (September 1860): 306–7.

42. M. O., "Za proshlyi god," *Voskhod* (March 1883): 31–48.

43. Quoted in Mitchell Hart, *Social Science and the Politics of Modern Jewish Identity* (Stanford, CA: Stanford University Press, 2000), 30.

44. V. Z. Zhabotinskii, "Pis'mo ob avtonomizme," *Evreiskaia zhizn'* 6 (1904): 116.

45. Ibid.

46. Ibid., 118.

47. Ibid., 122.

48. Vl. Zhabotinsky, "Obmen komplimentov: Razgovor," in Zhabotinsky, *Fel'etony* (St. Petersburg: Gerol'd, 1913), 181–94 (first published as Vl. Zhabotinsky, "Obmen komplimentov," *Odesskie novosti*, no. 8546 [October 16 (29), 1911]: 2).

49. Ibid., 182.

50. Gabriella Safran, "Jews as Siberian Natives: Primitivism and S. An-sky's *Dybbuk*," *Modernizm/Modernity* 13, no. 4 (2006): 635–55.

51. Nathaniel Deutsch, *The Jewish Dark Continent: Life and Death in the Russian Pale of Settlement* (Cambridge, MA: Harvard University Press, 2011), 29.

52. Ibid., 194.

53. Marina Mogilner, "'Toward a History of Russian-Jewish 'Medical Materialism': Russian-Jewish Physicians and the Politics of Jewish Biological Normalization," *Jewish Social Studies* 19, no. 1 (2012): 70–106.

54. Geoffery Cantor and Marc Swetlitz, eds., *Jewish Tradition and the Challenge of Darwinism* (Chicago: University of Chicago Press, 2006); Paul J. Weindling, "Race, Eugenics, and National Identity in the Eastern Baltic: From Racial Surveys to Racial States," in *Baltic Eugenics: Bio-Politics, Race, and Nation in Interwar Estonia, Latvia, and Lithuania 1918–1940*, ed. Bjorn Fedler and Paul Weindling (Amsterdam: Rodopi, 2013), 36.

55. Marina Mogil'ner, "Evreiskaia rasa v strane Sovetov," *Neprikosnovennyi zapas* 78, no. 4 (2011): 167–91; Nadia Abu El-Haj, *The Genealogical Science: The Search for Jewish Origins and the Politics of Epistemology* (Chicago: University of Chicago Press, 2012), 82–108.

56. Mitchell Bryan Hart, *The Healthy Jew: The Symbiosis of Judaism and Modern Medicine* (New York: Cambridge University Press, 2007), 14.

57. El-Haj, *Genealogical Science*, 64.

8

THE PREDATORY JEW AND RUSSIAN VITALISM
Dostoevsky, Rozanov, and Babel

Harriet Murav

THIS CHAPTER TRACES the peculiar fascination with the image of the bloodthirsty Jew in the broad context of the Mendel Beilis trial by focusing on three literary authors: Fyodor Dostoevsky, Vasilii Rozanov, and Isaac Babel. What happened in Kiev in 1913—the work of a "few honest and a few dishonest maniacs"—was not isolated from broader trends in Russian culture and had implications beyond that period.[1] To be sure, the image of the bloodthirsty Jew circulated widely in Russian culture, but I hope to show that what drew Dostoevsky, Rozanov, and Babel to this negative stereotype depended on their broader and more ambitious goals for themselves and for Russia and Russian literature.[2] The same words and images used by a rioter in the street and literary authors in their texts overlap to some limited extent, but there is a larger network of meaning and purpose behind the literary use, and this chapter seeks to trace its contours. I do not attempt to settle what amounts to a chicken-or-the-egg question—what came first, general circulation or specific usage on the part of these authors. In different ways, each of these writers was concerned with the "vitality" of the Russian and Jewish populations and cultures: the vitality of the Jews as a people was for Dostoevsky threatening; for Rozanov, inspiring; and for Babel, a factor in the literary salvation that he and Odessa could offer Russia. Dostoevsky and Rozanov rejected rationalist views of human society and culture. Both were deeply uncomfortable with the notion that human life could be reduced to mechanical laws and subject to mathematical predictability. Instead, the life of nations resembled the life of organisms, each with a unique personality. Although Babel did not write about politics and culture in the same way as Dostoevsky and Rozanov, he shared their antirationalist and antiutilitarian stance. In what follows, I show that the image of the bloodthirsty Jew in Dostoevsky, Rozanov, and Babel is linked to their vitalist tendencies.

Before turning to a more specific analysis, some preliminary remarks about the conceptualization of the terms "people," "nation," and "race" will be helpful. I focus in particular on Dostoevsky's time, because this is the period in which racialized and racial notions of nationhood began to appear. The organicist model of nationhood that emerged in this time is directly relevant to Rozanov's conceptualization of the Jews as well. As will become clear, organicism and vitalism depend on each other. In using the term "race," especially for the 1870s, I am relying on Eugene Avrutin's argument that the term does not always mean a set of biologically determined characteristics ascribed to a particular group.[3] Assigning an unchanging set of behaviors to a particular group is sufficient evidence of *racialized* attitudes, to use Avrutin's wording. Cultural and linguistic differences were used in racialized terms in the 1870s. Using Avrutin as a point of departure enables us to envision a spectrum, at one end of which racialized categories can be found, but without a biological justification, and at the other end, fully fledged notions of biological inheritance. As Avrutin argues, "administrative practices and social attitudes constructed and justified a hierarchy of human difference without biological theories of human development." Dostoevsky and Rozanov fall on different places of this continuum, and indeed, evidence of a shift can be found even in Dostoevsky's oeuvre.

Racialized Concepts

Evidence of the rise of the biological concept of inherited difference began to emerge in the Russian press in the late 1850s. The first step had to do with linguistic difference. Western European sources played a crucial role in these discussions. As Vera Tolz points out, Ernst Renan's study *The Origins of Languages* sharply distinguishes between the Aryan and Semitic races. Tolz also points to Nikolai Dobroliubov's article linking anatomy, physiology, and intellectual and moral activity. In this essay, published in *Sovremennik* in the late 1850s, Dobroliubov disseminated new conceptions of the relations among skull size, brain weight, the relative simplicity or complexity of the brain folds, and mental capacity.[4] According to Dobroliubov, women and "Negroes and other races stood incomparably lower in the development of their intellectual capacities than the peoples of the Caucasian race."[5] Dobroliubov's article and other similar essays were familiar to Dostoevsky, who drew on material published in it for his own journalistic work and as a source of the "half-baked" ideas that motivate Raskolnikov in *Crime and Punishment*.[6]

Arthur de Gobineau's four-volume *Essay on the Inequality of the Human Races*, originally published in France in 1853–1855, was one of the most important and widely read works on this subject at this time. Gobineau identifies three races: "the white, the black, and the yellow"; races referred to as "white" are also called Caucasian, Semitic, or Japhetic; black designates the "Hamites"; and yellow includes the "Altaic, Mongol, Finnish, and Tatar branches."[7] The names refer to Noah's sons, Japheth, Shem (Semites), and Ham.[8] Among the white races, the Aryan (Germanic) is superior. No civilization is possible without the white race, and in particular, the Germanic element: "where the Germanic element has never penetrated, our special type of civilization does not exist."[9] The prevalence of similar types of human beings in widely differing climatic and geographical conditions means that "human races do not take their qualities from any of the external forces."[10] The Slavs, according to Gobineau, "were nearer to us than Negroes," but were civilized only on the surface.

Although Gobineau was not translated into Russian until the twenty-first century, Dostoevsky could have encountered Gobineau's ideas in Russian-language discussions found in the "thick journals" of the 1860s. One likely conduit of Gobineau was Nikolai Gersevanov, as John Klier explains.[11] Gersevanov (1809–1871) had both a military and a literary career; the "Jewish question" was the subject of articles he published in *Severnaia pchela* and *Sankt-Peterburgskie vedomosti* in the early 1860s. The Jews belonged to the Semitic race and the Christian nations to the Indo-German or Japhetic. The differences between them were due to their racial origins. Gersevanov, writing in 1858, argued that what bound the Jews together was their hatred for other nations. Between the Christian nations, which belong to the Indo-German race, and the Jews, who were Semites, there lay "an entire abyss."[12] Dostoevsky relies on a similar argument in 1877.

Nikolai Danilevskii's work *Russia and Europe*, first published serially in 1869 and then in a separate edition in 1871 is another important point of departure for racialized conceptualizations of human groups.[13] Danilevskii rejected the prevailing view of the superiority of European culture and civilization, arguing instead for Russia's preeminence. He went so far as to downgrade Europe's geographic status from a continent to a peninsula.[14] As a young man, Danilevskii, like Dostoevsky, participated in the Petrashevskii circle; the two met again in the 1870s.[15] Danilevskii's importance for Dostoevsky's views has been well established in the critical literature.[16] I am adding another dimension to the discussion of the intellectual relationship between the two: Danilevskii's work is important for the organicist context that I seek to establish for Dostoevsky's changing conceptualization of the Jewish population in Russia. Indeed, Dostoevsky praised Danilevskii for the "degree of scientific method" the latter used in the exposition of Slavophile ideas that the two men shared.[17]

After his youth as a follower of Charles Fourier and before he became an avid Slavophile, Danilevskii, as Mark Bassin puts it, was "an accomplished botanist, ichthyologist, and biogeographer."[18] Emerging from the field of the natural sciences, Danilevskii used its methods to analyze the rise and fall of nations and peoples. A caveat about terminology is in order. Danilevskii refers to the concept of "people, tribe, race" (*plemia*) and the related term for "nation, people" (*narod*), as well as "race" (*rasa*). The first two overlap in his usage, but the third—*rasa*—also includes biological characteristics that determine moral, intellectual, and cultural capacities. Danilevskii's theories occupy a space that is not yet racialized, but nonetheless relies on the principles of observation, counting, and classification, and on evaluative instruments that measure the vitality and productivity of a given population. Just as every living thing in the natural world, from a species to an entire order—has a natural life span, so do nations, which "are born, reach various stages of development, age, become decrepit, and die."[19] China is an example of a healthy national body whose creative forces have withered, and which remains alive by means of a mere "animal vitality." Just as the natural sciences required advances in comparative anatomy, embryology, and physiology in order to classify more accurately the animal kingdom, a similar sort of advance is required in historical science. Grouping together the nations of ancient Greece and Rome with contemporary Germano-Latin nations is a category error, as is assigning universal human significance to the fate of the Germano-Latin nations. It would be comparable to classifying completely separate groups in the plant kingdom as rungs on the ladder of perfection of a single group.

History has three types of actors—the positive, the negative, and the neutral—according to Danilevskii. He includes the Egyptian, Greek, Roman, Jewish, and Germano-Latin types as making a positive contribution to human culture generally; others, including the Mongols and the Turks, were negative forces. The neutral groups, neither positive nor negative, are "merely ethnographic material in service to alien purposes." Some never emerge from "savagery [*dikost'*] or nomadism as in the case of the entire black race [*rasa*]."[20] A people may permanently occupy the place of "ethnographic material" in service to other peoples, without ever attaining the level of historical individuality, or they may enter and leave this condition as part of the natural cycle of collective human life. The first or ethnographic phase is a period of latency and preparation for further development, in contrast to the phase of civilization, which is a period when the accumulated energy of the prior phase is expended. When the creative energies of a particular group are exhausted, their decline back into a merely ethnographic form is not far off.

In contrast to Gobineau, Danilevskii's model of the life of peoples and nations allows for more change, but within limits, some of which are defined by race. Gobineau and Danilevskii also differ widely in their estimation of the importance of the Germanic element as an agent in the advance of the civilization of a particular people. Christianity, which has little significance in Gobineau's theory, is, according to Danilevskii, centrally important to the development of world history. The Germano-Latin or European peoples are not the gateway to universal human civilization. Like Gobineau, Danilevskii includes the Slavic language group among the "Aryan" languages, but unlike Gobineau, the Slavs, and not the Germanic peoples, are the key to the advance of civilization. The Slavic peoples, in contrast to others, embody all four types of historically significant activity: religious, cultural and aesthetic, political, and economic. In contrast to Europe, whose apparent vitality is an illusion created by the rapid succession of peoples occupying the same space, Russia has the advantage of never having had colonies, and Russians, the advantage of never seeking power. Instead of colonizing, Russia assimilated "into its flesh and blood all the alien habitations [*inorodcheskie poseleniia*] located on its borderlands."[21] In so doing, it created one continuous political, religious, economic, and cultural entity with one center and one ruler, the tsar. Danilevskii concluded that the sources of civilization in Europe had withered, but they were abundant in the Slav world, and Russia alone held the "new key" for a social and economic structure that could sustain the populations of the world.

Danilevskii does not use biologically deterministic notions to evaluate the potential of various peoples, with the exception of the "black races." However, his characterization of some peoples as mere ethnographic material and his argument that the ethnographic phase is a necessary stage in the development and disintegration of political and cultural individuality indicates his reliance on normative concepts that could be used to judge the capacities of peoples and populations within and beyond the borders of a particular state and subject to its policies. Danilevskii imagines this trajectory for his own system of knowledge. The definition of the qualities and characteristics of the different "cultural-historical types" could give rise to generalizations that then could give rise to "norms for the future."[22] And although he does not use the phrase in this context, his description of the happy process of assimilation whereby "alien" peoples are absorbed into Russian "flesh and blood" suggests rather strongly that these *inorodtsy* are indeed nothing but "ethnographic material," incapable of sustaining their own difference.[23]

Dostoevsky

The organicist model of nationhood was of singular importance to Dostoevsky, especially in the period of Russia's war against the Ottoman Empire. As in instances discussed earlier, Dostoevsky emphasizes ideas and beliefs: the key issue of the "Eastern Question" is Russian Orthodoxy. But even a cursory reading of the *Writer's Diary* for 1877 reveals Dostoevsky's faith not so much in Russian Orthodoxy as in the revitalizing force of a European war: he believes the war against Turkey will engulf all of Europe, and to a good end. The expansion of the war will make things better, even though more blood will be shed. The dominance of Roman Catholicism will end, to be replaced by Eastern Christianity. This universal war will mean the "last convulsion of old Europe on the eve of its great and certain renewal."[24] Ultimately Russia's role will be to unify all of Europe, but the first step is war. The war that Russia was already fighting was good for its national health. Here Dostoevsky invokes the organicist model of the Russian nation, venturing into a bizarre image of its present moribund state and revealing that Jews cannot be part of its future life: "the nation must live in the full sense of the word, i.e., it must have a genuine living life, fulfilling its natural mission, and not be merely a galvanized corpse in the hands of the Yids and the stock-exchange gamblers."[25] The Jews and the financiers attempt to manipulate the corpse of Russia, as if it were Victor Frankenstein's monster, but the Russian people will soon show their strength.

The war in Europe (the extension of the war against the Ottoman Empire) will not be a race war. However, racial notions of nationality appear explicitly in Dostoevsky's formulation of the rationale behind the coming war. Dostoevsky writes, "Europe is *almost* as dear to all of us as is Russia: Europe is the home of the whole tribe of Japheth, and our idea is the unification of all the nations of this tribe, and, eventually, in the distant future, of the tribes of Shem and Ham as well."[26] The tribes of Shem are the Semites; the tribes of Ham refers to blacks. The point of departure for the eradication of difference is the reinscription of difference, and according to racial and not political or geographic criteria, even though Dostoevsky does not use the term "race" (*rasa*). In his "Jewish Question" Dostoevsky characterizes the so-called Jewish idea (of exclusivity) as opposed to the European idea, but in this essay, his vision of the utopian future includes all. He will retreat from this position in the 1880 Pushkin speech.

In the 1877 "Jewish Question" Dostoevsky's characterizations of Jews do not depend on "biological theories of human development," to use Avrutin's phrase. Dostoevsky says that the Russian people, whom he came to know while he was in prison, do not show any signs of hating Jews on religious grounds. The Russian people excused and "almost approved" the seemingly bizarre manner in which their Jewish fellow-convict prayed. There is no "preconceived, a priori, religious hatred of the Jew, based on the charge that Judas betrayed Christ."[27] Dostoevsky denies that he or the ordinary Russian people hate Jews on religious grounds, but he provides an abundance of justification for hating them for other reasons. These reasons are not racist, but they are racialized.

In the very first paragraph of "The Jewish Question" Dostoevsky uses three different terms interchangeably to designate Jews as a group: *plemia* (tribe or race), *natsiia*, and *narod*, with the latter two meaning "people" or "nation," "ethnicity." There is little that is biologically racial in these terms in and of themselves.[28] The evidence of cultural, religious, and linguistic differences and distinctiveness in daily-life practices could be used to enhance group identity in a positive sense. Indeed, Jewish intellectuals from the early nineteenth to the early twentieth century set about gathering data about the Jewish people, sometimes using the language of race, to buttress their claims about their rights to Jewish nationhood.[29] Dostoevsky attributed Benjamin Disraeli's policies in the Balkans to his Jewish origins, and Disraeli, for his part, argued for the superiority of the "Jewish race" in works published in the 1850s.[30]

In "The Jewish Question" Dostoevsky simultaneously portrays Jews as implacable enemies of the Russian people and calls for their full rights. Dostoevsky cannot make up his mind as to whether or not assimilation will solve the Jewish question; he hesitates between a racialized and a racial definition of the Jews. The very essence of Jewish identity and the so-called Jewish idea, according to Dostoevsky, are both based on animosity toward non-Jews. These inherent Jewish characteristics are fixed and intractable, the same in every location where Jews are found, and passed on from generation to generation. Negative Jewish tendencies persist regardless of where Jews reside, or of the socioeconomic conditions of their lives. Just as Jews exploit the peasantry in Russia, they behave the same way toward the Latvian peasantry and toward the newly freed slaves in the United States of America. The self-imposed isolation of the Jews means for Dostoevsky that they are alien to Russians "by blood." He asks what would happen if there were not three million, but eighty million Jews in Russia? If Jews were in the majority—they would flay the skin from the peasants' backs. What distinguishes the Jewish attitude toward non-Jews is "mercilessness: they've been driven for so many centuries by their mercilessness to us, solely by their thirst for our sweat and blood."[31] Dostoevsky's use of blood, as in "bloodlines" and in the suggestion about Jewish bloodthirstiness, hovers between literality and metaphor throughout the 1877 essay.

This changes, however, in the late 1870s, when the mention of blood takes a more concrete meaning, beginning with the 1878–1879 ritual murder case in

Kutaisi.[32] The corpse of a young girl, Sara Iosifovna Modebdze, was discovered in the town of Sachkheri in April 1878, at the beginning of Passover. Nine Jews were accused of committing the murder, even though the initial report of the coroner indicated that her death was accidental. A series of articles were published in the newspaper *Grazhdanin*, alleging that Jews committed ritual murder. Dostoevsky had initially published *A Writer's Diary* as a column in this newspaper and had served as its editor in 1873–1874. Even though the Jewish suspects were acquitted, Dostoevsky thought otherwise. In a letter dated March 28, 1879, Dostoevsky wrote that the suspects were "undoubtedly guilty," and he added his own feeling of revulsion at the verdict: "How disgusting that the Kutaisi Yids were acquitted" (Kak otvratitel'no, chto kutaisskikh zhidov opravdali).[33]

The second significant event in this period was the publication of Dostoevsky's final novel *The Brothers Karamazov* (it appeared serially from 1879 to 1880). *The Brothers Karamazov* is probably best known for its portrait of Ivan. Ivan imagines Jesus's second appearance on earth during the Spanish Inquisition, and depicts the Grand Inquisitor sentencing Jesus to death a second time. Ivan is quoted as saying, "If there is no God, then everything is permitted." Ivan challenges Alyosha's faith in God by adducing a set of horrific atrocities against children, some of which Dostoevsky had already described in his *Writer's Diary*. And near the end of the novel, in a chapter titled "A Little Demon" (Besenok), Lise Khokhlakova asks Alyosha a question:

> "Alyosha, is it true that Jews steal children on Passover and kill them?"
> "I don't know."
> "I have a book here. I read in it about some trial somewhere, and that a Jew first cut off all the fingers of a four-year old boy, and then crucified him on the wall."[34]

> "Alesha, pravda li, chto zhidy na paskhu detei kradut i rezhut?"
> "Ne znaiu."
> "Vot u menia odna kniga, ia chitala pro kakoi-to gde-to sud, i chto zhid chetyrekhletnemu mal'chiku snachala vse pal'chiki obrezal na obeikh ruchakh, a potom raspial na stene."[35]

Leonid Grossman has shown that this description of the crucifixion of a child corresponds closely to the newspaper account of the Kutaisi case.[36] Alyosha's agnosticism on the question of ritual murder has generated an impassioned debate among Dostoevsky scholars, some arguing that Alyosha's hesitation throws doubt on the likelihood of the practice, and others saying that it suggests the possibility that Jews did in fact commit ritual murder.[37] I belong to the second camp. Alyosha's refusal to deny the Jews' alleged penchant for Christian blood and their cruelty in obtaining it indicates that these supposed crimes could be true, especially in light of all the other horrendous crimes committed against children in Dostoevsky's last novel, with which readers might have already been familiar from the newspapers and the author's own nonfiction writing. Readers accustomed to seeing episodes in Dostoevsky's novels that were ripped from the headlines would have no reason to doubt that Jews crucified children for the sake of their blood. The catalog of violence against children that is the basis for Ivan Karamazov's rejection of "God's world" could also serve as the basis for believing Jews committed ritual murder.

There is another way to evaluate what Dostoevsky meant when he had Alyosha profess ignorance about Jewish practices. Dostoevsky's theorizations about Jewish difference in the scene with Lise and Alyosha and in his *Writer's Diary* fed into Russian governmental policies of 1881 and beyond. Konstantin Pobedonostsev, a close associate of Dostoevsky and the procurator of the Russian Orthodox Holy Synod, consistently articulated the position that the Jewish population posed a threat to Russians. Other officials reasoned that the newly liberated peasants no longer had their masters to protect them against the rapacity of the Jews. To separate the Jewish and the peasant populations, the 1882 May laws prohibited Jews from living outside urban areas; subsequent legislation limited access to higher education and permission to reside in villages; other restrictions followed. I am not arguing that government officials such as Pobedonostsev promulgated anti-Jewish laws because they believed that Jews practiced ritual murder. I am arguing that Dostoevsky's ideas after his death in 1881 helped create an atmosphere in which suspicions against Jews were justified. Dostoevsky's views about Jews as bloodsuckers were not unique, however, in distinction from other figures who promulgated similar notions.[38] His negative depictions of Jews corresponded to his larger concerns about the vitality of Russia and the fate of Europe.

Vasilii Rozanov and the People of the Sun

Pobedonostsev was also active in the Multan peasant sacrifice case of 1892, which in some ways paralleled the Beilis case, not in the least because the opening speech of the prosecution raised the issue of Jewish ritual murder. The Udmurt peasants, like the Jews, were "aliens" (*inorodtsy*) and they were accused of using the body of their murder victim in a ritual sacrifice to their gods. The distinguished jurist Alexander Koni said that if the Multan peasants were guilty, then Russia was guilty of failing to civilize them.[39] For Rozanov and other prominent intellectuals and writers of the Russian Silver Age, in contrast, less civilization and not more—was precisely what was needed to cure Russia of its cultural and spiritual exhaustion.[40] Vasilii Rozanov (1856–1919), one of the most controversial writers of fin-de-siècle

Russia, was closely linked to Dostoevsky. He was a fervent admirer of Dostoevsky's fiction and argued that Dostoevsky sided with the Grand Inquisitor. That is, Rozanov believed that Ivan Karamazov was speaking for Dostoevsky when he said in his "Legend of the Grand Inquisitor" that the vast majority of human beings were incapable of accepting the freedom that Jesus offered and that they therefore were better off without it.[41] There is also a more intimate connection between the two writers: Rozanov was married to Dostoevsky's lover Apollonaria Suslova, who never agreed to a divorce, even after Rozanov began living and having children with another woman.

For Rozanov there is one respect in which the New Testament did not supersede the Old. The Hebrew Bible and the Semitic peoples generally understood that the secret of life was sexuality and the body, whereas in contrast, Christianity and the Aryan race had abandoned this wisdom in a misguided cult of asceticism.[42] Rozanov called the Semitic peoples "children of the sun," using Dostoevsky's language from "The Dream of a Ridiculous Man," the story of the fantastic journey of a denizen of St. Petersburg to a utopian paradise, whose inhabitants he calls "children of the sun."

Notorious for his writing on religion and sex, Rozanov attacked the sterile chastity of Christianity, preached by writers such as Leo Tolstoy in "The Kreutzer Sonata" and his novel *Resurrection*. In contrast, he extolled the carnality of the Jews, a people of the sun, as evidenced in the Jewish emphasis on the body and rituals pertaining to the body, which were key to their vitality as a people. (Russians were people of the "moonlight.") In his 1877 essay "The Jewish Question," Dostoevsky had also written about the excessive "vitality" of the Jews, "a people of such vitality, so unusually strong and energetic."[43] Rozanov's explanation for the excessive vitality of the Jews had to do with his theory of carnal Judaism. Jews possess secret knowledge of the divinity because they sanctify the body and sex. Circumcision, the central rite of biblical Judaism, not only signifies, but embodies, the human, fleshly link to the divine in the form of sacrifice (that is, the cut-off piece of flesh). The circumcised male is "betrothed" to God, and at the same time, that is, to God's female principle; his circumcision, which leaves a ring in his flesh, symbolizes his human sexuality. Israel is rewarded for its sacrifices with fertility.

The appendix to Rozanov's two-volume study, *The Family Question in Russia*, published in St. Petersburg in 1903, consists of drawings copied from Egyptian archeological sites, representing, according to Rozanov, the tender and erotic relations between humans and the natural world. Dostoevsky's "Dream," cited virtually in complete form, and Rozanov's commentary—make up the rest of the text. Rozanov remarks that the drawings show the Egyptians' love for each other, animals, and the sun, and, in addition, their heightened tactile sense.[44] *The Family*

Question in Russia, published ten years before the Beilis trial, reveals the preoccupations of its age, and the ideas and attitudes that Rozanov would transform into accusations of ritual murder.⁴⁵

At the beginning of the twentieth century, artists in Russia and Europe sought new sources for the resurrection of cultural life. They turned away from the West and from the scientific rationalism and materialist philosophy that had dominated the latter part of the nineteenth century in search of something older, more universal, and more tangible, something that could transform experience in the new century. Andrei Belyi traveled to Egypt, and Dmitrii Merezhkovskii wrote about the Greek god Dionysus. The affirmation of the force of life itself—vitalism—was not limited to Russia. These artists traveled metaphorically and literally in search of sources of renewal in so-called primitive cultures that were allegedly closer to humanity's archaic origins, and the art movement that they participated in bore the name "primitivism." Russian artists also referred to themselves as "Neo-Primitivists," attributing to themselves a unique advantage because of Russia's own "Asian" and "barbaric" legacy. The year of the Beilis trial, 1913, also saw the publication of the Neo-Primitivist manifesto.⁴⁶

In a series of articles written and published—during the 1911–1913 Beilis case—separately as *The Olfactory and Tactile Relation of Jews to Blood*, Rozanov transformed his theory of carnal Judaism, arguing that blood was not only central to the sacrificial system of the ancient temple, but remained central in Jewish practice of the twentieth century. Since the prosecution in the Beilis case hinted at a larger, systemic Judaic hatred of Christians, and detailed the specific form in which the alleged ritual murder must be committed, Rozanov's theorization of the significance of blood in Judaism was directly relevant to its argument. The Catholic priest Justin Pranaitis testified that a "dogma of blood" existed among the Jews, who were united in their hatred of Christians.⁴⁷ A combination of racial revenge and the belief that the killing of Christians hastened the coming of the Messiah motivated the murder of Iushchinskii. Pranaitis alleged that the compendium of Jewish mystical texts, the Zohar, detailed the particular method that was to be used in the killing, which involved thirteen stabs with a knife. Evidence of this pattern of wounding was found on Iushchinskii's body, according to the prosecution. Rozanov and Pranaitis were working along parallel lines, as their analyses of the pattern of wounds on the body reveals. Rozanov charged that the pattern of the wounding concealed a code in which each letter stands for a word, and the words together formed a sentence stating that Iushchinskii was a sacrificial victim.

In "The Secret Writing of the Jews," originally published in 1911, Rozanov alleges that the very manner in which the Hebrew language is written—that is, with consonants only—shows that the Hebrew Bible is a code written to conceal the conspiracy of the Jews, their plot to perform blood sacrifice. In a grotesque metaphor, Rozanov compares the consonants to bones, "plain for all to see." He likens the vowels to the blood that is kept secret. But it is the blood both literally and figuratively—the blood of sacrifice and the blood of the vowels—that give the Hebrew Scriptures life.

In 1913, the same year as the Beilis trial, Russian experimental poets were developing theories of the transrational meaning of language (*zaum*) and were writing poetry that consisted only of consonants. John Bowlt notes that in the years 1912–1914, "a number of Cubo-Futurists . . . painted their faces and other parts of their bodies with cryptic messages, codes, and ceremonial images of animals." He argues that in imitating the tattooing practices of primitive societies, the Cubo-Futurists were attempting to "establish contact with a divinity."[48] Among the signs used was the Star of David. The use of religious imagery, motifs, and terminology for secular artistic goals was a common practice of this epoch, and Jewish intellectuals and artists associated with both Jewish and non-Jewish artistic movements engaged in similar activities. I am not arguing that the artistic display used by the Cubo-Futurists of Burliuk's circle in any way supported Pranaitis's or Rozanov's allegations. I am arguing that Rozanov, like the avant-garde artists of his time, was repurposing mystical practice for his own interpretation of early twentieth-century Russian culture.

Rozanov's analysis of Jews and Judaism was nothing if not consistent. Just as the body requires the circulation of blood, so the collective body of Israel requires sacrifice to sustain itself as a community. Rozanov concluded that it did not matter whether Beilis committed the crime or not, indeed "individually, no one is responsible for Iushchinskii."[49] This resonates with the jury's finding at the trial: the murder had left the body in a state of "almost complete bloodlessness," but Beilis was innocent. Part of Rozanov's argument about the Beilis case had to do with his interpretation of the Jewish ritual of circumcision, which, according to Rozanov, was a form of blood sacrifice. Rozanov writes that the mohel, who cuts the infant's foreskin, extracts as much blood as possible from the penis—using his fingernails for the purpose—and sucks the blood with his mouth, allowing the blood to drip into a bowl, so that he and those participating in the ceremony can wash their faces with a mixture of this blood, wine, and narcotics. Rozanov underscores this point: "Around the tongue and lips of the mohel is the infant's blood, he feels it, hot, sticky, red, arterial—it must be arterial, and not the black blood of the veins, according to the general law and method of all Jewish sacrifice."[50] As Laura Engelstein writes, "the homoerotic element introduced here relates to Rozanov's argument elsewhere about the centrality of the phallus in Jewish culture and the heightened sexual vitality of the Jews." As Engelstein puts it, according to Rozanov, Jewish religious initiation took "the form of fellatio between men."[51]

Dmitrii Merezhkovskii provides some context for Rozanov's writings. Husband of the poet Zinaida Gippius, and a novelist and poet in his own right, Merezhkovskii spoke against the government's prosecution of the Beilis case, but his diagnosis of what ailed Russian and Western society bears directly on the larger cultural spectrum on which the Beilis case can be located. After the completion of the trial, Merezhkovskii published an essay, "Not Peace but the Sword," in which he argued that Christianity had lost its sense of the "visible and tactile reality" of the Resurrection.[52] The resurrected Christ had become a mere symbol. Merezhkovskii imagined a coming "Third Testament" that would restore the body to religion, and transform its earlier stages of human sacrifice, including that practiced by the Jews, into a new phase in which human flesh and God would meet again, in an affirmation of the "world, the flesh, and the earth."[53]

Rozanov's theories about the Jewish cult of blood sacrifice went further—much further than his contemporaries, who kicked him out of the Religious Philosophical Society because of his writings on the Jews. Silver Age literature and art and the ritual murder trial of Mendel Beilis do not stand in a cause and effect relationship. Rozanov thus represents the extreme end of a spectrum of attitudes and desires within which the charges against Beilis could have been believable and his acquittal insignificant. It is significant that the prosecution sought evidence of Jewish culpability in ritual murder both in the Bible and in Josephus, the first-century historian. Beilis's defense attorney Oskar Gruzenberg argued that what may or may not have happened three thousand years ago should have no bearing on the case against his client. The heady apocalypticism of the Silver Age, in contrast, saw no problem with beginning the argument against Beilis with the beginning, so to speak. Neither the messianic chauvinism of the right nor the apocalyptic revolutionism of the left gave much credit to the legal system as a source of meaning and value.

Rozanov died in 1919 having written both for and against the Black Hundreds, the Socialist Revolutionaries, and the Russian Revolution. He asked forgiveness from Jews for his position on the Beilis case. His literary legacy was not tarnished by his reputation, however. The Russian Formalist critic Viktor Shklovsky, among others, greatly admired Rozanov's nonfiction prose works, *Solitaria* and *Fallen Leaves*. By the end of the 1920s, however, Russian literary culture would no longer tolerate Rozanov. But he did not disappear altogether. Rozanovian traces may be seen in the work of Isaac Babel.

Babel, Rozanov, and Beilis

Babel saw himself as a source of a new southern vitality for Russian literature: he embodied Odessa's life-affirming forces of sunlight, warmth, and love.[54] In a short nonfiction piece called "Odessa," which Efraim Sicher characterizes as Babel's literary manifesto, the author chides Gorky for not being a true "minstrel of the sun" (*pevets solntsa*).[55] Russia's blood needed to be "refreshed," and the literary messiah who could accomplish this task would come from Odessa, from "the sun-drenched steppes, washed by the sea."[56] The distinction between the people of the moonlight and the "children of the sun," as I have shown, was central to Rozanov's thought; Babel's emphasis on the sun does not necessarily derive from Rozanov, however.

Babel's representation of bodies—both Jewish and not—has provoked controversy in the critical literature since the 1920s. He was both praised and excoriated for his use of what some considered the physiological excesses of his writing. Alexander Voronsky, for example, did not like Babel's portrait of Jesus's sexuality in the story "Pan Apolek," one of the *Red Cavalry* stories, because he had gone too far in his emphasis on "stinking flesh."[57] An early review of the story cycle admonished Babel for his overly aestheticized vision; the author had not yet assumed a properly Leninist perspective because he was still entranced by the "dead truth of rotting Talmuds." Indeed, the reviewer characterized Babel's worldview generally as "stinking of rot." It is not entirely clear what the reviewer intended to say, but Jewish carnality, and a Jewish attachment to the past, as well as a decadent combination of sexuality and death are the main targets of his attack on Babel.[58]

Babel's 1931 "Karl-Yankel" tells the story of the conflict in a Jewish family between Soviet Marxism and Judaism, as it plays out between the father of a newborn and his mother-in-law. As the twin names of the title indicate, the story concerns the double legacy of Marxism and Judaism. The infant Karl-Yankel "is to receive the Soviet kingdom," but his pious Hasidic grandmother needs an heir who can listen to her tell legends of the Baal Shem Tov, and while her son-in-law is away, she has Naftula Gerchik the mohel circumcise her grandson, adding "Yankel" to his name. It is likely that this dimension of the story is based on real-life cases in which fathers blamed their religious in-laws for carrying out circumcisions.[59] In the story, the child's father, outraged, takes the grandmother and the mohel to court.

In 1933 a Yiddish translation of Babel's story appeared in *Der apikoyres* (The Atheist). The illustration accompanying the work emphasizes the benefits of the "Karl" side of the controversy. The caption reads, "The struggle for the young generation." The "Karl" proponents are schoolchildren, some wearing the neckerchiefs of young Pioneers. A Torah scroll lies on the floor, abandoned and blasphemed. On the "Yankel" side are old Jews with side curls and beards; they carry the Torah in their arms. The figure in the foreground, wearing a bowler hat and carrying an umbrella—the costume used by the Moscow State Yiddish Theater to signify the luftmentsh—also carries the mohel's knife.

What is strikingly present in the story, and conspicuous by its absence in the accompanying illustration, is Babel's horrifying portrait of Naftula the mohel:

> When he sliced off what was his due, he did not strain off the blood through a glass funnel, but sucked it with puckered lips. The blood smudged his tousled beard. He appeared tipsy before the guests. His bearlike eyes twinkled cheerfully. Redheaded as the first redheaded man on earth, he whimpered a blessing over the wine. With one hand, Naftula pitched his vodka into his overgrown, crooked, fire-spitting pit, while in the other he held a plate. On this plate lay the little knife, reddened with the infant's blood, and some gauze. As he collected his money, Naftula went from guest to guest with his plate.... "Fat mamas," he howled for the whole street to hear, his little coral eyes glittering, "Go churn out some boys for Naftula."[60]

In this description of the satanic mohel, Babel seems to conjure the image of the predatory Jew from the late tsarist era, an image that circulated during the ritual murder trial of Mendel Beilis in 1913. Babel was in Kiev when the trial took place.

However, Babel's 1931 story "Karl-Yankel" refers most immediately to actual agitprop trials of circumcision that took place in the 1920s. In *Soviet and Kosher: Jewish Popular Culture in the Soviet Union: 1923–1929*, Anna Shternshis includes an account of the Odessa agitprop trial of circumcision that took place in 1928.[61] The mohel at the agitprop trial defended himself by pointing out that he had performed circumcisions on many members of the audience. Babel's Naftula does the same thing when he reveals that "Orlov," the chairman of the court, was born "Zusman," and that he, Naftula, performed his circumcision thirty years earlier. While the immediate source of Babel's story may well have been this purely theatrical trial of circumcision, the specter of the Beilis trial nonetheless haunts his text.[62] The agitprop trial does not exploit the alleged bloodlust of the Jews, but the 1913 Beilis trial did just that: the prosecution charged that the victim was killed in such a way as to yield the maximum amount of blood from his body.

The emphasis on the profuse flow of blood and the startling picture of Naftula's voracious mouth suggest that Babel was familiar with Rozanov's writings about the Beilis trial and the alleged practice of blood sacrifice among Jews. Babel read Rozanov, and if he did not refer to this article directly, he was familiar with the image of Jews as bloodsuckers found in other works by Rozanov.[63] Rozanov stressed the image of blood on the mohel's mouth: "around the tongue and lips of the mohel is the infant's blood; he feels it, hot, sticky, red."[64] Rozanov explicitly linked circumcision with the fecundity of the Jews, understanding circumcision as a form of sacrifice and fecundity as its compensation. In Babel's story, Naftula urges Jewish mothers to conceive boys to slake his thirst for their blood, and he is rewarded for his efforts. The courtyards "swarmed with children like the mouths of rivers with roe. Naftula dragged himself around with his bag, like a tax collector."[65] Lust for money and lust for blood, both of which circulate, are the twin hallmarks of the vampiric Jew. The link between the fecundity of the Jews and their penchant for blood—which Rozanov argued for in *Olfactory and Tactile Relation of Jews to Blood*—appears in Babel's "Karl-Yankel" as well.

Hasidism is another key link between Babel's story of 1931 and the Beilis trial of 1913. Karl-Yankel's grandmother attends a Hasidic synagogue and pays tribute to emissaries from Galician tsaddikim. Among the spectators who gather in the court in Babel's story are the Galician tsaddikim, convinced that "the Jewish religion" was on trial. Russian newspapers made Hasidism the particular target of the Beilis case: according to their reports, "tsadidkim instructed Jews how to employ kabbalistic symbols to extract the blood of Christian boys."[66] Efraim Sicher says that Naftula is "accused of being a fanatic follower of a villainous cult," but does not link "Karl-Yankel" to the Beilis trial.[67] Babel's use of a Rozanovian image of the bloodthirsty Jew in the 1930s is difficult to parse in this historical context. "Karl-Yankel," as Elissa Bemporad has pointed out, is a satire, and the image of Naftula is meant to provoke laughter. Babel might have thought that he was satirizing not only Jewish life, as Bemporad argues, but also anti-Jewish stereotypes of it.[68]

There is another possible reading of Naftula's role in "Karl-Yankel." His love for money, children, and childbirth can be characterized in a more positive light—not so much Rozanovian as Odessan. Naftula ought to be seen not in only the context of the Beilis trial and the negative image of the vampiric Jew that Rozanov portrayed. Instead, Babel's own earlier texts on children and childbirth should also be part of the broader context for this story. This is how Babel characterizes Odessan Jews in 1916: "Jews are a people who have learned a few simple truths along the way. Jews get married so as not to be alone, love so as to live through the centuries, hoard money so they can buy houses and give their wives astrakhan jackets, love children, because, let's face it, it is good and important to love children."[69]

The same elements that appear in grotesque form in Naftula appear here in a positive light. Jewish men love money so they can take care of their wives, who bear them children. The Jewish emphasis on the body appears here in the guise of a life-affirming domesticity. Two years after the publication of "Odessa" in 1918, Babel removes children and childbirth from a purely Jewish and domestic context and attaches the family question to the Bolshevik revolution more broadly. He attacked the deplorable conditions of the so-called Palace of Motherhood, arguing that it is important to "bear children well," and that "children must live."[70]

Babel's image of the mohel whose love of his profession borders on demonic lust provides an uncomfortable mirror for assimilated Jews and raises questions about the likely continuity of Jewish practice in the new Soviet world. The story ends on a wistful note. Looking at the baby, the narrator asks, "Is it possible that you will be happier than I?" Three years later, at the First Congress of the Soviet Writers' Union, Babel was to pronounce himself "a master of the genre of silence."

Babel's Naftula the mohel was a bit of grotesquerie, not the rapacious, bloodthirsty Jew of Dostoevsky's "Jewish Question," who would flay the skin off the peasants' backs. Naftula does not represent the Jewish population as a whole, and in this light he is quite distinct from the figure of the Jew that haunts both Dostoevsky and Rozanov. Naftula cannot be seen as evidence of some putative self-hatred on Babel's part. Dostoevsky's image of the predatory Jew was of a piece with his understanding of the organic life of nations and his presentiment of Europe's collapse, which necessitated Russia's mission to save the peoples of the Aryan race. This was Dostoevsky's apocalyptic vision in his 1881 Pushkin speech. Babel certainly did not share this view. Babel was closer to Rozanov, who saw in Judaism, if not in actual Jews, the sanctity of life—particularly the life of the flesh, sexuality, and fertility. Rozanov believed that the Russian Orthodox Church had abandoned what should have been its mission in its condemnation of the body and sex. The asceticism of the Russian Orthodox Church was not Babel's concern. Notwithstanding these differences, Babel, like Dostoevsky and Rozanov, confronted a version of scientific positivism that had no room for the life of the body. This was not the rational egoism and utilitarianism of Chernyshevsky, rejected by Dostoevsky and Rozanov, but a form of Marxism that emphasized production over reproduction and rendered the writer an "engineer of human souls."[71] The sorrow of Babel's narrator, who asks whether Karl-Yankel will be happier than he, reflects Babel's awareness that he was not going to bring Odessa's warmth to Soviet literature.

HARRIET MURAV is Professor of Slavic Languages and Literatures and Comparative and World Literatures at the University of Illinois Urbana-Champaign and editor of *Slavic Review*. She is the author, among other works, of *Music from a Speeding Train: Jewish Literature in Post-Revolution Russia* (2011) and the editor (with Gennady Estraikh) of *Soviet Jews in World War II: Fighting, Witnessing, Remembering* (2014). With Sasha Senderovich, she translated David Bergelson's 1929 novel *Judgment* (Mides-hadin).

NOTES

1. The phrase comes from Hans Rogger: "There had been an experiment, conducted by a small band of unsuccessful politicians and honest maniacs to see how far they could go in imposing their cynicism and madness on the state" ("The Beilis Case: Anti-Semitism and Politics in the Reign of Nicholas II," *Slavic Review* 25, no. 4 [1966]: 615–29). This chapter uses lengthy excerpts from my own earlier work on the Beilis trial. See Harriet Murav, "The Beilis Ritual Murder Trial and the Culture of Apocalypse," *Cardozo Studies in Law and Literature* 12, no. 2 (2000): 243–63. I am grateful to Peter Goodrich, ed., *Cardozo Studies in Law and Literature*, for his permission to use this material.

2. For a discussion of visual images of Russians and other ethnic groups in the late nineteenth century, including negative images of rapacious Jews, see Jeffrey Brooks, "The Russian Nation Imagined: The Peoples of Russia as Seen in Popular Imagery, 1860s–1890s," *Journal of Social History* 43, no. 3 (2010): 535–57. For a discussion of the image of the Jew as bloodsucker in the 1881 riots, see John Klier, *Russians, Jews, and the Pogroms of 1881–1882* (Cambridge: Cambridge University Press, 2011), 83–88.

3. Eugene M. Avrutin, "Racial Categories and the Politics of (Jewish) Difference in Late Imperial Russia," *Kritika: Explorations in Russian and Eurasian History* 8, no. 1 (2007): 13–40.

4. Nikolai Dobroliubov, "Organicheskoe razvitie cheloveka v sviazi s ego umstvennoi i nravstvennoi deiatel'nost'iu," *Sovremennik* 5 (1858): 1–30.

5. See Vera Tol'ts [Tolz], "Diskursy o rase: imperskaia Rossiia i 'Zapad' v sravnenii," in *Poniatiia o Rossii: K istoricheskoi semantike imperskogo perioda* (Moscow: Novoe literaturnoe obozrenie, 2011), 2: 145–93. I am grateful to Marina Mogilner for directing me to this source.

6. For a discussion of Dostoevsky's relation to the journal in the early part of the author's career, see Joseph Frank, *Dostoevsky: The Mantle of the Prophet, 1871–1881* (Princeton, NJ: Princeton University Press, 2002), 237.

7. Arthur de Gobineau, *The Inequality of Human Races*, trans. Adrian Collins (London: William Heinemann, 1915), 146.

8. John Klier, "The Jewish Question in the Reform Era Russian Press, 1855–1865," *Russian Review* 39, no. 3 (1980): 301–19.

9. Gobineau, *Inequality of Human Races*, 93.

10. Ibid., 121.

11. Klier, "Jewish Question in the Reform Era Russian Press," 316–17. For more on Gersevanov, see "N. B. Gersevanov," http://az.lib.ru/g/gersewanow_n_b/text_1911_bio.shtml/ (accessed February 20, 2014).

12. Gersevanov cited by Klier, "Jewish Question in the Reform-Era Russian Press," 315.

13. N. Ia. Danilevskii, *Rossia i Evropa, vzgliad na kul'turnye i politicheskie otnosheniia Slavianskogo mira k Germano-Romanskomu* (St. Petersburg, 1888). Unless otherwise noted, all translations are my own.

14. Mark Bassin, "Russia between Europe and Asia: The Ideological Construction of Geographical Space," *Slavic Review* 50, no. 1 (1991): 1–17.

15. Peter Sekirin, *The Dostoevsky Archive* (Jefferson, NC: McFarland, 1997), 332.

16. See, e.g., Frank, *Dostoevsky: The Mantle of the Prophet, 1871–1881*, 354–55, 483–84.

17. Dostoevsky, quoted in Joseph Frank, *Dostoevsky: The Miraculous Years, 1865–1871* (Princeton, NJ: Princeton University Press, 1995), 354.

18. Bassin, "Russia between Europe and Asia," 9. For a discussion of Danilevskii on Malthus and Darwin, see Daniel P. Todes, "Darwin's Malthusian Metaphor and Russian Evolutionary Thought, 1859–1917," *Isis* 78, no. 4 (1987): 537–51.

19. Danilevskii, *Rossia i Evropa*, 76.

20. Ibid., 93, 97.
21. Ibid., 532.
22. Ibid., 94.
23. The Russian term *inorodets* (alien) evolved from a narrowly defined legal category to a broader weapon in nationalist discourse. For a discussion, see John W. Slocum, "Who, and When, Were the Inorodtsy? The Evolution of the Category of 'Aliens' in Imperial Russia," *Russian Review* 57, no. 2 (1998): 173–90.
24. Fyodor Dostoevsky, *A Writer's Diary*, trans. Kenneth Lantz (Evanston, IL: Northwestern University Press, 1993), 23. For the original Russian, see F. M. Dostoevskii, *Polnoe sobranie sochinenii*, 30 vols. (Leningrad: Nauka, 1972–1990), 26:23.
25. Dostoevsky, *A Writer's Diary*, 1135; Dostoevskii, *Polnoe sobranie sochinenii*, 26:30.
26. Dostoevskii, *Polnoe sobranie sochinenii*, 25:23.
27. Dostoevsky, *A Writer's Diary*, 908.
28. For a discussion, see Nathaniel Knight, "Ethnicity, Nationality, and the Masses: Narodnost' and Modernity in Imperial Russia," in *Russian Modernity: Politics, Knowledge, Practices*, ed. David Hoffmann and Yanni Kotsonis (New York: Palgrave Macmillan, 1999), 41–66.
29. For example, S. An-sky's ethnographic expeditions in the Pale of Settlement in the years preceding World War I collected data on the folkways of the Jews. For a discussion, see Eugene M. Avrutin, Valerii Dymshits, Alexander Ivanov, Alexander Lvov, Harriet Murav, and Alla Sokolova, eds., *Photographing the Jewish Nation: Pictures from S. An-sky's Ethnographic Expeditions* (Waltham, MA: Brandeis University Press, 2009).
30. See, e.g., Benjamin Disraeli, *Lord George Bentinck: A Political Biography* (London: Colburn, 1852), 482–97. I am grateful to Bruce Rosenstock for directing me to this work.
31. Dostoevsky, *A Writer's Diary*, 913; Dostoevskii, *Polnoe sobranie sochinenii*, 25:84.
32. See David Goldstein, *Dostoevsky and the Jews* (Austin: University of Texas Press, 1981), 157–59.
33. Dostoevskii, *Polnoe sobranie sochinenii*, 30:59.
34. Fyodor Dostoevsky, *The Brothers Karamazov*, trans. Richard Pevear and Larissa Volokhonsky (San Francisco: Northpoint Press, 1990), 583–84.
35. Dostoevskii, *Polnoe sobranie sochinenii*, 14:24.
36. Leonid Grossman, "Dostoevskii i pravitel'stvennye krugi 1870-kh godov," *Literaturnoe nasledstvo* 15 (1934): 83–161.
37. Scholarly discussions of this question in particular and Dostoevsky's attitudes toward Jews generally have taken a variety of approaches. The first book-length study on the topic is Goldstein, *Dostoevsky and the Jews*. Joseph Frank's foreword to Goldstein apologetically calls Dostoevsky a "guilty anti-Semite" because, according to Frank, Dostoevsky knew his attitudes toward Jews violated his own Christian principles (ibid., xiv). Leonid Grossman's study of Avram Uri Kovner, first published in 1924, which contains an impassioned reflection on Dostoevsky and Judaism in its appendix, was reissued in Moscow in 1999. See Grossman, *Ispoved' odnogo evreia* (Moscow: Dekont, 1999). The twenty-first century has seen a continuing interest in the question: see, e.g., Maxim Shrayer, "The Jewish Question and The Brothers Karamazov," in *A New Word on The Brothers Karamazov*, ed. R. L. Jackson (Evanston, IL: Northwestern University Press, 2004); Raffaella Vassena, "The Jewish Question in the Genre System of Dostoevskii's 'Diary of a Writer' and the Problem of the Authorial Image," *Slavic Review* 65, no. 1 (2006): 45–65; and Susan McReynolds, *Redemption and the Merchant God: Dostoevsky's Economy of Salvation and Antisemitism* (Evanston, IL: Northwestern University Press, 2008).
38. For a discussion of Ivan Aksakov's exploitation of this image of Jews as well as its popular occurrence in the riots of 1881, see Omeljan Pritsak, "The Pogroms of 1881," *Harvard Ukrainian Studies* 11, nos. 1–2 (1987): 8–43.
39. A. F. Koni, *Izbrannye proizvedeniia* (Moscow: Iuridicheskaia literatura, 1956), 484.

40. For another discussion of these cultural phenomena, see L. F. Katsis, "Delo Beilisa v kontekste 'serebrianogo veka,'" in *Tsarskaia Rossiia i delo Beilisa*, ed. A. Kovel'man and M. Grinberg (Moscow: Gesharim, 1995), 412–34.

41. V. V. Rozanov, *Dostoevsky and the Legend of the Grand Inquisitor*, trans. Spencer E. Roberts (Ithaca, NY: Cornell University Press, 1972).

42. For a discussion of Rozanov's carnal theories of the Semitic peoples, see E. Kurganov and G. Mondry [Henrietta Mondry], *Rozanov i evrei* (St. Petersburg: Akademicheskii proekt, 2000). Adam Uhre argues that Rozanov is envious of the antiquity of Judaism. See Adam Uhre, "Rozanov, the Creation, and the Rejection of Eschatology," *Slavonic and East European Review* 89, no. 2 (2011): 224–27.

43. Dostoevsky, *A Writer's Diary*, 910.

44. Vasilii Rozanov, *Semeinii vopros v Rossii* (St. Petersburg, 1903), 510, n. 1.

45. For a similar contextualization of Rozanov's writing, see Henrietta Mondry, "Vasilii Rozanov and the Animal Body," *Slavic and East European Journal* 43, no. 4 (1999): 651–73.

46. For a discussion, see Sara Pankenier Weld, *Voiceless Vanguard: The Infantilist Aesthetic of the Russian Avant-Garde* (Evanston, IL: Northwestern University Press, 2014), 19–61.

47. *Delo Beilisa: Stenografischeskii otchet*, 3 vols. (Kiev: Pechatnaia S. P. Iakovleva, 1913), 1:31.

48. John E. Bowlt, "The Body Beautiful: The Artistic Search for the Perfect Technique," in *Laboratory of Dreams: The Russian Avant-Garde and Cultural Experiment*, ed. John E. Bowlt and Olga Matich (Stanford, CA: Stanford University Press, 1996), 53.

49. V. V. Rozanov, *Oboniatel'noe i osiazatel'noe otnoshenie evreev k krovi* (Stockholm: n.p., 1932), 64.

50. Ibid., 52.

51. Laura Engelstein, *The Keys to Happiness: Sex and the Search for Modernity in Fin-de-Siècle Russia* (Ithaca, NY: Cornell University Press, 1992), 324.

52. Dmitrii Merezhkovskii, *Polnoe sobranie sochinenii* (Moscow: Tipografiia I. Sytina, 1914), 13: 20.

53. Ibid., 13: 81.

54. For this argument, see Gabriella Safran, "Isaak Babel's El'ia Isaakovich as a New Jewish Type," *Slavic Review* 61, no. 2 (2002): 253–72.

55. Efraim Sicher, *Babel' in Context: A Study in Cultural Identity* (Boston: Academic Studies Press, 2012), 35. For the Russian original of Babel, see Isaak Babel, *Sobranie sochinenii*, 4 vols. (Moscow: Vremia, 2006), 1:47; for the English, see Isaac Babel, *The Complete Works of Isaac Babel*, trans. Peter Constantine (New York: W. W. Norton, 2002), 78.

56. Isaak Babel, *Sobranie sochinenii*, 1:48; *Complete Works of Isaac Babel*, 79.

57. Aleksandr Voronskii, *Literaturnye portrety* (Moscow: Federatsiia, 1928), 168–69.

58. P. Ionov, "I. Babel': Konarmiia," *Pravda*, June 27, 1926.

59. Elissa Bemporad, *Becoming Soviet Jews: Bolshevik Experiment in Minsk* (Bloomington: Indiana University Press, 2013), 137–43.

60. *Complete Works of Isaac Babel*, 621. For the Russian, see Babel, *Sobranie sochinenii*, 1:142–43.

61. Anna Shternshis, *Soviet and Kosher: Jewish Popular Culture in the Soviet Union 1923–1939* (Bloomington: Indiana University Press, 2006), 95.

62. The Beilis trial was the subject of many Yiddish theatrical productions in the early twentieth century. See Joel Berkowitz, "The 'Mendel Belis Epidemic' on the Yiddish Stage," *Jewish Social Studies* 8, no. 1 (2001): 199–225.

63. Efraim Sicher, *Style and Structure in the Prose of Isaak Babel'* (Columbus, OH: Slavica Publishers, 1985), 110.

64. Rozanov, *Oboniatel'noe i osiazatel'noe otnoshenie evreev k krovi*, 52.

65. *Complete Works of Isaac Babel*, 621.
66. Yohanan Petrovsky-Shtern, "An-sky and the Paradigm of No Return," in *The Worlds of S. An-sky: A Russian-Jewish Intellectual at the Turn of the Century*, ed. Gabriella Safran and Steven Zipperstein (Stanford, CA: Stanford University Press, 2006), 83–102.
67. Sicher, *Style and Structure in the Prose of Isaak Babel'*, 100.
68. Bemporad, *Becoming Soviet Jews*, 137–39.
69. *Complete Works of Isaac Babel*, 75.
70. Ibid., 499.
71. Eliot Borenstein, *Men without Women: Masculinity and Revolution in Russian Fiction, 1917–1929* (Durham, NC: Duke University Press, 2000).

9

CONNECTING THE DOTS

Jewish Mysticism, Ritual Murder, and the Trial of Mendel Beilis

Robert Weinberg

THE PROSECUTION OF Mendel Beilis for the murder of thirteen-year-old Andrei Iushchinskii in Kiev a century ago is perhaps the most publicized instance of "blood libel" since the torture and execution of Jews accused of ritually murdering the infant Simon of Trent in 1475. By the time of the trial in the fall of 1913, the Beilis case had become an international cause célèbre.[1] Like the trials of Alfred Dreyfus in the 1890s and the outcry that accompanied the Damascus Affair in the 1840s, the arrest, incarceration, and trial of Beilis aroused public criticism of Russia's treatment of Jews and inspired opponents of the autocracy at home and abroad to launch a campaign to condemn the trial. The persecution of the innocent Beilis mobilized forces along the political spectrum, from rabid antisemites on the extreme right to revolutionaries on the far left and to persons of all persuasions in between.

The killers of Iushchinskii—probably a gang of thieves whose leader was the mother of Iushchinskii's boyhood friend—savagely stabbed the boy some four dozen times in the head and upper torso with what the coroner believed was an awl. Some wounds penetrated bone, and one blow went so deep that the handle of the weapon left an impression on his skin. The corpse was significantly drained of blood, with perhaps only one-third of the normal amount of blood remaining in the body. The loss of blood and the placement of wounds prompted members of the Union of Russian People and the Union of the Archangel Michael, two of the empire's most zealous antisemitic and monarchist organizations, to declaim that Iushchinskii was a victim of ritual murder and to call for an investigation that focused on Jews. The government's case was predicated on the belief that the defendant and other unnamed perpetrators had killed the boy as a result of "religious fanaticism for ritual purposes."[2]

This chapter seeks to complicate our understanding of antisemitism in the early twentieth century. In particular, it explores the role played by mysticism and the occult, an understudied if not unacknowledged aspect of anti-Jewish thought and behavior on the eve of World War I. As I have noted elsewhere, belief in the supernatural and spirit world helped shape the worldview of many members of the cultural and intellectual elite in late imperial Russia who hoped to uncover the mystery of who murdered Andrei Iushchinskii.[3]

In many respects, the trial was a struggle between two irreconcilable ways of perceiving and living in the world. A mélange of competing and contradictory ways of apprehending the world, ranging from magic and superstition to forensic science, were in evidence during the trial. As one editorial in the rightwing *Russkoe znamia* pointed out, defenders of Beilis did not permit themselves to accept that there "could be ritual murders in the century of airplanes and trams."[4] The decision of the prosecution to rely on religious motives to prove its case against Beilis illustrates the extent to which the autocracy believed it was necessary to frame the trial in terms of the Jews' purported religious fanaticism to subvert the Christian foundations of society. The tsarist government relied on the testimony of witnesses who claimed that Judaism obligated Jews to obtain the blood of non-Jews for a variety of ritual purposes, including the baking of matzo. In particular, the prosecution sought to establish a link between the murder and the Kabbalah, or Jewish mystical thought.

Working in this intellectual climate, the prosecution put together its case against Beilis. The trial, however, was more than a struggle between two worldviews. Hillel Kieval notes in his contribution to this volume that the ritual murder accusation was not a static conception since its emergence in the twelfth century. Rather, the original religious foundation of the accusation became embedded in the culture of gentile society throughout Western and Eastern Europe by the early 1800s. Theology may have been the root of the belief that Jews purportedly needed gentile blood for the performance of religious rituals, but science and medicine, and not only religious texts, supposedly offered concrete evidence that a Jew or group of Jews had committed ritual murder. For example, in this volume, Andrew Reed in his essay on the Saratov Affair notes how investigators called on the expertise of local physicians to examine the wounds of the murdered boys and pass judgment on whether they displayed signs of ritual murder.

Government lawyers realized that the ritual murder accusation, easily dismissed by defenders of Beilis as a remnant of medieval religious prejudices and hatreds, needed to be supported by contemporary scientific and intellectual standards. Even a superstition from the twelfth century had to draw legitimacy from the authority of the written word and modern science. The ritual murder accusation had to be sustained in a manner befitting late imperial Russia's court system, which jurists in Europe and the United States held in high esteem. Hence, the prosecution turned to Ivan Sikorskii, an expert in the modern science of psychiatry, to develop its case against Beilis. Sikorskii was a prominent psychiatrist and professor emeritus at St. Vladimir University in Kiev who taught a course about the method used by Jews to murder Christian children. In his evaluation of the autopsy that constituted his testimony at the trial, Sikorskii asserted that the condition of Iushchinskii's corpse revealed the nationality of the murderers. He claimed that the youth was the victim of ritual murder carried out as the "racial revenge and vendetta of the Sons of Jacob" against gentiles. Sikorskii added that the murder was carried out with the aim of draining Iushchinskii's body of blood for religious purposes.[5]

Father Justin Pranaitis, a Roman Catholic priest with a checkered past and dubious credentials as an expert on Judaic texts such as the Talmud and the Zohar, served as another key government witness.[6] Drawing on the writings of other supposed specialists who wrote about the roots of Jewish ritual murder, Pranaitis insisted that Judaism dictated the ritual murder of gentiles, though Jews were careful not to spell this out in religious texts. He claimed that the Talmud prohibited putting into words the existence of such a tradition, leaving Jews to pass on knowledge of ritual murder via the spoken word. Even though he lacked legitimate credentials as an expert on the Talmud and other Judaic texts, Pranaitis passed himself off as an authority on Judaism. In *The Christians in the Jewish Talmud, or the Secrets of the Teachings of the Rabbis about Christians*, a pamphlet written in the early 1890s, Pranaitis claimed that Judaism required Jews to kill Christians. Several years before the murder of Iushchinskii, Pranaitis found refuge in Tashkent from the police in St. Petersburg for attempted extortion. But in 1911 he returned to the capital, where he began to distribute his pamphlet, thereby capturing the attention of other believers in the ritual murder accusation who then steered the police and prosecution toward a Jew as the culprit.

The indictment of Beilis drew on the ideas of Pranaitis and offered a concise statement of the priest's views: "All the rabbinical schools . . . are united by their hatred of non-Jews who, according to the Talmud, are not considered human beings but only animals in human form. The hatred and the spite that the Jews, from the point of view of their religious law, feel toward people of a different nationality and religion are especially strong toward Christians. Because of this sentiment, the Talmud allows and even commands the killing of non-Jews.... The extermination of non-Jews is commanded as a religious act ... that hastens the coming of the *Messiah*."[7]

When Pranaitis testified at the end of the trial, he tried to establish his scholarly credentials by grounding his testimony in a long-established tradition of likeminded thought. He claimed that his ideas on ritual murder had been sparked by a book written in the early nineteenth century by a converted Romanian Jew by the name of Neophyte (a term that refers to recent converts to Christianity). Neophyte, a former rabbi by the name of Noah Belfer who adopted his new moniker when he became a monk, claimed that he had knowledge of the secret practices of Jews. He laid out his views in *Argument against the Jews upon Their Law and Customs*, published in 1803.[8] Pranaitis drew liberally from Neophyte in his testimony, which went on for hours over the course of several days.[9]

Like Neophyte before him, Pranaitis found himself in good company when it came to his belief in this calumny against Jews. Also known as the "blood libel," the ritual murder accusation against Beilis was one in a long line of similar charges against Jews dating back to the Middle Ages. The canard that Jews engage in the murder of Christians, particularly young boys and girls, emerged in England in the twelfth century and soon spread to the continent, where Christians accused Jews of using Christian blood for religious rites and to mock the killing of Jesus. However, by the fourteenth and fifteenth centuries it fixated on the Jews' consumption of Christian blood either in sacramental wine or the baking of matzo. Not surprisingly, the ritual murder accusation tended to emerge around the time of Passover and Easter. The incidence of such accusations reached a crescendo in German-speaking Europe during the fifteenth century, frequently prompting Christians to attack their Jewish neighbors. By the sixteenth and seventeenth centuries, when ritual murder accusations began to die out in Central Europe, they gained a foothold in the Catholic regions of the Polish-Lithuanian Commonwealth. Nonetheless, the blood libel reemerged with a vengeance in parts of German-speaking Europe during the final decades of the nineteenth century. Dozens of well-documented incidents occurred between 1880 and the outbreak of World War I.[10]

Even though the Orthodox Christian tradition did not share the Western Christian churches' fixation on ritual murder, the blood libel eventually surfaced in the Russian Empire, which remained immune until the collapse of the Polish-Lithuanian Commonwealth in the late eighteenth century. It was then that large numbers of Jews, Catholics, and Uniates became imperial subjects as a result of the partitions of Poland, and by the early twentieth century the accusation had a secure footing among Russian and Ukrainian Orthodox believers. At the time of the Beilis trial the blood libel had sunk deep roots in Russian and Ukrainian culture and strengthened antisemitism on both the popular and official levels.

The testimony offered by Pranaitis reflected the attitudes of the intelligentsia toward Jews and the blood libel during Russia's Silver Age, the literary, intellectual, and artistic revival of the early twentieth century. In the last two decades scholars have explored the connection between Russian intellectual and cultural trends and antisemitism on the eve of World War I. In particular, several scholars have focused on the philosopher and writer Vasilii Rozanov's efforts to establish a link among the Jews' purported possession of secret and mystical knowledge, the role of blood in the Jews' experience of the divine, and ritual murder.[11] Rozanov believed that Jewish religious texts are a textual artifice to hide the ritual need of Jews to engage in blood sacrifice and mutilation of the body such as circumcision. He insisted that blood, which played a critical role in the sacrifices practiced by Jews in Jerusalem in the centuries before the destruction of the Second Temple, continued to occupy a central position in the practice of Judaism in the twentieth century. In one essay Rozanov maintained that Hebrew words, which are written without vowels, were designed as a code to disguise the fact that Jews colluded with each other to engage in ritual murder.[12] Jews, claimed Rozanov and others, possessed secret and mystical knowledge hidden in foundational Judaic texts such as the Hebrew Scriptures, Talmud, and Zohar. Other Silver Age writers alluded to blood rituals and the magical qualities of blood in their stories, plays, essays, and poems. For these intellectuals the Beilis case was replete with cultural symbolism and offered an opportunity to elucidate positions on Jews and Russians.

Other scholars have noted Rozanov's effort to establish a link between Iushchinskii's murder and Judaism. For example, Harriet Murav has written that for Rozanov "the wounds reveal a code of letters—each letter standing for a word, and the words taken together forming a magical sentence stating that this was a sacrificial victim to God."[13] Similarly, Judith Deutsch Kornblatt concurs that Rozanov embraced the view that lines connecting the stab wounds constituted Hebrew words that have an occult meaning that points to ritual murder. She also makes explicit references to the role that the Kabbalah purportedly played in this line of reasoning.[14] However, Murav and Kornblatt, do not, in my opinion, pay sufficient attention to the matter, particularly how the positioning of the wounds corresponded to letters and words that supposedly revealed, when decoded, the role of the Kabbalah in enjoining Jews to engage in the collective murder of innocent gentile youths. The detailed exegeses of the meaning of the messages embedded in the stab wounds served a purpose far beyond the confines of this particular trial. The scholarly language and claims of learned expertise were deployed in an effort to prove the guilt not only of Mendel Beilis, but of all Jews, especially adherents of Hasidism as participants in this heinous religious rite.

Wound patterns played a role in many ritual murder accusations, largely to demonstrate that the Jewish suspects purportedly stabbed the bodies of their victims in order to maximize the flow of blood into receptacles. Postmortem examinations and autopsy reports tended to be detailed in terms of identifying and locating every wound, including marks made by the pressure of fingers. Yet to the best of my knowledge, the Beilis Affair was the first time that accusers claimed that the wounds themselves represented letters and words that formed messages.

Elsewhere I have discussed how ordinary Russians and Ukrainians, along with tsarist authorities, underscored how astrology, the occult, and mysticism could solve the mystery of Iushchinskii's death.[15] Concerned citizens sent letters to police, prosecution, and defense attorneys with advice and insight gleaned from séances and hypnosis that purported to reveal who killed the youth. One letter writer in particular claimed that the wounds on Iushchinskii's right temple, neck, and torso, when connected by lines, corresponded to well-known constellations such as Aries, Ursa Major, Orion, Taurus, Draco, Ploughman, Canis Minor, and Northern Corona. In addition, the number of wounds corresponded to the number of the eight constellations. The author, however, did not offer any explanation and left it up to the police and prosecution to ascertain the astrological meaning.[16]

Another perspective on the significance of the wounds can be found in *The Olfactory and Tactile Relationship of Jews to Blood*, a collection of essays written and published during the Beilis Affair by Rozanov.[17] He looked for confirmation of ritual murder in the writings of other observers of the Beilis trial who were obsessed with demonstrating the veracity of the blood libel. In particular, Rozanov turned to the essay "'Echad': The Thirteen Wounds of Iushchinskii" by S. D-skii, whose identity is unknown, for corroboration. Rozanov included D-skii's essay in *The Olfactory and Tactile Relationship of Jews to Blood*, arguing that it offered convincing evidence of the Jewish conspiracy to engage in ritual murder.[18]

Judith Deutsch Kornblatt concluded, "D-sky's sources ... are less than reliable." She referred to his scholarship as "spurious," relying on "unnamed occultists and Christian cabalists" whose knowledge of Hebrew and Aramaic, the languages of the Talmud and Zohar, was dubious at best.[19] For example, Father Pranaitis claimed that he was an expert on the Talmud and Zohar, but he revealed his ignorance when defense lawyers cross-examined him during Beilis's trial. Likewise, the testimony of theologians, some Jewish and some not, demonstrated that the priest's knowledge of the Talmud was laughable.[20]

D-skii drew on essays, books, and translations of Jewish texts that supported his view that the positioning of wounds on the right temple of Iushchinskii corresponded to Hebrew letters. D-skii began his cryptographic analysis of Iushchinskii's wounds by asserting that the boy's killers stabbed him according to a "definite system."[21] First, he rotated a drawing of Iushchinskii's head ninety degrees to the right since the boy was found sitting up with his head dangling down and chin toward the chest. D-skii then connected the various wounds with lines (figure 9.1) and found that they spelled the following Hebrew letters: *Alef, Peh, Resh, Tav,* and *Shin* (ש ת ר פ א). The positioning of the five wounds also corresponded to the lower half of the ten *Sefirot* (singular *Sefirah*) that represent the creative forces connecting God to the material world (figure 9.2). Each *Sefirah* corresponds to a Hebrew letter, and when taken together, symbolize the unity of the spiritual and material worlds.[22] Finally, he also superimposed the lower half of the *Sefirot* on the thirteen stab wounds (figure 9.3) and concluded that "the puzzling punctures on the right temple of Iushchinskii were by no means accidental." In his words, they represented "a magical alphabetical formula."[23] According to D-skii's reading of the Zohar, the five Hebrew letters signified in Kabbalistic terms: Man (א), Mouth (פ), Head (ר), Chest (ת), and Arrow (ש). D-skii concluded that Iushchinskii "was killed by strikes to the head and chest like the calf sacrificed to Jehovah."[24] Moreover, he divined that the "secret meaning of *Shin* ... could be understood as weapons or a gun," and associated the letter to Lucifer. In addition, the number of wounds—thirteen—corresponded to a line in the Zohar that refers to thirteen wounds on a sacrificial animal whose mouth was tied shut.[25] (Evidence indicated that the killers of Iushchinskii had indeed tied something to his mouth, presumably to prevent him from screaming.) Furthermore, D-skii's analysis buttressed the view held by some believers in the blood libel that Lubavitcher Hasidim, with whom Beilis purportedly had intimate ties, were guilty of killing Iushchinskii since they constituted a "savage sect" of Judaism that engaged in "savage deeds" as outlined in the secret language of the Zohar.[26]

Finally, D-skii also drew on his purported facility with astrology when he wrote that the positioning of the wounds, when placed in a diagram of the signs of the zodiac, obeys the injunction in Exodus that Jews should obtain the blood of non-Jews during the month of Nisan, that is, at the time of Passover.[27] In sum, the positioning of the wounds on Iushchinskii's right temple was a secret code that revealed the sacrificial nature of the killing based on the Zohar's injunction that Jews kill Christians.

D-skii and Rozanov were not the only ones fascinated by the purported links between the murder and Jewish mystical writings. One author writing under the

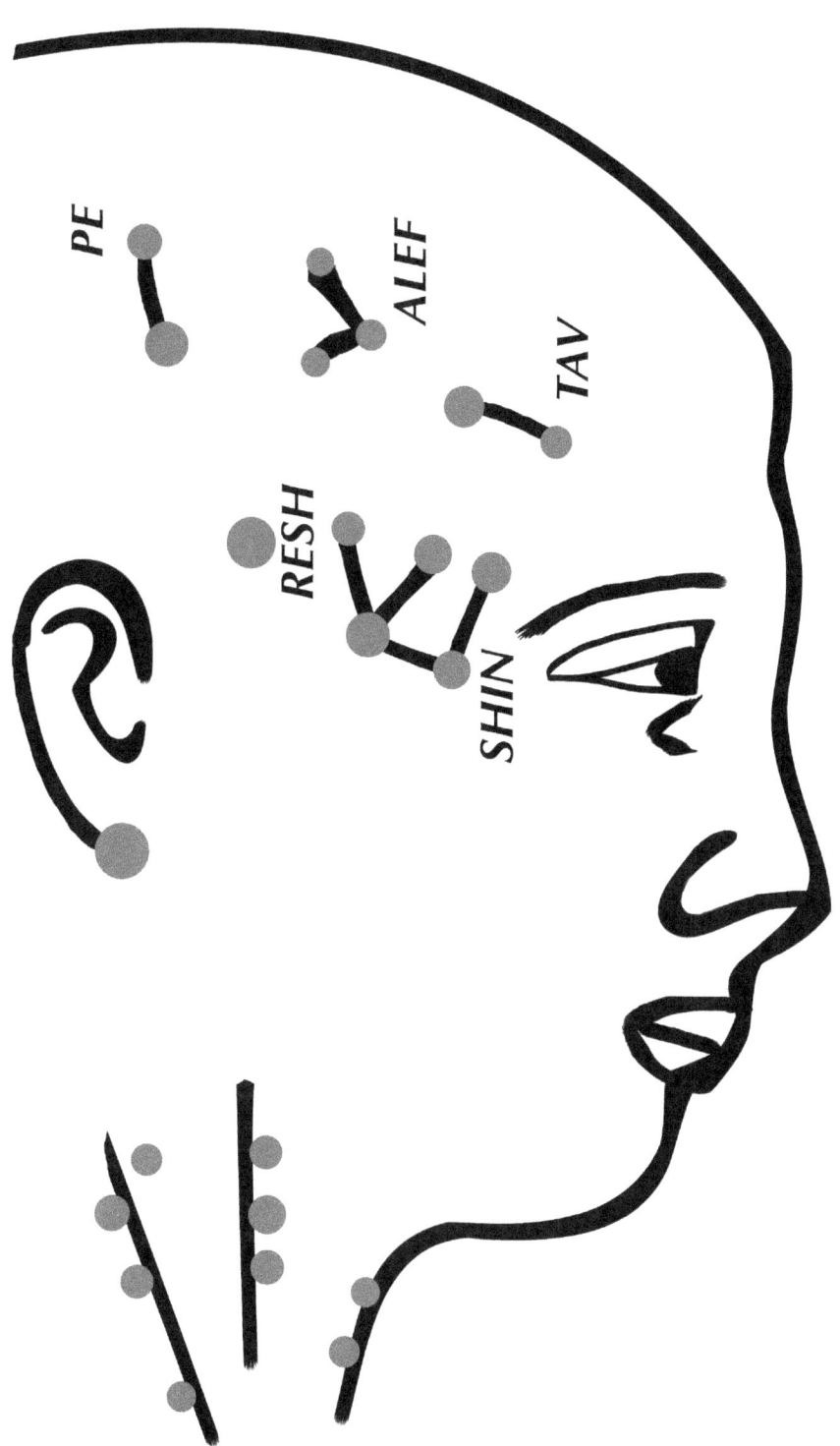

Figure 9.1. Five Hebrew letters formed by connecting wounds on Iushchinskii's head.

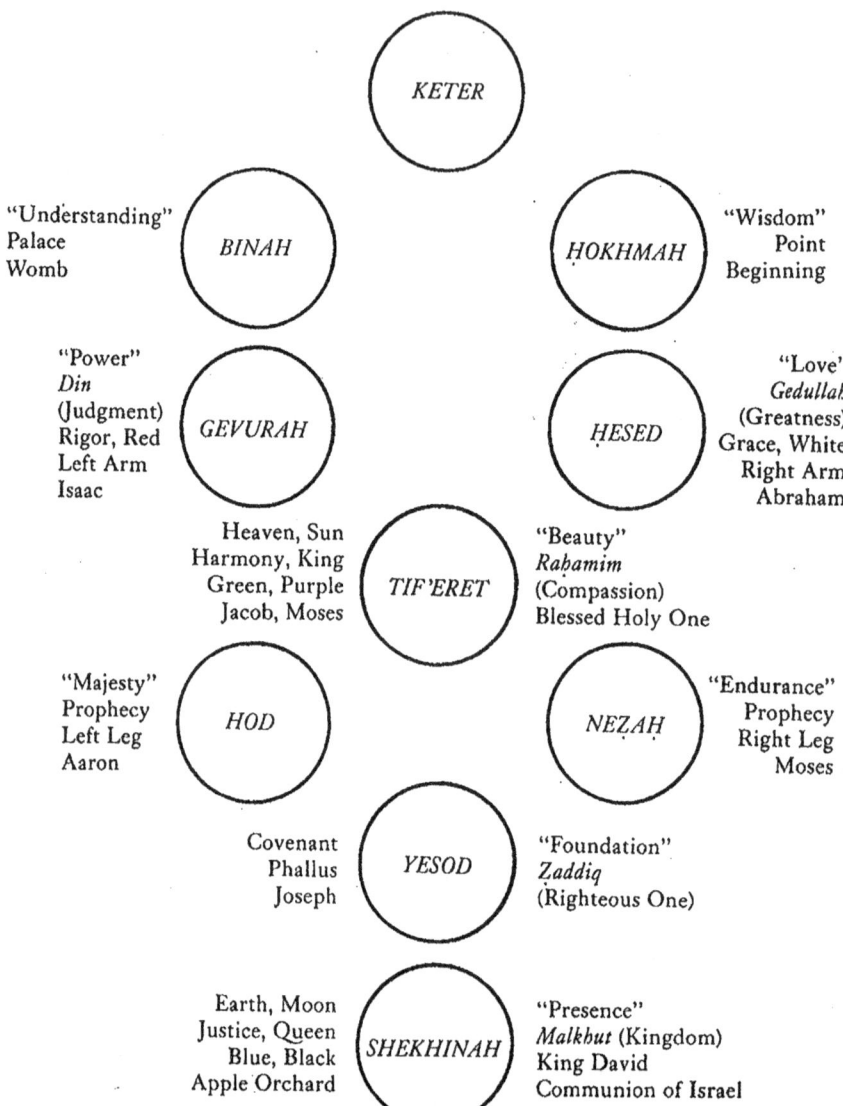

Figure 9.2. Diagram of the ten *Sefirot*. Source: *Zohar: The Book of Enlightenment*, trans. Daniel Chanan Matt (New York: Paulist Press, 1983), 35. Courtesy of Paulist Press.

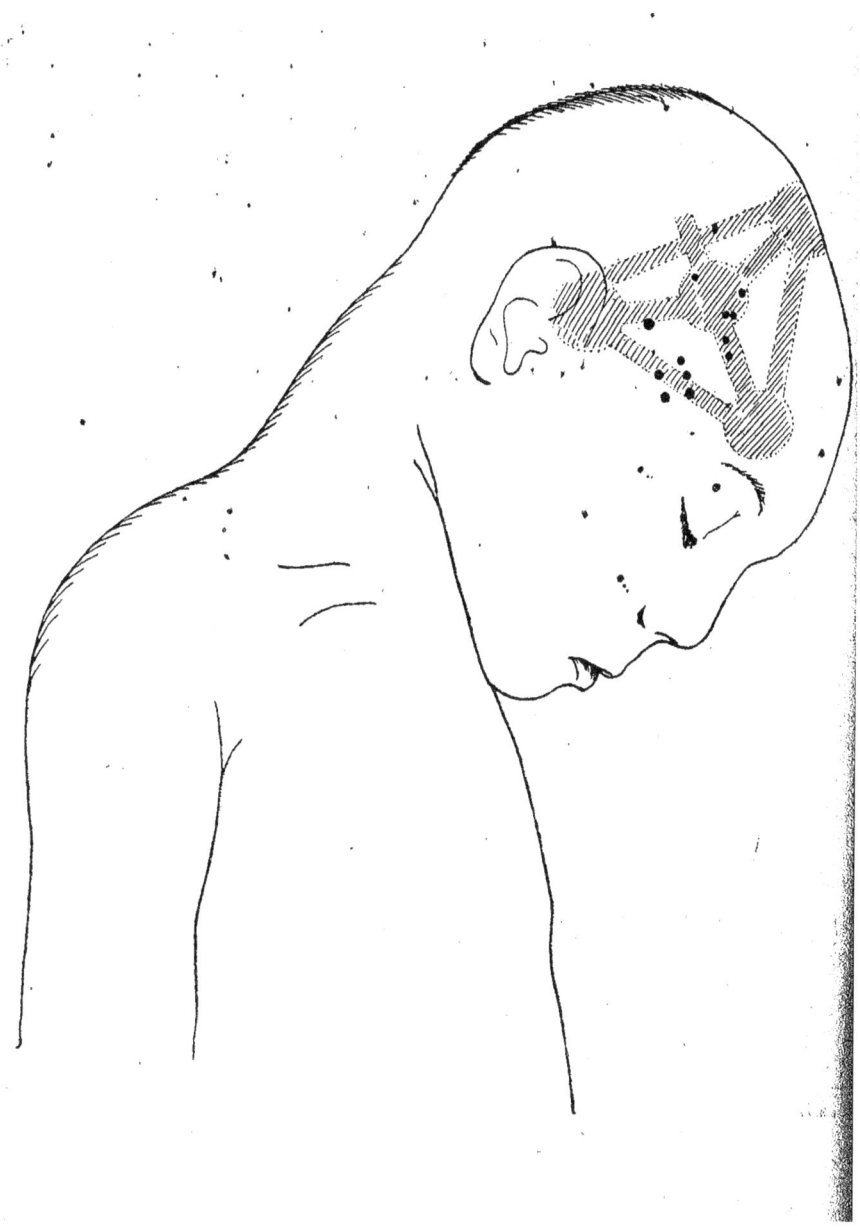

Figure 9.3. Lower half of ten *Sefirot* superimposed on head wounds. *Source*: D-skii, "Ekhad. Trinadstat' ran Iushchinskogo," in Vasilii Rozanov, *Obonitel'noe i oziasatel'noe otnoshenie evreev k krovi* (St. Petersburg: n.p., 1914), 226.

pseudonym Uranus claimed that the Kabbalah held the secret to Iushchinskii's murder. Like D-skii, Uranus believed that Jewish religious texts and traditions needed to be decoded in order to reveal their covert references toward ritual murder. He subjected the wounds on the right temple to an analysis similar to the one performed by D-skii and concluded that they were not "accidental." Uranus focused on six stab wounds that formed two triangles when connected by lines. When merged with each other, the triangles formed the Star of David, which, along with other letters formed from the wounds, signified blood sacrifice and devotion to the Devil.[28]

Fortunately for Beilis, the jury found him not guilty of participating in the murder of Iushchinskii. But the jury, composed primarily of peasants, did agree with the prosecution's argument that the killing had the hallmarks of a ritual murder. In this sense, the strategy of the prosecution to claim the ritual nature of the killing suceeded. Knowing the case against Beilis as a participant in the murder was based on perjured testimony, imaginary evidence, and innuendo, some police and members of the prosecution anticipated his acquittal. Hence, the government chose to focus on the supposed ritual nature of the murder, hoping to rely on popular belief and values to win its case. The prosecution had a reasonable expectation that the jury—and the general public, for that matter—would not question the veracity of the ritual murder accusation. It pinned its hope on the general ignorance (or, even more dangerously, the little, inaccurate "knowledge") and suspicion of Judaism and Jewish culture among the population at large. As a result, the government did not appeal the acquittal of Beilis for murder, content with the verdict that confirmed the ritual murder accusation. As one member of the prosecutorial team claimed at the end of the trial, "the main task of the trial has been proven, namely the ritual character of the murder."[29] Another lawyer who assisted the prosecution told a newspaper in Kiev that the "verdict satisfies us. It was necessary for us to establish that the murder had a ritual character and we achieved this goal. . . . Had the jury said the prosecution had not proven the ritual aspect of the murder, we would not have been satisfied even if the jurors had found Beilis guilty."[30]

The government's case regarding blood libel, unsurprisingly, did not fall on deaf ears as far as the jury was concerned. The jury accepted the prosecution's assertion that the murder could have been carried out by Jews intent on draining Iushchinskii of his blood for use in religious rituals. By the turn of the twentieth century, many literate and semiliterate, not to mention illiterate, gentiles did not question the preposterous assertion that Jews were not only capable of murdering children for ritual purposes but did so because their religion required them to do so. More than antisemitism and ignorance of Judaism were at work here. Many inhabitants of the Russian Empire, Jew and non-Jew alike, lived in a mental universe where magic potions, amulets, incantations, witchcraft, folk healing, and the occult played prominent roles in daily life. They lived in a world where logic, science, and reason clashed with ignorance, prejudice, and superstition, where the fear of the unknown challenged the science of the modern world.[31] As we have seen, even many highly educated and cultured people subscribed to the canard of the blood libel.

Government lawyers assumed that testimony about Jewish holy men, cryptic texts, and mystical knowledge would make it more likely for the jury and the public to accept their story of ritual murder. But they had to make a case that comported, at least on the surface, to rules of evidence, drawing from scientific knowledge and textual analysis to establish the veracity of ritual murder. The antisemitism reflected in the Beilis case may have served secular or political objectives (and was cloaked in the vocabulary of contemporary science) and therefore qualifies as a manifestation of what historians refer to as modern antisemitism. But the foundations of this antisemitism remained rooted in long-standing religious prejudices stemming from the late medieval period. State prosecutors used modern, state-of-the-art "science" to prove the existence of a deadly fantasy. In this way, the prosecution adorned a prejudice that stemmed from the medieval period with the trappings of the modern world. The Beilis trial cautions us to be careful not to draw distinct lines between modern and premodern forms of antisemitism.

ROBERT WEINBERG, the Isaac H. Clothier Professor of International Relations and History at Swarthmore College, is the author of *The Revolution of 1905 in Odessa: Blood on the Steps* (1994), *Stalin's Forgotten Zion: Birobidzhan and the Making of a Soviet Jewish Homeland* (1998), and *Blood Libel in Late Imperial Russia: The Ritual Murder Trial of Mendel Beilis* (2013).

NOTES

An earlier version of this chapter appeared in Maria Di Salvo, Daniel Kaiser, and Valerie Kivelson, eds., Word and Image in Russian History: Essays in Honor of Gary Marker *(Brighton, MA: Academic Studies Press, 2015). I thank the press for permission to reprint it here.*

1. The Beilis Affair stretched from March 1911, when Iushchinskii was murdered, to October 1913, when Beilis was acquitted of murder.

2. *Delo Beilisa: Stenograficheskii otchet*, 3 vols. (Kiev: Pechatnaia S. P. Iakovleva, 1913), 1:37.

3. See my "The Trial of Mendel Beilis: The Sources of 'Blood Libel' in Late Imperial Russia," in *Russia's Century of Revolutions: Parties, People, Places*, ed. Michael Melancon and Donald Raleigh (Bloomington, IN: Slavic Publishers, 2012), 17–36.

4. *Russkoe znamie*, no. 240 (October 25, 1913), 2.

5. University of Chicago, Regenstein Library Special Collections, Ludwig Rosenberger Collection 450 D/5 (spelling has been changed for consistency); *Delo Beilisa*, 2:252–64.

6. The Zohar ("radiance" or "splendor") is a collection of commentaries on the sections of the Torah read during weekly synagogue services and serves as the foundational work of Jewish mystical thought, Kabbalah.

7. *Delo Beilisa*, 1:32.

8. The book was a bestseller: it went through ten printings between 1803 and 1936. Before the Frankist controversy in the mid-eighteenth century, converted Jews did not assert that Jews engaged in ritual murder. However, after Jacob Frank accused Jews of engaging in ritual murder, proponents of the blood libel began to seek out Jews or converted Jews who claimed to have firsthand knowledge of or experience with ritual murder in order to substantiate their claims. I thank Hillel Kieval for pointing this out to me.

9. *Delo Beilisa*, 2:293–440.

10. A useful overview of the ritual murder accusation can be found in Helmut Walser Smith, *The Butcher's Tale: Murder and Antisemitism in a German Town* (New York: W. W. Norton, 2002), 91–133.

11. Harriet Murav, "The Beilis Ritual Murder Trial and the Culture of Apocalypse," *Cardozo Studies in Law and Literature* 12 (2002): 243; Judith Deutsch Kornblatt, "Russian Religious Thought and the Jewish Kabbala," in *The Occult in Russian and Soviet Culture*, ed. Bernice Glatzer Rosenthal (Ithaca, NY: Cornell University Press, 1997), 75–95; Laura Engelstein, *The Keys to Happiness: Sex and the Search for Modernity in Fin-de-Siècle Russia* (Ithaca, NY: Cornell University Press, 1992), 299–333; Henrietta Mondry, *Exemplary Bodies: Constructing the Jew in Russian Culture since the 1880s* (Brighton, MA: Academic Studies Press, 2009), ch. 3; and Leonid Katsis, *Krovavyi navet i russkaia mysl'* (Moscow: Mosty kul'tury, 2006).

12. See "Iudeiskaia tainopis'," in Vasilii Rozanov, *Obonitatel'noe i osiazatel'noe otnoshenie evreev k krovi* (St. Petersburg, 1914), 1–11.

13. Murav, "Beilis Ritual Murder Trial," 248.

14. Kornblatt, "Russian Religious Thought," 91.

15. Weinberg, "Trial of Mendel Beilis," 17–35.

16. Derzhavnyi arkiv Kyïvs'koï oblasti, f. 183, op. 5, d. 4, l. 180.

17. Rozanov, *Oboniatel'noe i osiazatel'noe otnoshenie*.

18. D-skii, "'Ekhad': Trinadstat' ran Iushchinskogo," in Rozanov, *Obonitatel'noe i osiazatel'noe otnoshenie*, 215–61. Ekhad or echad is the Hebrew word that signifies the oneness or unity of God.

19. Kornblatt, "Russian Religious Thought," 91.

20. See *Delo Beilisa*, 2:293–440.

21. D-skii, "Ekhad," 217.

22. Ibid., 218–35.

23. Ibid., 227.

24. Ibid., 234.

25. Ibid., 234–35.

26. Ibid., 244.

27. Ibid., 235–38.

28. Uranus, *Ubiistvo Iushchinskogo i kabbala* (St. Petersburg: n.p., 1913).

29. *Kievskaia mysl'*, no. 301 (October 31, 1913): 4.

30. *Vecherniaia gazeta*, no. 162 (October 29, 1913): 1.

31. See Eugene Avrutin's contribution to this volume.

10

A HALF-FULL CUP?

Transnational Responses to the Beilis Affair

Jonathan Dekel-Chen

IN JULY 1911 the imperial Russian police in Kiev arrested a Jewish man named Mendel Beilis (1874–1934). This otherwise unremarkable, middle-aged superintendent of a brick factory remained behind bars for the next two years while awaiting trial for the murder of a local twelve-year-old Christian boy named Andrei Iushchinskii. At the time of the arrest, agents of the Russian state—the police and judiciary in particular—set in motion what became an explosive series of events that would shake the foundations of the Russian Empire over the next two years. No less important, and closer to the core of this chapter, the arrest of Beilis and subsequent events ignited an expansive international response to what was perceived in much of Europe and the United States as an antisemitic assault by the Russian autocracy on the human rights of the Jewish minority in tsarist Russia.

Although no evidence linked Beilis to the killing of Iushchinskii and police investigators had earlier identified the likely (non-Jewish) culprits, the state prosecutor—with the sanction of Russia's minister of justice—indicted Beilis for ritual murder. During four weeks from late September to late October 1913, Beilis's trial became the focus of stormy public debate in Russia that transcended the contours of the legal proceedings themselves. On one side stood groups of conservatives and hypernationalists close to the autocracy; these men hoped to use the trial as a means of mobilizing old hatreds against Jews in order to bring peasants and other common folk in Russia closer to Tsar Nicholas II at a time of great political volatility. The autocracy had barely survived the Revolution of 1905, while social and economic challenges plagued much of the country, leaving the specter of future upheavals lurking everywhere. Added to these problems, Russia's peasant majority seemed profoundly dissatisfied with the regime and enormous foreign debt remained a chronic threat to the national economy still struggling with the transition to modernization after three decades of rapid industrialization. Following months of violent confrontations, the Russian army managed to suppress the Revolution of 1905 but not before strikers and protesters had forced Nicholas II to create a national parliament (State Duma) with wide electoral suffrage. While mostly devoid of real power, from its first convening in 1906 the Duma had become a public platform for fiery criticism of the tsar and the state. Despite repeated attempts by the regime to create a more compliant parliament through unilateral changes in the electoral system, Duma deputies continued to heap scorn on the autocracy. No less problematic for the tsar, a proliferating daily press disseminated this criticism in reports on these proceedings to an increasingly large reading public thirsty for news.[1]

Given this dangerous state of affairs in 1911, the Beilis Affair became a lightning rod issue in Russia. From the point of view of political conservatives, it mattered very little whether Beilis had actually perpetrated the murder of Andrei Iushchinskii. Rather, by demonizing him before and during the trial as a scheming, treacherous Jew, they hoped to unify Russians behind their tsar against new and old "enemies" supposedly capable of monstrous crimes. Thereby, it was hoped, the regime could benefit by creating a common enemy at a time of continuing political uncertainty while positioning the tsar as a bulwark of Christian values against the purportedly growing power of Jews in the economic life of the empire. On the other side of the debate ignited by the Beilis trial stood liberal Russians appalled by the actions of the tsar's government and its shadowy, judeophobic supporters on the extreme right. For liberals, this sort of behavior embodied the worst features of a reactionary autocracy. Moreover, Russia's liberal activists and journalists believed that the cynical manipulation of Russia's legal system by agencies of the state intent on convicting Beilis on preposterous charges of ritual murder bore ominous implications for the future of their beloved country.

The Beilis Affair echoed loudly long after the jury set him free in 1913. Following weeks of trial and deliberations he was declared innocent of all charges, but the jurors nonetheless remained convinced that young Iushchinskii had been a victim of ritual murder, thereby leaving a shadow of possible guilt over Jews. For non-Jewish Russians, particularly liberals, the case remained a signpost of the ever-present dangers of conservatism lurking in dark corners near the centers of authority as well as a painful reminder of how Europeans and Americans could easily see Russia as a primitive, backward land.[2] For local Jews, the verdict of the Beilis case—which had absolved the defendant but then potentially made all Jews suspects in this crime—reminded them of their precarious position in the Russian Empire. Consequently, the result of the trial gave Jews legitimate cause for concern. But it was no less true that the preceding decades had witnessed an overall movement among the empire's Jews from the tail toward the middle ground of national economic and professional life.[3] For Jews throughout the diaspora, the Beilis Affair had multiple effects. First, the renewal of the blood libel in Russia sparked by the trial seemed to indicate the incorrigible nature of the tsarist regime toward its Jews. Second, and more important for this chapter, the apparent success of the international mobilization on behalf of the defendant Beilis seemed to suggest a new, effective stage of Jewish intercession against repressive regimes.[4]

Unlike Robert Weinberg's chapter in this volume, mine does not deal with ritual murder per se, the details of the accusations made against Beilis, or the trial. The domestic significance of the trial, as well as the trajectory of judeophobia in Russia before and after, are also mostly outside the scope of this chapter. Instead, the focus is on the mobilization of international advocacy on behalf of Beilis and some later ramifications from that campaign. I also consider how specific advocacy actions for Beilis compared to older patterns of intercession among Western Jews to aid co-religionists in Eastern Europe and the Ottoman Empire. As will be seen, the international campaign for Beilis's acquittal brought a small, but significant, shift to how transnational Jewish intercessors in the West mobilized; this crisis simultaneously moved them toward greater proactivity and pushed them toward coordination of efforts with leaders in their target Jewish communities in the East.[5] I also show that this mobilization may have been no less important to Jewish life in the years thereafter—in Eastern Europe and in the West—than the ritual murder accusations brought against the defendant and the particulars of his trial. In sum, this chapter deals only peripherally with the development of ritual murder myths, their transmission, the accusations they sparked and the violence they caused. Rather, I suggest how this one episode— the Beilis Affair—demonstrates the wider, lasting effects on international developments unleashed by relatively isolated, rather absurd, and cynical cases.

THE BEILIS AFFAIR SEEN FROM A *LONGUE DURÉE*

The place of the Beilis Affair in the arc of Jewish transnational intercession in the modern era is the core of this chapter. I am not alone in this respect among the authors in this volume. For example, Gennady Estraikh mentions the lasting reverberation of the Beilis case in Soviet public discourse before and during the Gindin case in Moscow in 1922. My chapter takes a similar path, but in a separate arena—the enduring implications and afterlife of the Beilis Affair among transnational Jewish intercessors once the particulars of the case had moved into the realm of memory.

Reactions among transnational intercessors were important because the year of Beilis's acquittal, 1913, marked a pivotal chronological intersection. Until that time, intervention efforts by prominent Jews in the West had been characterized for the most part by episodic mobilizations among relatively few, prominent men on behalf of endangered co-religionists in various locations around Eastern Europe or in the Ottoman lands. From 1914 onward, by contrast, much larger attempts became the norm. The first modern transnational campaign occurred as a result of what came to be known later as the Damascus Affair of 1840. Here, two well-known Jews, Moses Montefiore in England and Adolphe Crémieux in France, used the popular press with great effect to mobilize public opinion in their home countries, thereby applying pressure on their own governments and on the Ottoman sultan to free a group of wrongly accused Jews imprisoned in Damascus on charges of ritual murder.[6] Their successful campaign in 1840 stood in contrast to a failed effort in 1856 at intercession during the Mortara Affair, when eminent Jews in Europe could not convince the Vatican to return a kidnapped Jewish child from Bologna to his parents.[7] The collective sense of frustration engendered by this episode led within four years to the establishment of the Alliance Israélite Universelle, the first transnational Jewish organization with a mandate to intercede on behalf of imperiled co-religionists abroad.[8] Several years later (1869–1872), many of these same Europeans, together with counterparts in the United States, mobilized to deal with a refugee crisis in the port city of Memel (Klaipeda), Lithuania, where thousands of desperate East European Jews had congregated to escape famine. In response, German, French, English, and American activists for the first time coordinated action to at once balance short-term relief for refugees with the need to correct the fundamental deficiencies of traditional Jewish society through targeted vocational training and resettlement programs.[9]

The communities of activists in the Jewish world expanded still further in response to widespread anti-Jewish violence that ripped through Russia after the assassination of Tsar Alexander II, then again after the highly publicized pogrom in Kishinev in 1903 and the anti-Jewish savagery that accompanied the Russian Revolution of 1905. In parallel to these reactive interventions, the Alliance and other European philanthropic organizations provided educational support to Jewish communities in the Muslim world, while other transnational organizations— among them Baron de Hirsch's Jewish Colonization Association in Paris and the Hebrew Immigrant Aid Society in New York—initiated programs in the last decades of the nineteenth century to resettle Jews from the East in new lands to the West.[10]

In retrospect, we know that such efforts before 1911 were later overshadowed by mass mobilizations for the relief of millions of Jews who suffered from World War I. These and additional activists continued their intensive efforts for East European Jews in distress until the early 1920s in response to the continued suffering wrought by the Russian Civil War, then as a result of Soviet Russia's short, brutal war against newly independent Poland, and the unprecedented pogroms that these conflicts triggered. During the interwar era, Jewish transnational philanthropists launched and/or sustained large agrarian resettlement projects and vocational training programs abroad. Transnational philanthropic activity intensified still further following the defeat of Nazi Germany and the magnitude of need among Europe's surviving Jewish remnant. Threaded throughout these many decades of cross-border activism was a parallel strand of intercession and philanthropic work among Zionists dedicated to the creation of a Jewish homeland and/or sovereign state in the Land of Israel.[11]

Given its chronological position on the eve of World War I, the Beilis Affair must be contextualized within these developments. This chapter, therefore, explores how the case influenced not just the practice of transnational intercession but also, and perhaps more importantly, the state of mind it produced among generations of subsequent intercessors in the West. One thing we already know at the outset: the acquittal of Beilis in 1913, and the reckoning it sparked among Russia's liberals, did not dispel long-held suspicions about Jews among the nation's conservatives or, perhaps, in the general population of the empire.[12]

Into the Breach: Transnational Intercession in Defense of Beilis

In terms of collective memory among Jews and non-Jews, the international response to the Beilis trial is captured in an illustration produced at the time about the outcome of the case (figure 10.1). In keeping with contemporary stereotypes and what probably was an understandably anti-Russian orientation in the Yiddish-language publishing house in New York that produced the postcard, Tsar Nicholas II taunts the fleeing Beilis, "Go, Mendel, you're free! Rejoice with your American friends, but I won't waste any time in getting even for your acquittal with the Russian brothers you have left behind." The thrust of the cartoon is the implied threat that loomed over Russian Jewry, even after the conclusion of the trial. My primary interest here, however, is in the tsar's reference to Beilis's foreign friends, who constitute the main actors in this chapter.

In light of recent memory among Jews at the time inside and outside the Russian Empire, the arrest and trial of Beilis seemed to signal the potential coming of a new, frightening wave of repression. Escalating outbreaks of agitation and

Figure 10.1. Yiddish postcard, circa 1913: "In Memory of the Beilis Trial: Beilis Not Guilty, Jews Guilty." *Source*: Artwork by Mitchel Loeb. Printed by Progress Publishing Company, New York. *Credit*: YIVO.

mob violence had plagued large parts of Eastern Europe from the 1880s, climaxing between 1903 and 1906. Blood libel accusations—eerily similar to those leveled by the Russian authorities against Beilis—had sparked or intensified many of these anti-Jewish episodes.[13] With the benefit of hindsight, we now know that the Beilis trial was the final case of the anti-Jewish blood libel trial in Europe; activists at the time, however, did not have this luxury. They acted in response to what they *did* know: a conviction in a ritual murder case could spark accusations elsewhere and perhaps a wave of unwanted westward migration among panicked East European Jews. The potential for intensified immigration was already a burning issue for Jews in the West, who were showing signs of ambivalence about the masses of co-religionists who had been disembarking on their shores from Eastern Europe for nearly three decades.[14] Hence, for Jewish elites in Russia and their allies abroad—still dealing with the shadow of antisemitism "from above" manifested in the Leo Frank Affair in the United States and the Alfred Dreyfus Affair in France among Jewish elites in the West—the Beilis trial was a kind of "Alamo" in terms of core Jewish interests.[15] For their part, liberals in Russia came to see the Beilis Affair as a way to bludgeon the autocracy for the worst, most embarrassing features of its conservatism.

The disturbing upswell of European antisemitism around the turn of the twentieth century unfolded in parallel to conflicting political trends inside Russia. Most important for our purposes: liberalism had seemed to be gaining traction in Russia, reflected by embryonic parliamentarianism, significant local autonomy embodied in the zemstvo system begun during the emancipation of serfs and other nationwide reforms under Tsar Alexander II, and gradual improvements in public education as well as a degree of economic progress sparked by rapid industrialization.[16] Russia had by no means transformed into an open, liberal society by the early 1910s. Rather, the empire remained repressive toward its myriad minority groups and any opposition to the tsar; the vast majority of its peasant population teetered just above subsistence farming; the state bureaucracy functioned erratically outside of the major cities; and the regime manipulated the nation's fledgling electoral system to protect the autocracy. But positive signs did exist, even for Jews. For example, the horrors of the 1905–1906 pogroms had passed with no major recurrences while an energetic, vocal liberal press openly debated the "Jewish question" and called for Russia to jettison judeophobia.[17]

Most Russian Jews, however, remained insecure about the future. Some had experienced upward socioeconomic mobility but most still barely eked out a living. For many, emigration or political radicalism seemed to be the only viable responses to their misfortune. Nevertheless, Jewish university students did not mobilize for Jewish issues in the decade or so before World War I. When Russian Jews did organize responses, these usually arose among older elites. While it seems that young Jews did coordinate strikes at their schools during the Beilis trial, the fact remains that during the Duma years (1906–1914) Jewish students did not display the political fervor of the previous decade, when they had spearheaded protests against antisemitic policies and anti-Jewish violence.[18] One explanation for the comparative inaction among young Jews may be that the well-publicized intercessions from the West during previous decades had created expectations about the inevitability of such support during the Beilis crisis.

Contours of Action

Since 1840 elite West European Jews interceded in Eastern Europe in ways that went beyond straightforward charity or relief. They employed a kind of informal, stateless diplomacy with an eye toward public opinion, mobilized by the press. Around the turn of the twentieth century, larger multiclass organizations in the West joined in these efforts.[19] Their "deliverables" ranged from material relief on the ground in Eastern Europe to political advocacy in Western capitals as well as attempts to curb anti-Jewish policies through financial leverage. Whatever the successes or failures in each of these cases, repeated intercessions created a precedent of transnational action that meant many things to many people by 1911. Among Western activists, the revival of the blood libel in Kiev signaled a need for renewed mobilization, not only in defense of the hapless defendant Mendel Beilis, but, as in the Damascus Affair some seventy years earlier, because the ritual murder accusation in Kiev triggered reactions in the West akin to a call to the defense of the Jewish people as a whole.

Looking back at a nearly forgotten study of American-Jewish intervention in late imperial Russia adds a fascinating layer to this story. It reveals that during the same period as the transnational mobilization for Beilis, North American individuals, companies, and government agencies perpetrated what many would consider atrocities against African Americans and migrant Chinese laborers at home. Moreover, these men and others engaged in brutal campaigns against insurgents and innocents in the Philippines. Similar things could be said about British, Belgian, Portuguese, Dutch, and French behavior in their North African, South American, and Asian colonies. So, in effect, we are talking about the mobilization of public opinion and governmental action by local Jewish communities in the West at a time when their home nations were, at best, ambivalent toward "others" at home and abroad. Added to this ethical morass, the Russian government often emphasized this double standard when confronted with demands from foreigners for protection of *its* Jews.[20] All of this meant that when mobilizing public opinion in their home countries for human rights abroad, Jews in the West often faced uphill *domestic* struggles.

The Beilis Affair transpired closely on the heels of a politically loaded episode of transnational advocacy. A preeminent Jewish leader of the time, the banker Jacob Schiff, had clashed with US President William Howard Taft earlier in 1911 over renewal of the commercial treaty between the United States and Russia, originally signed in 1832. Schiff urged Taft to abrogate the treaty as a means to pressure Tsar Nicholas II to reverse anti-Jewish policies, such as the Pale of Settlement, as well as to stop harassment perpetrated by the tsar's officials against American-Jewish tourists of Russian descent. This effort, together with a separate intercession by another Jewish luminary of the time, Louis Marshall, led to an overwhelming vote in the US House of Representatives in December to terminate the 1832 treaty and a congressional threat to cease trade entirely with Russia.[21] Therefore, from the start of Beilis's trial, Russia's elites were already sensitized to linkages between anti-Jewish repression and their country's standing in the international arena as well as the potential damage to Russia's economic security if foreign loans could not be secured.[22]

Let us now consider British responses to the June 1906 pogrom in Białystok—half a decade before the Beilis Affair—as a slightly earlier test case for the potential and limits of Jewish influence on the formation and conduct of foreign policy. Here, a ferocious wave of violence erupted, leaving two hundred Jews dead, hundreds wounded, and massive destruction of property. Following shortly after the horrific pogroms that accompanied the 1905 Revolution (and only three years after the highly publicized, and widely denounced, pogrom in Kishinev), the Białystok pogrom sparked intense condemnation of the tsar's government from the Duma and relatively diverse parts of Russian society. But pressure on the Russian regime did not stop here. Rather, direct appeals from prominent Russian Jews to leaders of the Jewish community in London quickly resulted in action.[23] In short order, articles in the *Times* stoked public outrage against the suspected collusion of the tsar's regime in anti-Jewish violence. An upswell of anti-Russian sentiment in Parliament, together with direct pressure from influential Jewish personages such as Lord Rothschild, did figure somewhat into the formation of Britain's subsequent Russian policy. But there were limits to what could be accomplished by mobilization of political connections and the press. In the end, Britain's overall foreign policy goals in a tumultuous international arena still took precedence over what would today be considered human rights issues. In 1906, whatever the pressures applied from mainstream newspapers and wealthy Jewish leaders to do more to protect Russia's Jews, Britain's Liberal government still preferred improved relations with Russia as a bulwark against the growing power of the German-Habsburg alliance. This prioritization led Her Majesty's government to the conclusion of the Triple Entente approximately one year later. Hence, in 1906–1907 pressures on behalf of Russian Jews may have colored but did not determine British policy.[24] The question remains, however: what did the transnational intercession on behalf of Mendel Beilis achieve?

What the Beilis Affair Changed

The reappearance of a ritual murder accusation in 1911 touched a nerve among intercessors in the West, whereas 1913 marks a turning point in regard to public relations. As mentioned earlier, mobilization of the press was not new. But defenders of Beilis exhibited new sensibilities, as shown by Lucien Wolf, the preeminent Jewish informal diplomat of his time in Britain. First, he demonstrated a refined analysis of public opinion. In a letter to the Board of Deputies of British Jews (the elected representative organization of British Jewry) in October, Wolf suggested that the board refrain from public pronouncements or appeals to the British government around the Beilis Affair. He advised avoiding saturation of the press while showing "the Board and the *Jewish Chronicle* that we have not been idle."[25] The community's newspaper had been voicing for some time its desire to see more strident actions. Here we learn that the respected intercessor was listening to this criticism while also developing a more nuanced tactical vision for mobilizing the press.

On another level, during the Beilis Affair Wolf began to formulate longer-term public relations *strategies*, not just tactical *responses*. This shift comes forth in a December 1913 correspondence—just weeks after the formal acquittal—dealing with an offer from a newspaper owned by William Randolph Hearst, the *New York American*, to finance the publication of Beilis's memoir, as well as his emigration to the United States. Wolf shared his concern with a leader of Polish Jewry that "nothing should be published [by the *American*] which would constitute a scandalous or ridiculous anti-climax to the recent Blood Ritual [sic] case."[26] In this way, a longer-term public relations strategy had an afterlife once the ritual murder crisis itself had receded.

In the case of the London House of Rothschild, the Beilis case prompted a particularly energetic response. While very active for decades in Jewish affairs throughout Europe and the Middle East, responses to specific crises around the Jewish world among the various Rothschild houses were not always in unison, nor did they always fit a predictable pattern.[27] Nathaniel, head of the London branch of the family at the time of the Beilis Affair, corresponded on the case with Cardinal Rafael Merry del Val, the Vatican's secretary of state. Lord Rothschild asked the Vatican to authenticate papal bulls that rejected the ritual murder accusation. As a result of their communication, the cardinal confirmed that an encyclical from Pope Innocent IV had declared the blood libel baseless, as a matter of principle. This letter (written on October 18, 1913) was reprinted in the mass-circulation *Standard* daily newspaper. Ten days later, an admiring *Pall Mall Gazette* poked fun at the power of the Rothschilds to elicit such a response from the Vatican. Nathaniel Rothschild also prepared a public letter of protest about the Beilis trial, signed by many dozens of British notables.[28]

How, if at all, did the ritual murder accusation against Beilis change the way Russian-Jewish leaders defended their own? An often-overlooked scholar of Eastern Europe concluded more than fifty years ago that the case resulted in the emergence of a new kind of mobilization. Evidently, the "primitiveness" of the charges shocked Russian-Jewish communal elites into a new kind of activism through which they no longer waited to be rescued by brethren from abroad. Rather, starting in 1911 Russian-Jewish elites organized not just for the legal defense of Beilis. Because they believed that the ritual murder accusation constituted a threat beyond the mere fate of Beilis, they now mobilized in defense of the integrity of the whole community.[29] While this interpretation may underrate previous attempts at Jewish self-defense, a greater point arises: transnational advocacy henceforth was a conversation between local communities and overseas intercessors. This conversation—not always cordial—pushed transnational advocacy toward a more modern application of aid wherein relationships between givers and recipients embodied at least a modicum of coordination, if not equity. Until then, foreign intercessors had operated in nearly complete detachment from local leaderships in the East where they interceded, rarely believing that much could be gained through cooperation with target communities. Thereafter, at least an attempt to synchronize action between transnational intercessors and local leaders (if they could be found) became a nearly universal feature of Jewish cross-border philanthropy and advocacy.

What the Affair Did Not Change

Since at least the mid-eighteenth century, when prominent European Jews attempted to reverse Empress Maria Teresa's expulsion of Prague's fourteen thousand Jews (based on her belief that they had betrayed her), intercessors have formulated action in complex international arenas, often at odds with national interests in their home countries and often without consensus among themselves.[30] A similar environment greeted Beilis's supporters in 1911. Specifically, any activism for his defense—and, thus, in conflict with the intents of St. Petersburg—had to account for the emergent Triple Entente against Germany and the Habsburg Empire. So whether one mobilized support in Paris or London, the winds of war swirling around Europe restricted one's range of action. On the other side of the geopolitical divide, foreign policy priorities in Berlin and Vienna belied an aggressive public relations campaign by German or Austrian Jews; aggressive tactics might offend Russian national pride, and thereby push Russia further into the arms of the probable enemies of Germany and Austria in the looming global conflict. In the early 1910s European war seemed increasingly likely, but no one wanted to ignite it over a "Jewish" issue, not even to do battle against heinous blood libel accusations in Russia.[31]

Once it did move into action, however, transnational intercession for Beilis seemed to affirm, and somewhat enhance, earlier efforts. For example, the Alliance Israélite Universelle formed in 1860 to correct the inability among activists four years earlier to pressure the Holy See during the Mortara Affair. Now in 1913—fifty-three years later—Nathaniel Rothschild had successfully solicited from the Vatican a formal, written rejection of the blood libel. This pronouncement may not have directly influenced the verdict of the Russian jury in the Beilis trial—after all, the jurors in this case were almost certainly not Catholics. But the highly publicized letter from Rome did elevate Beilis's defense onto the moral high ground in world public opinion.[32] It is equally clear from the Beilis Affair that old networks of individual intercession remained mostly unchanged. As a case in point: a Rothschild-initiated action that resulted in the Vatican's repudiation of the blood libel; that appeal was in fact authored by Lucien Wolf, at the time a prominent journalist with deep ties to Jewish organizational life in Britain.[33]

In ways that resembled prior efforts, tactical agreement coalesced slowly about how to confront the ritual murder accusation in Kiev. This hesitancy is no surprise; the practice of transnational advocacy was still in its infancy and had no clear-cut infrastructure. True, the other national advocacy organizations in the largest Western Jewish communities—the American Jewish Committee (AJC) in New York, the Hilfsverein der deutschen Juden in Germany, and the Alliance in France—all believed that something must be done. But in 1911 no nationwide mechanisms existed to coordinate action in any of these countries, certainly not to manage a transcontinental campaign. Added to that, American Jewry was preoccupied with other, mostly domestic issues during the two years before the trial: the 1912 presidential campaign, the Leo Frank case, and the campaign to abrogate the 1832 treaty.[34] Some voices demanded quick, "forcible" action against the Russian regime, while others cautioned against public protests that might invite antisemitic backlash at home or more intransigence in Russia.[35] Most understood the importance of coordination but had trouble convincing others to surrender autonomy and prestige on behalf of a greater good.[36]

At first glance, transnational action for Beilis indeed looked like "more of the same" compared to what had come before. Judging by outcomes, however, the campaign for Beilis seems somewhat more professional and successful. The AJC and Hilfsverein orchestrated efforts in major Western newspapers that emphasized human rights and repression while minimizing more troublesome questions that arose from the reemergent ritual murder accusation.[37] Moreover, the campaign showed sophistication in its focus on those messages that applied maximum moral pressure on the Russian regime, namely on the tsar, while reducing the risks of political reprisals against Russian (or Western) Jews.[38] Central among these efforts was "An Open Letter to the Czar [sic]" dispatched by prominent American clergymen and published by the *Independent* newspaper in September 1913, reprinted (or commented upon) shortly thereafter in multiple American newspapers.[39] The "Letter" implored the tsar: "The Jews [in Russia] have experienced during your reign persecutions far more cruel than those which prevailed during the Middle Ages.... You have gone much farther than your father in your anti-Jewish policies. How can you ... tolerate, in the land in which you hold absolute sway, such refinement of barbarity and brutality and yet venture to face the rulers of civilized powers as their equal? ... Open your eyes! Observe the fruits that freedom bears under other skies."[40]

In a separate branch of the campaign, Jacob Schiff and other activists cultivated more realistic approaches to advocacy when responding to the ritual murder charges leveled against Beilis: the goal of the campaign should not be an unachievable "breaking" of the Russian autocracy. Rather, the intercessors reoriented themselves toward attaining incremental gains in response to the ritual murder accusations, whose cumulative results would improve the lives of Russia's Jews.[41] While transnational pressure probably contributed little toward Beilis's acquittal, the political fallout from the trial did convince Western Jewish leaders that more could be done in the future to force concessions from the tsar.[42]

A Troubling Afterlife

For better or worse, up to now this episode in transnational advocacy has conformed more or less to what a scholar might expect to find; the activists succeeded in some respects, while accomplishing less in others. No one, however, expected what followed the conclusion of the trial. We now briefly explore a significant epilogue in this story of transnational intercession that transpired *after* Beilis went free. The accepted historical narrative of posttrial events—based mostly on Beilis's own retelling—held that his Zionist commitment propelled the family's emigration to Ottoman-controlled Palestine in 1914 once he became convinced that his safety and livelihood had been permanently compromised in Russia.[43] This move, so the old narrative goes, demonstrated that Beilis's nationalistic fervor outweighed more pragmatic considerations, even if he was promised some assistance upon arrival in Palestine. After all, it was no secret that physical conditions in Palestine at the time left much to be desired. Moreover, the decision to go there required that Beilis first decline potentially lucrative financial opportunities offered to him in the United States and Europe.[44] Further along in the accepted narrative of the posttrial period, the Jewish and Arab communities in Palestine initially welcomed Beilis as a celebrity, he acclimated quickly but economic hardship forced him—like many other immigrants at the time—to relocate to New York, where he hoped to gather money from supportive Jewish communities and donors. A variety of sources in Kiev, Europe, and Palestine had promised Beilis funds but, by his account, did not deliver them.[45] Finally, so the story goes, once he was in the United States the community embraced him as a people's hero.

The archives suggest a sharply different scenario. Years of interaction with Beilis, in fact, damaged attitudes among American activists toward relief for East European Jews in subsequent crises. This bore serious implications in the East and West given that the overall needs for intercession in the Jewish world only increased after 1913. What happened? Just as the smoke cleared following his acquittal, the AJC learned from the Hilfsverein in Berlin that Beilis was considering offers to perform in vaudeville if he did not receive significant financial aid for his family from Western Jewish organizations. Indeed, Beilis had made veiled threats in this regard. The possibility that Beilis might actually appear on sensationalist stages in North America worried the AJC. Whether or not Beilis knew it, three popular Yiddish-theater productions about his case had run in New York during 1913.[46] The headquarters of the AJC was in Manhattan; its leaders surely understood the potential popularity of a vaudeville show starring the man himself and what harm this sort of parody might do to Jewish interests. From England, Lucien Wolf cautioned that Beilis "should not be exploited by music hall proprietors and people of that description."[47] To avoid this embarrassment, the American Jewish Committee in fact did what it could to ensure that Beilis relocated to the Yishuv (the pre-1948 Jewish community in Palestine), not to New York; this included a quiet allotment of several thousand dollars, to be augmented by contributions from European organizations, for the emigration of the Beilis family to Palestine and its upkeep there.[48] By Beilis's account, these funds had been exhausted by 1920, making his move to New York imperative.[49]

That move, however, did not solve the dilemmas Beilis presented for his American intercessors. In short, emigration to Palestine did not bring harmony. For the next seven years (1913–1920), Beilis repeatedly implored Jewish organizations in the West for financial relief. He hinted that failure to provide sufficient support for the self-described "martyr" would force the family to relocate to the United States. These letters accused a variety of Zionist notables (inside and outside Palestine) of deception and suggested that the Palestine Committee and others had misappropriated charitable contributions intended for him.[50] An otherwise level-headed and empathetic Louis Marshall (on behalf of the AJC) bridled against what seemed like outrageous monetary demands from Beilis, particularly at a time when American Jews were engaged in fundraising for masses of suffering Jews in Eastern Europe and for the building of a national homeland in Palestine, recently promised by the British Mandatory authorities.[51] Once resettled in the United States with his family in 1921—a move facilitated with yet more assistance from philanthropic organizations—Beilis continued to write Marshall requesting compensation for recent misfortunes.[52] Although already considered a nuisance and at risk for squandering whatever aid he did receive, the AJC transferred the balance of a special fund of $5,000 that it had raised for him.[53]

The final segment of this posttrial saga picks up in New York in 1928. Beilis, now approximately fifty-four years old, issued desperate appeals to the AJC, threatening suicide if his family's economic distress was not remedied. By this time, however, the AJC had learned to avoid direct support; instead, it referred his case to the Jewish Social Service Association.[54] Evidently unable to maintain complete detachment from Beilis, the AJC asked members of its Executive Committee to contribute to a one-time $500 fund and tried (unsuccessfully) to find him new employment despite his failures to hold a job in the United States.[55] These efforts ended in January 1930, when the Jewish Social Service Association notified the AJC that "the time had come when the Beilis family should stand on their own feet."⁵⁶ Henceforth, the archival record suggests that the family dropped entirely off the radar screen of Jewish philanthropic organizations.

I now raise the question that I had originally thought to consider solely in regard to events around Beilis's arrest, trial, and acquittal: should this epilogue be seen as a watershed in transnational Jewish advocacy? Perhaps. It reveals disaffection among the intercessors for precisely the same target—in this case an individual—for whom they had previously interceded. From my wider research, it appears that this sort of souring among transnational activists became increasingly common. Also, tactical *dis*agreement emerged between advocacy organizations in North America and Europe only *after* the trial: in late 1913 the AJC flatly refused a request from the Hilfsverein to raise 100,000 rubles (approximately $49,000 at the time) to convince Beilis *not* to go into vaudeville. The AJC did raise up to $5,000 and informed the Europeans to gather on their own whatever else they deemed necessary in dealing with Beilis.⁵⁷

One can only conjecture on what obscured these unpleasant events until now. For his part, Beilis's autobiography ended its recounting of events just before his arrival in the United States.⁵⁸ Whatever the answer, this posttrial chapter—now adjusted to the archival record—had a lasting impact on transnational advocacy. The frictions it caused are significant because many of those activists exasperated with Beilis were the same men who formulated, launched, and sustained huge philanthropic campaigns for East European Jewry during the interwar period. How did Beilis color their attitudes when moving forward? At the risk of speculation, I offer the following possibilities. Perhaps their frustrations with Beilis help explain why for much of the next two decades these heads of Jewish communities in the West increasingly acquiesced to immigration restrictions by their home governments and increasingly sought solutions for their needy co-religionists *in* Eastern Europe or in other sites outside their own countries.⁵⁹ Perhaps it is better for this epilogue of the Beilis Affair to remain in the shadows. I shudder to think what creative antisemites and ardent blood libelists might do today with this information.

JONATHAN DEKEL-CHEN is a Senior Lecturer in Modern History at the Hebrew University of Jerusalem and academic Chair of its Leonid Nevzlin Research Center for Russian and East European Jewry. His work has been widely published at prestigious university presses and in scholarly journals. During the 2015–2016 academic year, he was an Israel Institute Visiting Professor in the Department of History and the Institute for Israel and Jewish Studies at Columbia University.

NOTES

Research for this chapter was supported, in part, by the Israel Science Foundation (Grant no. 462/05).

1. For more on the proliferation of literacy in fin-de-siècle Russia, see Jeffrey Brooks, *When Russia Learned to Read* (Princeton, NJ: Princeton University Press, 1985).

2. For analysis of liberal views about Jews in the Russian-language popular press at this time, see Jonathan Dekel-Chen, "Liberal Answers to the 'Jewish Question': Then and Now," in *Church and Society in Modern Russia*, ed. Elise Wirtschafter and Manfred Hildermeier (Wiesbaden, Germany: Harrassowitz, 2015), 133–56.

3. For a study of this process, see Benjamin Nathans, *Beyond the Pale: The Jewish Encounter with Late Imperial Russia* (Berkeley: University of California Press, 2002).

4. The term "intercession" is usually translated in Hebrew as *shtadlanut*; the term "intercessor," as *shtadlan*.

5. For the purposes of this chapter, I use the term "international" to denote global phenomena and the term "transnational" to denote specific cross-border actions taken by intercessors or others.

6. For details, see Jonathan Frankel, *The Damascus Affair: "Ritual Murder," Politics, and the Jews in 1840* (Cambridge: Cambridge University Press, 1997).

7. For details, see David Kertzer, *The Kidnapping of Edgaro Mortara* (London: Picador, 1997).

8. For more on this process, see Eli Bar-Chen, "Two Communities with a Sense of Mission: The Alliance Israélite Universelle and the Hilfsverein der deutschen Juden," in *Jewish Emancipation Reconsidered: The French and German Models*, ed. Michael Brenner, Vicki Caron, and Uri R. Kaufman (Tubingen: Mohr Siebeck, 2003), 111–17.

9. For further discussion, see Yaakov Kelner, *The Start of Global Jewish Social Planning: Institutional Intervention on Behalf of Russian Jewry in the Early 1870s* [Hebrew] (Jerusalem: Hebrew University, 1975).

10. For descriptions of these activities before 1911, see Ronald Sanders, *Shores of Refuge: A Hundred Years of Jewish Emigration* (New York: Henry Holt, 1988).

11. For a more detailed overview of this transition, see Jonathan Dekel-Chen, "Activism as Engine: Jewish Internationalism, 1880s–1980s," in *Religious Internationals in the Modern World: Globalization and Faith Communities since 1750*, ed. Abigail Green and Vincent Viaene (Basingstoke: Palgrave Macmillan, 2012), 269–91.

12. Benjamin Nathans, "The Other Modern Jewish Politics: Integration and Modernity in Fin de Siecle Russia," in *The Emergence of Modern Jewish Politics: Bundism and Zionism in Eastern Europe*, ed. Zvi Gitelman (Pittsburgh: University of Pittsburgh Press, 2003), 27. For a canonical work on the intersections between judeophobia and politics in late imperial Russia, see Hans Rogger, "The Beilis Case: Anti-Semitism and Politics in the Reign of Nicholas II," *Slavic Review* 25, no. 4 (1966): 615–29. See also Ezekiel Leikin, trans. and ed., *The Beilis Transcripts: The Anti-Semitic Trial That Shook the World* (Northvale, NJ: Aronson, 1993).

13. These included Hungary (Tiszaeslár, 1882), Poland (Chojnice, 1899), and Austrian-ruled Bohemia (Polná, 1899). See Hillel J. Kieval, "Blood Libels and Host Desecration Accusations," *YIVO Encyclopedia of Jews in Eastern Europe*, accessed November 4, 2016, www.yivoencyclopedia.org/article.aspx/Blood_Libels_and_Host_Desecration_Accusations. For further discussion, see *Anti-Jewish Violence: Rethinking the Pogrom in East European Jewish History*, ed. Jonathan Dekel-Chen, David Gaunt, Natan Meir, and Israel Bartal (Bloomington: Indiana University Press, 2011).

14. For examples, see Myron Berman, *The Attitude of American Jewry towards East European Jewish Immigration, 1881–1914* (New York: Arno Press, 1980), 516–23; and Alfred J. Kutzik, "The Social Basis of American Jewish Philanthropy" (PhD diss., Brandeis University, 1967), 984–89.

15. For more on these points, see Christoph Gassenschmidt, *Jewish Liberal Politics in Tsarist Russia, 1900–1914* (New York: New York University Press, 1995), 112; and Albert S. Lindemann, *The Jew Accused: Three Anti-Semitic Affairs (Dreyfus, Beilis, Frank) 1894–1915* (New York: Cambridge University Press, 1991).

16. The zemstvo reform of 1864 came in response to the abolition of serfdom in Russia three years earlier. The zemstvo system created a network of elected, mostly autonomous local governing bodies charged with administration of the Russian countryside—and later its cities—instead of the state or nobles, which no longer had the means or authority to govern Russia's vast hinterland. For details of this extraordinary model of rural governance, see Terence Emmons and Wayne S. Vucinich, eds., *The Zemstvo in Russia: An Experiment in Local Self-Government* (Cambridge: Cambridge University Press, 1982).

17. For details, see Dekel-Chen, "Liberal Answers."

18. Nathans, *Beyond the Pale*, 302.

19. For details, see Jonathan Dekel-Chen, "Philanthropy, Diplomacy, and Jewish Internationalism," in *The Cambridge History of Judaism*, vol. 8; *The Modern Period, c. 1815–c. 2000*, ed. Mitchell Hart and Tony Michels (New York: Cambridge University Press, forthcoming 2017); and Eli Lederhendler, "Democracy and Assimilation: The Jews, America, and the Russian Crisis from Kishinev to the End of World War I," in *The Revolution of 1905 and Russia's Jews*, ed. Stefani Hoffman and Ezra Mendelsohn (Philadelphia: University of Pennsylvania Press, 2008), 245–54.

20. Gary Dean Best, *To Free a People: American Jewish Leaders and the Jewish Problem in Eastern Europe, 1890–1914* (Westport, CT: Greenwood, 1982), 3–4, 7, 10.

21. Evyatar Friesel, "Jacob H. Schiff and the Leadership of the American Jewish Community," *Jewish Social Studies* 8, nos. 2–3 (2002): 64; Gassenschmidt, *Jewish Liberal Politics*, 113.

22. Frederick C. Giffin, "American Reactions to the Beilis Case," *Social Science* 55 (Spring 1980): 90–91.

23. These included Duma members Maxim Vinaver, N. I. Katsenelson, and Shmaria Levin.

24. At most, British statesmen agreed to privately pressure Russian authorities about anti-Jewish policies. See Shmuel Galai, "The Jewish Question as a Russian Problem: The Debates in the First State Duma," *Revolutionary Russia* 17, no. 1 (2004): 52–53.

25. Archive of the YIVO Institute, New York (hereafter YIVO), Lucien Wolf and David Mowshowitch Papers, Record Group (hereafter RG) 348, b. 12, f. 105, Wolf to Alexander, October 22, 1913. Founded in 1841, the *Jewish Chronicle* is the oldest newspaper published by the British Jewish community.

26. YIVO, Lucien Wolf and David Mowshowitch Papers, RG 348, b. 12, f. 105, Wolf to Dr. [Joseph] Bychowsky, December 12, 1913.

27. For examples, see Simon Schama, *Two Rothschilds and the Land of Israel* (London: Collins, 1978); and Mattityahu Mintz, "The Jewish Facet to the Withdrawal of the Rothschilds from the April 1891 Loan to Russia [Hebrew]," *Tsion* 54 (1989): 401–35. Additional banking houses (and centers of power) of the Rothschild family existed in Paris, Vienna, Frankfurt, and elsewhere.

28. Signatories on the letter of protest included the duke of Norfolk, Alfred Lyttleton, Montagu Bulter, Lord Cromer, Lord Llandaff, and Lord Rosebery. See Miriam Rothschild, *Dear Lord Rothschild: Birds, Butterflies, and History* (Philadelphia: Balaban, 1983), 36. Some government officials, such as Lord Morley, Lord Lansdowne, Lord Crewe, and Lord Loreburn declined to sign.

29. Zoşa Szajkowski, "The Impact of the Beilis Case on Central and Western Europe," *Proceedings of the American Academy for Jewish Research* 31 (1963): 198.

30. For details, see François Guesnet, "Textures of Intercession: Rescue Efforts for the Jews of Prague, 1744–1748," *Simon Dubnow Institute Yearbook* 4 (2005): 355–77.

31. For more on this point, see Szajkowski, "Impact of the Beilis Case," 199–205.

32. Ibid., 206–7.

33. YIVO, Lucien Wolf and David Mowshowitch Papers, RG 348, b. 12, f. 105, Wolf to Rothschild, October 1, 1913. After World War I, Wolf became the best-known and most influential informal British-Jewish diplomat of his time.

34. Giffin, "American Reactions," 89–90.

35. See the correspondence between Herbert Friedenwald and David de Sola Pool (New York Board of Jewish Ministers), May 17 and May 23, 1912, Archive of the American Jewish Committee, New York (AJC Archive), General Correspondence, 1906–1932, box 4, folder 17.

36. AJC Archive, General Correspondence, 1906–1932, b. 4, f. 18, Schneiderman to Nathan, September 11, 1913. Among other things, Harry Schneiderman (assistant secretary of AJC) implored Nathan to convince Leo Motzkin to share information about the trial.

37. AJC Archive, General Correspondence, 1906–1932, b. 4, f. 17, Schiff to Friedenwald, February 9, 1912; AJC Archive, General Correspondence, 1906–1932, b. 4, f. 17, Schiff to Friedenwald, February 13, 1912.

38. AJC Archive, General Correspondence, 1906–1932, b. 4, f. 17, Schiff to Friedenwald, February 9, 1912; AJC Archive, General Correspondence, 1906–1932, b. 4, f. 17, Friedenwald to Schiff, February 14, 1912; AJC Archive, General Correspondence, 1906–1932, b. 4, f. 17, Friedenwald to Pereira Mendes, September 23, 1913; AJC Archive, General Correspondence, 1906–1932, b. 4, f. 17, Schneiderman to Nathan, November 13, 1913. For specific references to these types of articles in the *London Times* (May 6, 1912) and in the *New York Times* (October 9, 1913), see Robert Weinberg, *Blood Libel in Late Imperial Russia: The Ritual Murder Trial of Mendel Beilis* (Bloomington: Indiana University Press, 2014), 109, 124–25.

39. Jacob Schiff seems to have been the first to suggest this sort of public petition in February of that year. See AJC Archive, General Correspondence, 1906–1932, b. 4, f. 17, Schiff to Friedenwald, February 9, 1912. This folder contains clippings of these editorials from several newspapers.

40. Quoted in "The Beilis Affair," *American Jewish Yearbook* 16 (1914–1915): 85–89.

41. AJC Archive, General Correspondence, 1906–1932, b. 4, f. 17, Schiff to Bernstein, November 11, 1913; AJC Archive, General Correspondence, 1906–1932, b. 4, f. 17, Schneiderman to Nathan, November 13, 1913.

42. Henry Feingold, *"Silent No More": Saving the Jews of Russia. The American Jewish Effort, 1967–1989* (Syracuse, NY: Syracuse University Press, 2007), 7.

43. The primary source for this was Beilis's autobiography; see *The Story of My Sufferings* (New York: Mendel Beilis Publishing Co., 1926).

44. Ibid., 210–16, 226.

45. For example, 41,000 francs from prominent German Jews to purchase a house. See ibid., 236–38. Beilis added that the Rothschilds and Justice Louis Brandeis had made implicit promises of financial aid. These disappointments with his co-religionists evidently brought Beilis to title the final chapter of his autobiography, "Many Promises and Few Fulfillments."

46. For more on this phenomenon, see Joel Berkowitz, "The 'Mendel Beilis Epidemic' on the Yiddish Stage," *Jewish Social Studies* 8, no. 1 (2011): 199–225.

47. YIVO, Lucien Wolf and David Mowshowitch Papers, RG 348, b. 12, f. 105, Wolf to Bychowsky, December 12, 1913.

48. AJC Archive, General Correspondence, 1906–1932, b. 4, f. 17, Schneiderman to Nathan, November 13, 1913; AJC Archive, General Correspondence, 1906–1932, b. 4, f. 17, Marshall to Executive Committee of AJC, December 29, 1913; AJC Archive, General Correspondence, 1906–1932, b. 4, f. 18, Marshall to Simon, January 2, 1914; AJC Archive, General Correspondence, 1906–1932, b. 4, f. 17, Marshall to Simon, February 5, 1914.

49. Beilis, *Story of My Sufferings*, 238–41.

50. AJC Archive, General Correspondence, 1906–1931, b. 4, f. 16, Beilis to AJC, November 25, 1919; AJC Archive, General Correspondence, 1906–1931, b. 4, f. 16, Beilis to AJC, April 23, 1920; AJC Archive, General Correspondence, 1906–1931, b. 4, f. 16, Beilis to AJC, November 24, 1920. Beilis promised at this time that he would make no more financial demands on the AJC if it helped him emigrate to the United States. See also AJC Archive, General Correspondence, 1906–1931, b. 4, f. 21, Beilis to Marshall, November 22, 1921.

51. AJC Archive, General Correspondence, 1906–1932, b. 4, f. 21, Marshall to Schneiderman, April 20, 1921.

52. AJC Archive, General Correspondence, 1906–1932, b. 4, f. 21, Beilis to Marshall, August 20, 1922; AJC Archive, General Correspondence, 1906–1932, b. 4, f. 21, n.n. [Schneiderman's secretary] to Marshall, August 28, 1922.

53. AJC Archive, General Correspondence, 1906–1932, b. 4, f. 21, Marshall to Schneiderman, November 23, 1921; AJC Archive, General Correspondence, 1906–1932, b. 4, f. 21, Marshall to Beilis, November 23, 1921; AJC Archive, General Correspondence, 1906–1932, b. 4, f. 21, Schneiderman to Marshall, November 28, 1921.

54. AJC Archive, General Correspondence, 1906–1932, b. 4, f. 15, memorandum on Beilis, October 17, 1928; AJC Archive, General Correspondence, 1906–1932, b. 4, f. 15, Schneiderman to Taussig, June 6, 1929.

55. AJC Archive, General Correspondence, 1906–1932, b. 4, f. 15, Bressler to Schneiderman, December 3, 1928; AJC Archive, General Correspondence, 1906–1932, b. 4, f. 15, Schneiderman to Tausig, June 6, 1929; AJC Archive, General Correspondence, 1906–1932, b. 4, f. 15, Waldman to Gottlieb, December 26, 1929; AJC Archive, General Correspondence, 1906–1932, b. 4, f. 15, Gottlieb to Waldman, December 30, 1929. The Bank of the United States declined to employ Beilis due to a lack of English skills.

56. AJC Archive, General Correspondence, 1906–1932, b. 4, f. 15, Taussig to Schneiderman, January 6, 1930.

57. AJC Archive, General Correspondence, 1906–1932, b. 4, f. 18, Marshall to Simon, January 2, 1914.

58. For a comparable case of a "blind spot" in the historical record, see Jonathan Dekel-Chen, "The Agricultural Settlement around the Black Sea: A Lost Chapter of Jewish Interwar History [Hebrew]," *Zmanim* 93 (2006): 70–80.

59. This contrasted with the unequivocal position in early 1914 of the AJC in favor of unrestricted Jewish immigration from Russia, Romania, and Galicia. See AJC Archive, General Correspondence, 1906–1932, b. 4, f. 17, Marshall to Simon, February 5, 1914.

11

SIMULATING JUSTICE

The Blood Libel Case in Moscow, April 1922

Gennady Estraikh

Moscow: Capital City of Russia

The blood libel episode that occurred in Moscow in March and April 1922—a year after the Lenin government's turn from the postrevolutionary War Communism system to the New Economic Policy (NEP)—has not gained sufficiently close academic attention so far, though descriptions of it can be found in memoirs and newspaper reports. Notwithstanding the fact that the 1922 case hardly contains tragic elements and rather has the trademarks of a farce, it deserves a place in Soviet history as a precursor to more salient incidents of anti-Jewish violence and abuse in the second half of the 1920s.[1] In his analysis of antisemitic occurrences in postrevolutionary Belarus, Arkadi Zeltser concludes that "the rises and falls in interethnic tension in Soviet society correlated with the shifts in the level of general social tension."[2] Indeed, the 1922 case can be seen as a litmus test of Jewish-gentile social relations in early Soviet Moscow, when the bulk of the city's population, many of them recent migrants from various parts of the erstwhile Russian Empire, lived in difficult conditions, huddled together in overcrowded "communal apartments," barracks, and dormitories. Although the economic situation in the capital was better than in other parts of Soviet Russia, even those residents who had a job (unemployment was close to 12 percent) usually struggled to buy food and other necessities.[3] The Soviet poet David Samoilov visualized Moscow at that time as a "morally despondent city, which was involved in 'expropriation of expropriators,' had lost [its] moral principles, [and] condoned the terror of the 1920s and the liquidation of the church and cultural values."[4]

Boris Bogen, the pioneer historian of Jewish philanthropy, who came to Moscow as a representative of the American Jewish Joint Distribution Committee, wrote that in the beginning of 1922 the NEP, which allowed for the reappearance of private property and free commerce, "was already in force, but its efforts were not yet viable. The few stores that were open were provision-houses, but the confidence of the dealers in the possibility of doing business and in the safety of their wares was so limited that every night they would pack their goods up and take them home with them until morning."[5] The newly opened opportunities for trade and small-scale manufacturing appealed to Jews who had similar occupations before the revolution. Their visible, sometimes ostentatious, success intensified antisemitism in Soviet society to the point that being a Nepman became synonymous with being a Jew.[6]

By that time, the Soviet capital came to be known as a "Jewish city," because during World War I and particularly after the revolution, the share of Jews in the general population of the city rapidly increased, from 0.4 percent in 1912 to 2.7 percent in 1920 and 5.6 percent in 1923.[7] In the popular imagination, the share of Jews in the Moscow population was much higher. A character in a story by Lidia Seifullina asserts: "Nowadays Moscow is a Jewish city, Russians are not allowed to reside there. They can't get the right of residence [*pravo zhitel'stva*]."[8] In September 1923 Zalman Wendroff, the Soviet Yiddish journalist who wrote for the foreign press, cited demographic estimates, which placed the number of Moscow Jews at 450,000–500,000 (in actuality, close to 86,000 by 1923), or 35 percent of the city's population. He also emphasized that, although thousands of Moscow Jewish residents found gainful employment in the byzantine apparatus of the Soviet state and in the growing sphere of private business, many local Jews were desperately poor and often remained dependent on the Moscow Society for Helping Jews in Need (Moskovskoe obshchestvo po okazaniiu pomoshchi nuzhdaiushchimsia evreiam).[9]

The Moscow Society for Helping Jews in Need worked under the auspices of the Moscow Jewish Religious Community, which provided an institutional umbrella for the synagogues, the Dorogomilovo Cemetery (on the Mozhaisk Highway), and other communal bodies catering to the interests and needs of the traditional segment of the local Jewish population. Albert Fuks, chairman of the Community, was a former "sworn attorney" (*prisiazhnyi poverennyi*), as lawyers were called in imperial Russia. Fuks had a reputation as a seasoned Jewish civic activist leader; in prerevolutionary years he headed the Moscow branch of the influential Society for the Promotion of Culture among the Jews of Russia.[10]

Meir Gindin (or Hindin in some Yiddish-language sources), the seventy-five-year-old protagonist of our story, certainly belonged to the traditional segment of

Moscow Jewry. A *shammes*, or synagogue sexton, he was also a member of the *hevrah kadishah* (burial society) and supported himself by delivering corpses to the Dorogomilovo Cemetery, the only Jewish burial ground in Moscow. Thus, Albert Fuks assigned him to take the body of the eight-year-old boy named Hirsh Rabinovich from a morgue and to transport it to the cemetery. The boy had died of pneumonia on March 21, 1922, and his father, a physician who, together with his wife and four children, recently returned from emigration, lacked money to pay for the burial. Rats inundated the morgue where the deceased was kept, and by the time Gindin received the body, it had numerous traces of rat bites. In violation of the law, the old man wrapped the corpse in a bed sheet and a blanket and carried it to Lubianka Square, planning to take a tram to the cemetery. However, he stumbled while trying to enter the tramcar, fell down, and dropped his load. Some people in the crowd found the package suspicious and turmoil ensued. As a result, Gindin ended up at the nearest police (or, in Soviet terms, *militia*) station, from where the corpse was send to forensic experts, who confirmed, first, that the boy had died of natural causes, and, second, that the boy was circumcised.[11] Clearly, the incident should have been over, and press reports specifically highlighted the boy's unmistakable Jewishness. Nonetheless, it is likely that the public and/or police suspected that Gindin might have been carrying a murdered Christian boy.

Coincidentally, Lubianka Square, the site of Gindin's arrest, housed the headquarters of the Soviet secret police, which in February 1922 was reshaped into the State Political Directorate (GPU in Russian abbreviation). At the same time, the GPU became responsible for conducting a new antireligious campaign, which marked a radical change in the government's attitude to religion: from acute propaganda to an offensive underpinned by state repression.[12]

The following pages describe and analyze how Soviet authorities reacted to antisemitic incidents that took place at the time when, first, the religious segment of the population, most notably Russian Orthodox believers, felt themselves attacked by the state, and second, the memories of the Mendel Beilis case (1911–1913) remained fresh among many people in Russia and abroad.[13]

Confiscation of Church Valuables

In 1922 the decision of the Soviet government to seize church valuables for famine relief added fodder to antisemitic feelings, which were rife at that time, though their pervasive existence usually remained deniable by the regime and invisible to foreign observers.[14] Yet Marguerite Harrison, an American journalist and spy who arrived in Russia in February 1920 and spent eighteen months there, wrote about "the universal detestation of the Jews by the peasant population, who still do not feel safe from Jewish exploitation, and attribute all the evils of Bolshevism to the Jews."[15] Feelings against Jews ran high among the sailors, predominantly of peasant stock, who in March 1921 participated in the Kronstadt rebellion that pushed Lenin and his government to implement the NEP.[16] Even the very fact that, thanks to such organizations as the Joint Distribution Committee (which until late 1922 operated in Russia under the umbrella of the American Relief Administration), Jews would often get more help from abroad than other segments of the population aroused antisemitic sentiments among residents of Moscow and other places.[17]

Many people affixed blame for the confiscation of church valuables on Jewish communists, despite the fact that the campaign targeted all religious institutions, including those of Jews. According to the US commissioner in Riga (the Latvian capital was an important center for information gathering about the Soviet state), "inventories of valuables at Churches of other faiths have also been made, and especially at synagogues, so as to put an end to anti-Jewish agitation."[18] Still, even terminologically the Orthodox Church appeared as the prime target of the confiscations: the official documents and the press wrote about *tserkovnye tsennosti* (church valuables) rather than, say, "valuables of religious institutions." The daily *Izvestiia*, published by the Central Executive Committee, Soviet Russia's highest legislative and administrative body, explained that although synagogues, "especially the so-called choral synagogues," had significant quantities of religious silverware, they were in this sense much poorer than churches. Therefore it was suggested to persuade observant Jews to contribute to famine relief with the payments that were traditionally paid for an *aliyah*, the honor of reciting the blessing before and after the reading of a section of the Torah.[19]

At any rate, the scale of confiscation of synagogue valuables certainly paled in comparison to the scale of that in the realm of Orthodox churches and monasteries. Meanwhile, the idea that Jews played a central role in executing this campaign had gained wide traction. In April 1922 the New York socialist Yiddish daily *Forverts* (Forward) published an interview that Maxim Gorky, who was sojourning in Berlin at that time, gave to the bestselling Yiddish writer Sholem Asch. Gorky accused Jewish Bolsheviks of being "tactless," and argued that "irresponsible striplings, rather than all of them, participate[d] in defiling sacred places of the Russian people."[20] The US commissioner in Riga reported on April 21, 1922, that "opposition to the confiscation of Church property . . . is causing anti-Jewish feeling, as the Jews are held to be responsible for the Decree."[21]

On March 28 and 29, 1922, a segment of the local population in the city of Smolensk resisted the efforts of local authorities to confiscate church valuables. Characteristically, the resistance at once began to develop into a pogrom: Jewish market stalls were destroyed, and there was an attempt to throw two Jews from a bridge. Prompt intervention by the police and cadets of a military school prevented more serious harm. *Der emes* (Truth), the Yiddish daily of the Central Bureau of the Communist Party's Jewish Sections, tried to rationalize the event, arguing that the crowd turned against Jews because large numbers of the "Jewish bourgeoisie" were engaged in speculation.[22]

Meir Gindin's Interrupted Trudge

Against this backdrop Meir Gindin soon reappeared in the limelight. This happened when an eleven-month-old boy died of pneumonia in Moscow. As in the case of Hirsh Rabonivich, the deceased baby's family, which carried the name Kaplan and came from famine-stricken Ukraine, did not have money to bury the deceased. Oddly, Albert Fuks had failed to learn a lesson from the recent incident that occurred with Gindin and once again sent the impecunious man to take care of the boy's body. This time, on April 4 (eight days before Passover and twelve days before Easter), Gindin wrapped the corpse in a cloth and put it into a linen sack. It seems that he decided to walk the few miles to the cemetery, thereby saving 300,000 rubles, which was the hyperinflated cost of a tram ride (an ongoing monetary reform had been replacing the high-denomination banknotes).

Gindin's journey to the cemetery was interrupted at Theater Square, a short distance from Liubianka Square. Romanova, a points woman on the tramways, stopped the old man and demanded that he show her the contents of the sack. When Gindin told her to mind her own business, the woman raised a shout claiming that the Jew was carrying a murdered child. A large crowd quickly assembled, attracted by the woman's clamor. With public tensions running high, some people immediately sided with Romanova and were ready to take the law into their own hands. A couple of individuals even swore to God that they had seen Gindin murder the boy. Three members of the crowd played particularly active roles: Yefremenko, an adult peasant; Serafimov, an eighteen-year-old theater-ticket scalper; and a well-dressed woman with the surname, Bendel, of her husband, a converted Jew. Later it became known that the Dorogomilovo Cemetery was the resting place of Mrs. Bendel's Jewish father. However, all this did not stop her from shouting with the crowd: "Beat the Jews!"[23]

Ultimately, Gindin survived the ordeal thanks to several worthy—or to borrow *Izvestiia*'s description "conscientious"—people who called a patrolman. As a result, despite the resistance of the crowd, the old man was brought to the nearby police station. No doubt, the setting, in the heart of Moscow, next to the GPU's headquarters, had a role in how events then unfolded. In a remote part of the city, Gindin's chance to reach the cemetery without trouble was much slimmer. Meanwhile, the police identified Romanova, Yefremenko, Serafimov, and Bendel as the prime troublemakers and apprehended them, though Bendel was soon released and played no role in future events. In general, it seems that the policemen had no doubts that they were dealing with a mundane, albeit somewhat bizarre, situation. However, in order to cool down the electrified crowd, they decided to send for medical experts and a Russian Orthodox priest from the nearby church of the Nativity of the Virgin, in Stoleshnikov Lane. In addition, they invited four representatives of the crowd (their names did not appear in newspaper reports) to observe the investigation. The ad hoc commission came to the conclusion that, first, the body revealed no evidence of violent death, and, second, the boy was definitely Jewish.[24]

Although the press mentioned only the militia's involvement, it is absolutely clear that other, much more influential institutions of Soviet power, most notably the GPU and the Communist Party apparatus, took charge of dealing with this incident. It is known that, following Lenin's instruction, the Party should direct court sentencing.[25] The veteran of the Party and member of the Moscow Party Committee Innokentii Stukov, appointed to act as the public prosecutor, also played a leading role in the concurrent campaign aimed at confiscating church valuables.[26] Particularly remarkable was the rapid nature of the investigation. The trial opened without any delay, on the next day, April 5, and was staged within a stone's throw distance from the GPU—at the Polytechnic Museum, a popular, capacious site for cultural and political events.

On April 6 *Izvestiia* came out with a short article signed by Mikh. K. Most probably it was Mikhail Kol'tsov (Fridliand), a talented, Kiev-born essayist, later a central figure in Soviet journalism. He addressed his readers:

> Did you think that the old types of [Prime Minister Pyotr] Stolypin and [one of the main instigators of the blood libel case against Mendel Beilis, Minister of Justice Ivan] Shcheglovitov had already gone to their last resting places or evaporated, vanished in darkness?
>
> It turns out that they are still alive. They hold on, persist, although they—the old notorious personages of the Beilis trial—keep out of sight, hibernate somewhere....
>
> A decade has passed relatively quietly.... The war followed by the revolution and the proletariat dictatorship had boarded up, riveted their slandering mouths that spewed out poisonous venom.

According to the author, the "old types" reappeared in the climate of the NEP and, most important, "in the tense days, when church valuables are being seized in order to help those who suffer from famine."[27] The "reappearance" of the characters from the dramatis personae of the Beilis trial is also mentioned in the article written for *Forverts* by Samson Koldovsky, a Moscow-based representative of the

Joint Distribution Committee, who believed that the Gindin affair had revealed "the suppurating wound of contemporary Jewish life in Russia, as well as of all Russian life." In Koldovsky's detailed descriptions of the affair, Romanova is typified as a reincarnation of Vera Cheberiak, the central character in the Beilis case, who headed the gang of thieves and was allegedly responsible for taking the life of the boy Andrei Iushchinskii. The non-Jewish foreign press also pointed out the parallels between the two cases. *The New York Times* made it plain in its article's title, "A Beilis Case in Moscow" (April 9, 1922), and reminded, or informed, its readers that "Beilis arrived in the United States in February of last year."

The Beilis Affair had been present in the Soviet public discourse, too. Cheberiak, executed in Kiev in 1918, had been the subject of a short film, released in 1917. In 1921 the State Publishing House produced in Moscow a revised edition of Vladimir Bonch-Bruevich's book *A Mark of the Age: The Murder of Andrei Iushchinskii and the Beilis Case*, based on the author's reports written during the trial. The Soviet press kept writing about the 1913 trial in Kiev and the more recent court cases of prosecuting and punishing those persons who participated in the conspiracy against Beilis. A couple of such incidents took place in Moscow and were well publicized. In September 1919 Oskar Vipper, the prosecutor during the Beilis trial, faced a revolutionary tribunal that sentenced him to confinement in a concentration camp "until the full strengthening of the communist system in the Russian Republic."[28] In May and June 1922 the press reported the case of the former Kiev agent provocateur Mikhalin, who later changed his name to Makhalin, joined the Communist Party and had a career in the government bureaucracy, advancing to the position of chairman of Moskustarprom (the Moscow Department of Artisanal Industry).[29] For all that, some actors in the Gindin case might have never heard about the Kiev trial, so that traditional prejudices rather than an experience gained from the Beilis Affair triggered their reaction to seeing an old Jew carrying a child's body in his bag.

The Trial

Yekaterina Kuskova, the prominent liberal economist and politician, remembered that the trial had "attracted huge interest" among Moscow residents.[30] On April 5 and 6 about 1,500 people of various walks of life filled the auditorium of the Polytechnic Museum to its full capacity. A month later, the same lecture hall of the museum would be used for another court trial—of Orthodox Church leaders who had "failed" to donate church valuables to aid those stricken by the famine. Both trials fulfilled agitational purposes. The authorities clearly wanted to send a message that such items associated with legacies of the past would be not tolerated in Moscow or elsewhere in Soviet Russia.[31] According to Koldovsky, on the first day of the trial the majority of the public was non-Jewish, whereas on the second day Jews dominated among the audience. However, he did not explain the reason for this change of the spectators' ethnic composition. It seems that there was no predetermined list of audience members, whereas the authorities would regulate the audience composition during the show trial of the Socialist Revolutionaries staged in Moscow two months later.[32]

The judge, public prosecutor, and jurors had been carefully selected. The Yiddish poet and essayist Daniel Charney, who lived in Moscow in the early 1920s, emphasized that all of them were ethnically Russian.[33] Characteristically, Lenin instructed Mikhail Kalinin, the titular head of the Soviet state and a man of impeccable Russian origin, rather than the Jewish Leon Trotsky to act as the official spokesman on the subject of the campaign of confiscating church valuables.[34] It is known that around that time Lenin was generally concerned about the prominent role that Jews played in the Soviet apparatus.[35]

The judge, Ivan Smirnov, had worked at Moscow bakeries before World War I and was a soldier during the war. He joined the Bolshevik Party in 1917 and from 1919 occupied high positions in the capital city's revolutionary tribunals and courts. Koldovsky praised him as a top, even-keeled judge and an unassuming person who dressed in a simple proletarian-style shirt. Two factory workers, who assisted the judge, sat dressed in their overcoats. Perhaps they simply did not have any appropriate clothes under their overcoats and, like Ilya Ehrenburg, kept their overcoats "on all the time, afraid to allow the skirts of the overcoat to part by some incautious movement."[36] In Soviet Russia, the three-man bench had replaced the jury system that existed in late imperial Russia (in the fall of 1913, an all-Christian jury acquitted Beilis). Significantly, defense lawyers were not mentioned in the press report. Lenin's hostility toward the defense lawyers left an imprint on the early Soviet legal system, based on the principle that laws were just as long as they served the interests of the revolution.[37] Therefore, from the very beginning, the regime saw the judicial system as its instrument of governance and did not allow the court to function independently from the executive branch.

The trial itself, particularly Gindin's erratic explanations, provoked a lot of laughter from the audience. Even the surname of the points woman on the tramways, Romanova, who started the commotion by asking Gindin to show her the contents of the bag, made the audience laugh: "Some surname! Must be a member of the tsar's family!" In his concluding remarks, the prosecutor urged everyone to "overcome the darkness and medieval nature of the accusation—a legacy of tsarist and religious obscurantism. I hope you walk away not only laughing, but also with sadness in your souls."[38]

The *Washington Post* wrote that, according to the "official soviet Rosta News agency," the "attempted pogroms in Moscow" were associated with "'Black Hundred' monarchists" who were "carrying out antisemitic propaganda in connection with the requisition of church treasures. The news agency declares the apparent object is to strengthen opposition to the requisition."[39] Yet the court failed—and it seems that it even did not make an attempt—to reveal direct links between the three accused members of the public and any "Black Hundred" monarchist organization. Moreover, the question remained unanswered: why did Romanova assume that Gindin was carrying the body of a child? The Soviet press reproduced the decision of the court that:

> found all the accused guilty and pronounced sentence as follows: [the three instigators of the commotion] Romanova, Yefremenko, and Serafimov were accused of antisemitic agitation, but since they all were unwitting tools of experienced adherents of the Black Hundreds movement and enemies of the Soviet regime, they were sentenced to a severe public reprimand. Gindin—his guilt was proven, but it was impossible to punish a decrepit and hungry old man, engaged in carrying corpses to the cemetery to earn a crust of bread. The court could not punish him, but recommended that the Social Security administration should immediately ensure that he was supplied with the necessary means of subsistence.[40]

At the same time Albert Fuks was accused of gross dereliction of duty for allowing Gindin to carry corpses that were not dressed in shrouds. Charney explained that the accusation was spurious because the Jewish community simply could not obtain linen to make shrouds. He recalled how Jacob Maze, chief rabbi of Moscow, asked Shimon Dimanshtein, people's commissar for Jewish affairs in Lenin's government and a former star student at a Lubavitch yeshiva, to help procure linen to give a proper Jewish burial to the dead. However, Dimanshtein either could not or was unwilling to grant the rabbi's request.[41] The Soviet apparatus considered such people as Fuks particularly dangerous, believing that they, as representatives of the bourgeois intelligentsia and former public figures who lost their influence during the years of revolution, used religious communal bodies, which remained a legal form of communal activity, to once again play a role in Jewish life.[42]

Stukov, the public prosecutor, told Fuks that as an educated person he had to remember the lessons of the Beilis trial. Stukov did not find convincing Fuks's explanation that the community had no means of transportation: their horse, coach, and even the *mitas* (stretchers for carrying corpses) had been confiscated in 1918 and since then the community had not been allowed to collect money to buy such things. Although Stukov argued that Fuks should be punished by imprisonment, the court, after five hours of deliberation and, conceivably consultations with the higher echelons of power, decided that a year of compulsory labor, without detention, would suffice.[43] In reality, it meant that Fuks could keep his regular job while forfeiting part of his wage (up to 25 percent) and certain social insurance claims.[44] Ultimately, he was destined to reach the age of eighty by the time of his arrest, on January 4, 1938, which led to his execution on April 8, 1938. His "crime" was classified as "counterrevolutionary activity."[45] Both Innokentii Stukov (1887–1936) and Ivan Smirnov (1891–1938) would be liquidated, too, also as counterrevolutionary elements.

In the Aftermath of the Trial

The leading article published on April 9, 1922, in *Izvestiia*, edited at that time by the veteran Bolshevik Iurii Steklov (Ovshii Nakhamkis), expressed dissatisfaction with the mild verdict delivered by the court. The editorial suggested that justice would have been better served if the three antisemitic culprits—Romanova, Yefremenko, and Serafimov—had been sent to a political literacy course, keeping them disenfranchised until they successfully completed their studies. The newspaper emphasized that antisemitism, a "legacy of the past," was particularly menacing if it found support among the toilers. The editorial also reminded readers that the "notorious Beilis Affair had caused a singularly destructive moral blow to tsarism, placing it beyond the limits of even such a civilization as the bourgeois one," and that antisemitism was equally shameful as "the horrible cases of cannibalism brought about by starvation-induced mental disorders. On the other hand, the myth of ritual murder is also a concomitant of some kind of psychosis, mental disorder or, at least, spiritual darkness."[46]

Der emes referred to the Beilis case in the title of its reports published on April 7 and 9, 1922: "Beylisyade in ratn-Rusland ummeglekh!" (A [new] Beilisiad in Soviet Russia is impossible!). Writing in *Der emes*, in an article titled "At the Gindin-Beilis Trial," Moyshe Rafes, a former Bundist leader turned into a Comintern functionary, broached a somewhat different, conspiratorial view of the event:

> It is a devilish plan—to try to start a second blood libel process in the fifth year of Russia's Soviet regime, in the heart of the worldwide proletarian revolution.
> Petty bourgeois elements are raging in the country. The New Economic Policy has brought back the competition and, as a result, refreshed antisemitic spirits. Counterrevolutionary circles think that their time is close at hand and they feel more confident. . . .
> Soviet Russia accommodates today a hodge-podge of various epochs. Elements of communism fight with state capitalism as well as with decrepit landlord feudalism. This became clear when the resistance of priests to the seizure of church valuables surfaced in the last few weeks. . . . Antisemitism, a response of the dark forces, is the vehicle that medieval feudalism can use to incite the broad masses against communism.

Rafes knew how to explain Romanova's curiosity concerning the content of Gindin's bag: the whole incident had been carefully organized, and he expected the prosecution to stress the fact that a counterrevolutionary *organization* stood behind the ostensibly spontaneous turmoil.[47] Charney, however, presumed that no such organization was behind this incident. Rather, one could simply see that there was a body in the sack.[48] The press presented yet another explanation: Gindin wanted to catch his breath, and when he put down the load he carried the string holding the point of the bag untied and the boy's head came into view.[49]

In any case, the organizers and executors of the trial did not choose to pursue the conspiratorial line of indictment. Either they did not have enough supporting material to do so (the police could not properly conduct an investigation due to the rushed nature of the trial) or, more likely, the authorities were wary of possible protests and did not want to aggravate the already tense situation. In April hundreds of Moscow parishioners tried to protect their churches, showing resistance to the militia and army units.[50] At that moment prejudices such as the blood libel could be rendered less important than the rebellious mood of the Christian masses. Significantly, the trial accused both Jews and non-Jews of backwardness and obscurantism, with the blood libel as only one of the examples of such "relics of the past."

Antisemitism began to be considered as a separate serious issue only in the second half of the 1920s, when the authorities faced a potent and dangerous tide of verbal and violent attacks against Jews, especially as migration, coupled with professional and social mixing, brought together an increasing number of Jews and non-Jews. For instance, in Moscow the Jewish population grew from 86,000 in 1923 to 132,000 in 1926.[51] The blood libel continued to influence the thinking of antisemites. At the end of 1928 or the beginning of 1929 the Communist Party organization at the Naphtha Syndicate's Moscow offices (the Soviet foreign trade syndicate that had offices abroad) issued a reprimand to one of its members—a woman who argued that there were instances when Jews had abducted Christian children in order to use their blood in matzo.[52] In 1930 an American communist witnessed a public trial in Poltava, Ukraine, against a woman accused of spreading the blood libel.[53]

Although the vast majority of such cases would not be brought for trial, thirty-eight proceedings involving antisemitism passed through the courts of Moscow city and (only in four instances) province during a single year ending on September 30, 1928. In the end, out of seventy defendants, ten were acquitted, and fourteen were sentenced to loss of freedom, whereas the majority defendants were fined, sentenced to compulsory labor, or given a public reprimand.[54] In fact, the Soviet Criminal Code, adopted on June 1, 1922, did not have special provisions regarding antisemitism, therefore such crimes were judged under the terms of "assault and battery," "abusive insult," or "hooliganism."[55] At the same time, antisemitism was not a taboo topic of Soviet press coverage and other forms of media and propaganda. According to William Korey, a historian of antisemitism in the Soviet Union: "During the twenties, especially toward the end of that decade, the regime continued to make strong efforts to contain the virus of anti-Jewish bigotry. If . . . severe sentences for anti-Semitic offences were rare, nonetheless educational campaigns were energetically conducted by party organs, and various pedagogical efforts were undertaken."[56] This intense and vociferous campaign had eclipsed the 1922 episode which, in hindsight, can be seen as an ignored and forgotten forewarning of ensuing developments. But even earlier, in 1922, the speed of "performing justice" and the reputation of a crusader against antisemitism, reinforced by distancing itself from anything remotely reminding the Beilis case, allowed the regime to turn the Gindin affair into a nonevent and focus on the main task of the day: weakening religious institutions.[57] This explains, in particular, why out of the five culprits in the "Gindin case" only Albert Fuks, chairman of the Moscow Jewish Religious Community, received an actual punishment.

GENNADY ESTRAIKH is Clinical Professor at the Skirball Department of Hebrew and Judaic Studies, New York University. From 1988 to 1991, he was the managing editor of the Moscow Yiddish literary monthly *Sovetish Heymland*. In 1991, he moved to Oxford, England, where he defended his doctoral dissertation and worked at the Oxford Institute of Yiddish Studies. His publications include *Soviet Yiddish: Language Planning and Linguistic Development* (1996), *In Harness: Yiddish Writers' Romance with Communism* (2005), *Yiddish in the Cold War* (2008), *Yiddish Literary Life in Moscow* (2015), the coedited volume *1929: Mapping the Jewish World* (2013, winner of the National Jewish Book Award), and *Children and Yiddish Literature: From Early Modernity to Post-Modernity* (2016).

NOTES

1. See, e.g., Gennadii Kostyrchenko, *Tainaia politika Stalina: Vlast' i antisemitizm* (Moscow: Mezhdunarodnye otnosheniia, 2001), 100–111; Elissa Bemporad, "Empowerment, Defiance, and Demise: Jews and the Blood Libel Specter under Stalinism," *Jewish History* 26, no. 3–4 (2012): 343–61.

2. Arkadi Zeltser, "Ethnic Conflict and Modernization in the Interwar Period: The Case of Soviet Belorussia," in *Anti-Jewish Violence: Rethinking the Pogrom in East European History*, ed. Jonathan Dekel-Chen, David Gaunt, Natan M. Meir, and Israel Bartal (Bloomington: Indiana University Press, 2010), 183.

3. "Vi lebt zikh in Moskve?," *Moment*, March 8, 1922; Irina N. Gavrilova, *Naselenie Moskvy: Istoricheskii rakurs* (Moscow: Mosgorarkhiv, 2001), 109.

4. David Samoilov, *Pamiatnye zapiski* (Moscow: Vremia, 2014), 26.

5. "Dr. Boris D. Bogen Described Russian Condition on His Return to This Country," *Reform Advocate*, December 30, 1922.

6. Ekaterina Foteeva, "Copying with Revolution: The Experiences of Well-to-do Russian Families," in *Living through the Soviet System*, ed. Daniel Betraux, Paul Thompson, and Anna Rotkirch (New York: Routledge, 2004), 88.

7. Gavrilova, *Naselenie Moskvy*, 420.

8. Lidia Seifullina, *Vykhval'* (Moscow: Gosudarstvennoe izdatel'stvo khudozhestvennoi literatury, 1931), 166.

9. V. N. Drof [=Zalman Wendroff], "Yidn in Moskve," *Haynt*, September 10, 1923. Exaggerated figures for the size of the Moscow Jewish population are also noted later—e.g., "over 300,000" in Eliyahu Shulman, "A Sholem-Aleykhem-ovnt in Moskve," *Literarishe bleter*, July 24, 1936.

10. See Iurii Snopov, "Evreiskaia obshchina Moskvy v 1920–1930-e gg.," *Diaspory* 3 (2004): 80–99. According to other sources, Fuks became chairman of the Community later, whereas in 1922 he was one of the Community's leaders—see, e.g., Arkadii Zeltser, "The Belorussian Evsektsiia and Jewish Religious Life in 1927: A Change in Policy," *Jews in Eastern Europe* 1, no. 35 (1998): 58.

11. "Nedopustimye poriadki," *Izvestiia*, April 5, 1922; Samson Koldovsky, "Di komedye mitn aliles-dam in Moskve," *Forverts*, May 6, 1922.

12. Simon Pirani, *The Russian Revolution in Retreat, 1920–1924: Soviet Workers and the New Communist Elite* (London: Routledge, 2008), 144.

13. Robert Weinberg, *Blood Libel in Late Imperial Russia: The Ritual Murder Trial of Mendel Beilis* (Bloomington: Indiana University Press, 2013).

14. Solomon M. Schwarz, *Antisemitism in the Soviet Union* (New York: American Jewish Committee, 1948), 3.

15. Marguerite E. Harrison, *Marooned in Moscow: The Story of an American Woman Imprisoned in Russia* (New York: George H. Doran, 1921), 148.

16. Paul Avrich, *Kronstadt 1921* (Princeton, NJ: Princeton University Press, 1970), 155, 178–80.

17. Bertrand M. Patenaude, *The Big Show in Bololand: The American Relief Expedition to Soviet Russia in the Famine of 1921* (Stanford, CA: Stanford University Press, 2002), 51; R. A. Latypov, "'Kul'turnyi shok' v mezhdunarodnykh otnosheniiakh: Opyt raboty ARA v Sovetskoi Rossii v 1921–1923 gg.," *Novyi istoricheskii vestnik* 12 (2005): 18.

18. Boleslaw Szczesniak, ed., *The Russian Revolution and Religion: A Collection of Documents concerning the Suppression of Religion by the Communists, 1917–1925* (Notre Dame, IN: University of Notre Dame Press, 1959), 74.

19. "Tserkovnye tsennosti golodaiushchim," *Izvestiia*, April 14, 1922. See also Vladimir Goridovets, "Iz"iatie tsennostei u religioznykh obshchin v Vitebskoi gubernii v 1922 godu," *Vestnik tserkovnoi istorii* 3–4 (2012): 308–46.

20. See Mikhail Agursky and Margarita Shklovskaia, *Iz literaturnogo naslediia: Gor'kii i evreiskii vopros* (Jerusalem: Hebrew University, 1986).

21. Szczesniak, *Russian Revolution and Religion*, 74.

22. "Sobytiia v Smolenske," *Pravda*, April 4, 1922; "Attempted Pogrom at Smolensk Confirmed by Soviet Organ," *Reform Advocate*, April 29, 1922.

23. Koldovsky, "Di komedye mitn aliles-dam in Moskve."

24. "Nedopustimye poriadki."

25. James Ryan, "Cleansing NEP Russia: State Violence against the Russian Orthodox Church in 1922," *Europe-Asia Studies* 65, no. 9 (2013): 1811–12.

26. *Iz"iatie tserkovnykh tsennostei v Moskve v 1922 godu: Sbornik dokumentov iz fonda Revvoensoveta Respubliki* (Moscow: Pravoslavnyi Sviato-Tikhonovskii gumanitarnyi universitet, 2006), 28.

27. Mikh. K., "Neudavshaiasia provokatsiia. Nechist'," *Izvestiia*, April 6, 1922.

28. "Revoliutsionnyi tribunal. Delo Vippera," *Izvestiia*, September 20, 1919. See also E. V. Zhogoleva and A. D. Proshliakov, "Izmenenie obstanovki posle vstupleniia prigovora v zakonnuiu silu," *Vestnik Iuzhno-Ural'skogo gosudarstvennogo universiteta, seriia Pravo* 18 (90) (2007): 37.

29. "Razoblachennyi provokator," *Izvestiia*, May 14, 1922; "Delo provokatora Makhalina," *Izvestiia*, June 2, 1922.

30. See Vladimir Khazan, *Osobennyi evreisko-russkii vozdukh: K problematike i poetike russko-evreiskogo literaturnogo dialoga v XX veke* (Moscow: Gesharim, 2001), 313.

31. Elizabeth A. Wood, *Performing Justice: Agitation Trials in Early Soviet Russia* (Ithaca, NY: Cornell University Press, 2005), 82.

32. Julie A. Cassiday, *The Enemy on Trial: Early Soviet Courts on Stage and Screen* (DeKalb: Northern Illinois University Press, 2000), 46.

33. Daniel Charney, *A yortsendlik aza* (New York: Tsiko, 1943), 305.

34. *Iz"iatie tserkovnykh tsennostei v Moskve v 1922 godu*, 26–27. See also *Arkhivy Kremlia: Politbiuro i tserkov': 1922–1925* (Novosibirsk: Sibirskii khronograf, 1997), 1:142.

35. Gennady Estraikh, "Letters to the Editor," *East European Jewish Affairs* 23, no. 1 (1993): 123.

36. Ilya Ehrenburg, *Men, Years, Life: First Years of Revolution, 1918–1921* (London: MacGibbon and Kee, 1962), 139.

37. Eugene Huskey, *Russian Lawyers and the Soviet State: The Origins and Development of the Soviet Bar, 1917–1939* (Princeton, NJ: Princeton University Press, 1986), 36, 37, 42, 75.

38. An. Charov, "Neudavshaiasia provokatsiia," *Pravda*, April 7, 1922; "Stavka na temnotu," *Izvestiia*, April 9, 1922. See also Zinovy Zinik, *The Mushroom-Picker*, trans. Michael Glenny (London: Heinemann, 1987), 91.

39. "Moscow Pogroms Are Foiled," *Washington Post*, April 7, 1922.

40. See the English-language rendering in Zinik, *Mushroom-Picker*, 92.

41. Daniel Charney, "Tshikave protsesn in Moskve," *Tsukunft*, October 1941, 37.

42. Zeltser, "Belorussian Evsektsiia," 56–57.

43. Charov, "Neudavshaiasia provokatsiia"; Koldovsky, "Di komedye mitn aliles-dam in Moskve."

44. Schwarz, *Antisemitism in the Soviet Union*, 97.

45. *Rasstrel'nye spiski: Moskva, 1937–1941, "Kommunarka," Butovo* (Moscow: Memorial, 2000), 421.

46. "Pozornoe iavlenie," *Izvestiia*, April 9, 1922. In 1931, Statin, too, characterized antisemitism as "the most dangerous survival of cannibalism"—see, e.g., *New York Times*, January 15, 1931.

47. Moyshe Rafes, "Af 'Hindin-Beilis' protses," *Der emes*, April 7, 1922.

48. Koldovsky, "Di komedye mitn aliles-dam in Moskve"; Charney, *A yortsendlik aza*, 304.

49. "Sovet-gerikht farvorft mit farakhtung a blut-bilbl, vos antisemitn hobn gepruvt aroyfvarfn oyf yidn," *Forverts*, April 9, 1922.

50. *Iz"iatie tserkovnykh tsennostei v Moskve v 1922 godu*, 16–18.

51. Lev G. Zinger, "Dvizhenie evreiskogo naseleniia SSSR," *Voprosy biologii i patologii evreev* 2 (1928): 127.

52. Schwarz, *Antisemitism in the Soviet Union*, 27–28.

53. Melech Epstein, "Pages from My Stormy Life: An Autobiographical Sketch," *American Jewish Archives* 14, no. 2 (1962): 148.
54. Schwarz, *Antisemitism in the Soviet Union*, 95–97.
55. Ibid., 92.
56. William Korey, "The Origins and Development of Soviet Anti-Semitism: An Analysis," *Slavic Review* 31, no. 1 (1972): 115.
57. Ryan, "Cleansing NEP Russia," 1808.

❈ 12 ❈

THE BLOOD LIBEL AND ITS WARTIME PERMUTATIONS
Cannibalism in Soviet Lviv

Elissa Bemporad

IN THE SUMMER of 1945 the city of Lviv, liberated from the Germans and incorporated by the Soviets into the Ukrainian Soviet Socialist Republic, became the arena of a ritual murder accusation against the Jews. According to the allegations, local Jews had kidnapped Polish and Ukrainian children, murdered them, and hidden their corpses within the confines of one of the local synagogues. Instigated by the rumors, a crowd of four hundred people gathered from the Lviv Krakovskii marketplace by the neighboring synagogue, on Vuhilna Street 3. Amid the commotion and a number of physical attacks against Jewish passersby, passionate assertions resounded through the crowd. These included statements of disappointment that Hitler had not come to Lviv some twenty years earlier, which would have prevented the Jews from killing children. Some voiced their rage over the traces of blood of the allegedly murdered children in the synagogue courtyard. Others cried that Jews stole children, slaughtered them and turned their bodies into food to sell at the marketplace.[1] Without the prompt intervention of the Lviv city police, these accusations most likely would have spiraled into a pogrom, as anti-Jewish violence triggered by blood libel rumors had become a common feature in the postwar (and post-Holocaust) Eastern European landscape immediately following the defeat of the Germans and the establishment of Soviet power.

Instances of anti-Jewish violence elicited by false blood libel allegations occurred in at least a dozen Polish cities and towns in 1945 and 1946. The first one took place in Cracow, on August 11, 1945, when Jews were accused of abducting and murdering thirteen (or perhaps as many as eighty) Christian children and hiding their corpses in the local synagogue. Jewish property came under attack, a fire was set inside the synagogue, and at least one Jew was killed and many were wounded.[2] During the pogrom of July 4, 1946, that erupted in the city of Kielce following a ritual murder accusation, forty-two Jews were killed and over forty were injured.[3] While there are numerous and substantial studies on the blood libel in postwar Poland, there is virtually no research on the ritual murder accusation in those territories that—like the city of Lviv—came under Soviet occupation after World War II. Historically a multiethnic city inhabited mostly by Poles and Jews, and a smaller percentage of Ukrainians, Lviv was first occupied by the Soviet Union in the fall of 1939 under the terms of the Ribbentrop-Molotov Pact of August 23, 1939, and subsequently invaded by the German army in June 1941. Exploring the distinct features of the events in Lviv, as well as the similarities with other instances of anti-Jewish violence that occurred in postwar Poland, this micro study provides new insight into the history of the blood libel in twentieth-century Eastern Europe. First, by contextualizing the Lviv case within the history of the blood libel under the Soviets before and during the war, it discusses the different dynamics in the Soviet government's response to the ritual murder accusation. Second, this chapter reveals the changes that occurred in the allegation itself, shedding light on the complicated interplay among the blood libel accusation, World War II, and the new fragile and social environment that emerged in Soviet Lviv under communism. If the events in Lviv underscored the persistence of traditional antisemitism embedded in religious prejudice, they also confirmed that the unique treatment of the Jews at the hands of the Germans in occupied Ukraine nurtured the existing notion of their ethnoreligious and political otherness. The encouragement of expressions of antisemitic beliefs and behaviors under German occupation yielded distinctive permutations in the traditional blood libel, eliciting the emergence of a new notion of Jewish ritual murder. This notion had less to do with religious rituals and practices and more with the everyday realities of hunger and privation.

Finally, this chapter explores how the memory of destruction and the reality of displacement generated by the war, in conjunction with the renewed brutal policies of Sovietization, could result in unexpected alliances between Poles and Ukrainians. Despite their recent history of ethnic conflict and reciprocated massacres, Poles and Ukrainians could come together by identifying a common religious and political enemy, Jewish and communist at the same time. While the allegation of ritual murder should not be considered the archetypal expression of antisemitism in Soviet society (both the interwar Soviet Union and newly annexed territories, including Lviv), it deserves close attention. The blood libel accusation can in fact be used as a canvas to explore neighborhood sociology, memory and habits of violence, questions of cultural transmission, and state responses to antisemitism in Soviet society.[4]

The General Soviet Context

Little is known about the history of the ritual murder accusation in the Soviet Union, about its endurance, its permutations, and the responses it generated among government authorities. The available scholarship on Soviet Jewry, and on the history of antisemitism, seems to suggest that after the 1911–1913 Beilis Affair, likely the most notorious ritual murder accusation in pre-Holocaust Europe, the blood allegation died out, completely and without much blare.[5] In fact, the blood libel remained an issue in Soviet society that authorities had to deal with throughout the interwar period.[6] The assumption that the blood libel petered out under the Soviets is strengthened by two important and closely intertwined ruptures in the politics of antisemitism and manifestations of anti-Jewish violence that occurred from late imperial Russia to the Bolshevik regime. First, the Bolsheviks' aggressive struggle against antisemitism—launched at once by Lenin as he regarded "the pogroms and the Beilis case" as part of the worst legacy of tsarist Russia— inevitably curbed and changed expressions of antisemitism, especially in the 1920s and early 1930s.[7] Leon Trotsky himself, who typically shunned any reference to his Jewish background, spoke out fervently against the Beilis case, criticizing the tsarist legal system and branding antisemitism as a political tool in the hands of the counterrevolution. In the midst of the Civil War, the Sovnarkom, or Council of People's Commissars, outlawed antisemitism. As Chairman of the Sovnarkom, Lenin signed the decree on July 27, 1918, and openly avowed "to take uncompromising measures to tear the antisemitic movement out by the roots. Pogromists and pogrom-agitators are to be placed outside the law."[8] In the midst of the Russian Civil War (1918–1921), with anti-Jewish pogroms that resulted in more than 150,000 casualties, the decree on antisemitism read by Lenin and recorded on phonograph records, was disseminated across cities and villages through the gramophones of the "propaganda trains."[9] After the revolution, therefore, the Bolsheviks' rejection and condemnation of antisemitism was clear-cut, categorical, and one of the most visible features of the new regime, maintained at least on the official level throughout the interwar period.

The second notable rupture in manifestations of antisemitism from tsarist to Soviet times relates to the virtual disappearance—at least during the 1920s and 1930s—of outbreaks of mass violence against Jews. In tsarist Russia, pogroms occurred in waves in cities and towns, and then spread to the countryside and the surrounding villages during the 1880s, following the assassination of Tsar Alexander II, and during the early twentieth century, in particular at the time of the Russian Revolution of 1905. During the reigns of Alexander III and Nicholas II, Russia possibly became "the land of the pogroms." After the Civil War, under Soviet rule, public attacks and displays of violence against Jews receded significantly. While the blood libel accusation persisted in Soviet society throughout the 1920s and 1930s, with instances occurring in cities such as Moscow, Minsk, Kaniev, Tula, Poltava, and Kharkiv, it did not dovetail with the pogrom.[10] The only instances of blood libel accusations that elicited a violent attack against the entire Jewish community occurred in the 1920s in Central Asia, a region in which Bolshevik infrastructure was arguably weaker and not as well entrenched as in the European regions of the Soviet Union.[11] In tsarist Russia, in contrast, the rumors of a missing Christian child allegedly taken by the Jews for ritual murder accusation had easily sparked and justified anti-Jewish violence.[12]

The accusation of ritual murder constitutes one of the most extreme manifestations of antisemitism. Lying at the core of the Western tradition of anti-Judaism, the belief in this legend required no evidence at all, as Gavin Langmuir has eloquently shown.[13] The alleged crime had never occurred. It was nevertheless deeply embedded in the popular consciousness of Christian Europe and particularly rooted in the religious and literary output during medieval and early modern times. The blood legend traveled efficiently through word of mouth, preserving its well-known tropes through folklore and anti-Jewish religious and (later) racial mythologies; and, from time to time, it was reinvigorated (or exploited) by modern media and mass politics.[14] Overlapping with other religiously based traditional anti-Jewish accusations—such as the "Christ-killers" charge of deicide, or that of an existing anti-Christian conspiracy, ranging from the Black Death to the *Protocols of the Elders of Zion*—ritual murder could also intersect with the notion of Żydokomuna or Judeo-Bolshevism, the idea that Soviet communism was really part of a wider Jewish scheme to seize power. In the words of Zvi Gitelman, "The 'Judeo-Bolshevik' myth contains at least five rationales for hostility toward the Jews: they are aliens, foreigners; they are subversive and dangerous; they are anti-Christian; Jews are internationalists rather than patriots; and they threaten the economic foundations of society. All these traits are attributed to communists as well. For those so inclined, this proves that the Jewish and communist conspiracies are either the same or very closely related."[15]

In general, the examination of the blood libel under the Soviets helps us gain insight into the nature, as well as the limits, of modernization and secularization within the Bolshevik system. The accusation of ritual murder against the Jews also grew out of the unintended link between the Soviet anti-Judaism campaigns (which targeted circumcision and kosher butchering) and grassroots, popular antisemitism. Cyclical outbursts of antisemitism, which included the blood libel accusation, were common before 1941 and represented a clear challenge to the Bolsheviks' attempt to modernize and secularize Soviet society by force and intense speed.[16] In fact, they became a relatively typical popular response to the violence of Sovietization, the compulsory "brotherhood of peoples" imposed by the Bolsheviks on Soviet citizens, and the economic hardship and destitution that many suffered during the 1920s and 1930s. This is captured, for example, in the lines of a folk poem in Ukrainian, produced at the height of the construction of socialism in the capital of Soviet Ukraine. In the poem, which contains echoes of the blood libel myth, the Jews have taken over the city of Kyiv: they appear as the foreign "other," the exploitative profiteer, the bloodsucker, who "sucks out the blood of the people like water."[17]

> Look, as you go to Kyiv,
> How they live there, the Jews.
> They sit in their shops,
> And eat white rolls.
> They drink wine from Georgia
> And live in prosperity.
> No, delicious rolls do not satisfy them.
> No, strong wine does not quench them.
> Then they feed on the fortune of the people
> And suck out its blood like water.
>
> Glian' u Kyiv pidy.
> Jak zhivut tam zhidy.
> V magazinakh sidiat,
> Bili bulki idiat.
> Vina z Gruzii p'iut,
> U dostatkakh zhivut.
> Ni, ne bulki smachni napikhaiut,
> Ni, ne vina mitsni zalivaiut.
> To idiat voni doliu narodu.
> Z n'ogo krov visisaiut jak vodu.[18]

In Soviet-occupied Lviv the historical memory of the blood libel accusation certainly played a significant role in the events of the summer of 1945. But the ritual murder accusation against the Jews also intersected with the recent memory of the "war of extermination" launched by the Germans in 1941–1944. The Nazi occupation, and the exceptional treatment of the Jews therein, unleashed a legitimization of antisemitism that persisted after the war. It also further promoted the metamorphosis of the blood libel, which had been underway by the end of the nineteenth century in Russia, and removed it, at least in part, from its traditional religious context. The events in Lviv resulted thus from the interplay between the impact of the Nazi occupation and the return of Soviet and communist power in the city.

Where Old and New Blood Libels Meet

During World War II the Soviet Union saw the return of virulent popular antisemitism—first in Nazi-occupied territories, then in distant evacuation centers in Central Asia, and eventually in the Russian interior.[19] In clear opposition to the interwar politics of antisemitism, the Communist Party did not respond forcefully to instances of anti-Jewish violence. It paid little heed, for example, to the anti-Jewish pogrom that caused havoc in the streets of Kyiv in September 1944.[20] In the words of a Jewish witness to the events who had left Kharkiv for Kyiv in March 1944, and then had fled Kyiv for Palestine in 1945: "Even now, when Jews return to their places of residence, they don't receive any help from anyone. Ukrainians meet the returning Jews with open hostility. During the first few weeks following liberation . . . no Jew would go out alone at night. . . . In Kyiv sixteen Jews were killed during a pogrom set off by the murder of a military official by a woman, who was said to be Jewish (even though she wasn't)."[21] Unlike the 1920s, there was no public campaign against antisemitism in the Soviet Union after the war, when one was desperately needed. The experience of a "total ethnic war" fueled antisemitism among the population in German-occupied territories. In the words of Amir Weiner, "the constant exposure to relentless, exterminatory, antisemitic rhetoric and practices" under the Germans inevitably bolstered the memory of existing imagery of anti-Bolshevik propaganda, which in turn intersected with wartime anti-Jewish propaganda.[22] Both anti-Bolshevik propaganda from the Civil War period and anti-Jewish propaganda from World War II featured a ritual murder subtext, as the blood libel trope converged with the myth of *Żydokomuna*.[23] Furthermore, the unique brutality with which Jews were treated in Nazi-occupied territories confirmed their "otherness" and lack of humanity, reinforcing traditional religiously based antisemitism. This appears powerfully, for example, in a drawing by a Ukrainian worker, dated November 1941, in which Stalin, holding a knife in his hand and surrounded by hundreds of skulls, is toiling on behalf of the bloodthirsty Jew, the embodiment of the Judeo-Bolshevik. The drawing's text reads: "Stalin is the bloody enemy of the people and brought destruction to the whole world! A sea of blood flows from the people, in the name of the regime of the Jews and the communists. Stalin is the hireling of the Jews; Stalin is the bloody enemy of the people."[24] While this is not an iconographic representation of ritual murder, it does capture the "othering" process undergone by the Jews during World War II, as the prime actors in this modern version of ritual murder carried out in the name of communism.

The fear that the renewal of Soviet occupation of postwar Ukraine could intersect with the widespread myth of Jewish communism, was clearly conveyed by the first secretary of the Central Committee of the Communist Party of Ukraine and head of the Council of People's Commissars of Ukraine, Nikita Khrushchev. Following the liberation of Kyiv from the Germans on November 6, 1943, Maria Chelminskaia, a Polish Jewish communist who had fled to the city during the war and who, under a false identity, had remained active in the local communist underground movement throughout the Nazi occupation, was employed in the Secretariat of the Central Committee of the Communist Party of Ukraine.[25] Because of her allegiance to the Party, Maria was considered politically reliable and a trustworthy player in the re-Sovietization of Kyiv. However, her ethnic identity, which she eventually disclosed in the questionnaire (*anketa*) she filled out for the job application, ultimately cost her the position. When confronted with the secret directive to restrict the employment of Jews in positions of responsibility in Ukraine, Maria in disbelief wrote to Khrushchev. His reply clearly captures the zeitgeist with regard to antisemitism and notions of Judeo-Bolshevism:

> I understand that as a Jew you contemplate this question from a subjective point of view. But we are objective. Jews in the past committed many sins against the Ukrainian people. And the people hate them for this reason. Jews are not needed in our Ukraine. I also believe that for Ukrainian Jews who survived Hitler's attempt to exterminate them, it would be better not to return here . . . better yet if they moved to Birobidzhan. . . . We are in Ukraine, you know? Do you understand? This is Ukraine. And we are not interested in the Ukrainian people interpreting the return of the Soviet authorities as the return of the Jews. All I can do for you is to return the questionnaire to you. Fill out a new questionnaire without mentioning your Jewish background. Use your false documents, in which you appear as a pure Ukrainian [*chistokrovnaia ukrainka*].[26]

The return of Soviet power to the territories recently liberated from the Germans and annexed to the Soviet Union should not appear as the "return of the Jews."

World War II drastically swayed the habits and discourses of violence in the German-occupied territories of the Soviet Union. Here, Nazi propaganda often encouraged the exploitation of the blood libel theme, frequently in conjunction with the Judeo-Bolshevik myth of communism as the embodiment of the Jewish spirit and lust for power. The 470-page book *The Jewish Ritual Murder*, by Nazi Party member Max Helmutt Schramm, is a case in point. The book was distributed in occupied Ukraine to promote anti-Bolshevik propaganda and invigorate antisemitism among those handling the Jewish question by exploiting the blood allegation.[27] To take another single but prominent example, in August 1943, the Ukrainian-language daily newspaper *Ukrainskiy kurer* published in Kyiv during the German occupation, featured a detailed analysis of the murder of Tsar Nicholas II and his family. Published on "the twenty-fifth anniversary of the murders at Ekaterinburg," and titled "The Jews' Right Hand," the account presented the assassination of the tsarist family as a ritual murder carried out by Jewish Bolsheviks. "The decision to execute the tsar," stated the author of the article, "was sanctioned by the Jewish *kahal* [community] long before [the revolution] . . . [and was executed by] the *zhidok* [little kike] Yankel Sverdlov, one of the most powerful people in the Kremlin under Lenin."[28] Although the order to execute the Romanov family came directly from Lenin, the telegram from Moscow with the directive was indeed signed by Sverdlov, who was Jewish, and who in 1918 was chairman of the Central Executive Committee of the Congress of Soviets of the Russian SFSR. In its account of the murder, the Ukrainian newspaper provided the names and ethnicity of the "major killers" of the tsarist family, identifying seven out of nine as Jewish. In fact, only two of the executioners were of Jewish origin: Yakov Yurovski, at the time head of the Cheka, the Bolshevik Secret Police, and Filipp Goloshchekin, a member of the Petrograd Military Revolutionary Committee. The author of the article went on to state, "The execution of the royal family can be unmistakably described as a Jewish ritual performance . . . the ritual murder of the Aryan race . . . of the Aryan spirit . . . as indicated by the mysterious kabalistic signs found in the basement [of the building in which the tsar was executed]."[29] A perfect symbiosis between the Judeo-Bolshevik myth, in which the Jew represented the political enemy, and the more traditional ritual murder reemerged forcefully in the early 1990s when, following the collapse of the Soviet Union, the nationalist organization Pamiat' (Memory) issued in its homonymous publication (with a print run of a hundred thousand) several accounts about the "Jewish execution" of the Romanov family. The execution was cast as "ritual murder."[30]

If Nazi propaganda in the occupied territories of the Soviet Union often exploited the blood libel theme, ritual murder accusations turned up even in those regions, such as Central Asia, which were not directly affected by the German military occupation and were thus removed from wartime propaganda.[31] Soviet Kirghizia, for example, which saw a momentous growth in its Jewish population from the small prewar Bukharan and Ashkenazi communities, as thousands of refugees fleeing Nazi-occupied territories settled there, experienced the blood allegation, albeit reforged by the wartime reality.[32] The refugees included both

Soviet citizens (Jews and non-Jews alike) and Jews with Polish citizenship. When in the summer of 1942, a group of twenty Jewish women, wives of Red Army military personnel who were fighting at the front, addressed a letter to Stalin and the Central Committee of the Kirghiz Communist Party, complaining about antisemitism among the local population in the cities of Tokmak and Frunze, they noted the following: "during the days of the [Great] Patriotic War, when all peoples should be always united and engaged in a common effort to strengthen the rear and help the front, here [in our city] we observe and experience in person terrible medieval antisemitism.... [Accusations that] Jews are killing kids of other nations, drinking their blood, and using their body parts to make soup."[33]

Wartime food shortages, rumors about cannibalism on the Eastern Front, hearsay of the blood libel allegation, as well as the actual murder of two children in the city of Tokmak, served as the background—and perhaps pretext—for the accusations. These were well-removed from the more traditional Passover plot, which involved the abduction of Christian children, and the drawing and use of their blood for religious purposes, in particular for the baking of matzo. The investigation conducted by the party authorities in Tokmak and Frunze, and the ensuing report by the People's Commissariat for Internal Affairs (NKVD), both confirmed the plea by the Jewish women. The report stated that widespread antisemitic comments resulting in harassment and physical violence targeting Jews fell into three categories: (1) "Russians are dying at the front because of the Jews"; (2) "prices are high because of the Jews"; and (3) "Jews are killing the children of other nationalities, drinking their blood, and using their body parts to make soup."[34] The secularization of the blood libel was thus well underway, as food containing human flesh and blood replaced the matzo, in a murder that was no longer "ritual" in nature, but "merely" predatory and merciless cannibalism. The NKVD report also singled out one instance in which the librarian in Tokmak's children's library accused the head physician of the local pediatric hospital—who was Jewish—of collecting "fresh children's blood."[35] No remark about the possible ritual needs for the blood was included in the report.

The Soviet authorities' immediate response to the events in Tokmak and Frunze seems rather unusual, especially when compared to the utter lack of response elicited by a blood libel accusation that occurred in Soviet Kirghizia one year later, in mid-1943. When the Jewish woman accused of abducting and killing a child appealed to the local authorities, protesting the absurd allegations made against her, not only was her grievance disregarded, but the regional prosecutor dismissed her from her job.[36] One possible explanation for the prompt reaction of the NKVD authorities lies in the specific timing of the 1942 letter, addressed to

Stalin at a critical stage in the war. The affair could have caused some embarrassment for the USSR, which hoped that American Jewry would sway the US government to join the Soviet war effort.[37] By the spring of 1943, in contrast, the United States had already joined the war effort, and the Soviets had prevailed at Stalingrad against the Germans. Against the backdrop of the momentous war effort, and with a victorious Red Army, blood libels, and antisemitism in general, turned into a trivial matter for Soviet authorities.[38]

There Is Human Blood in the Synagogue in Lviv!

In the contentious and fragile geopolitical reality of postwar communist Eastern Europe, the ritual murder accusation recurred forcefully through different forms and permutations, both in historically Soviet areas and in newly annexed Soviet territories. The ritual murder accusation that erupted in the summer of 1945 in the city of Lviv took place in the wake of the return of hundreds of Jewish refugees, most of them Polish Jews who evacuated to Central Asia during the war and who sought repatriation to Poland in 1945. For the Jewish refugees resettlement came with major obstacles, disappointments, growing tensions with the local population over questions of restitution of Jewish property, and the psychological trauma caused by the demise of one of the major centers of Jewish life in pre-Holocaust Europe. If in September 1939, there were over 150,000 Jews living in Lviv, constituting 33 percent of the urban population, in the summer of 1944, following the Red Army's liberation of the city, only 2,571 Jews remained.[39]

But the Jewish refugees were also relocating to a city in which most of its non-Jewish inhabitants had experienced major violence and intense ordeal under German occupation, to a city that underwent massive population changes and radical transformations under the newly established Soviet rule.[40] A predominantly Polish city during the interwar period, after 1944 Lviv endured ruthless Sovietization and ethnic cleansing. Over the postwar period the city became predominantly Ukrainian, ethnically and linguistically.

Many Jews took shelter in the synagogue building on Vuhilna Street 3, one of the only synagogues left in postwar Lviv. From June 14, 1945, to July 14, 1946, the Lviv Police Department, the Lviv Public Prosecutor's Office, the Prosecutor's Office of the Ukrainian Soviet Socialist Republic, and the NKVD investigated the accusation that Jews were allegedly killing Polish and Ukrainian children in the synagogue and then hiding their bodies in the building's basement.[41] In the results of the preliminary investigation, the senior investigator of the Lviv Prosecutor's Office stated, as if to reassure officials about the thoroughness and diligence of his search: "no body was found in the building of the synagogue, nor in the nearby apartments [where Jews lived, including the local rabbi], nor in the basement or cellars, nor in the sewer pipes. . . . No evidence or witnesses of the killing of children in the synagogue was discovered."[42] The police found instead large quantities of chicken feathers and traces of chicken blood of the poultry slaughtered according to Jewish ritual in the synagogue courtyard. The fact that in 1945 the Jews in Lviv performed ritual slaughter in the synagogue courtyard might have been, at least for some, evocative of an alleged Jewish adeptness with blood rituals, and reminiscent of the other alleged Jewish ritual, namely the blood libel. According to the second round of investigations, the accusation originated in the marketplace located next to the synagogue, where hundreds had gathered, and where many engaged in "counterrevolutionary disturbance" (*agitatsiia*).[43]

The police report recorded the details of the incident, which gained momentum as Jews were leaving the synagogue building. At the time of the accusation one Polish woman declared that the bodies of Polish children with slit throats (*pererezannye gorla*) were found in the synagogue. She then substantiated her charge by stating that the police had already arrested a large number of Jews for this crime. In response to the allegation a group of people chased a Jewish woman through the marketplace and attempted to kill her because, as they shouted, "Poles hid [you] from the Germans and [you] killed Polish children!"[44] Another person involved in the unrest at the marketplace, reportedly stated, "there should have been a Hitler twenty years ago [in Lviv], that way the Jews would not be killing our children; that Jews steal our children, slaughter them and then turn them into sausages to sell; that in the synagogue courtyard there is the blood of the murdered children."[45] One complainant argued that he saw the bodies of eighteen Polish and Ukrainian children in the synagogue;[46] another one concluded that the bodies were in fact sixteen, and as he physically attacked a Jewish passerby, he encouraged the residents of Lviv "to set fire to the synagogue and kill all the kikes, because they kill [our] children."[47] Another complainant argued that the number of bodies in the synagogue amounted to six hundred. Soviet authorities proceeded with a criminal case against those responsible for rousing "national hatred." A second search of the synagogue's premises followed to ascertain that indeed no murder of children had taken place. The NKVD eventually arrested five people of Ukrainian and Polish nationality "for incitement of national hatred against the Jewish people" (v rozzhiganii natsional'noi rozni napravlennoi protiv evreiskogo naroda).[48] One of them in particular disquieted Soviet authorities: twenty-five-year-old Ivan M. Fedak, a Ukrainian who had worked for the Germans from 1941 until the Soviets liberated the city and served in the police force in Lviv, as well as in the SS Division Halychyna.[49] The Lviv Prosecutor's Office found out that Fedak not only had engaged "in blackmail and contraband under the Germans, but that he had also taken part in the massacres of Jews and Red

Army soldiers."[50] The trial confirmed the guilt of the five defendants, who were charged with "counterrevolutionary disturbance and incitement of national hatred against the Jewish people." They were sentenced to two years in prison.

A few observations seem apt when analyzing this instance of ritual murder accusation. First, the Lviv blood libel/ritual murder accusation should be considered within the general context of ethnic relations among Ukrainians, Poles, and Jews under Soviet rule.[51] Not unlike other instances of antisemitism in post-Holocaust Eastern Europe (which in several places, in Poland in particular, escalated into actual pogroms with Jewish casualties) the ritual murder accusation in Lviv in 1945 also found its trigger in the heightened tensions between Jews and non-Jews, in the collaboration of the local population with the Germans, in the three years of anti-Jewish propaganda disseminated by the Nazis, and in the appropriation of Jewish property and the Jewish struggle to have it returned. In a letter to Minister of Foreign Affairs Viacheslav Molotov, the head of the Jewish Anti-Fascist Committee, Solomon Mikhoels, noted: "In so many places—Berdichev, Balta, Zhmerink, Vinnitsa . . . [Holocaust] survivors still live on the territory of the former ghettos. Their homes are not being returned to them; nor is the property that has been stolen from them."[52] In their slow, late, and arbitrary response to these postwar "abnormal" conditions, Soviet authorities eventually demanded the "return of homes and property" to their prewar rightful owners.[53] Frustrated for being forced to return the property they had seized from their Jewish neighbors, local residents who had prospered during the war could take revenge by playing up rumors of Jewish ritual murder.

Second, while there was no direct mention of a specific Jewish religious ritual, the fact that the alleged murders of Polish and Ukrainian children took place within the space of the synagogue implied some ritual aspect of the assumed crime, both for the initiators of the accusation and for the targets of the accusation. The day of the incident did not coincide with any specific Jewish religious holiday. The Jews who were leaving the synagogue might have assembled there for the customary Thursday morning Torah scroll reading (June 14, 1945, was a Thursday), or they might have participated in one of the special services held to commemorate the victims of the Holocaust, a practice that became rather widespread immediately after the war. However, it seems that the ritual aspect of the alleged murder is markedly secondary and mostly inferred. The allegation of cannibalism, in contrast, spurred by the hunger and miserable conditions that so many had experienced during and after the war, looms prominently. This is a form of cannibalism disconnected from the assumed religious context of Passover, for example. The social memory of widespread cannibalism during the Holodomor, the Ukrainian famine of 1932–1933, and the siege of Leningrad may have played a role in the abuse of the accusation. Moreover, there seems to have been an actual case of cannibalism in Nazi-occupied Lviv: archival documents mention wartime rumors about human body parts being sold at the city's marketplace, which eventually set off a German investigation and the ensuing arrest of several people involved in the case. Since those Jews who had not yet been exterminated by the Germans and their collaborators did not have free access to the marketplace, those arrested were obviously not Jewish.[54]

While deeply entrenched in the alleged Jewish practice of religiously driven blood rituals, the Lviv case was therefore also the outcome of wartime violence. Real instances of cannibalism and food shortages removed the blood libel from its ritual aspect and promoted the emergence of a new notion of Jewish murder, with no direct mention of ritual. The Lviv case was in this respect not unique. In fact, blaming Jews for committing "a modern ritual murder," or acts of cannibalism against non-Jewish children, and profiteering by selling human flesh at the marketplace, became somewhat common in the immediate postwar months and years. In the summer of 1945, in the city of Kryvyi Rih in Dnipopetrovsk oblast in central Ukraine, a group of Ukrainians and Russians was arrested by the Soviet secret police. They were accused of distributing flyers throughout nearby cities about an alleged Jewish gang involved in "taking Russian children, killing them, and then making sausages and meat pies out of the children's flesh to sell at the marketplace" (voruia russkikh detei, ubivali ikh, a iz detskogo miasa vydelyvali miasnye kolbasy i pirozhki, kotorymi torgovali na rynke).[55] "The oppressors of the Russian and Ukrainian people," as the Jewish murderers were referred to, were also accused of using the children's flesh to make soap to sell at the marketplace.[56] The latter was an allusion to instances of Germans converting human remains of Jewish corpses into soap during World War II, which were rumored to have occurred.[57] During the NKVD investigation, one of the women tried, prosecuted, and arrested in connection with the antisemitic incidents in Dnipopetrovsk oblast admitted that in July 1945, while working as a teacher in the Children's Home of Dubno, she placed the following note in the auditorium: "Children, love your own people, and hate the kikes [*zhidy*], who will skin you alive [*oni s vas shkuru sderut*]."[58]

Third, the reaction of local authorities to the Lviv blood libel was much firmer and swifter than it was to blood libels in Central Asia, to the 1944 pogrom in Kyiv, or, for that matter, to the copycat events that took place in Cracow in August 1945 and elsewhere in Poland during 1945 and 1946. In Lviv Soviet authorities prosecuted the accusers and maintained law and order. There seems to be a deep connection between the presence of a weak Soviet infrastructure and ability to exert control over society—such as, for example, in the regions of Central

Asia and in the recently liberated city of Kyiv—and outbreaks of anti-Jewish violence. Unlike in many places in Poland in 1945 and 1946, a pogrom was averted in Lviv. Because of prompt police involvement, the calls to burn down the synagogue and murder the Jews were not as successful as they were in Cracow or Kielce. Part of the newly annexed Soviet territory, Lviv had not been Soviet before World War II. Consequently, the authorities did not trust the local Polish and Ukrainian inhabitants, whom they suspected of collaboration with the Germans. The Soviets identified the ritual murder accusation, and zoological antisemitism in general, with Fascism and Nazism.[59] From their perspective the accusers were not only antisemitic, but anti-Soviet as well; after all, in Lviv Ukrainians and Poles had been living under Nazism since 1941, and allegedly had cultivated their bourgeois and fascist tendencies. From the Soviet perspective, the situation in Lviv in 1945 was essentially the same as in southern Russia and Ukraine in 1920 during the Civil War. Violent antisemitism was discredited as a weapon used by the political enemy.

Fourth, whether the participants in this "theatrical performance of violence" in Lviv actually believed that Jews engaged in killing children or not is hard to tell. It is, however, noteworthy that they resorted to this specific form of antisemitic accusation as opposed to other expressions. I would suggest that the blood libel accusation became a collective performative act with a ritual character, an act in which the collective shared knowledge and practices were put on stage in order to reaffirm, and perhaps recreate, the familiar social order destroyed by the Germans during the war, and then wiped out by the new political system. In spite of the growing violence and ethnic cleansing sparked during Operation Vistula (with 218,711 Poles forcibly evacuated from Lviv alone from 1944 through 1946), Poles and Ukrainians found commonalities—perhaps even Christian ones reinforced by a common Catholic identity to oppose to Russian Orthodoxy—to reject the Soviets.[60] Similar dynamics of a Polish-Ukrainian alliance through anti-Jewish violence had already emerged in Lviv during the pogrom of 1941.[61] In 1945 Poles and Ukrainians forged a subcommunity of common interests and fears that was religiously and culturally based, as well as politically grounded. In this micropolity of anti-Soviet resentment, discussing ritual murder became acceptable for the populace but not necessarily for the government, as the blood libel merged with anticommunist accusations, as the traditional blood libel narrative legitimized the claim of Judeo-Bolshevism. In the minds of many the depraved crimes of the Jews and of the communists became intertwined. Poles and Ukrainians of newly Sovietized Lviv could now unite and take revenge on Jews who had always engaged in killing their children by means of the traditional blood libel, the new wartime ritual murder, or Judeo-Bolshevism. In the midst of a postwar crisis of identity, borders, and political powers, memories of blood libel stories could easily intersect with fears of cannibalism and Judeo-Bolshevism.

ELISSA BEMPORAD is the Jerry and William Ungar Chair in East European Jewish History and the Holocaust, and Associate Professor of History at Queens College of the City University of New York. She is the author of *Becoming Soviet Jews: The Bolshevik Experiment in Minsk* (2013). In 2015 and 2016 she was the National Endowment for the Humanities Fellow at the Center for Jewish History.

NOTES

1. Derzhavniy arkhiv Lvivskoi oblasti (hereafter DALO), f. R-239 (Office of the Public Prosecutor, Lviv Oblast, Office of the Public Prosecutor of the Ukrainian SSR), op. 2, d. 24, l. 13 (Resolution, July 19, 1945).

2. Anna Chichopek, "The Cracow Pogrom of August 1945," in *Contested Memories: Poles and Jews during the Holocaust and Its Aftermath*, ed. Joshua D. Zimmerman (New Brunswick, NJ: Rutgers University Press, 2003), 221–38. For more on pogroms coupled with blood libel accusations in postwar Poland, see David Engel, "Patterns of Anti-Jewish Violence in Poland, 1944–1946," in *Yad Vashem Studies* 26 (1998): 43–85; István Deák, Jan T. Gross, and Tony Judt, eds., *The Politics of Retribution in Europe: World War II and Its Aftermath* (Princeton, NJ: Princeton University Press, 2000); and Jan T. Gross, "After Auschwitz: The Reality and Meaning of Postwar Antisemitism in Poland," in *Studies in Contemporary Jewry* 20 (2005): 199–226.

3. On the Kielce pogrom, see Jan T. Gross, *Fear: Antisemitism in Poland after Auschwitz: An Essay in Historical Interpretation* (New York: Random House, 2006).

4. On ritual murder accusations as a canvas to explore neighborhood sociology, memory, and habits of violence see, e.g., Helmut Smith, *The Butcher's Tale: Murder and Anti-Semitism in a German Town* (New York: W. W. Norton, 2003). On instances of blood libel in interwar and post-World War II Soviet society and on the ambivalent Soviet response to these accusations, see Elissa Bemporad, "Empowerment, Defiance, and Demise: Jews and the Blood Libel Specter under Stalinism," *Jewish History* 26, nos. 3–4 (2013): 343–61.

5. On the Beilis Affair, see Ezekiel Leikin, ed., *The Beilis Transcripts: The Anti-Semitic Trial That Shook the World* (Northvale, NJ: Jason Aronson, 1993); Albert Lindemann, *The Jew Accused: Three Anti-Semitic Affairs (Dreyfus, Beilis, Frank), 1884–1915* (Cambridge: Cambridge University Press, 1992); Hans Rogger, *Jewish Policies and Right-Wing Politics in Imperial Russia* (Berkeley: University of California Press, 1986), esp. ch. 3; and Robert Weinberg, *The Blood Libel in Late Imperial Russia: The Ritual Murder Trial of Mendel Beilis* (Bloomington: Indiana University Press, 2014).

6. On the persistence of the blood libel in Soviet society in the 1920s and 1930s, see Bemporad, "Empowerment, Defiance, and Demise," 346–54.

7. Vladimir I. Lenin, "The National Equality Bill," in Lenin, *Collected Works* (Moscow: Progress Publishers, 1972), 20: 172–73. On Lenin and the Jewish question, see also Lenin, "Critical Remarks on the National Question," in ibid., 17–51; Lenin, *Lenin on the Jewish Question*, ed. Hyman Lumer (New York: International Publishers, 1974); and Yohanan Petrovsky-Shtern, *Lenin's Jewish Question* (New Haven, CT: Yale University Press, 2010), esp. ch. 3.

8. Lenin, *Lenin on the Jewish Question*, 142. See also "Vnimanie bor'be s antisemitizmom," *Pravda*, February 19, 1929, 1.

9. Yuri Larin, *Evrei i antisemitizm v SSSR* (Moscow: Gosudarstvennoe izdatel'stvo politicheskoi literatury, 1929), 35.

10. Bemporad, "Empowerment, Defiance, and Demise," 346–54.

11. Larin, *Evrei i antisemitizm v SSSR*, 124, 127.

12. See John Doyle Klier and Shlomo Lambroza, eds., *Pogroms: Anti-Jewish Violence in Modern Russian History* (Cambridge: Cambridge University Press, 1992); Edward H. Judge, *Easter in Kishinev: The Anatomy of a Pogrom* (New York: New York University Press, 1995); Klier, *Russians, Jews, and the Pogrom Crisis* (Cambridge: Cambridge University Press, 2011); Jonathan Dekel-Chen, David Gaunt, Natan Meir, and Israel Bartal, eds., *Anti-Jewish Violence: Rethinking the Pogrom in East European History* (Bloomington: Indiana University Press, 2010); and Darius Staliunas, *Enemies for a Day: Antisemitism and Anti-Jewish Violence in Lithuania under the Tsars* (New York: Central European University Press, 2015).

13. See, e.g., Gavin Langmuir, *History, Religion, and Antisemitism* (Berkeley: University of California Press, 1990); and Langmuir, *Toward a Definition of Antisemitism* (Berkeley: University of California Press, 1996). See also David Nirenberg, *Anti-Judaism: The Western Tradition* (New York: W. W. Norton, 2013): see, esp., 203–7, 261; and Hannah R. Johnson, *The Blood Libel: Ritual Murder Accusation at the Limit of Jewish History* (Ann Arbor: University of Michigan Press, 2012).

14. On the intersections between blood libel and folklore, see Alan Dundes, ed., *The Blood Libel Legend: A Casebook in Antisemitic Folklore* (Madison: University of Wisconsin Press, 1991). On the origin of the ritual murder accusation in Western Europe in the Middle Ages, and the ways in which the blood libel accusation managed to take hold through different adaptations of the same allegations, see Emily M. Rose, *The Murder of William of Norwich: The Origins of the Blood Libel in Medieval Europe* (Oxford: Oxford University Press, 2015). On the interplay among attacks against Jewish religious rituals, racially based antisemitism, and modern politics in nineteenth- and twentieth-century Germany, see Robin Judd, *Contested Rituals: Circumcision, Kosher Butchering, and Jewish Political Life in Germany, 1843–1933* (Ithaca, NY: Cornell University Press, 2007).

15. Zvi Gitelman, "Was Communism a Jewish Conspiracy? The Evidence from Eastern Europe," paper delivered at the Conference on "Judeo-Bolshevism": The Crystallization of an Antisemitic Political Concept, Jerusalem, Yad Vashem, March 24, 2014.

16. On instances of outbursts of violent antisemitism in the interwar period, see, e.g., Arkadi Zeltser, "Ethnic Conflict and Modernization in the Interwar Period: The Case of Soviet Belorussia," in *Anti-Jewish Violence: Rethinking the Pogrom in East European History*, 182; and N. Lagorev, *Antisemitizm i bor'ba s nim* (Moscow: Gosudarstvennoe iuridicheskoe izdatel'stvo, 1930), 26–27.

17. On the image of the Jew as "bloodsucker," see Joanna Tokarska-Bakir, "The Figure of Bloodsucker in Polish Religious, National, Left-Wing Discourse in the Years 1945–1946: A Study in Historical Anthropology," *Dapim: Studies on the Holocaust* 29, no. 2 (2013): 75–106. See also Misha Mitsel, "Shtetl-Kiev v 1958 godu (opyt rekonstruktsii sobytiy)," in *"Shtetl" jak fenomen evreiskoi istorii*, ed. G. Aronov (Kyiv, Ukraine: Institut iudaiki, 1999), 180–86, esp. 181.

18. A graduate student in the Faculty of Philology at Kiev State University by the name of G. Kudeli collected this and other similar folk poems, which were sent to the Central Committee of the Communist Party of Ukraine by the university's rector, in July 1958. See Mitsel, "Shtetl-Kiev," 181.

19. Yuri Slezkine, *The Jewish Century* (Princeton, NJ: Princeton University Press, 2004), 331.

20. Misha Mitsel, *Evrei Ukrainy v 1943-1953 gg: Ocherki dokumentirovannoi istorii* (Kiev, Ukraine: Dukh i litera, 2004), 63-66.

21. Ibid., 65-67.

22. Amir Weiner, *Making Sense of War: The Second World War and the Fate of the Bolshevik Revolution* (Princeton, NJ: Princeton University Press, 2002); "Blut-bilbl," *Eynikayt*, April 25, 1947, 3.

23. The anti-Bolshevik propaganda output from the Civil War and the Polish-Soviet War, included depictions of Leon Trotsky as the murderous leader of the Red Army, portrayed with enormous paws dripping in blood, reminiscent of the Devil, or holding a weapon soaked in blood. See, e.g., the antisemitic and anti-Bolshevik poster "Bolshevik Freedom," depicting Trotsky sitting on a pile of skulls, in Eduard Fuchs, *Die Juden in der Karikatur: Ein Beitrag zur Kulturgeschichte* (Munich: Albert Langen, 1921), 281.

24. YIVO Institute Archives, Record Group 222 (Institut der NSDAP zur Erforschung der Judenfrage), box 17, f. 142, p. 200.

25. Leon Leneman, *La tragédie des Juifs en U.R.R.S.* (Paris: Desclée De Brouwer, 1959), 175-79; and Solomon Schwarts, *Evrei v Sovetskom Soiuze s nachala vtoroi mirovoi voiny (1939-1965)* (New York: Izdatel'stvo Amerikanskogo evreiskogo rabochego komiteta, 1966), 257-58.

26. See Misha Mitsel, *Evrei Ukrainy*, 26-27; and Leneman, *La tragédie des Juifs*, 179; Schwarts, *Evrei v Sovetskom Soiuze*, 257-58.

27. On Helmut Schramm, see Darren O'Brian, *The Pinnacle of Hatred: The Blood Libel and the Jews* (Jerusalem: Vidal Sassoon International Center for the Study of Antisemitism, 2011), 25-30, 32-35, 37-49.

28. "Sprava ruk zhidivskikh," *Ukrainskyi kur'er*, no. 17 (August 10, 1943): 3.

29. Ibid.

30. A. M. Volkovskii, "Sud naroda ili ritual'noe ubiistvo?," *Pamiat'*, no. 3 (1993): 7, quoted in Jonathan Brent, *Inside the Stalin Archives: Discovering the New Russia* (New York: Atlas, 2008). On the history of Pamiat', see Marlène Laruelle, *Le Rouge et le noir: Extrême droite et nationalisme en Russie* (Paris: Éditions du CNRS, 2007).

31. Iakov S. Khonigsman, "*Liudy, gody, sobytiia: Stat'i iz nashei davnei i nedavnei istorii*" (Lvov, Ukraine: L'vovskoe obshchestvo evreiskoi kultury im. Sholom Aleykhema, 1998), 113-14. On wartime propaganda and the Jews, see, e.g., Shimon Redlich, *Propaganda and Nationalism in Wartime Russia: The Jewish Antifascist Committee in the USSR, 1941-1948* (Boulder, CO: East European Quarterly, 1982).

32. See Zeev Levin, "Antisemitism and the Jewish Refugees in Soviet Kirgizia, 1942," *Jews in Russia and Eastern Europe* 1, no. 50 (2003): 191-203.

33. Ibid., 8.

34. Ibid.

35. Ibid., 10-13.

36. See Nisn Rozental, *Yidish lebn in ratnfarband* (Tel Aviv, Israel: Y. L. Peretz, 1971), 164-69.

37. See Levin, "Antisemitism and the Jewish Refugees," 11-13. On manifestations of antisemitism directed against World War II Jewish refugees from Ukraine and Belorussia who evacuated to the regions of Central Asia, see Leonid Smilovitsky, *Jewish Life in Belorussia during the Final Decade of the Stalin Regime, 1944-1953* (Budapest: Central European University Press, 2014), 19.

38. See Antony Beevor and Luba Vinogradova, eds., *A Writer at War: Vasily Grossman with the Red Army, 1941-1945* (New York: Pantheon, 2005), 344-45.

39. Mitsel, *Obshchiny iudeiskogo veroispovedaniia v Ukraine, Kiev-Lvov, 1945-1981 gg.* (Kiev, Ukraine: Sfera, 1998), 12-13. For more on the Jewish community in Soviet Lviv from 1944 to

1962, see Tarik Cyril Amar, "Yom Kippur in Lviv: The Lviv Synagogue and the Soviet Party State, 1944–1962," *East European Jewish Affairs* 35, no. 1 (2005): 91–110.

40. On the history of the city caught up between different political regimes and forces during the twentieth century, see Tarik Cyril Amar, *The Paradox of Ukrainian Lviv: A Borderland City between Stalinists, Nazis, and Nationalists* (Ithaca, NY: Cornell University Press, 2015).

41. DALO, f. R-239, op. 2, d. 24, ll. 1–48 (Case against Ivan Mikhailovich Fedak, Mikhail Yulianovich Badak, Matvei Vasilevich Kobrinskii, Mariia Ilinichna Skribaicho, and Anna Filippovna Shmigel, accused of igniting national hatred against the Jewish people).

42. DALO, f. R-239, op. 2, d. 24, l. 6 (Resolution, June 18, 1945).

43. DALO, f. R-239, op. 2, d. 24, ll. 9–10 (Resolutions, July 18, 1945; August 2, 1945).

44. DALO, f. R-239, op. 2, d. 24, l. 12 (Resolutions, July 20, 1945).

45. DALO, f. R-239, op. 2, d. 24, l. 13 (Resolution, July 19, 1945).

46. DALO, f. R-239, op. 2, d. 24, ll. 14–15 (Resolution, July 19, 1945).

47. DALO, f. R-239, op. 2, d. 24, l. 18 (Indictment, August 22, 1945).

48. DALO, f. R-239, op. 2, d. 24, ll. 3 (Protocol of the Investigation, June 14, 1945).

49. On the establishment and role of the SS Division Halychyna during the German occupation, see David R. Marples, *Heroes and Villains: Creating National History in Contemporary Ukraine* (Budapest: Central European University Press, 2007), 183–93.

50. DALO, f. R-239, op. 2, d. 24, l. 4 (Resolution, July 18, 1945).

51. For more about the city under Soviet rule, see Amar, *Paradox of Ukrainian Lviv*, esp. ch. 4–6.

52. Mitsel, *Evrei Ukrainy*, 22.

53. Ibid., 23.

54. See DALO, f. R-239, op. 2, d. 24, l. 8 (Resolution, July 18, 1945). On cannibalism and memories of cannibalism in the Soviet context, see, e.g., Steven Bela Vardy and Agnes Huszar Vardy, "Cannibalism in Stalin's Russia and Mao's China," *East European Quarterly* 41, no. 2 (2007): 223–38; Tamara Polishchuk, ed., *Stolytsia vidchaiu: Holodomor 1932–1933 rr. na Kharkivshchyni vustamy ochevydtsiv: Svidchennia, komentari* (Kharkiv, Ukraine: Berezil', 2006); Pitirim A. Sorokin, *Man and Society in Calamity: The Effects of War, Revolution, Famine, Pestilence upon Human Mind, Behavior, Social Organization, and Cultural Life* (New York: E. P. Dutton, 1946); Andrea Graziosi, Lubomyr A. Hajda, and Halyna Hryn, eds., *After the Holodomor: The Enduring Impact of the Great Famine on Ukraine* (Cambridge, MA: Harvard University Press, 2013); Ruslan Pyrih, ed., *Holodomor 1932–1933 rokiv v Ukraini: Dokumenty i materialy* (Kyiv, Ukraine: KMA, 2007); and V. A. Smolii, ed., *Holod 1932–1933 rokiv v Ukraini: Prychyny ta naslidky* (Kyiv, Ukraine: Naukova dumka, 2003). On the one reported case of cannibalism in the Warsaw ghetto, see Samuel D. Kassow, *Who Will Write Our History? Emanuel Ringelblum, the Warsaw Ghetto, and the Oyneg Shabes Archive* (Bloomington: Indiana University Press, 2007), 213.

55. Mitsel, *Evrei Ukrainy*, 127–29.

56. Ibid., 128.

57. See, e.g., Ilya Ehrenburg and Vasily Grossman, eds., *The Complete Black Book of Russian Jewry* (New Brunswick, NJ: Transaction Publishers, 2003), 82.

58. Mitsel, *Evrei Ukrainy*, 129.

59. The phrase "zoological antisemitism" was first used by the distinguished Soviet physicist Andrei Sakharov in 1968 to describe the thinking of Stalinist bureaucrats. It suggests an extremely virulent and primitive form of judeophobia. See William Korey, *The Soviet Cage: Anti-Semitism in Russia* (New York: Viking, 1973), 18–19.

60. See Marples, *Heroes and Villains*, 214–18. While Ukrainian Uniates belong to the Eastern Catholic Church and practice the Eastern rite, they share the same allegiance to the pope as Polish Catholics.

61. On the emergence of a Polish-Ukrainian alliance in the midst of anti-Jewish violence in Lviv during the war, see John-Paul Himka, "The Lviv Pogrom of 1941: The Germans, Ukrainian Nationalists, and the Carnival Crowd," *Canadian Slavonic Papers* 53, nos. 2–4 (2011): 209–43.

~ 13 ~

WAS THE DOCTORS' PLOT A BLOOD LIBEL?

Jeffrey Veidlinger

To what extent can the Doctors' Plot, Stalin's 1953 campaign against Jewish doctors, be seen as a blood libel? Of course, Jews were not accused of using Christian blood for ritualistic purposes or of reenacting the crucifixion, so in a strict sense the Doctors' Plot was not a blood libel on par with the medieval prototype. But the accusation that Jewish doctors were poisoning leading Kremlin officials borrowed many medieval and early modern motifs from the blood libel trope and injected them with more modern antisemitic accusations and stereotypes. In fact, the common name ascribed to the episode, *delo vrachei*, commonly translated as Doctors' Plot—but perhaps closer to Doctors' Affair—is a misnomer. There were no doctors plotting. In reality, it can more accurately be described as the "Medical Libel"—a libelous charge made against medical practitioners.

A close reading of the two most important news reports on the arrest of the doctors released respectively by the state news agency Telegraphic Agency of the Soviet Union (TASS) and *Pravda*, the official newspaper of the Communist Party of the Soviet Union, reveals the skill and dexterity with which the regime drew on existing prejudices and stereotypes in order to render a patently absurd accusation palatable and even believable. The Doctors' Plot, I contend, skillfully combined atavistic and well-worn beliefs about the Jewish lust for blood with more modern tropes about the Jewish pursuit of wealth, warmongering, dual loyalties, and conspiratorial penchants in order to create a modern document with historical resonance that could usher in a new campaign against the Jews.

The resulting libel, I argue, was melded into a response to the early geopolitical realities of the Cold War and the development of the State of Israel.

Scholarship on the Doctors' Plot has exposed the internal machinations of the regime and the agents of state security, as well as the workings of Stalin's mindset. These studies have shed extensive light on how the regime obtained confessions, connected and twisted disparate ideas into outlandish conspiracies, and fabricated counterrevolutionary allegations. These studies have also shown how the plot advanced Stalin's political goals in both the domestic and international spheres. This chapter builds on that scholarship by offering a reading of the final product of the plot, the two articles that publicized it, in order to demonstrate how the Doctors' Plot combined well-worn tropes of the blood libel with the Soviet leadership's anxieties over diaspora nationalities and obsession with conspiratorial espionage.[1]

The Doctors' Plot, which is often viewed as the culmination of Stalin's postwar campaign against the Jews, was first publicized on January 13, 1953, when *Pravda* published on its front page an article titled "Vicious Spies and Murderers under the Mask of Academic Physicians." TASS also issued a press release that day, which appeared on page 4 of *Pravda*, under the title, "Arrest of a Group of Doctor-Wreckers."[2] The TASS report began with an ominous libel: "Some time ago, the organs of state security uncovered a terrorist group of doctors who had the goal of shortening the lives of active leaders in the Soviet Union by providing them with harmful treatment." Both articles charged the doctors with plotting to poison leading Kremlin officials, and maliciously misdiagnosing and mistreating Andrei Zhdanov, the chief of ideology of the Central Committee of the Communist Party, leading to his death in 1948, and Aleksandr S. Shcherbakov, a former secretary of the Central Committee, who died of a heart attack on May 10, 1945, the day after Victory Day.

There was, indeed, a conspiracy at work here. However, it was not the work of a group of Jewish doctors, but rather the efforts of the Central Committee of the Communist Party, working in tandem with the Ministry of State Security and Stalin himself, to portray the challenges confronting the Soviet Union in the postwar period as the malevolent work of a cabal of physicians. The conspiracy was finalized in a Central Committee meeting of January 9, 1953, at which the precise terms of the Doctors' Plot were discussed and the means of disseminating news of the invented conspiracy were settled. The article that appeared in *Pravda* was written predominantly by Dmitry Shepilov, the editor in chief of *Pravda*, and was extensively edited and approved by Stalin himself.[3]

The names of the doctors cited as ringleaders in the *Pravda* article were all identifiably Jewish and, in all but one case, were identified only by last name, as though to emphasize their ethnic roots: "Vovsi, B. Kogan, Feldman, Grinshtein, Etinger, and others." By referring to the accused parties only by family name, the article encouraged readers to universalize the guilt to all Jews: it was not just *a specific* Vovsi, Feldman, Grinshtein and Etinger, but rather the Vovsis, Feldmans, Grinshteins, and Etingers of the world who could be imagined as guilty. In this sense, the names function as archetypes, much as Rabinovich functioned as the Jewish everyman in many well-known Soviet jokes. Even the initial "B" that *Pravda* provided to differentiate the physician Boris Kogan from his brother Mikhail Kogan, who was also a prominent physician implicated in the plot, did little to delimit the number of Kogans that could be held responsible. It is likely no coincidence that *Pravda* chose to highlight such obviously Jewish names among those accused.

Indeed, each of these family names was easily recognizable as Jewish, and the first name on the list—Vovsi—was also well known as the original surname of the Yiddish actor Solomon Mikhoels. Mikhoels had been murdered by Stalin's agents on the night of January 12–13, 1948, exactly five years before the revelation of the Doctors' Plot. Notably, Mikhoels death was purported at the time to have been a tragic accident—he was run over by a truck in Minsk—and he was publicly mourned, given a state funeral, and lauded in the press. Then, the following year, his name suddenly disappeared from all publications. Only now, on the front page of *Pravda*, was he being referred to as a "well-known bourgeois nationalist."

Miron Vovsi, Mikhoels's cousin was, before his November 1952 arrest, the former chief internist for the Soviet Army and a prominent physician at the Kremlin Hospital. Neither Vovsi, Grinshtein, nor Feldman had been involved in the medical treatment of either Shcherbakov or Zhdanov, making their inclusion in the list of primary perpetrators curious. Meanwhile, the *Pravda* article did not include the names of several non-Jews that were included in the TASS release and had been involved in the medical treatments of Zhdanov and Shcherbakov.

Although the news releases came as a shock to most observers, Stalin had secretly been plotting the campaign for several years, allowing it to evolve and snowball based on a combination of changing political circumstances and the predilections of his own fantasies. The Doctors' Plot belongs to the type of antisemitism that the historian Gavin Langmuir once categorized as "chimerical."[4] Unlike Langmuir's identification of xenophobic antisemitism, which blamed all Jews for the misdeeds of a few, chimerical antisemitism was based entirely on a falsehood. It was, like the accusation of ritual murder, a complete libel without even a kernel of truth. It was also, in Langmuir's perception, the most dangerous form of hatred.

The libel began, as archival discoveries have made clear, with a letter that Lidia Timashuk, the head of the EKG department in the Kremlin Hospital, had penned soon after Zhdanov's death in August 1948 to Lieutenant General Nikolai Vlasik, the head of Stalin's personal security service until his 1952 removal from the position and subsequent arrest in connection with the Timashuk letter.[5] Timashuk incorrectly alleged that the doctors treating Zhdanov had misdiagnosed the results of his EKG and had allowed him to take on more activity than he should have been permitted, resulting in a myocardial infarction (heart attack). Stalin ordered the letter to be filed away, probably recognizing that it could come in use at some point in the future. Years later he would revive it in order to establish a record of allegedly malicious doctors.[6]

Zhdanov's death occurred just as Stalin was embarking on a massive purge directed against the Jewish population of the Soviet Union. The year began with the assassination of Solomon Mikhoels on the night of January 12–13, 1948, and culminated in late 1948 with the arrest of leading Jewish political, cultural, and intellectual personalities associated with the Jewish Anti-Fascist Committee (JAFC), including the writers Peretz Markish, Dovid Bergelson, and Dovid Hofshteyn, and the actor Benjamin Zuskin. The physicians Lina Shtern and Boris Shimeliovich were both arrested in January 1949 as a result of their connections to the JAFC, though neither was accused of misusing their medical licenses. In January 1949 a campaign against a group of mostly Jewish theater critics was publicized with a January 28 article in *Pravda* titled "About One Anti-patriotic Group of Theater Critics." Like the publicity that surrounded the Doctors' Plot, the campaign against the theater critics began with an article in *Pravda* using antisemitic motifs but making no explicit references to the Jewish nationality of the accused. Throughout 1949 and 1950 arrests of leading Jewish intellectuals and public figures continued, including the November 1950 arrest of the physician Yakov Etinger.

Before he died in prison after a night of enhanced interrogation, Etinger, who had been one of several consulting physicians in Shcherbakov's case, had been forced to confess to shortening the life of Shcherbakov in order to promote Jewish nationalist interests. Within this forced confession, the Ministry of State Security, acting under Stalin's close observation, managed to turn Etinger into the linchpin in the concoction of a case that connected the allegation of bourgeois nationalism associated with the JAFC to a bourgeoning campaign against Jewish doctors. The libelous charge that Soviet Jews were acting at the bequest of US intelligence agencies to promote Jewish nationalist causes was a crucial component of the *in camera* trial of the JAFC in the spring of 1952, which led to the secret execution of thirteen defendants on August 12, 1952. In November of that same year,

Rudolf Slansky, the secretary general of the Czech Communist Party, and thirteen other politicians, eleven of whom were Jewish, were publicly tried in Prague on trumped up charges of promoting Zionist espionage and plotting to murder Czech President Klement Gottwald.[7]

All these cases—particularly those well-publicized as press events—helped prepare the ground for the Doctors' Plot by aggravating latent suspicion of Jewish state loyalty. They provide evidence that, as Jonathan Brent and Vladimir Naumov write, "the conspiracy against the Jewish doctors must be viewed in a much wider context than that of Stalin's personal antisemitism. It became a tool of his foreign and domestic policy."[8] At the same time, the plot drew together motifs and prejudices long associated with the blood libel.

By early 1953 the Ministry of State Security publicly identified a core group of thirty-seven doctors (seventeen of whom were Jewish). After the release of the news report, authorities arrested hundreds of Jewish doctors over the next two months. Some scholars believe that the plot was connected to a wider plan to deport Soviet Jews from major cities to Soviet Central Asia and other destinations to the east. Indeed rumors proliferated at the time that Russia's Jews would soon be deported, and in fact, in early 1953 construction began on four new work camps in Kazakhstan and Siberia. In any case, the Doctors' Plot ended with Stalin's death on March 5, 1953, and the subsequent exoneration of the arrested doctors.[9]

The trope of doctors secretly poisoning leading political figures was not new at the time and built on widespread associations between Jews and physicians, dating back to the Middle Ages. As the historian Cecil Roth demonstrated in an article he coincidentally published several months after the Doctors' Plot was revealed in 1953, some two thousand Jewish physicians practiced medicine in medieval Europe.[10] These physicians were widely believed to have access to secret sources of knowledge or were regarded as possessing supernatural powers, and therefore often fell under suspicion. Medical cures in the medieval mind were widely associated with magic or Kabbalah and medicinal ointments and syrups were associated with supernatural potions. Illnesses were commonly believed to be the work of demons, and some believed that the special relationship Jews allegedly had with the Devil helped them expel the evil forces of disease. Medicine, then, was regarded as an esoteric art, accessible only to the initiated, and commonly associated with Jews. When treatments failed, it was very easy to blame the doctor, whose expertise already seemed arcane. More threateningly, the idea that doctors possessed secret knowledge often elicited widespread fear that they could potentially use it as a powerful malicious force.

Jewish doctors had famously been accused of poisoning their patients in the distant past. There are numerous episodes of medieval authorities arresting and even burning at the stake Jewish doctors on charges that they had poisoned their patients. Holy Roman Emperor Charles the Bald's court physician was accused of poisoning the emperor in 877, a reported eighty-six Jews were accused of working with physicians to poison the Bohemian population in 1161, and in 1610 Jewish physicians in Vienna were accused of poisoning their patients.[11] As Martin Luther wrote of the Jews: "If they could kill us all, they would gladly do so, aye, and often do it, especially those who profess to be physicians. They know all that is known about medicine in Germany; they can give poison to a man of which he will die in an hour, or in ten or twenty years; they thoroughly understand this art."[12] Political figures were imagined as common victims of Jewish doctors. As Frank Heynick notes, the Catholic Church of Valladolid in 1322 warned that Jewish physicians, "under guise of medicine, surgery, or apothecary commit treachery with much ardor and kill Christian folk when administering medicine to them."[13] The baptized Jew Rodrigo Lopez, who served as Queen Elizabeth's personal physician, was publicly hanged in 1594 on suspicions that he was trying to poison the monarch. Oddly enough, although the case of Lopez was widely publicized at the time, contemporary reports hardly mentioned his Jewish heritage. Allegations that Jews use disease to harm the general population also reappeared in the infamous *Protocols of the Elders of Zion*, which first appeared in Russian as *The Great within the Minuscule and Antichrist* in 1903. In this text, among other allegations, the Jews are accused of disturbing the people's relations with their government "by the inoculation of diseases."[14] These anti-physician libels, which were commonly directed against Jews, share with the traditional blood libel the accusation that Jews would deliberately despoil gentile bodies. Given the high percentage of physicians in the Soviet Union who were of Jewish heritage—some 20 percent in 1939—it was not difficult to revive this preexisting association between Jews and medicine.[15]

The libels against the doctors also included the accusation that the physicians were corrupting the practice of medicine and science in general. These accusations came at a time when the Soviet Union was working to present itself as a world leader in science and technology, a claim that would culminate with the 1958 launch of Sputnik, the first artificial satellite. Specifically, the doctors were accused of having, in the words of the TASS press release, "defiled the honor of science" and in the *Pravda* article of having "dishonored the holy banner of science." At the same time, both the TASS and *Pravda* reports credit modern scientific forensic techniques with uncovering the plot: the allegations are backed by "documentary materials, research findings of medical experts, and declarations of those arrested," according to the TASS release. In this sense, the rhetoric follows some of the observations that Hillel Kieval has made about nineteenth-century

Central European blood libel accusations in Tiszaeszlár and Xanten. As Kieval argues, "medicine and the experimental sciences, in fact, presented a vocabulary that prosecutors as well as defenders increasingly found indispensable."[16] It demonstrates, again quoting Kievel, "the continued attractiveness of nonrational, conspiratorial thinking" and shows that "the modern ritual murder trial was to be structured by powerful, if implicit, rules of expression and authority: it could only be articulated through the epistemological categories and idioms of a culture that understood itself to be both rational and scientific."[17] Similarly, although the essence of the Doctors' Plot accusation relied on well-established medieval tropes—Jewish doctors secretly poisoning gentiles—the presentation and epistemological categories were modernized through the use of scientific language, while at the same time playing on latent public anxieties and suspicions of science and physicians.

The Doctors' Plot relied on the notion that the conversion or assimilation of the Jew was only a façade, and that with vigilance, the true face of the Jew could be unmasked. The component of secrecy is crucial to any conspiracy. As Eva Horn and Anson Rabinbach noted in a special issue of the *New German Critique* dedicated to conspiracy theories: "No outsider may know who the members are, which is what distinguishes the conspiracy as a political agency from other secretive groups with agendas such as political parties or commercial firms."[18] Both the TASS and *Pravda* articles draw on the motif of umasking hidden identities. The *Pravda* article's title, "Vicious Spies and Murderers under the Mask of Academic Physicians" alludes already to the notion of Jews masking their true identities. The TASS article also draws on similar themes, identifying the nine doctors as "hidden enemies of the people" who "concealed" Zhdanov's myocardial infarction.

This notion of unmasking the true identity of the Jew dates back to medieval images of the Jewish convert. Conversion rarely absolved a former Jew of the accusation that he or she possessed Jewish traits. Jewish converts in sixteenth-century Spain did not lose their "Jewishness" simply by converting to Christianity; in fact, these "New Christians," or "Marranos," were often regarded as being even more dangerous because their Jewishness was now masked behind a façade of Christianity. In addition, they continued to be suspected of retaining ties to their former communities. Even converted Jews were often accused of poisoning the souls of good Christians. The notion of unmasking Jewish plots also reappears hundreds of years later in the *Protocols of the Elders of Zion*, in which the bogus "Elders" assert, "Our power in the present tottering conditions of all forms of power will be more invincible than any other, because it will remain invisible until the moment when it has gained such strength that no cunning can any longer undermine it."[19] Jewish power, it is asserted, is again most dangerous because it is clandestine. Finally, Nazi propaganda portrayed assimilated German Jews as even more dangerous than more easily recognizable Eastern European Jews precisely because they first had to be unmasked before they could be combatted. Just as converted Jews in the early modern era were regarded as being unable to fully shed their Jewishness, regardless of their level of piety, so Jews in the postwar Soviet Union remained under suspicion, regardless of the zealousness with which they had embraced the communist creed. In some respects this compulsion to unmask can also be linked to the 1930s campaign to uncover enemies of the people, in which Stalin famously warned of the "wolf in sheep's clothing." Soviet citizens were warned that the enemy lurked behind masks, concealing their true identity. It was the task of a conscious proletarian to "tear off each and every mask from reality," as the slogan of the proletarian writers' association put it.[20]

In addition to borrowing medieval tropes of antisemitism, the Ministry of State Security and the authors of the plot's narrative responded to modern geopolitical insecurities by twisting the accusation into a bizarre international conspiracy typical of twentieth-century Soviet and Eastern European show trials. The doctors were accused of working with foreign intelligence agencies and, according to TASS, of being "associated with the international Jewish bourgeois-nationalist organization, the 'Joint,' created by American intelligence in order to direct material aid to Jews in foreign countries. At the same time this organization, at the behest of American intelligence, undertook broad espionage, terrorism, and other injurious activity in a series of countries, including the Soviet Union." The report continued to state that Vovsi had confessed to "receiving directives from the United States about exterminating the leading cadres of the Soviet Union through the 'Joint' via the doctor Shimeliovich in Moscow and the well-known Jewish bourgeois nationalist Mikhoels." Other members of the alleged conspiracy were accused of being "long-standing members of British intelligence." The *Pravda* article expanded on the TASS release by noting that the Joint is the "filthy face of the Zionist espionage organization" acting "under the mask" of charity. In the next paragraph, the Joint was referred to as a "terrorist espionage organization."

The Joint Distribution Committee, which had in fact channeled large sums of aid to the Soviet Union in collaboration with Soviet authorities over the preceding three decades, was presented as merely a cover for clandestine espionage. The organization, as well, was only referred to by the mysterious name Joint rather than by its full name, the Joint Distribution Committee, which sounds much more benign and limited in its goals. It is also irrelevant that the Joint was precisely a non-Zionist organization, and was therefore very far from the "face of the Zionist espionage organization." "Now," the article continued, "everybody can see what type of 'charity' and 'world friendship' hides under the mask of the 'Joint.'" Like the *Protocols*, this allegation underscored the belief that the ideas of modern liberalism, self-help, and charity were merely slogans designed to deceive the public so that the Jewish cabal can implement its ulterior motives.

The allegation that Jewish charity work was a front for more malicious espionage and terrorist activity was not a new allegation, and indeed, it is one that continues to this day. Neither was the Joint the only Jewish philanthropic organization to have served as a focal point for antisemitic conspiracy theories. *The Protocols of the Elders of Zion*, which contained some of the most recognized allegations of a vast Jewish conspiracy for global dominance, are sometimes ascribed to anxieties surrounding the Alliance Israélite Universelle, which like the Joint was devoted to providing charitable services for Jews around the world. The second volume of Henry Ford's notoriously antisemitic *The International Jew* similarly accused the Jewish philanthropist and financier Jacob Schiff in particular of using his charity work to advance Bolshevism in Japan.[21] Jewish philanthropy is often imagined as a cover for Jewish political machinations and interventions. Indeed, these themes continue to this day on the internet, where philanthropic Jewish organizations are routinely derided as cogs in a global Jewish conspiracy. For instance, the top Google search results for Jacob Schiff include several antisemitic websites. One result, under the title "The Genocidal Jewish Supremacist Jacob H. Schiff," a blog post by Christopher Jon Bjerknes, alleges, in conspiratorial terms reminiscent of the Doctors' Plot language, that "Schiff implemented Rothschild's plan to genocide the Russian People and steal the wealth of the Russian nation."[22]

In fact, though, the Joint had long provoked a crisis of faith among the communist faithful, as it begged the question of why a society that purported to have solved most economic conundrums would continue to require foreign aid to provide for basic agricultural necessities and means of production. The Joint was also intricately connected to the failed project of establishing a Jewish homeland in the Crimea, an idea briefly entertained by Soviet Foreign Minister Viacheslav Molotov and promoted by Mikhoels. It was this connection that provided some of the basis for the secret trial of the JAFC and, through Mikhoels's cousin Vovsi, fodder for the crucial link between the JAFC and the doctors. It was probably also a factor in the November 1952 arrest of Molotov's wife, Polina Zhemchuzhina, whose Jewish heritage rendered even her suspect. Her 1948 encounter with Golda Meir, then the Israeli minister plenipotentiary to Moscow, provided additional fodder for accusations of dual loyalty.[23]

The *Pravda* article drew from these motifs to argue that the accused Jewish doctors were utilizing their global influence in order to foment war: "The movers and shakers of the United States and their British junior partners know that they cannot achieve dominance over other nations through peaceful means." Unable to carry out their mission peacefully, the plotters were accused of "feverishly preparing for a new world war." The accusation continued that "they energetically send spies inside the USSR and the people's democratic countries; they attempt to accomplish what the Hiterlites could not do—create in the USSR their own subversive 'fifth column.'" The notion that Jews are the primary instigators of war not only echoes the early twentieth-century *Protocols of the Elders of Zion* and the *International Jew*, but was also a common motif of antisemitic writings on the world wars. In his famous January 30, 1939, speech to the Reichstag, for instance, Adolf Hitler prophesied that "if the international Jewish financiers in and outside Europe should succeed in plunging the nations once more into a world war, then the result will not be the bolshevization of the earth, and thus the victory of Jewry, but the annihilation of the Jewish race in Europe."[24] Similarly, grumblings in the Soviet Union sometimes blamed the Jews for bringing the Soviet Union into the war. By warning that the Jewish doctors were once again conspiring to instigate another world war, the libel of the Doctors' Plot revived these powerful and persistent tropes. These tropes also all echoed typical conspiracy theories, in which large-scale events are imagined as being under the secret control of a small group of individuals. This particular allegation adds the over-the-top insult that the group of accused Jewish doctors was attempting to finish the job that Hitler began—a particularly offensive implication to a community still reeling from the trauma of the Holocaust.

The doctors' motivations are presented as being in line with popular perceptions and stereotypes of Jewish motivations. The Jewish doctors have sold out science and their country not out of patriotism or genuine Zionist fervor, but for venal reasons. They are accused of working for foreign governments solely for hire: "having sold their bodies and souls, they appeared as hirelings, paid agents" who were "bought by American intelligence." In this way, the doctors are not even given the dignity of being presented as traitors who were motivated by ideological or political convictions; they are portrayed as having been motivated solely for money. The allegation that Jews are capable of gross immoralities in their never-ending pursuit of wealth is also a timeworn canard, perhaps made most famous by Shakespeare's *Merchant of Venice*, but certainly one of the most familiar of antisemitic tropes.

While many of these aspects are universal to conspiracy theories and antisemitic accusations and are not specifically derived from the blood libel, it is worth noting the extent to which Christian theological thinking, although staunchly rejected by the communist elite, continued to inform the Soviet worldview in important ways. Soviet confessions and rituals, for instance, borrowed extensively from Christian theological traditions. The Ministry of State Security relied on inquisitorial practices and procedures in terms of both the torture it utilized to extract confessions and the importance it ascribed to confessions in constructing legal cases. The myth of ritual murder also remained relevant in the Soviet Union and did not end in Russia with the hapless Mendel Beilis. As Elissa Bemporad has shown, the notion that Jews engage in ritual murder remained a persistent belief throughout the Soviet period. Indeed, the general public seems to have had little difficulty being convinced of the veracity of the Doctors' Plot: the newspaper articles that claimed to unveil it unleashed a wave of fear throughout the Soviet Union, as people chose to avoid medical help for fear of their doctors across the country.[25] Like the blood libel, the accusation of murder—whether ritualized or medicalized—was the first step in inaugurating mass panic and hysteria, which would make subsequent repressive measures more palatable to the terror-stricken populace.

The Doctors' Plot and other postwar Soviet anti-Jewish atrocities were not only motivated by existing ethnic, racial, and religious antisemitism, but were also part of a more general Soviet persecution of "diaspora nationalities." After the United Nations, with the support of the Soviet Union, voted in favor of the establishment of the State of Israel in November 1947, and after the actual foundation of the State of Israel in May 1948, the Jews of the Soviet Union became not just a national minority, but a diaspora nationality, a national minority with a territorial homeland located outside the Soviet Union. Like all other diaspora nationalities they were instantly subject to repression as potential fifth columns. In the 1930s and the immediate aftermath of World War II, Stalin had deported and repressed Poles, Finns, Crimean Greeks, Koreans, Volga Germans, and others whose loyalty could potentially lie with a titular state beyond the borders of the Soviet Union. With the establishment of the State of Israel as a Jewish homeland, the loyalty of all Soviet Jews also fell into question. The widespread excitement that Soviet secret police observed among Soviet Jews about Israel further convinced the authorities that Jewish loyalty was suspect.[26]

Thus, although the political context was obviously very different from that of the traditional blood libel, there were some very important similarities. As Gavin Langmuir argued, blood libels were rooted in religious zeal, "motivated and explicitly justified by the irrational fantasies of paranoid people whose internal frontiers of faith were threatened by doubts they did not admit."[27] The key component that Langmuir identified here is that blood libels occur at moments in which faith is threatened by doubt. Similarly, the historian David Nirenberg has written of the blood libel in the Middle Ages that the accusation of ritual murder was a "common tool with which critics of monarchy represented the dangers they believed protection of Jews posed to Christian society."[28] He argues that ritual murder accusations helped make sense of "the gap between worldly politics and some posited (albeit strategically) Christian ideal."[29] Nirenberg's gap, like Langmuir's crisis of faith, can both serve as viable characterizations of the Soviet Union in the late 1940s and early 1950s.

The battle of Stalingrad and the beginning of the Russian counteroffensive against the Germans in 1943 initiated a period of euphoria in Russia. The war was moving toward victory, the siege of Leningrad was lifted in January 1944, and in May 1945 the Red Army captured Berlin. Despite unprecedented suffering and human loss, Stalin's massive industrialization campaign seemed to have paid off. In the rhetoric of the time, communism had been victorious over Fascism. But Victory Day did not immediately bring about a new utopian era. Instead, the country was hit with a massive famine in 1946, and the project of rebuilding proved to be more onerous and difficult than many had imagined in the euphoric days of 1945. All too many Soviet soldiers returned from war to find their homes destroyed and their families perished.

In 1946 Nicholas Timasheff famously wrote of "The Great Retreat," a process that he argued began in 1934, but whose contours could only have been realized in the postwar era.[30] Similarly, Vera Dunham wrote in 1976 of what she termed a "Big Deal," a postwar alliance between the regime and the middle class that allowed for mutual coexistence under the guise of a totalitarian system.[31] Both texts—one written in the immediate postwar period and the other thirty years later—share the assumption that as the Soviet state's early revolutionary euphoria gave way to an ossified bureaucracy, it inaugurated a crisis of faith in its ideals. Fundamentally, by the early 1950s, the Soviet state could no longer present itself as a utopia in the making—"the First Socialist Society"—struggling against the imperialist powers for survival, but rather had become a mammoth bureaucratic state beset with quotidian difficulties and paralyzed by a superpower status that was poorly reflected in the living standards of its citizens. Its success bred contentment, but hardly euphoria.

At the same time, there was another state—Israel—emerging on the global scene that was being touted as a utopia, a solution to thousands of years of suffering, and that was captivating Jewish youth throughout the Soviet Union. In fact, the Soviet Ministry of Foreign Affairs was inundated with requests from young Jews throughout the country seeking permission to emigrate and join in the heroic battle for the State of Israel. Official diplomatic discussions with foreign governments centered around the issue of "reunification of families," but internal correspondence within the ministry shows that the state understood that the desire of many Jews to leave the Soviet Union was not just motivated by family concerns. Even if family reunification was the driving motivation, virtually every Soviet Jew had some family member abroad, and so the migratory chain could have been endless. In fact, the movement among Jews to "make Aliyah"—to migrate to Israel—in the late 1940s and early 1950s represented a crisis of faith for the communist leadership. In February 1952, Deputy Minister of Foreign Affairs Andrei Gromyko sent a top secret note to Stalin warning of a "mass exodus of Jews from the USSR to Israel." The Soviet authorities recognized that such a mass emigration would pose a direct threat to Soviet ideology. USSR Ambassador to the United Nations Iakov Malik told Israeli Minister of Foreign Affairs Moshe Sharett when the two met in New York that "the emigration of Soviet people to a country with different social conditions would contradict the basic principles of the Soviet state."[32] The desire of Jews to emigrate instilled doubt in the superiority of the Soviet system. In Langmuir's terms, the internal frontiers of faith were threatened by doubt. The timing of the Doctors' Plot occurred at a moment of doubt in the unique mission of the Soviet Union, and thereby conforms to the model of the blood libel, which tended to emerge during similar periods of doubt, when political realities failed to match ideological and religious expectations.

The Doctors' Plot can also be seen as rooted in the psychological phenomenon that, in reference to the medieval blood libel, the folklorist Alan Dundes has termed projective inversion: "Projective inversion refers to a psychological process in which A accuses B of carrying out an action which A really wishes to carry out him or herself."[33] In the case of the blood libel, Dundes argues that Christians accuse Jews of reenacting the crucifixion through ritual murder as a means of projecting their own guilt at having partaken of the blood and flesh of their savior through transubstantiation in the ritual of the Eucharist. Rather than feel guilt themselves for ritually partaking of the body and blood of Christ, he continues, Christians have engaged in projective inversion by scapegoating the Jews. "By means of this projective inversion," he writes, "it is not we Christians who are guilty of murdering an individual in order to use his blood for ritual religious purposes (the Eucharist), but rather it is you Jews who are guilty of murdering an individual in order to use his or her blood for ritual religious purposes, baking matzah."[34] It is not difficult to imagine Stalin, and the Ministry of State Security more broadly, projecting their own murder of "leading Kremlin cadres" during the purges and Great Terror onto the Jews in a similar manner. In this sense, Dundes's projective inversion is not just symbolic—as in the Eucharist—but is very real. The leadership of the state security apparatus was, in fact, blaming the Jews for the crimes they themselves had committed. Whether or not the roots of the postwar antisemitic campaigns can be seen in such psychological terms, the applicability of Dundes's theory provides further attestation of the structural similarities between the blood libel and the Doctors' Plot. The Doctor's Plot was not a blood libel, but it borrowed many of the tropes and motifs that had made the blood libel a formidable and durable tool.

JEFFREY VEIDLINGER is Joseph Brodsky Collegiate Professor of History and Judaic Studies and Director of the Frankel Center for Judaic Studies at the University of Michigan. He is the author of *The Moscow State Yiddish Theater: Jewish Culture on the Soviet Stage* (2000), *Jewish Public Culture in the Late Russian Empire* (2009), and *In the Shadow of the Shtetl: Small-Town Jewish Life in Soviet Ukraine* (2013).

NOTES

1. For previous studies on the plot, see Jonathan Brent and Vladimir P. Naumov, *Stalin's Last Crime: The Plot against the Jewish Doctors, 1948–1953* (New York: HarperCollins, 2003); G. V. Kostyrchenko, *Tainaia politika Stalina: Vlast' i antisemitizm* (Moscow: Mezhdunarodnaia otnosheniia, 2001), 629–94; Arkady Vaksberg, *Stalin against the Jews* (New York: Knopf, 1994), 238–80; Louis Rapoport, *Stalin's War against the Jews: The Doctors' Plot and the Soviet Solution* (New York: Free Press, 1990); and Yakov Rapoport, *The Doctors' Plot of 1953* (Cambridge, MA: Harvard University Press, 1991). For more on the related campaign against the Jewish Anti-Fascist Committee, see Joshua Rubenstein and Vladimir P. Naumov, eds., *Stalin's Secret Pogrom: The Postwar Inquisition of the Jewish Anti-Fascist Committee* (New Haven, CT: Yale University Press, 2001).

2. The TASS release was published in *Pravda* as "Arest gruppy vrachei-vreditelei," *Pravda*, January 13, 1953. The more extensive *Pravda* article appeared as "Podlye shpiony i ubiitsy pod maskoi professorov-vrachei," *Pravda*, January 13, 1953.

3. For details, see Brent and Naumov, *Stalin's Last Crime*, 287.

4. Gavin I. Langmuir, *Toward a Definition of Antisemitism* (Berkeley: University of California Press, 1990), 334.

5. For more on the arrest of Vlasik, see Brent and Naumov, *Stalin's Last Crime*, 272–82.

6. For more on Stalin's reaction to the Timashuk note, see ibid., 54–92.

7. For more on the case of the Jewish Anti-Fascist Committee, see Rubenstein and Naumov, *Stalin's Secret Pogrom*. On the Slansky Affair, see Igor Lukes, "The Rudolf Slansky Affair: New Evidence," *Slavic Review* 58, no. 1 (1999): 160–87.

8. Brent and Naumov, *Stalin's Last Crime*, 119.

9. For more on the possible deportation of the Jews, see Brent and Naumov, *Stalin's Last Crime*, 294–97. For a critical analysis of the "myth of deportation," see Kostyrchenko, *Tainaia politika Stalina*, 671–85.

10. Cecil Roth, "The Qualification of Jewish Physicians in the Middle Ages," *Speculum* 28, no. 4 (1953): 834.

11. Joshua Trachtenberg, *The Devil and the Jews: The Medieval Conception of the Jew and Its Relation to Modern Anti-Semitism* (Philadelphia: Jewish Publication Society, 1983), esp. 88–108. For more on medieval medicine and the Jews, see John M. Efron, *Medicine and the German Jews: A History* (New Haven, CT: Yale University Press, 2001), 13–33; Joseph Shatzmiller, *Jews,*

Medicine, and Medieval Society (Berkeley: University of California Press, 1994); and Frank Heynick, *Jews and Medicine: An Epic Saga* (Hoboken, NJ: Ktav Publishing, 2002). On the blood libel, see R. Po-Chia Hsia, *The Myth of Ritual Murder: Jews and Magic in Reformation Germany* (New Haven, CT: Yale University Press, 1988); and Francesca Matteoni, "The Jews, the Blood, and the Body in Late Medieval and Early Modern Europe," *Folklore* 119, no. 2 (2008): 182–200.

12. Cited in Efron, *Medicine and the German Jews*, 25. For numerous other examples of Jewish doctors being accused of harming their patients, see ibid., 24–27, 50–57.

13. Heynick, *Jews and Medicine*, 124.

14. Stephen Eric Bronner, *A Rumor about the Jews: Antisemitism, Conspiracy, and the Protocols of Zion* (Oxford: Oxford University Press, 2000), 21.

15. For the percentage of Soviet Jews in medicine, see Yuri Slezkine, *The Jewish Century* (Princeton, NJ: Princeton University Press, 2004), 225.

16. Hillel J. Kieval, "The Rules of the Game: Forensic Medicine and the Language of Science in the Structuring of Modern Ritual Murder Trials," *Jewish History* 26, no. 3–4 (2012): 289.

17. Ibid., 306.

18. Eva Horn and Anson Rabinbach, "Introduction," *New German Critique* 103 (2008): 1.

19. Cited in Bronner, *Rumor about the Jews*, 11–12.

20. See Sheila Fitzpatrick, *Tear Off the Masks! Identity and Imposture in Twentieth-Century Russia* (Princeton, NJ: Princeton University Press, 2005), esp. 65.

21. Henry Ford, *The International Jew: The World's Foremost Problem* (Dearborn, MI: Dearborn Publishing Co., 1920), 2: 48.

22. Christopher Jon Bjerknes, "The Genocidal Jewish Supremacist Jacob H. Schiff," *Jewish Racism* (blog), January 29, 2008, http://jewishracism.blogspot.com/2008/01/genocidal-jewish-supremacist-jacob-h.html.

23. Rubenstein and Naumov, *Stalin's Secret Pogrom*, 46–47.

24. Norman H. Baynes, *The Speeches of Adolf Hitler, April 1922–August 1939* (London: Oxford University Press, 1994), 1, pt. 3:741.

25. See Elissa Bemporad, "Empowerment, Defiance, and Demise: Jews and the Blood Libel Specter under Stalinism," *Jewish History* 26, nos. 3–4 (2012): 343–61. For some more examples, see Kostyrchenko, *Tainaia politika Stalina*, 667–71; Rapoport, *Stalin's War*, 158–63; and Aleksandr Lokshin, "The Doctors' Plot: The Non-Jewish Response," in *Jews and Jewish Life in Russia and the Soviet Union*, ed. Yaacov Ro'i (Ilford, UK: Frank Cass, 1995), 157–67.

26. For more on this point, see Jeffrey Veidlinger, "Soviet Jewry as a Diaspora Nationality: The 'Black Years' Reconsidered," *East European Jewish Affairs* 33, no. 1 (2003): 4–29.

27. Gavin Langmuir, "At the Frontiers of Faith," in *Religious Violence between Christians and Jews: Medieval Roots, Modern Perspectives*, ed. Anna Sapir Abulafia (London: Palgrave, 2002), 153.

28. David Nirenberg, *Anti-Judaism: The Western Tradition* (New York: W. W. Norton, 2014), 204.

29. Ibid., 206.

30. Nicholas S. Timasheff, *The Great Retreat: The Growth and Decline of Communism in Russia* (New York: E. P. Dutton, 1946).

31. Vera Sandomirsky Dunham, *In Stalin's Time: Middleclass Values in Soviet Fiction* (Cambridge: Cambridge University Press, 1976).

32. See Veidlinger, "Soviet Jewry as a Diaspora Nationality," 21–22.

33. Alan Dundes, "The Ritual Murder or Blood Libel Legend: A Study of Anti-Semitic Victimization through Projective Inversion," in *Blood Libel Legend: A Casebook in Anti-Semitic Folklore*, ed. Dundes (Madison: University of Wisconsin Press, 1991), 353.

34. Ibid., 354.

⁕ 14 ⁕

THE SANDOMIERZ PAINTINGS OF RITUAL MURDER AS *LIEUX DE MÉMOIRE*

Magda Teter

IN 1710 JEWS in the Polish town of Sandomierz were accused of killing a small boy. It was the beginning of an exceedingly complex three-year trial, at the end of which several Jews of Sandomierz lost their lives. While the 1710 trial in Sandomierz was one of many, now forgotten, trials that took place in the Polish-Lithuanian Commonwealth in the eighteenth century, three hundred years later, this trial has not fallen into oblivion and still reverberates in Polish society and beyond.[1] Its reminders, visible in the local Cathedral Church and in the Church of St. Paul, where a series of paintings referring to the tales of ritual murder can be found, controversially blend history and the present, and color the perception of Jewish-Christian relations in Sandomierz and, more broadly, in Poland. The paintings in Sandomierz, especially the painting *Infanticidia* (figure 14.1) on the western wall of the Cathedral Church depicting scenes of Jews killing Christian children, have become a site of memory (*lieu de mémoire*) on which the memory of Jewish-Christian relations in Poland rests; a place where the past is remembered and distorted; a battlefield where memory and history fight against a desire to forget.[2] As a result the painting(s) became a source of protests and tensions between the Catholic Church in Poland, and especially in Sandomierz, and the Jewish community and progressive Catholics.[3]

As the French historian Pierre Nora has argued, *lieux de mémoire* exist because the *milieux de mémoire*, the physical social setting on which history and memory rest, which had been part of everyday life, have disappeared.[4] For centuries Jews

Figure 14.1. Painting *Infanticidia* by Carlo de Prevo and Andreas Erixson, before 1737. *Photograph*: Roman Chyła, Sandomierz.

were an integral part of the Polish landscape, Poland's society, history, culture, and economy. But since the end of World War II, despite efforts to revive the Jewish community in Poland, there has been no Jewish community that would have been an inseparable part of the country's everyday reality the way it had been for centuries until 1939.[5]

According to Nora, the *lieux de mémoire* are material reminders of the historical past, "the ultimate embodiments of memorial consciousness."[6] They represent "moments of history torn away from the movement of history," and they are linked to historical ruptures. The memory about Jews in Poland, and about that long-gone past, is now located in several *lieux de mémoire*, such as Kazimierz, the Jewish part of Cracow, Auschwitz, and other death camps, and in the Sandomierz painting(s). All have become powerful, and problematic, sites of memory.[7]

But memory and the *lieux de mémoire* associated with it necessarily simplify the past, heighten emotions, and mute the past's different colors, shades, and textures. *Lieux de mémoire*, though ostensibly focused on the past, are not really concerned with history. Rather, they are about the present. An example with Sandomierz as the centerpiece comes from a crime novel published in Polish in 2011 but now also available in English, *The Grain of Truth*, and as a film:

Sandomierz is the center of the so-called legend of blood . . . the capital of the universe for the idea of ritual murder. The place where accusations of kidnapping children and the resulting pogroms were once as regular as the seasons of the year. The place where the Church endorsed that sort of bestial attitude, virtually institutionalized it. The place where to this day there's a painting hanging in the cathedral showing Jews murdering Catholic children. As part of a series about Christian martyrdom. The place where everything possible has been done to sweep that bit of history under the carpet. Now, as I think about it, my God, that is as revolting as it gets. . . . For years he [the murder victim's husband] has tried to have the painting removed, or at least get it provided with an appropriate sign saying it was still here as a memento of Polish antisemitism, a reminder of what hatred can lead to.[8]

All the efforts of the victim's husband were in vain because "the Church," the book continues, "has its own way of dealing with things like that. They have not taken it down or put up a sign. When there was too much fuss about it, they hid it behind a screen . . . and pretended it doesn't matter." As these passages demonstrate, the less than accurate representation of the eighteenth-century blood libels in Sandomierz became linked, "as a memento of Polish anti-Semitism," to the difficult, more recent past, engendering polemics and emotions on all sides, and making it difficult to engage not only with the history of the paintings and the events behind them, but also with the larger topic of Jewish-Christian (or more specifically Jewish-Catholic) relations.[9]

But memory has its counterpart—oblivion. If, as David Lowenthat has argued, "the past validates the present," then the Poland that emerged after World War II—largely ethnically and culturally homogenous—needed a new way of looking at its past.[10] And although all nations seek to remember some aspects of the past and forget others, given the near total destruction of its Jewish community, Poland became uniquely positioned to reconceptualize and effectively distort its past. It could, so it seemed, forget its multiethnic, multicultural past and embrace a past of a homogenous Polish society.[11] As Sławomir Kapralski has shown, Poland could now choose to preserve, marginalize, or erase its Jewish past.[12] And each town did so in a variety of ways: some destroyed what was left of the Jewish past (synagogues, cemeteries), and some preserved the structures, appropriating them for other uses.

Discussion of the Jewish past in Poland was difficult during the decades following World War II. The communist regime's insistence on the narrative that Nazis committed crimes against "humanity," and on representing the victims of the Nazi death camps as citizens of almost all European countries without specifying that they were overwhelmingly Jewish, helped deepen the silence about the destruction of Polish Jews and their long history in Poland.[13] During the decades following the war, both the communist regime and the Catholic Church at times either remained silent or harnessed antisemitism to bolster their position in Polish society.[14] It was politically expedient *not* to confront the past.

It was not till the 1980s that the situation began to change, at least in the circles of Catholic and Jewish intellectuals, who had begun engaging in a dialogue as a paradoxical result of the 1968 events.[15] For the first time in decades, new publications and films appeared about Jewish culture and the Polish Jewish past.

The silence about Poland's Jewish past fostered by the communist era ossified the language used to discuss Jews. Unable to evolve with the new post–World War II spirit that was palpable in the West, in part because of the absence of a significant Jewish community willing and able to talk about its traditions, culture, and history, the Polish language used to discuss Jews remained the language of the past. Poland did not have a way to speak about Jews except in the language of the interwar period, still using the theologically loaded term *starozakonni,* literally "the people of the Old Testament," or the term whose roots go back to the nineteenth century *wyznawcy religii mojżeszowej* (the believers in the religion of Moses). In the new, postcommunist Poland, Poles had to learn a new way of speaking, and even today some of these old expressions still persist even among well-meaning Poles.

A by-product of Polish "rediscovery" of its Jewish past was also the topic of Jewish-Christian relations and dialogue, an open awareness of intensified antisemitism of the interwar period, and open discussions about the destruction of the Jews during World War II. They all influenced the reading of the Sandomierz paintings, reducing it to a symbol of a much-simplified version of a much richer Polish-Jewish past. And so the controversy over the painting was really not about the three-hundred-year-old past; it was about the present.[16] Sandomierz became a battlefield between contesting collective identity and self-image: some denied, or wished to forget, Poland's antisemitic past, some wanted Poland to reckon with it. The Sandomierz paintings, preserved in Christian spaces, unlike the increasingly restored synagogues, which were seen as purely Jewish spaces, became "nodes," or even "knots," in the entangled histories of Jews and Poland.[17] Those who wanted to expiate for Polish antisemitism and for the lost Jewish past in the country saw the paintings as "a memento of Polish anti-Semitism" to the chagrin of those who wanted to forget Poland's Jewish past and the complex relations between Polish Jews and Christians.[18]

But presenting the painting(s) in terms of "Polish antisemitism" is somewhat reductionist. Their historical meaning is far more complex, predominantly because it is very closely tied to the story of Simon of Trent, a boy whose death in 1475 spurred not only a trial of the Jews of Trent but also a cult, whose cultural and ecclesiological legacy cannot be ignored. In fact, this legacy is also one that may have helped foster dialogue and solutions.

No other case of ritual murder accusations against Jews inspired such rich literary production as did the 1475 case of Simon of Trent, and none other left an equally impressive—quantitatively and qualitatively—iconographic legacy. The iconographic legacy from Trent was tantamount to the invention of "an iconographic vocabulary" of ritual murder.[19] The iconography and the literary output were related and led to an inclusion of Simon of Trent in the revised 1583 liturgical calendar *Martyrologium Romanum*, and then to the official recognition of the cult by Pope Sixtus V in 1588, which set a precedent that would later make it difficult, if not impossible, for popes to openly protect Jews from similar accusations.

But Simon's status was not uncontested. With the rise of the printing press, which helped disseminate images and stories of venerated figures, Pope Sixtus IV decided to intervene in the rise of the pilgrimage site devoted to "little Simon." Sixtus IV worried that Bishop Johannes Hinderbach's efforts, which in Hinderbach's mind were in line with medieval customs, could lead to something "that might result in injury to God or contempt of the Apostolic See."[20] In his letter to Bishop Hinderbach from October 10, 1475, for the first time Sixtus IV applied explicitly the legal concepts of authorized public worship of saints to the term *beatus*, previously loosely used for local cults, prohibiting people from calling the boy *beatus*, from preaching in public about him and about miracles related to him, and from disseminating images of him. In disapproving of the "public proclamation of Simon as a martyr," even though no liturgy was attached at the time to the veneration of Simon, Pope Sixtus IV interpreted the existing law in a new way, effectively condemning any "public manifestation" of veneration without prior approval of the Holy See.[21] This marked the first step of what would by the seventeenth century become a formal process of beatification and made Simon a precedent in canon law.

Despite Sixtus IV's efforts to stem the cult of little Simon, thanks to the patronage of Bishop Hinderbach, the cult flourished in Trent, at least until the bishop's death in 1486. And though it declined in the first half of the sixteenth century, it reentered the pilgrim's consciousness in the second half of the sixteenth century, following the Council of Trent. Among the 517 officials of the Catholic Church who participated in the council, some expressed, as a seventeenth-century writer would later recall, great interest in Trent's "most blessed innocent martyr," promoted then by Cardinal Cristoforo Madruzzo, the bishop of Trent and Brixen during the Council.[22]

In 1570, seven years after the conclusion of the Council, Laurentius Surius (or Lorenz Sauer), a German Carthusian hagiologist and historian, published in Cologne a collection of the lives of saints, *De probatis sanctorum historiis* (Approved Histories of the Saints) based on the magnum opus of Luigi Lippomano, a bishop of Verona and a participant in the Council of Trent. Surius's opus was organized (in contrast to Lippomano's work, which was ordered chronologically) in a monthly order, allowing users to follow the lives of saints in an annual cycle. It also included, for the first time, under March 24, an account of Simon's death.[23] Surius's lives of saints became a European bestseller, no doubt thanks to its monthly order, inspiring new adaptations, and providing materials for other chroniclers, including Cesare Baronio and Raynaldo Odorico, thereby helping secure for Simon a permanent place in authoritative Christian histories of the world. (The Counter-Reformation chroniclers were not the first to turn to Simon. Simon had entered northern European consciousness already in the fifteenth century, when the story of Simon of Trent featured prominently in Hartmann Schedel's 1493 *History of the World* published in Nurnberg [figure 14.2], which provided one of the most iconic images of Simon, but Schedel's chronicle did not have much influence after 1500.)[24]

The Council of Trent decided, in response to Protestant attacks on the cult of saints in the Catholic Church, to affirm the validity of the worship of saints and to consider regulating them, and called for a review of liturgical books.[25] Thus, the breviary was revised in 1568, and the missal in 1570.[26] In 1580 Pope Gregory XIII also ordered a reform of the liturgical calendar *Martyrologium Romanum*.[27] Until then many versions of *Martyrologium Romanum* existed that "were not perfect, or without errors."[28] Pope Gregory XII formed a commission of scholars that included, among others, Roberto Bellarmino and Cesare Baronio.[29] Cesare Baronio's name would be attached to the 1586 edition of the calendar.[30]

Baronio wanted to include "the names of the saints celebrated and honored all over the Christian world," and carefully evaluated all saints and martyrs, adding some and deleting others.[31] Some of his decisions were met by controversy; others were accepted without any opposition.[32] When the revised *Martyrologium Romanum* first appeared in 1583, it had the pope's imprimatur and emphasized that it was "restored in accordance with the truth of church history."[33]

Since many editions of the calendar had existed prior to the publication of the newly revised *Martyrologium Romanum*, on January 14, 1584, Pope Gregory XIII issued a *breve* titled *Emendato iam*, in which he prohibited the use or publication of any other version of *martyrologium* but the latest one and banned any new additions to the calendar. Local figures venerated in local churches but not included in this new and authorized version of *Martyrologium Romanum* were to

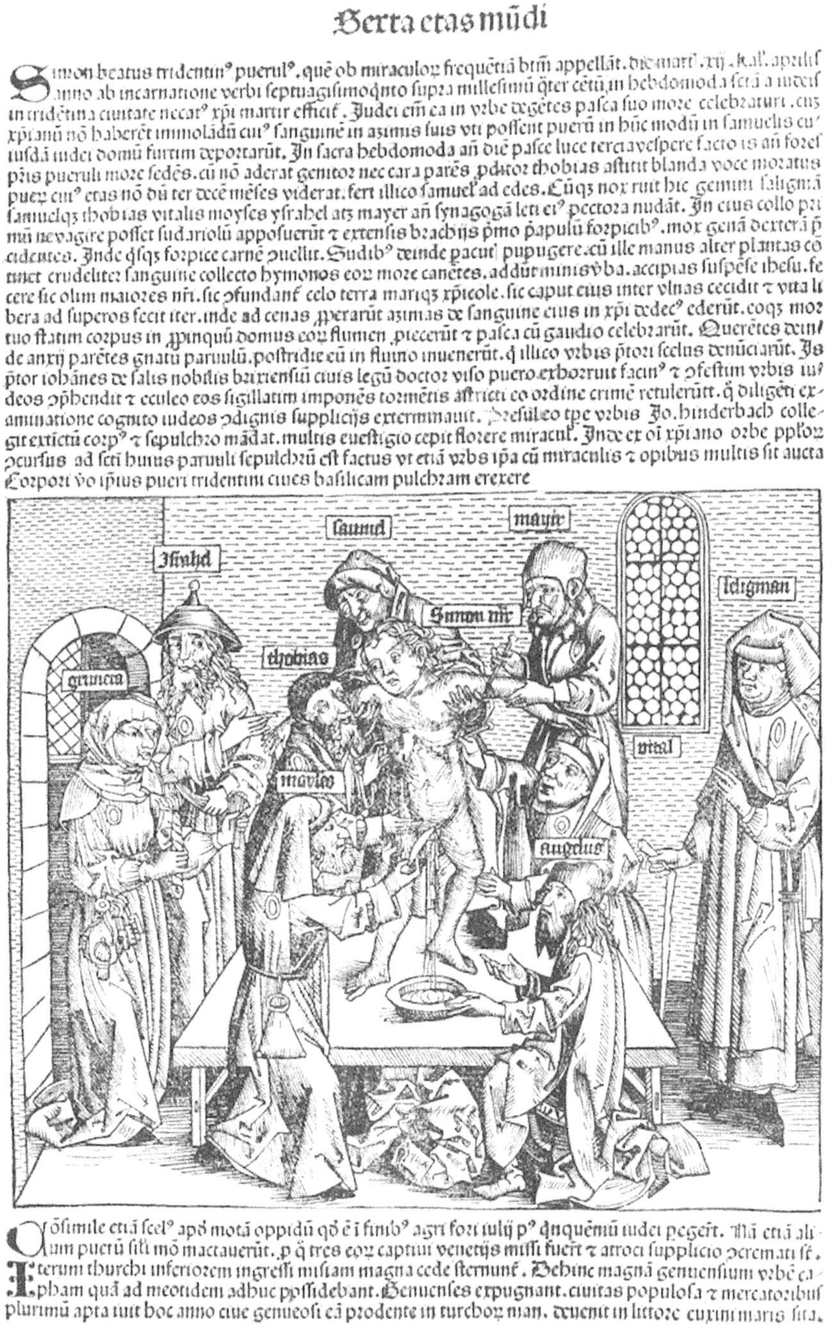

Sexta etas mūdi

Simon beatus tridentin⁹ puerul⁹. quē ob miraculoꝝ frequētiā btm̄ appellāt. die marti .xij. kal'. aprilis anno ab incarnatione verbi septuagisimoqnto supra millesimū q̄ter cētū, in hebdomoda scā a iudeis in tridētina ciuitate necat⁹ xp̄i martir efficit. Judei em̄ ea in vrbe degētes pasca suo more celebraturi. cū xp̄ianū nō haberēt immolādū cui⁹ sanguinē in azimis suis vti possent puerū in hūc modū in samuelis cuiusdā iudei domū furtim deportarūt. In sacra hebdomoda añ diē pasce luce tercia vespere facto is añ fores p̄ris puerulꝰ more sedēs. cū nō aderat genitor nec cara parēs, pditor thobias astitit blanda voce moratus puer: cui⁹ etas nō dū ter decē mēses viderat. fert illico samuel ad edes. Cūq3 nox ruit hic geminū saligmā samuelq3 thobias vitalis moyses ysrahel atq3 mayer añ synagogā leti ei⁹ pectora nudāt. In eius collo pri mū ne vagire posset sudariolū apposuerūt ⁊ extensis brachijs p̄mo p̄putiū forpicib⁹. mox genā dexterā p̄ cidentes. Inde q̄sq3 forpice carnē euellit. Sudib⁹ deinde pacuti pupugere. cū ille manus alter plantas cō tinet crudeliter sanguine collecto hymnos eoꝝ more canētes. addūt minis v̄ba. accipias suspēse ihesu. fecere sic olim maiores n̄ri. sic ↄfundant celo terra mariq3 xp̄icole. sic caput eius inter vlnas cecidit ⁊ vita libera ad superos fecit iter. inde ad cenas p̄perarūt azimas de sanguine eius in xp̄i dedec⁹ ederūt. coq3 mortuo statim corpus in p̄pinquū domus eoꝝ flumen p̄iecerūt ⁊ pasca cū gaudio celebrarūt. Querētes deinde anxij parētes gnatū paruulū. postridie eū in flumo inuenerūt. q̄ illico vrbis p̄tori scelus denūciarūt. Is p̄tor iohānes de salis nobilis brixiensiū ciuis legū doctor viso puero exhorruit facin⁹ ⁊ ↄfestim vrbis iudeos ↄphendit ⁊ eculeo eos sigillatim imponēs tormētis astricti eo ordine crimē retulerūt. q̄ diligēti examinatione cognito iudeos ↄdignis supplicijs exterminauit. Presul eo tp̄e vrbis Jo. hinderbach collegit extictū corp⁹ ⁊ sepulchro mādat. multis e vestigio cepit florere miracul'. Inde ex oī xp̄iano orbe pploꝝ ↄcursus ad scti huius paruuli sepulchrū est factus vt etiā vrbs ip̄a cū miraculis ⁊ opibus multis sit aucta Corpori v̄o ip̄ius pueri tridentini ciues basilicam pulchram erexere

Nōsimile etiā scel⁹ apd motā oppidū qd ē ī finib⁹ agri fori iulij p⁹ qnquēniū iudei pegerūt. Nā etiā alium puerū sibi mō mactauerūt. p q̄ tres eoꝝ captiui venetijs missi fuerūt ⁊ atroci supplicio ↄcremati sūt.

Iterum thurchi inferiorem ingressi misiam magna cede sternunt. Dehinc magnā genuensium vrbē caphā quā ad meotidem adhuc possidebant. Genuenses expugnant. ciuitas populosa ⁊ mercatoribus plurimū apta fuit hoc anno ciue genueosi eā prodente in turchoꝝ man. deuenit in littore euxini maris sita.

Figure 14.2. Simon of Trent in Hartmann Schedel, *Liber Chronicarum*. Nuremberg: Anton Koberger, 1493. *Source:* The author's private collection.

be listed separately.³⁴ Crucially, the revised and authoritative calendar now also included Simon of Trent under March 24. Simon appeared in the main body, not under a separate section devoted to local cults. He now belonged to the official church calendar.

The 1586 edition, published under Baronio's name, underscored the new calendar's validity. A letter "To the Candid Reader" by the Dutch bishop William Damasus Lindanus affirmed that the book had been reviewed by church authorities and contained nothing that would contradict "orthodox faith and doctrine." In fact, the revisions and emendations were made so that the faithful could worship the martyrs and saints assured of the verity of the eloges contained therein and not worry about "vain," "apocryphal," even "superstitious" tales that may have "contaminated" earlier versions of the *Martyrologium*.³⁵

With such heavy scrutiny of the content of the new *Martyrologium Romanum*, the inclusion of Simon of Trent was no accident; it was a deliberate affirmation of the cult, a result no doubt of heavy lobbying by interested parties from Trent. With Simon thus part of the official liturgical calendar, in 1588 Pope Sixtus V had no choice but to grant an *officium* (a liturgy) in Simon's name. What was once from Rome's perspective a "rogue" local cult now became a cult fully embraced by the pontiff and the Roman Curia and had serious consequences for subsequent responses from the Church to blood libels against Jews.

The impact of the inclusion of Simon in *Martyrologium Romanum* was felt in the limitations it posed on papal condemnations of similar anti-Jewish accusations without undermining papal authority, and the legitimacy of the liturgical calendar. The change of Simon's status resulting from reform of *Martyrologium Romanum* and from broader reforms of the canonization procedures, thus, tied hands of subsequent popes to intervene openly in condemning similar accusations against Jews, despite medieval papal condemnations of the charges. It was only during the Second Vatican Council in 1965, when the Church began to revise its Tridentine policies, that church authorities abolished Simon's cult, and with it came, for the first time in centuries, an open condemnation of anti-Jewish accusations of ritual murder.

The cult's formal recognition in the late sixteenth century led to a wave of publications about Simon and to new efforts to popularize the cult.³⁶ Pilgrims helped in that regard, too. In 1668 Michel Angelo Mariani reported hearing about the faithful venerating Simon not only in Italy, France, and Germany, but also in Poland and Flanders.³⁷ He was certainly correct; the cult of Simon was known in Poland. The 1608 edition of Ambrogio Franco's *Martirio di S. Simone di Trento* found its way to Poland; a copy, which had earlier been in the Camedule Monastery in Cracow, is now held in the Jagiellonian Library in Cracow. Polish pilgrims and travelers visiting Rome stopped in Trent on their way there, and some even settled in the region. The painter Marcin Teofilowicz, known in Italy as Martino Teofilo Polacco, was active in Trentino. His oeuvre includes paintings of Simon of Trent. One, "Madonna with a child, Saint Francis and Little Simon," was in fact placed in the church established in the house of a community leader, Samuel, which served at the time as a synagogue; another, now in Spormaggiore, was "The Coronation of the Virgin," which prominently featured local saints, including in the right bottom corner Simon of Trent.[38]

But perhaps the most notorious role in the spread of Simonine iconography in Poland was played by Stefan Żuchowski, a Polish priest from Sandomierz, who visited Trent in 1699 on his way to Rome, one year after he spearheaded a trial of Jews in his hometown, where he was a canon, accusing them of murdering a Christian child. Visiting Trent just a year after the trial must have resonated with Żuchowski. He would have surely seen Simon's body and relics, and the numerous works of art on public view: the representation of Simon's kidnapping painted above the entry door to Simon's house on Via Simonino, the 1668 series of paintings by Pietro Ricchi in the chapel devoted to Simon in St. Peter's Church. He would have also seen the spaces and paintings in the former synagogue, a church during Żuchowski's sojourn.[39]

A few years after his return to Sandomierz, Żuchowski again became embroiled in a lengthy trial against Jews living in Sandomierz, leaving behind not only grief and pain among the Jewish community in town, but also literary and iconographic traces of the tragic events, with which we still grapple. Żuchowski published two books about the trials he had spearheaded and sponsored a series of sixteen grand paintings inspired by the liturgical calendar *Martyrologium Romanum* for the collegiate church, now a cathedral, in Sandomierz. Twelve of the paintings represented scenes of martyrdom for each month and day.[40] Four additional paintings showed local instances of "martyrdom," including the now notorious painting *Infanticidia*, a vivid painting representing Jews killing a Christian child (figure 14.1). And although this painting was indeed intended to illustrate the two cases of ritual murder Żuchowski championed in Sandomierz, its presence within the series of paintings titled *Martyrologium Romanum* tied it to the Trent story, as traditionally martyrological calendars sought to connect local martyrs with the universal liturgical calendar accepted by the Church.[41] Indeed, the placement of the four paintings in a separate space seems to have complied with the requirement that figures venerated in local churches be listed separately.[42]

Yet, if the painting *Infanticidia* in Sandomierz alluded to Simon of Trent only indirectly by association with *Martyrologium Romanum*, far more explicit

Figure 14.3. A painting depicting "Tobias the Jew" from a series of paintings in the Church of St. Paul in Sandomierz. *Photograph*: Roman Chyła, Sandomierz, 1996.

were seven paintings in the chancel of the church of St. Paul's in Sandomierz.[43] These paintings, despite claims in Poland that they represent local events, most definitely depicted the Trent story. Until their restoration, frames on at least three of them contained inscriptions in Latin.[44] One, on the painting showing the kidnapping of the child, read (figure 14.3): "Tobias Judaeus puerum rapit et eum synagogam clam inducit" (Tobias the Jew snatches the boy and furtively leads him to the synagogue).[45] There was *no* Tobias in Sandomierz, nor was there one in any of the known ritual murder trials in Poland. But there was a Tobias in Trent—a major figure known for his purported role in kidnapping Simon, and he was widely represented in iconography (figure 14.2). Moreover, the text found on the frame closely echoed the opening words from the liturgy for Simon of Trent, which read: "Tobias iniquus rapuit beatum Simonem et eum in Synagogam clam deduxit" (Hostile Tobias kidnapped the blessed Simon and brought him furtively to the synagogue).[46] The text in Sandomierz is shorter but the difference may simply stem from the space available on the frame—the much longer text from the liturgy would not fit.

Other inscriptions were more general and mentioned no specific names. One depicted a meal at a table and once bore the line "Dicunt judaei perforavimus venas pueri nunc in contemptum Jesu Sanguinem eius bibamus" (Jews say, we pierced the boy's veins, now we drink his blood in contempt of Jesus). This line closely resembles a sentence from Simon's *officium* used to celebrate mass in his honor in Trent: "Tenentes puerum saeui carnifices, *dicebant ad invicem perforemus venas eius et sanguinem eius bibamus*" (Holding the boy, the ferocious tormenters were saying to one another we shall pierce his veins and drink his blood).[47] The line in Sandomierz seems to be a conflation of two lines in the Simonine liturgy—"in contemptum Iesu" can be found in a few lines in the liturgy after the verse referring to the drinking of blood.[48]

The painting depicting the scene of the boy's death in St. Paul's Church in Sandomierz also displayed iconographic Simonine clues—including the white scarf with which Simon was said to have been strangled (figures 14.4 and 14.5)—and once contained an inscription: "Extensus in modum crucis puer ac *forticibus* [forcipibus] et *acutus* [acubus] toto corpores *sanciatus* [sauciatus] elevatis oculis in coelum sanctum emisit spiritum" (The boy, extended in the form of the cross and hurt all over the body with pincers and nails, having lifted his eyes toward heaven, gave up his holy spirit).[49] Like the two other inscriptions, this too is an almost verbatim rendition of a phrase found in the *officium* (table 14.1).[50] And like the other inscriptions, this one also omits the name Simon.

The differences between the text of the Simonine liturgy and the inscriptions in Sandomierz may be explained by the space available on the frames, efforts to tie the story of Simon to local events, or perhaps even memory lapses by the Italian painter, Carlo de Prevo, who at the time had lived and worked in Poland for decades.[51] But if it was the painter's memory, understandably shaky after decades

Figure 14.4. St. Paul's Church in Sandomierz, an image displaying motifs from Simonine iconography, for example, a white scarf. *Photograph:* Roman Chyła, Sandomierz.

Figure 14.5. Simon of Trent in the Church of Santa Maria Rotonda in Pian Camuno, Val Camonica, Italy, fifteenth century. *Photograph:* Luca Giarelli, public domain, Wikimedia.

Table 14.1. Comparison between the inscriptions in St. Paul's Church and *Officium Proprium S. Simonis Innocentis*

Inscriptions in the Church of St. Paul in Sandomierz	*Officium Proprium S. Simonis Innocentis*
Tobias Judaeus puerum rapit et eum synagogam clam inducit (Tobias the Jew snatches the boy and furtively leads him to the synagogue).	*Tobias iniquus rapuit beatum Simonem et eum in Synagogam clam deduxit* (Hostile Tobias kidnapped the blessed Simon and brought him furtively to the synagogue).[1]
Dicunt judaei perforavimus venas pueri nunc in contemptum Jesu Sanguinem eius bibamus (Jews say, we pierced the boy's veins, now we drink his blood in contempt of Jesus).	*Tenentes puerum saeui carnifices, dicebant ad invicem perforemus venas eius et sanguinem eius bibamus* (Holding the boy, the ferocious tormenters were saying to one another we shall pierce his veins and drink his blood. Two lines later the phrase "in contemptum Jesu" is used).[2]
Extensus in modum crucis puer ac forticibus [forcipibus] et acutus [acubus] toto corpore sanciatus [sauciatus] elevatis oculis in coelum sanctum emisit spiritum (The boy, extended in the form of the cross and hurt all over the body with pincers and nails, having lifted his eyes toward heaven, gave up his holy spirit).	*Extensus in modum crucis beatus Simon, et diris forcipibus et acubus toto corpore sauciatus elevatis oculis in caelum sanctum emisit spiritum.* (The blessed Simon, extended in the form of the cross and hurt all over the body with pincers and nails, having lifted his eyes toward heaven, gave up his holy spirit).[3]

[1] *Officium Proprium S. Simonis Innocentis*, 7, 14.
[2] Ibid., 7.
[3] Ibid.

of living away from his homeland, it may suggest that de Prevo, who designed the series and about whose life before coming to Poland little is known, may have hailed from Trent, or its surroundings, and thus had been familiar with the Simonine cult and iconography. For even though Stefan Żuchowski visited Trent in 1699 on his way to Rome, and may have even brought a copy of the *officium* back home, he could not have retained as detailed a knowledge of Simonine iconography as is on display here.

Indeed, the painting of Tobias in the Church of St. Paul in Sandomierz bears an eerily close resemblance to one of the scenes of a painting, datable to 1594, *San Simonino da Trento* by Pietromartino di Anversa, originally in the "third altar on the left" of the Church of Santa Maria dei Fossi (or degli Angeli) in Perugia, now at the Galleria Nazionale there (figure 14.6).[52] The painting by Pietromartino was no doubt created in light of the renewed interest in Simon's story following the formal recognition of his cult in the 1580s. The color schemes and scenery are similar in the two paintings. The vestment and position of Tobias, as well as the vestment and position of the child, are almost the same (see figures 14.2 and 14.6). Also similar are the buildings, with a bell tower, a gate, and open shops.[53]

There are also differences between the paintings in the Sandomierz Church of St. Paul and that from Perugia by Pietromartino di Anversa. But the differences, too, underscore the significance of the story and early Simonine iconography for both works. Pietromartino's painting suggests that he was intimately familiar with the Simonine story and iconography developed after 1475. The painting from Perugia shows Simon dressed in accordance with historical records—a gray tunic and a white apron. In Sandomierz, Simon is shown wearing a red tunic with a white apron. Red, or crimson, was a symbol of Christ's tunic and was used in both literary imagery and in Simonine iconography to connect the alleged child victims with representations of Christ; it is, in fact, characteristic of the developed iconography of Simon of Trent.[54]

The prominent presence of barrels in the painting by Pietromartino di Anversa, as well as in many other Simonine paintings, may help explain the barrel motif in the Sandomierz paintings. However, a much closer parallel may be the iconography found in the iconography of Atilius Regulus (d. 250 BCE), who is said to have been executed by being put in a barrel spiked with nails and rolled down a hill in Carthage. The story was frequently rendered pictorially in print in the sixteenth and seventeenth centuries (figure 14.7).[55] A similar fate awaited Saint Erasmus of Formia, who, according to the Golden Legend, was put in a barrel spiked with iron nails and rolled down a hill (though in this instance he was saved by an angel). A barrel spiked with nails also appears in one of the stories in Yehuda ibn Verga's *Shevet Yehudah*, according to which a king places Jews accused of ritual murder in a barrel with nails protruding inside.[56]

In Sandomierz the link to the Simon of Trent story was quickly forgotten, and then entirely lost. A 1915 book described the paintings as "an illustrated history of the little boy, Jerzy Krasnowski, killed in Sandomierz in 1710."[57] Some two decades later a Polish writer, Jarosław Iwaszkiewicz, also saw the paintings as a reflection of the trials in Sandomierz, when he referred to the visible river in one of the paintings as the Vistula.[58] Today, too, scholars have described them as

Figure 14.6. Pietromartino di Anversa, *Simonino da Trento* (1594), originally in "third altar on the left" of the Church of Santa Maria dei Fossi (or degli Angeli) in Perugia, now at the Galleria Nazionale in Perugia.

Figure 14.7. Atilius Regulus in a barrel, an engraving by Georg Pench (1535). *Source:* Metropolitan Museum of Art, New York, Harris Brisbane Dick Fund, 1917. Accession number: 17.3.1277, http://www.metmuseum.org/art/collection/search/432151.

"representing the martyrdom of Jerzy Krasnowski," the boy whose death led to the lengthy 1710–1713 trial.[59] Finally, the restoration of the paintings in the Church of St. Paul entirely removed any traces of this connection, as the texts on the frames that linked the paintings in the church of St. Paul to Simon of Trent were painted over. Now, to contemporary viewers the story represented there is *entirely* local, with no outside connection, no historical and iconographic legacy. To be sure, even in the eighteenth century, when these paintings were commissioned and created, their content was chosen in the context of the local trials of Jews. (Indeed, at least one alludes to the local story by displaying a child inside a barrel.) The fact that the descriptions of these paintings do not mention Simon's name only underscores the conscious play on both Simon's story and the local trials even in the eighteenth century when they were executed. But unlike today, when the connection between Sandomierz and Trent is entirely forgotten, in the eighteenth century the connection to events from Trent would have served to justify, frame, and amplify the accusations against Jews in Sandomierz. Paradoxically, as the town today addresses its past and seeks to shake off that legacy, the restored paintings *now* seem entirely about Sandomierz.

But there is another important connection to Simon of Trent. The history of the cult of Simon and its abolishment in 1965 in the wake of the Second Vatican Council reflect the changing relations between Jews and the Catholic Church. Similarly, the fate of the Sandomierz paintings seems to reflect the changing state of Catholic-Jewish relations and dialogue in Poland, and Poland's gradual embrace of the teachings of the Second Vatican Council especially since the 1980s.[60]

The timing of the new tone in Jewish-Catholic relations ushered in by the 1965 declaration "Nostra Aetate" (In Our Times), a seminal document redefining Jewish-Catholic relations, and the transformative Second Vatican Council coincided with antisemitic agitation in Poland that resulted in the 1968 marginalization and forced migration of thousands of Jews still living in Poland. When the Vatican Commission for Religious Relations with the Jews issued its "Guidelines and Suggestions for Implementing the Conciliar Declaration Nostra Aetate, no. 4" in 1974, Poland was in no position to receive them.[61]

But in the 1980s, on the heels of political changes related to the Solidarity movement, the relations between Jews and the Catholic Church in Poland began to change as well.[62] In 1986, inspired by Pope John Paul II's visit to the synagogue in Rome and his appreciation for "our dearly beloved brothers," a Commission for the Dialogue with Judaism was established by the Polish Episcopate; it became a full-fledged council in 1996.[63] In 1990 the Polish Episcopate issued a pastoral letter to be read in churches, which, in the spirit of Nostra Aetate, emphasized the Jewish roots of Christianity, and condemned antisemitism.[64] And yet, lest it appear revolutionary and thus be rejected, the letter did not only refer to the Second Vatican Council and Nostra Aetate, but also grounded the message in the Church's Tridentine tradition.⁶⁵

This new openness and rapprochement also resulted in new sensitivity to painful events. The Kielce pogrom of 1946 emerged from oblivion, the "deinternationalization" of Auschwitz-Birkenau began, along with other disputes such as the Jedwabne controversy. Soon, the Sandomierz paintings, one of few reminders of premodern anti-Jewish sentiments and persecutions, also came into focus. In 2000 one of the main actors was the late Stanisław Musiał, SJ, who was also one of the original members of the Episcopate Commission for the Dialogue with Judaism, and its secretary from 1986 to 1991, published in a major Polish daily an exposè of the painting.⁶⁶ Soon, the Episcopate Committee for the Dialogue with Judaism and the Polish Council for Christians and Jews became involved. Proposals were made, even for a text of a plaque to be affixed next to the painting, but no executable solution was found.

In 2006, after years of resurging controversies, the painting in the town's cathedral was covered, an original controversy over a plaque now became a controversy with much higher stakes. While a plaque could have been affixed without much publicity, the removal of the cover, thus making the painting visible again, could not have been done discreetly. In January 2014 the painting was finally unveiled, and a plaque that had been agreed on during the first flare-up was affixed next to it. It was done in the presence of Chief Rabbi of Poland Michael Schudrich and Israeli Ambassador Zvi Rav Ner, along with several bishops, including Bishop Mieczysław Cisło, the head of the Episcopate Commission for the Dialogue with Judaism, during the celebration of the Day of Judaism, a day observed each year by the Catholic Church in Poland with the aim of fostering a dialogue with Judaism and the Jewish community.⁶⁷ Among the goals of the Day of Judaism, celebrated in Poland since 1997, is to "propagate exposition" of biblical texts, "which in the past may have been interpreted in an anti-Jewish and anti-Semitic way" in the spirit of the legacy of the Second Vatican Council and Nostra Aetate, "to explain to the faithful the tragedy of the Jewish extermination," and "to present anti-Semitism as a sin."⁶⁸

In Sandomierz the events on January 16, 2014, seemed to mark a turning point in the long-rankling controversy and the almost decade-and-a-half-long stalemate. Indeed, one could not be unmoved when a group of young clerics from the local Catholic seminary sang a popular Israeli song in Hebrew "Hevenu Shalom Aleikhem," during a Catholic service in this small (and in January very sleepy) town in southeastern Poland. The Israeli ambassador to Poland, Zvi Rav Ner, could be seen singing along with a smile. The 2014 celebration of the Day of Judaism in Sandomierz and the uncovering of the controversial painting with the previously agreed-on and prominently displayed description were greeted with a sigh of relief by all. Credit for this accomplishment has to be given to Sandomierz Bishop Krzysztof Nitkiewicz. Participating in the events, Chief Rabbi of Poland Michael Schudrich called the unveiling of the controversial painting and the new plaque "a wise solution," and he emphasized that Jewish-Catholic relations had never been better than they were now. Though the solution may not have been fully satisfying to all, this was an important step that helps normalize further the relations between Jews and Catholics in Poland, and in Sandomierz, and facilitates more discussions among Polish Catholics and Jews about their shared, and often difficult, past.

To be sure, beyond Poland those efforts at rapprochement between Jews and Catholics have been taking place since the years preceding the Second Vatican Council and since the 1990s in Poland.[69] In Sandomierz they had never succeeded in breaking the stalemate. But Sandomierz helps make a case for historians lending a hand in situations difficult to overcome (in the interest of full disclosure, I was one of the participating historians in Sandomierz) very much in line with the 1974 Vatican "Guidelines and Suggestions for Implementing the Conciliar Declaration Nostra Aetate," stressing the importance of, in the words of the Vatican Commission for Religious Relations with Jews, "research into the problems bearing on Judaism and Jewish-Christian relations."[70]

A year before the historic celebration of the Day of Judaism in Sandomierz, a smaller gathering took place just steps from the cathedral. Scholars from Poland and the United States discussed questions of the history and historiography of Jewish-Christian relations, Jews in Christian art, and the local context for the divisive painting, in a symposium called "Jewish-Christian Relations in History, Memory, and Art: European Context for the Paintings in the Sandomierz Cathedral."[71] The symposium was the result of an unprecedented collaboration between the Diocese of Sandomierz, and especially Bishop Nitkiewicz, and an American academic institution.[72] On a cold January day in 2013, when the cobbled streets of the beautiful town were lightly covered by snow, participating scholars traced Sandomierz iconography to its Italian roots, notably to the history and iconography of Christian martyrologies, and to the iconography of the most notorious example of a blood libel, the 1475 case of Simon of Trent. What the 2013 symposium succeeded in doing was to help untangle the past from the present and find a language to discuss the painting openly, as a work of its time and place, facilitating steps that a year later allowed the young clerics to sing Hebrew songs, and the bishop to deliver a moving homily marking the Day of Judaism 2014—in the very cathedral that had been the source of bitter controversies.[73] In 2015 the diocese organized another international symposium, this one about the declaration

Nostra Aetate, hosted in the local seminary. To be sure, the change is not fast and dramatic. Rather it is the fruit of deliberate, patient efforts by the Church authorities, many of whom sincerely act "in the service of dialogue," local citizens, and scholars.[74] But the change is palpable. Perhaps now the history of the Sandomierz paintings and of the town itself may serve as a legacy of the evolution of contemporary Jewish-Christian relations in Poland. And perhaps Sandomierz may move from a symbol of antisemitism to become a model of Jewish-Catholic dialogue. Only time will tell.

In some way, Sandomierz represents an example of what the literary scholar Michael Rothberg called a "knotted intersection of history and memory."[75] The paintings in their original historical context used the past to validate the present by turning to the story of Simon of Trent, and they served to validate the Sandomierz trials. Over time that historical connection with Trent was lost, and the paintings began to represent a local past. But with the loss of Jewish community in Poland—the *milieu de mémoire*—the living memory of a more complex history has been lost as well. What remained were the *lieux de mémoire*, sites of memory, where a moment from the past became a symbol of the totality of history.

MAGDA TETER is Professor of History and the Shvidler Chair in Judaic Studies at Fordham University. She is the author of *Jews and Heretics in Catholic Poland* (2006); *Sinners on Trial* (2011); and numerous articles in English, Polish, Italian, and Hebrew. Her work has been supported by the John Simon Guggenheim Memorial Foundation (2012) and the Harry Frank Guggenheim Foundation (in 2007 and 2012). She currently serves as the vice president for publications of the Association for Jewish Studies.

NOTES

1. Joanna Tokarska-Bakir, *Legendy o krwi: Antropologia przesądu, z wagą* (Warsaw: WAB, 2008).

2. On the idea of battlefields of memory in post–World War II Poland, see Sławomir Kapralski, "Battlefields of Memory: Landscape and Identity in Polish-Jewish Relations," *History and Memory* 13, no. 2 (2001): 35–58.

3. The image of the painting is available in Hillel Kieval, "Blood Libels and Host Desecration Accusations," *YIVO Encyclopedia*, accessed November 4, 2016, http://www.yivoencyclopedia.org/article.aspx/Blood_Libels_and_Host_Desecration_Accusations.

4. Pierre Nora, "Between Memory and History: Les Lieux De Mémoire," *Representations*, no. 26 (1989): 7; Nora, *Realms of Memory* (New York: Columbia University Press, 1992), 1.

5. On these efforts, see, e.g., Katka Reszke, *Return of the Jew: Identity Narratives of the Third Post-Holocaust Generation of Jews in Poland* (Boston: Academic Studies Press, 2013); and Stanisław Krajewski, *Poland and the Jews: Reflections of a Polish Polish Jew* (Cracow: Austeria, 2005).

6. Nora, "Between Memory and History," 12.

7. One could add Jedwabne, following Jan Gross's book *Neighbors*, and its impact on Poland and its reckoning with its Polish-Jewish past: Jan Tomasz Gross, *Neighbors: The Destruction of the Jewish Community in Jedwabne, Poland* (New York: Penguin, 2002); Antony Polonsky and Joanna B. Michlic, *The Neighbors Respond: The Controversy over the Jedwabne Massacre in Poland* (Princeton, NJ: Princeton University Press, 2004); Jan Gross, *Fear: Anti-Semitism in Poland after Auschwitz: An Essay in Historical Interpretation* (New York: Random House, 2006).

8. Zygmunt Miłoszewski, *Ziarno prawdy*, Mroczna Seria (Warsaw: WAB, 2011), 78; translated as *A Grain of Truth* (London: Bitter Lemon Press, 2013), 73–74.

9. This debate is succinctly summarized in Anna Landau-Czajka, "The Last Controversy over Ritual Murder? The Debate over the Paintings in Sandomierz Cathedral," *Polin* 16 (2003): 483–90.

10. David Lowenthal, *The Past Is a Foreign Country* (New York: Cambridge University Press, 1985), 41.

11. Kapralski, "Battlefields of Memory"; Brian Porter-Szucs, *Faith and Fatherland: Catholicism, Modernity, and Poland* (New York: Oxford University Press, 2011), ch. 9.

12. Kapralski, "Battlefields of Memory."

13. See, e.g., Michael C. Steinlauf, *Bondage to the Dead: Poland and the Memory of the Holocaust* (Syracuse, NY: Syracuse University Press, 1997); Krajewski, *Poland and the Jews*, 48.

14. Porter-Szucs, *Faith and Fatherland*; Gross, *Fear*. The communist regime and the Church learned that quickly following the Kielce pogrom. There is a growing body of scholarship both in Poland and in the United States and Europe about this topic.

15. Paradoxically, perhaps the 1968 events fostered interest in Jewish matters and awakened Jewish identity among many "hidden" Jews in Poland (Krajewski, *Poland and the Jews*).

16. This is discussed in detail in Tokarska-Bakir, *Legendy o krwi*; and Landau-Czajka, "Last Controversy over Ritual Murder?"

17. On "knots" of memory, see the critique of Pierre Nora's *lieux de mémoire* by Michael Rothberg, "Between Memory and Memory: From Lieux de Mémoire to Noeuds de Mémoire," *Yale French Studies* 118/119 (2010): 3–12.

18. See, e.g., Landau-Czajka, "Last Controversy over Ritual Murder?"; Miłoszewski, *Ziarno prawdy*; and Tokarska-Bakir, *Legendy o krwi*.

19. Dominique Rigaux, "L'immagine di Simone di Trento Nell'arco Alpino Lungo Il Secolo XV: Un Tipo Iconografico?," in *Il principe vescovo Johannes Hinderbach (1465–1486) fra tardo medioevo e umanesimo: Atti del convegno promosso dalla Biblioteca Comunale di Trento, 2–6 Ottobre 1989*, ed. Iginio Rogger and Marco Bellabarba (Bologna, Italy: Edizioni Dehoniane, 1992), 488. On early printed iconography, see David Areford, *The Viewer and the Printed Image in Late Medieval Europe* (Farnham, UK: Ashgate, 2010), ch. 4. The most comprehensive overview of Simonine iconography in northern Italy to date is Valentina Perini, *Il Simonino: Geografia di Un Culto* (Trent, Italy: Società di studi trentini di scienze storiche, 2012). On the Trent trial, see R. Po-chia Hsia, *Trent 1475: Stories of a Ritual Murder Trial* (New Haven, CT: Yale University Press, 1992); and Wolfgang Treue, *Der Trienter Judenprozess: Voraussetzungen, Abläufe, Auswirkungen (1475–1588)* (Hanover, Germany: Hahn, 1996).

20. Fidel Gonzalez Fernandez, "Prefazione," in *Le cause di canonizzazione nel primo periodo della Congregazione dei Riti (1588–1634)*, ed. Giovanni Papa (Rome: Urbaniana University Press, 2001), 1; Shlomo Simonsohn, *The Apostolic See and the Jews: Documents, 1464–1521* (Toronto: Pontifical Institute of Mediaeval Studies, 1990), 99:1277.

21. Fabiano sac Veraja, *La beatificazione: Storia problemi prospettive* (Rome: S. Congregazione per le Cause dei Santi, 1983), 2:18. For the text of the letter, see Simonsohn, *Apostolic See and the Jews*, 1231.

22. Michelangelo Mariani, *Il glorioso infante S. Simone: Historia panegirica* (Trent: Zanetti Stampator Episcopale, 1668), 173–74.

23. Laurentius Surius, *De probatis sanctorum historiis: Partim ex tomis Aloysii Lipomani partim etiam ex egregiis manuscriptis codicibus, quarum permultae antehàc numquàm in lucem prodiere, optima fide collectis* (Cologne, Germany: Apud Geruinum Calenium et haeredes Quentelios, 1571), 387–90.

24. This image, in turn, had been inspired by the earliest visual representations of ritual murder in print, which appeared immediately after Simon's death. See, e.g., Areford, *Viewer and the Printed Image*.

25. Giovanni Papa, *Le cause di canonizzazione nel primo periodo della Congregazione dei Riti (1588–1634)* (Rome: Urbaniana University Press, 2001), 15–26.

26. Robert Bireley, "Early-Modern Catholicism as a Response to the Changing World of the Long Sixteenth Century," *Catholic Historical Review* 95, no. 2 (2009): 238; Natalia Nowakowska, "From Strassburg to Trent: Bishops, Printing, and Liturgical Reform in the Fifteenth Century," *Past and Present* 213, no. 1 (2011): 7. For a musicological study of the liturgical reforms following the Council of Trent, see Theodore Karp, *An Introduction to the Post-Tridentine Mass Proper* (Middleton, WI: American Institute of Musicology, 2007).

27. Pio Paschini, "La Riforma Gregoriana Del Martirologio Romano," *La Scuola Cattolica* 51 (1923): 201–3.

28. Ibid., 198.

29. Ibid., 198–99.

30. Cesare Baronio, *Martyrologivm Romanvm, ad novam kalendarii rationem, et ecclesiasticæ historiæ veritatem restitutum Gregorii XIII. Pont. Max. Ivssv editvm. Accesservnt notationes, atque Tractatio de Martyrologio Romano. Avctore Cæsare Baronio Sorano Congreg. Oratorij Presbyt* (Rome: Ex Typographia Dominici Basae, 1586).

31. Paschini, "La Riforma Gregoriana," 274.

32. Baronio recounted his difficult job of making the call whether to retain or expunge someone in the *martyrologium* (ibid., 276).

33. Cesare Baronio, *Martyrologium Romanvm ad nouam kalendarij rationem, & ecclesiasticae historiae veritatem reftitutum Gregorii XIII Pont. Max. iussu editum* (Rome: ex typographia Dominici Basae, 1583).

34. Baronio, *Martyrologivm Romanvm* (1586).

35. Ibid.

36. See, e.g., Antonio Gesti, *Martirio di S. Simone di Trento nel quale si tratta de la gran crudeltà che usarono gli empi ebrei in martirizarlo, et come è stato posto nel catalogo de santi e la solenne processione fatta nella sua prima festa con molti miracoli fatti da esso santo* (Trent, Italy: Per i fratelli de Gelmini, 1589); and Gesti, *Martirio di S. Simone di Trento nel quale si tratta de la gran crudeltà che usarono gli empi ebrei in martirizarlo, et come è stato posto nel cattalogo de santi e la solenne processione fatta nella sua prima festa con molti miracoli fatti da esso santo* (Trent, Italy: Per Gio[vanni] Battista Gelmini da Sabbio, 1593).

37. Mariani, *Il glorioso infante*, 204. The 1608 edition of Ambrogio Franco's *Martirio di S. Simone di Trento* was found in Poland; there is currently a copy in the Jagiellonian Library in Cracow, which had earlier been in the Camedule Monastery in Cracow.

38. Laura Dal Prà, "L'immagine di Simonino nell'arte Trentina dal XV al XVIII secolo," in Rogger and Bellabarba, *Il principe vescovo Johannes Hinderbach*, 469, figs. 20–21.

39. Stefan Żuchowski, *Process kryminalny o niewinne dziecie Jerzego Krasnowskiego iuz to trzecie, roku 1710 dnia 18 sierpnia w Sendomirzu okrutnie od Zydow zamordowane. Dla odkrycia iawnych kryminalow zydowskich, dla przykladu sprawiedliwosci potomnym wiekom* (Sandomierz, Poland: n.p., after 1718), 88.

40. On the Sandomierz "Martyrologium" in the context of liturgical calendars, see Henryk Wąsowicz, "Martyrologium sandomierskie na tle kalendarzy świąt," in *Stosunki chrześcijańsko-żydowskie w historii, pamięci i sztuce: Europejski kontekst dzieł w katedrze sandomierskiej*, ed. Magda Teter and Urszula Stępień (Sandomierz, Poland: Wydawnictwo diecezjalne, 2013).

41. For the most recent and most comprehensive discussion of the Sandomierz paintings, see Teter and Stępień, *Stosunki chrześcijańsko-żydowskie*. On the history of the calendar, see Wąsowicz, "Martyrologium sandomierskie."

42. Baronio, *Martyrologivm Romanvm* (1586).

43. On these paintings, including images, see Magda Teter, "Stosunki chrześcijańsko-żydowskie z perspektywy historii oraz czasu: sandomierskie obrazy w ikonograffi europejskiej," in Teter and Stępień, *Stosunki chrześcijańsko-żydowskie*, esp. 42–51, figs. 19–23.

44. Jan Wiśniewski, *Dekanat Sandomierski* (Radom, Poland: Jan Kanty Trzebiński, 1915), 177.

45. Images in color are available in Teter, "Stosunki chrześcijańsko-żydowskie," esp. 42–51, figs. 19–23.

46. *Officium proprium S. Simonis innocentis, et martyris tridentini: per totam dioecesin trid. a secularibus, & regularibus die xxiiii Martii celebrandum* (Tridenti, Italy: Ex typographia episcopale, 1655), 7.

47. Ibid., 7.

48. Ibid., 7. See also on 9: "Dixerunt impii Judaei in contumeliam Iesu, quem Christiani Deum colunt, huius pueri sanguinem exhauriamus."

49. The transcription provided in Wiśniewski's book contains errors; they may be errors of transcription, or typographical errors incurred in print, or errors of memory that were the responsibility of the painter (*Dekanat Sandomierski*, 177).

50. *Officium proprium S. Simonis Innocentis*, 14.

51. Or errors of transcription by Wiśniewski.

52. Francesco Santi, *Dipinti, sculture e oggtti dei secoli XV–XVI* (Rome: Libreria dello Stato, 1989), 221–22; Perini, *Il Simonino*, 339.

53. Teter, "Stosunki chrześcijańsko-żydowskie," appendix with color illustrations.

54. Mariani, *Il glorioso infante*, 43–44. The imagery of resurrected Christ often included a red tunic: Dieric Bouts the Elder, *Resurrection* (1450–1460), Norton Simon Museum of Art, Pasadena; Piero della Francesca, *Resurrection* (1463–1465); Michael Wolgemut, *Resurrection* (c. 1485), Alte Pinakothek, Munich.

55. See, e.g., an etching by Salvatore Rosa (1661–1662) at the Metropolitan Museum of Art, accessed November 4, 2016, http://www.metmuseum.org/collection/the-collection-online/search/400203. See also the prints by Sebald Beham (ca. 1518–1530), Georg Pencz (1535), Antonio Fantuzzi (1540–1545), and Diana Scultori (after Giulio Romano's work in Palazzo Te' in Mantua, 1547–1612), at the British Library, accessed November 10, 2016, http://www.britishmuseum.org/research/collection_online/search.aspx?searchText=Atilius+Regulus+. I thank Haya Bar-Itzhak from Haifa University for pointing me in this direction.

56. Jacob de Voragine, *The Golden Legend: Or, Lives of the Saints*, translated by William Caxton. Vol. 7 (London: J.M. Dent and Company, 1900), 7:267–73; "The Eighth Tale" in Solomon Ibn Verga, *Sefer Shevet Yehudah*, ed. Meir Wiener, 2 vols. (Hanover, Germany: Sumptibus C. Rumpleri, 1856). In the nineteenth century, this mode of torture was employed by slave owners in America. In 1838, the abolitionist paper the *Emancipator* published in five installments an account by a runaway slave, "Recollections of Slavery by a Runaway Slave," in which he described how "One day master sent me to his plantation on an errand, and I saw a man rolling another all over the yard in a barrel, something like a rice cask, through which he had driven shingle nails. It was made on purpose to roll slaves in. He was sitting on a block, laughing to

hear the man's cries." The text is available on *Documenting the American South*, posted 2003, accessed, November 11, 2016, http://docsouth.unc.edu/neh/runaway/runaway.html.

57. Wiśniewski, *Dekanat Sandomierski*, 177; also quoted in Jolanta Żyndul, *Kłamstwo krwi: Legenda mordu rytualnego na ziemiach polskich w XIX i XX wieku* (Warsaw: Cyklady, 2011), 241.

58. Żyndul, *Kłamstwo krwi*, 241.

59. Tokarska-Bakir, *Legendy o krwi*, 402.

60. On this, see, e.g., Joanna Michlic, "'The Open Church' and 'the Closed Church' and the Discourse on Jews in Poland between 1989 and 2000," *Communist and Post-Communist Studies* 37 (2004): 461–79. Extensive work on Sandomierz was done by Joanna Tokarska-Bakir (*Legendy o krwi*, 395–455). See also Landau-Czajka, "Last Controversy over Ritual Murder?" On Jewish-Catholic dialogue in Poland, see Krajewski, *Poland and the Jews*; and Archbishop Henryk Józef Muszyński, *Początek wspólnej drogi: Dialog katolicko-żydowski w Polsce w latach 1986–1994* (Gniezno, Poland: Pelplin, 2015).

61. The English text of the December 1, 1974, guidelines is available on the Council of Centers on Jewish-Christian Relations (hereafter CCJR) website, accessed, November 11, 2016, http://www.ccjr.us/dialogika-resources/documents-and-statements/roman-catholic/vatican-curia/277-guidelines.

62. Krajewski, *Poland and the Jews*, 141–62.

63. The most detailed description to date of the early stages is Muszyński, *Początek wspólnej drogi*. Pope John Paul II's April 13, 1986, address in Rome is available at CCJR, accessed, November 11, 2016, http://www.ccjr.us/dialogika-resources/documents-and-statements/roman-catholic/pope-john-paul-ii/305-jp2-86apr13.

64. Muszyński, *Początek wspólnej drogi*, 382–85. The full text is available on the website of the Centrum Dialogu i Modlitwy w Oświęcimiu, http://www.cdim.pl/pl/edukacja/zasoby-edukacyjne/teksty/52-oficjalne-teksty-kocioa-katolickiego/85-1990-11-30-episkopat-polski-list-pasterski-z-okazji-25-rocznicy-nostra-aetate (accessed November 11, 2016).

65. One statement referred to the teachings of the Council of Trent: "Katechizm Soboru Trydenckiego tak ujmuje sprawę odpowiedzialności za śmierć Chrystusa: 'Chrześcijanie grzesznicy są bardziej winni śmierci Chrystusa w porównaniu z niektórymi Żydami, którzy w niej mieli udział: ci ostatni istotnie nie wiedzieli, co czynią, podczas gdy my wiemy to aż nadto dobrze' (pars 1, cap. 5, questio 9). Deklaracja Nostra aetate przypomina tradycyjną naukę Kościoła, że "Chrystus ... mękę swoją i śmierć podjął dobrowolnie z bezmiernej miłości, za grzechy wszystkich ludzi" (Nostra aetate, tamże)." The full text of the 1990 letter is available on the website of the Centrum Dialogu i Modlitwy w Oświęcimiu, http://www.cdim.pl/pl/edukacja/zasoby-edukacyjne/teksty/52-oficjalne-teksty-kocioa-katolickiego/85-1990-11-30-episkopat-polski-list-pasterski-z-okazji-25-rocznicy-nostra-aetate (accessed November 11, 2016).

66. Tomasz Wiścicki, "Jak wygląda dialog katolicko-żydowski w Polsce?," January 13, 2015, http://ekai.pl/dossier/x85611/jak-wyglada-dialog-katolicko-zydowski-w-polsce/?print=1. A summary of the controversy is Agnieszka Sabor, Michal Okonski, "Oszczerstwo krwi," *Tygodnik Powszechny* 10, no. 2904 (2005): 11, and Landau-Czajka, "Last Controversy over Ritual Murder?"

67. See Magda Teter, "Painting Inspires Dialogue between Jews and Catholics in Poland: Small Town of Sandomierz Celebrates Day of Judaism," *Jewish Daily Forward*, March 7, 2014, http://forward.com/articles/193793/painting-inspires-dialogue-between-jews-and-cathol/?p=all.

68. For a collection of official church statements on the occasion of celebrating the Day of Judaism from 1998 to 2014, see Archbishop Stanisław Gądecki, *Dzieci jednego Boga: Przesłania na dzień judaizmu w kościele katolickim w Polsce (1998–2014)* (Poznań, Poland: Święty Wojciech, 2015).

69. John Connelly, *From Enemy to Brother: The Revolution in Catholic Teaching on the Jews, 1933–1965* (Cambridge, MA: Harvard University Press, 2012).

70. Vatican Commission for Religious Relations with the Jews, "Guidelines and Suggestions for Implementing the Conciliar Declaration Nostra Aetate, no. 4," December 1, 1974, http://www.ccjr.us/dialogika-resources/documents-and-statements/roman-catholic/vatican-curia/277-guidelines.

71. Teter and Stępień, *Stosunki chrześcijańsko-żydowskie*.

72. The academic institution was Wesleyan University, where I taught until 2015.

73. Krajewski, *Poland and the Jews*, 199.

74. Bishop Mieczysław Cisło, "W służbie dialogu," in *Początek wspólnej drogi: Dialog katolicko-żydowski w polsce w latach 1986–1994*, ed. Archbishop Henryk Józef Muszyński (Gniezno, Poland: Pelplin, 2015).

75. Rothberg, "Between Memory and Memory," 8.

INDEX

Page numbers in italics refer to figures.

Agafonov, Boris, 133–34
Agafonov, Nikolai Iakovlevich, 134
agitprop trials, Soviet, 165
AJC. *See* American Jewish Committee
Alexander I (Tsar of Russia), and Velizh ritual murder investigation, 68–69
Alexander II (Tsar of Russia): assassination of, anti-Jewish violence following, 188, 222; Great Reforms under, 191; ritual murder accusations during reign of, 74; Saratov ritual murder trial and, 88, 89; suppression of Uniate Church under, 70n17
Alexander III (Tsar of Russia), 222
Alliance Israélite Universelle, 188, 195, 196, 246
American Jewish Committee (AJC), 196, 197–98, 199, 203n50
American Jewish Joint Distribution Committee. *See* Joint Distribution Committee
American Relief Administration, 207
animal slaughter, ritual murder compared to, 123–25
Annals of the Persecution of Israel (Gurland), 50
An-sky, S., 43, 44, 50, 145, 169n29
anthropology: medieval superstition and, 140; role in ritual murder trials, 9, 131, 133; Russian scholars in, 132–37; and self-fulfilling prophecies, 146; seminal works in, 131–32
antisemitism: anti-Bolshevik propaganda and, 224–26, 235n23; Beilis trial and, 183; Catholic Church and, 3–4, 5, 7, 103–4; Catholic Church's condemnation of, 269; "chimerical," 240; in early Soviet Union, 206–7, 223; economic arguments and, 96, 103, 104, 205; Fascism and Nazism identified with, 232; modern, 6–7, 11, 95, 103–4, 173, 183, 190; Nazi occupation and legitimation of, 220, 223–25, 229, 230; and ritual murder accusations, 62, 68, 222; Soviet authorities' stance against, 13, 212, 213, 214–15, 221;

227–28, 229–32; World War II and, 223–33; xenophobic, 240; "zoological," 232, 236n59. *See also* literature, antisemitic
Aronson, Mirka, 57, 59, 60, 61, 63, 64, 65, 67
art: medieval Christian, depiction of Jews in, 21, 22. *See also* images, of Jewish ritual murder
Asch, Sholem, 207
assimilation of Jews: debates on, 143–44; suspicion regarding, and Doctors' Plot, 244–45; weak degree in Eastern Europe, 104
astrology, role in Beilis trial, 177, 178
Atilius Regulus, iconography of, 266, *268*
Austria-Hungary (Habsburg Empire), ritual murder trials in, 9, 111, 112, 118–22
Avrutin, Eugene M., 5, 152, 156

Babel, Isaac, 9, 151, 152, 164–67; "Karl-Yankel," 164–67; "Odessa," 164, 166; Rozanov and, 163
Bar-Itzhak, Haya, 4, 120
Baronio, Cesare, 258, 260
barrel, lined with nails: iconography of, 266, *268*; punishment of slaves in, 275n56; in ritual murder accusations, 97, 266, 269
Bary, József, 119
Bassin, Mark, 154
Beilis, Mendel, 112, 185; acquittal of, 182, 186, 189; arrest of, 185; emigration to Palestine, 197, 198; emigration to U.S., 189, *190*, 194, 197, 198–99; international advocacy on behalf of, 187–88, 189; memoir of, 194, 202n45
Beilis ritual murder trial, 111, 140–42, 172–83; antisemitism reflected in, 183; and Babel's writings, 165, 166; Bolsheviks on, 221; confirmation of Jewish guilt in, 141, 163, 182–83, 186–87, 189; cultural trends in Russia and, 151, 161, 162, 163, 176; debates triggered by, 186; "expert" witnesses at, 8–9, 140–41, 161, 173, 174–75; indictment in, 174–75;

279

Beilis ritual murder trial (cont.)
and Jewish transnational intercession, 11, 187–90, 193–99; Jewish university students during, 191; jury in, 182; length of, 183n1; Merezhkovskii on, 163; Moscow trial compared to, 13, 209, 210, 213; Multan trial compared to, 140, 147n7, 159; outcome of, 182, 186, 189; political context of, 185–86, 189, 190–91; prosecution in, 173–74, 182, 183; religious prejudice and, 7, 8; Rogger on, 168n1; role of science in, 8–9, 140–41, 183; Rozanov on, 161, 162, 163, 176, 177; and Russian-Jewish activism, 194; Saratov trial's outcome and, 90; scapegoating in, 141–42; superstition vs. science in, 173, 183; wound pattern analysis in, 172, 176–82, *179–81*; Yiddish postcard on, *190*; Yiddish theatrical productions on, 170n62, 197–98

Bekhterev, Vladimir Mikhailovich, 140

Belarus: postrevolutionary, antisemitism in, 204. *See also* Velizh

Belarusian nationalism, 103

Belfer, Noah (Neophyte), 175

Bellarmino, Roberto, 258

Belyi, Andrei, 161

Bemporad, Elissa, 13, 166, 248

Bergelson, Dovid, 241

Bergmann, Werner, 106

Berlin, Hirsh, 60, 65, 66

Berlin, Shmerka, 60–61, 62, 63, 64, 65, 66, 67

Berlinskii, Itska, 79

Berman, Yankel, 84

Bernardino of Siena, 21

Bezalel, Rabbi Judah Leib ben. *See* Maharal of Prague

Białystok pogrom, 192–93

Bible, Hebrew: evidence for Jewish ritual murder in, claims regarding, 86, 163; *golem* in, 43–44; Rozanov on, 160, 162

Bjerknes, Christopher Jon, 246

Black Hundreds movement, 212

blood, and Judaism/Jewish identity: in circumcision ritual, 7, 162–63, 165–66, 176; Dostoevsky on, 157; Nicholas I's special commission on, 87–88; in ritual murder concept, 81, 124–25, 175; Rozanov on, 161, 162, 166, 176; Russian Ministry of Internal Affairs report on, 81

blood, and nationhood: early modern understanding of, 7, 131; Jewish discourse on, 143–45

blood, ethnography of, 22, 31

blood libel: Holocaust as, 46, 146; Jewish counter-legend to, 4, 39, 40, 41–49, 52–53, 120. *See also* ritual murder, Jewish

bloodthirsty Jew, trope of: in Russian culture/literature, 9–10, 151, 158–59, 162–63, 165–66; in Ukrainian folk poem, 223

Bochnia: expulsion of Jews from, 19, 24; witch trial in, 19, 22, 32n6

Bodin, Jean, 26–27

Bogdanov, Anton, 79, 80, 84, 86, 88

Bogen, Boris, 205

Bolshevism, association of Jews with, 207, 222, 224–26, 232, 235n23

Bonch-Bruevich, Vladimir, 210

Bowlt, John, 162

Brent, Jonathan, 242

Breza, Jan, 23

Brothers Karamazov, The (Dostoevsky), 158–59, 160

Buber, Salomon, 47

Bulota, Andrius, 104

Buschhoff, Adolf, 110, 112, 114–18, 125; relations with neighbors, 110, 112, 114–15; as suspect in ritual murder, 116–18, 123

butchers (ritual slaughterers), Jewish, as suspects in ritual murder, 114, 119, 123–25

Bychkov, Vasilii Mikhailovich, 82

cannibalism, allegations of: blood libel replaced by, 227; as demonization of the other, 21, 30; against Jews, 13, 14, 230–31

capitalism, and Jewish domination, anxieties about, 6, 8

Casimir III the Great (King of Poland), 51, 81

Catherine the Great (Empress of Russia), 73

Catholic Church: and antisemitism, 3–4, 5, 7, 103–4; changing relations with Jews, 269–72; condemnation of ritual murder libel, 66, 71n36, 194, 195, 260; and Jewish ritual murder libel, 3–4, 5, 40; and Sandomierz church paintings, 253, 255; Second Vatican Council and, 260, 269, 270; and Simon of Trent's cult, 257–60, 269; teachings about Jews, 126n5

Central Asia, ritual murder accusations in, 222, 226–28

charity, refusal of, ritual murder charges as revenge for, 65, 67–68

Charles the Bald (Holy Roman Emperor), 243

Charney, Daniel, 211, 212, 214

Cheberiak, Vera, 210
Chelminskaia, Maria, 225
Chernyshevsky, Nikolai, 167
children, frequent death of: in imperial Russia, 58–59; in medieval Christian society, 40. *See also under* ritual murder
Chmielnicki pogroms, 50, 55n39
Chmielowski, Benedykt, 22
Christian(s)/Christianity: early, defamatory clichés applied to, 21, 30, 33n20; folklore of, and ritual murder accusations against Jews, 2, 3, 4, 5, 27, 39–40; projective inversion of ritual in, 40, 250; and Soviet worldview, 247–48. *See also* Catholic Church; Eucharist
Christ-killers, charges against Jews as, 104, 126n5, 222
circumcision: in Babel's "Karl-Yankel," 164, 165; as blood sacrifice, 7, 162–63, 165–66, 176; and carnality of Judaism, Rozanov on, 160, 162–63; Soviet agitprop trials of, 165; used as evidence in ritual murder trials, 9, 77–78, 79, 85
Cisło, Mieczysław, 270
Clark, Stuart, 22, 27
Cohn, Norman, 21
collective memory, Jewish blood libel legends and, 52–53
collective performative acts, ritual murder accusations as, 232
Cologne (Germany), 113, 258
communism: and feudalism, in Soviet Russia, 213; Jews and, conspiracy theories regarding, 8, 13, 222, 224–25 (*see also* Judeo-Bolshevism); ritual murder carried out in name of, 225 (*see also* Doctors' Plot)
community, Jewish: Beilis trial and, 141, 163, 182–83, 186–87, 189; collective memory of, Jewish blood libel legends and, 52–53; impact of ritual murder trials on, 4, 24, 31, 141, 182–83, 186–87, 189 confessions, extracted through torture: in medieval Europe, 1–2, 3, 22; modern justice system and inadmissibility of, 112; in Soviet Union, 239, 241, 248
Congress of Antisemites, 123
conspiracy, Jewish: Catholic-oriented publications on, 103–4; Doctors' Plot and allegations of, 241, 245–47; liberalism/capitalism and anxieties about, 6, 8, 246; Perovskii report of 1853 on, 84; *Protocols of the Elders of Zion* on, 8, 222, 243, 244, 246, 247; Rozanov on, 162; theories of, 222; World War II blamed on, 247

converted Jews: medieval images of, 244; suspicions regarding, 79, 83–84, 244–45; testimony on ritual murder, 98, 175, 184n8
Council of Trent, 257, 258
Cracow (Poland), ritual murder accusations in, 25, 220, 231
Crémieux, Adolphe, 12, 188
Crimea, failed project of Jewish homeland in, 246
Crime and Punishment (Dostoevsky), 153
crucifixion: of Christ, Jews held responsible for, 104, 126n5, 222; in Jewish ritual murder, images of, 81, *258*, *263*, *264*; in Jewish ritual murder, popular beliefs regarding, 40, 125, 158, 159, 250
Cubo-Futurists, 162
Czartoryski, Kazimierz Florian, 23
Czech Communist Party, anti-Jewish purges in, 242
Czech nationalism: and ritual murder trial, 118. *See also* Polná; Prague

Dal', Vladimir, 4, 8, 80, 82–83
Damascus Affair, 86, 112, 172, 188, 192
Danilevskii, Nikolai, 153–55
Darwin, Charles, 131
Day of Judaism (Poland), 270–71
Dekel-Chen, Jonathan, 10, 11
deliverance legends, Jewish, 39
de Preo, Carlo, 263–65
De probatis sanctorum historiis (Approved Histories of the Saints), 258
Derzhavin, Gavriil, 66
Dimanshtein, Shimon, 212
Dimša, Petras, 97, 98
Disraeli, Benjamin, 157
Dobroliubov, Nikolai, 152
Doctors' Plot, 13–14, 238–41; as blood libel, 238, 240, 248, 249–50; events leading up to, 241–42, 249–50; and international conspiracy allegations, 241, 245–47; medieval tropes used in, 242–43, 244, 245
Dostoevsky, Fyodor, 156–59; antirationalist stance of, 151–52; Danilevskii and, 153–54; on Jewish question, 156–57, 167, 169n37; on Jewish ritual murder, 158–59; racialized concepts and, 153–54, 157; Rozanov and, 160; and trope of bloodthirsty Jew, 9, 158–59; on vitality of Jews, 151, 160
dream(s), in Jewish blood libel legends, 41, 63
"Dream of a Ridiculous Man, The" (Dostoevsky), 160

Dreyfus, Alfred, 172, 190
Drohobycz, Adil Kikinesh of, 46–52
D-skii, S., 177–78, 182
Dundes, Alan, 40, 250, 251
Dunham, Vera, 249
Durnovo, N. S., 80, 83, 87
Düsseldorf (Germany), 113

Easter. *See* Passover
East European Jews: assimilation of, weak degree of, 104; immigration of, Western Jews' ambivalence regarding, 190, 199, 203n59; transnational intercession on behalf of, 10–13, 187, 188–89, 191–93
economic activities, Jewish: suspicions/resentment of, 96, 103, 104, 205; and ritual murder accusations, 62, 68
Ehrenburg, Ilya, 211
El-Haj, Nadia Abu, 146
Elijah (prophet): in Jewish blood libel legends, 41; at Passover seder, 54n11
Elijah of Chelm, Rabbi, 44
Elisavetgrad pogrom, 5
Elizabeth I (Queen of England), 243
emancipation of European Jewry, and ritual murder discourse, 6, 12, 111
emancipation of serfs, in Russia, 191, 201n16; and relations with Jews, 159
Engelstein, Laura, 162–63
England: execution of Jewish physician in, 243; pogroms in imperial Russia and, 192–93; reaction to Beilis trial, 193–94; ritual murder accusations in, 2, 175
Erasmus of Formia, Saint, 266
Eremeeva, Anna, 57, 60, 63
Essay on the Inequality of the Human Races (Gobineau), 153
Estherke (beloved of Casimir the Great), 51
Estraikh, Gennady, 13, 187
ethnography: of blood, 22, 31; medieval superstition and, 140; role in ritual murder trials, 9, 131, 133; and self-fulfilling prophecies, 146. *See also* anthropology
ethnolinguistic nationalisms, 103
Etinger, Yakov, 241
Eucharist: as cannibalistic feast, pagan Romans on, 21; merger with Passion and Nativity, in ritual murder trials, 22; projective inversion of, ritual murder accusations against Jews as, 40, 250; witch trials involving, 23, 24. *See also* host desecration

evolutionism, 131–32, 146; Russian scholars and, 132–33, 138
Exchange of Compliments (Jabotinsky), 144–45
execution: of Jews, for alleged ritual murder, 23, 35n41, 48, 49; of witches, 24
expulsion of Jews: complicity of local authorities in, 29; from Prague, 195; ritual murder accusations and, 4, 19, 21, 24, 31

faith, crises of, and ritual murder accusations against Jews, 248, 250
Family Question in Russia, The (Rozanov), 160–61
famine(s), in early Soviet Union: cannibalism during, 230; and confiscation of church valuables, 206, 207, 209, 210, 213, 214; and ritual murder accusations, 249
Farkás, Gábor, 120
Fedak, Ivan M., 229
Ferrer, Vincent, 21
folklore: evil, 40. *See also* legend(s); oral culture
folk medicine, role in Jewish communities, 68
Ford, Henry, 246
forensic medicine, in ritual murder trials, 2, 6, 7, 9, 112, 130
Fourier, Charles, 154
France: Dreyfus Affair in, 190; Jewish advocacy in, 188, 196; witch trials in, 21, 68
Franco, Ambrogio, 260
Frank, Friedrich, 111, 126n5
Frank, Jacob, 184n8
Frank, Leo, 190, 196
Frankel, Jonathan, 74, 91n10
Frankfurter, David, 30
Frazer, James, 131, 132, 134, 140, 141, 142, 146
Frunze (Kirgizia), antisemitism in, 227
Fuchs, Alexandra Andreevna, 135
Fuchs, Karl Friedrich, 135
Fuks, Albert, 205, 206, 208, 212–13, 215
Fulda (Germanic town), ritual murder accusation in, 2
Funkenstein, Amos, 40

Gelbak, Leib, 143
Gelbert, Josel, 100, 101, 102
Georgia, ritual murder trial in, 111, 158
Geraci, Robert, 147n7
Germany: assimilated Jews in, Nazi propaganda on, 245; Jewish advocacy organization in, response to Beilis trial, 196, 197, 199; Nazi, legitimation of antisemitism by, 220, 223–25,

229, 230; peasant attitudes toward Jews in, 116; ritual murder trials in, 9, 110, 111, 112, 113–18, 123, 175; witch trials in, 68. *See also specific locations*
Gersevanov, Nikolai, 153
Giers, Aleksandr Karlovich, 87, 88
Gindin, Meir, 205–6, 208, 211, 212
Gippius, Zinaida, 163
Gobineau, Arthur de, 153, 155
Golden Bough, The (Frazer), 132, 142
Golden Rose of Lwów, 49
Golem legends, 39, 43–46, 54n17
Golitsyn, Count Aleksandr, 66
Goloshchekin, Filipp, 226
Gorky, Maxim, 164, 207
Gottwald, Klement, 242
"Great Russian" chauvinists, 84
Gregory XII, Pope, 258
Gregory XIII, Pope, 258
Grodno, ritual murder charge in, 66
Gromyko, Andrei, 250
Grossman, Leonid, 158
Grotius, Hugo, 19, 29, 33n20
Gruzenberg, Oskar, 163
Guglina, Minareiza, 79–80
guilt, projective inversion of: ritual murder accusations against Jews as, 40, 250; in Soviet antisemitic campaigns, 250–51
Gurland, H. J., 50

Habsburg Empire. *See* Austria-Hungary
Halbwachs, Maurice, 52
Handler, Andrew, 121
Handt, Wilhelm van de, 115
Harrison, Marguerite, 206
Hasid, Rabbi Judah, 44
Hasid, Rabbi Samuel, 44
Hasidism: Beilis trial and targeting of, 166, 177, 178; mysticism associated with, 68; suspicions regarding, 86
Hearst, William Randolph, 194
Hebrew Bible. *See* Bible
Hebrew Immigrant Aid Society, New York, 188
Hegmann, Heinrich, 115
Hegmann, Johann, 110, 113–14, 117, 123
Heinrich Institoris, 21–22, 27
heretics, defamatory clichés applied to, 21, 30, 33n20
hermeneutical Jew, of medieval Christian theology, 22
Herodotus, 135

Herzen, Alexander, 134–35
Herzl, Theodor, 143
Heynick, F., 243
Hilfsverein der deutschen Juden, 196, 197, 199
Hilsner, Leopold, 112, 118, 123, 125
Hinderbach, Johannes, 257
Hindin, Meir. *See* Gindin
Hirsch, Baron de, 188
History of the World (Schedel), 258, *259*
Hitler, Adolf, 247. *See also* Nazism
Hofshteyn, Dovid, 241
Holocaust, blood libels and, 46, 146
Holocaust survivors: golem legend among, 45–46; in Soviet Union, 230, 247
Holy Roman Empire, ritual murder libel in, 2
Horn, Eva, 244
host desecration, by Jews: medieval stories of, 4; trials for, in early modern Poland, 19, 23, 24, 32n3; witch trials and accusations of, 19, 22, 24–25, 32n6
Hrůzová, Anežka, 118, 123, 124
Hsia, R. Po-chia, 22, 26
Hubicki, Szymon, 19, 28
human sacrifice: anthropologists/ethnographers on, 9, 131, 132, 141; Jewish, Perovskii report on, 86; Jewish, popular stereotype of, 140; logic of, in Russian nationalism, 142; as scapegoating, 132–33, 141; Votiak, accusations of, 133–39. *See also* ritual murder

Idel, Moshe, 44, 54n24
IFA. *See* Israel Folktale Archives
images, of Jewish ritual murder, 257; in Ministry of Internal Affairs report, 81; in Nuremburg, 22; in Sandomierz, 4–5, 253, *254*, 261–63, *262*, *263*, 266–69, 270–71; Simon of Trent's cult and, 4–5, 257, *259*, 261, *264*, 266, *267*, 271, 272
images, of Jews, in medieval Christian art, 21, 22
immigration: of East European Jews, Western Jews' ambivalence regarding, 190, 199, 203n59; of Mendel Beilis, 189, *190*, 194, 197, 198–99; of Soviet Jews, to Israel, 249–50
infanticide: in early modern Russia, 58–59; among Jews, biblical story used as proof of, 86; medieval superstitions regarding, 21, 23, 26. *See also* ritual murder, Jewish
Infanticidia (Sandomierz painting), 253, *254*, 261
Innocent IV, Pope, on ritual murder libel, 66, 71n36, 194

Index

inquisition: in medieval ritual murder trials, 1–2; Soviet practices compared to, 248. *See also* torture
Institoris, Heinrich, 21–22, 27
international assistance, Jewish, 10–13, 188–89; anxieties regarding, 207, 245–47; Beilis trial and, 11, 187–90, 193–99
international conspiracy, allegations of, Doctors' Plot and, 241, 245–47
International Jew, The (Ford), 246, 247
Israel: blood group population genetics in, 145, 146; establishment of, 248, 249; propaganda against, blood libel and, 14; Soviet Jews' emigration to, 249–50
Israel Folktale Archives (IFA), 41, 53n10, 54n17
Italy: ritual murder accusations in, 14. *See also* Trent
Iurlov, Fedor, 79, 84, 88
Iushchinskii, Andrei, 172, 185; grave of, 14; killers of, 172; wounds of, 172, 176–82, *179–81*
Iushkevicher, Iankel, 79–80, 84, 85, 86, 88
Ivanov, Emel'ian, 56, 57, 59, 64
Ivanov, Fedor, 56, 57, 58
Ivanovna, Mar'ia, 79
Iwaszkiewicz, Jarosław, 266

Jabotinsky, Vladimir (Zeev), 144–45
JAFC. *See* Jewish Anti-Fascist Committee
Jaworski, Rudolf, 104
Jew(s): Babel on, 166–67; depiction in medieval Christian art, 21, 22; as diaspora nationality, 248; Dostoevsky on, 156–59, 167, 169n37; nationalism of, blood libel and, 146; as the other, 103, 224–25; racialized concepts of, 141, 142–43, 153, 157; restrictions on residence of, 62, 71n21; Rozanov on, 160–63, 167; vitality of, Russian writers on, 151, 160, 163, 166, 167. *See also specific topics and locations*
Jewish Anti-Fascist Committee (JAFC), trial of, 241, 246
Jewish blood libel legend, 4, 39, 40, 41–49, 52–53, 120
Jewish Colonization Association, 188
"Jewish Question, The" (Dostoevsky), 156–57, 160, 167
Jewish ritual murder. *See under* ritual murder
Jewish Ritual Murder, The (Schramm), 225–26
John Paul II, Pope, 269
Joint Distribution Committee, 205, 207, 210; Doctors' Plot and allegations against, 245–46

Josephus (historian), 163
Judaism: carnal, Rozanov's theory of, 160, 161, 162–63, 166; major texts of, suspicion regarding, 7–8, 17n19; and ritual murder of gentiles, Pranaitis on, 174–75. *See also* blood, and Judaism; Kabbalah; Talmud; Zohar
Judeo-Bolshevism, myth of, 207, 222, 224–26, 232, 235n23
Judith (apocryphal heroine), 51
Junkermann, Heinrich, 9, 117–18, 123

Kabbalah, 184n6; and ritual bloodletting: Beilis trial testimonies on, 182; popular beliefs regarding, 7–8; Russian writers on, 176
Kalinin, Mikhail, 211
Kanin, Stepan, 75, 76, 78
Kapralski, Sławomir, 255
Karamzin, Nikolai Mikhailovich, 135
"Karl-Yankel" (Babel), 164–67
Karniolin-Pinskii, Matvei Mikhailovich, 81
Kasachevskaia, Daria, 64–65, 67
Katz, Hirsh, 97, 98
Kavelin, A. A., 81
Kazan: alleged Jewish atrocities in, 82; Votiak people in vicinity of, charges against, 133–39
Kazan University, ethnographers affiliated with, 135, 136, 137–38
Kermenskii (investigating officer in Tel'shi), 98
Khovanskii, Nikolai Nikolaevich, 69
Khrushchev, Nikita, 225
Khvol'son, Daniil Avraamovich, 87, 88, 91n10, 93n49, 93n59
Kielce pogrom, 220, 270
Kierel, Szymon, 22
Kiev (Kyiv): anti-Jewish pogrom of 1944 in, 224; Beilis trial in, 111, 172; Nazi occupation of, 224–26; return of Soviet power in, 225; trope of bloodthirsty Jew in, 223. *See also* Beilis ritual murder trial
Kieval, Hillel, 6, 9, 173, 243–44
Kiev University, 140
Kikinesh, Adil, 46–52
Kikinesh, Moshe, 46, 47, 48
Kirghizia, ritual murder accusations in, 226–28
Kishinev pogrom, 193
Kisin, Abram, 63
Klaipeda (Lithuania), refugee crisis in, 188
Kleczew (Poland), witch trials in, 19
Klier, John, 80, 92n27, 153
Kmita, Jan Achacy, 19
Kochetov, Ioakim Semenovich, 82–83

Kogan, Boris, 240
Kogan, Mikhail, 240
Kokhanskii, Vasilii, 59
Koldovsky, Samson, 209–11
Kölling, Bernd, 117
Kol'tsov, Mikhail, 209
Koni, Alexander, 159
Konitz (Germany), ritual murder trial in, 111, 112, 118
Korey, William, 215
Kornblatt, Judith Deutsch, 176, 177
Korolenko, Vladimir, 133
Kovno (Lithuania): restrictions on Jewish residence in, 62, 71n21. *See also* Tel'shi
Kraków (Poland). *See* Cracow
Krasnowski, Jerzy, 266–69
Kriuger (Saratov provincial secretary), 84–85, 86, 88
Kronstadt rebellion, 207
Kryvyi Rih (Ukraine), ritual murder accusation in, 231
Kucharzowa, Katarzyna, 24
Kumzovna, Karolina, 97, 98
Kunia, ritual murder accusation in, 25
Kušeliauskas, Serafinas Laurynas, 104
Kuskova, Yekaterina, 210
Kutaisi, ritual murder trial in, 111, 158
Kuznetsov, S. K., 136
Kyiv. *See* Kiev

Laba, Shlomo, 45
Lambek, Michael, 30
Langmuir, Gavin, 222, 240, 248, 250
legend(s): Christian, of Jewish ritual murder, 2, 3, 4, 5, 27, 39–40, 68, 69n5, 111; definition of, 39; Jewish, in response to ritual murder libel, 4, 39, 40, 41–49, 52–53, 120; as sites of memory, 52–53; of witchcraft, 3, 27
Leib, Aryeh, 46
Lenin, Vladimir, 207, 209, 211, 221, 226
Leningrad, siege of, 230
Leo Frank Affair, 190, 196
Levison, Vasilii Andreevich, 87, 88
liberalism: backlash against, and antisemitism, 7, 8, 246; in imperial Russia, Beilis trial and, 186, 189, 190, 191
lieux de mémoire (sites of memory), 253, 254, 272; legends as, 52–53
Limor, Ora, 40
Lindanus, William Damasus, 260
Lippomano, Luigi, 23, 258

literature, antisemitic: Lithuanian, 103–4; Polish, 25–26, 27–28, 96–97, 98, 99; Russian, 8, 9–10, 81, 89, 156–63, 164–67
Lithuanian lands: antisemitic ideology in, 103–4; blood libel in, 95–96, 105; reenactment of Christ's Passion in, 96. *See also* peasants, Lithuanian; Polish-Lithuanian Commonwealth
Liutostanskii, Ippolit, 91n10
Lokotkov (Saratov suspect), 78, 88
Lopez, Rodrigo, 243
Łosice (Poland), ritual murder accusation in, 23, 24
Lowenthat, David, 255
Lublin (Poland): restrictions on Jewish residence in, 62; ritual murder trials in, 1–2, 19, 24, 28; witch trial in, 19
Lukashevich (inspector), 60, 65
Luther, Martin, 243
Lviv: cannibalism in, allegations of, 230–31; historical memory of blood libel in, 223; Nazi occupation and legitimation of antisemitism in, 223–24, 229, 230; pogrom of 1941 in, 232; Polish-Ukrainian alliance against Jews in, 220, 232; ritual murder accusation in, 13, 228–33; under Soviet rule, 228; during World War II, 220, 228
Lwów, Golden Rose of, 49

Maciejowski, Bishop, 19
Madruzzo, Cristoforo, 257
magic: Judaism associated with, 22, 68; vs. science, in ritual murder trials, 173, 183
Magnitskii, Vasilii Konstantinovich, 137
Maharal of Prague (Rabbi Judah Leib ben Bezalel), 54n12; legends about, 41–46
Maksimov, Sergei Vasilyevich, 135–36
Maksimova, Avdot'ia, 64
Malik, Iakov, 250
Malleus maleficarum (Hammer of witches), 21–22, 27, 36n66
Mariani, Michel Angelo, 260
Maria Teresa (Empress of Austria-Hungary), 195
Markish, Peretz, 241
Marshall, Louis, 192, 198
Martha (daughter of Boethus), 50
martyrdom: in Jewish blood libel legends, 46–52; of victims of alleged ritual murder, 14, 23, 25. *See also* Simon of Trent
Martyrologium Romanum, 257, 258–60
Maslov, Mikhail, 75, 76–78, 85, 86

Matteoni, Francesca, 31
Maze, Jacob, 212
medicine: Doctors' Plot and, 243; Jewish race from perspective of, 143; medieval superstition and, 140, 242; use in ritual murder trials, 2, 6, 7, 8–9, 76–78, 173–74, 244
medieval Europe: Jewish converts in, suspicion regarding, 244; Jewish physicians in, 242–43; ritual murder trials in, 1–2, 4, 17n19, 175, 249; witch trials in, 3, 18–20, 22, 23–24, 27, 30, 35n32
Meir, Golda, 246
Memel (Lithuania), refugee crisis in, 188
memory: collective, Jewish blood libel legends and, 52–53; sites of *(lieux de mémoire)*, 253, 254, 272
Merchant of Venice (Shakespeare), 247
Merezhkovskii, Dmitrii, 161, 163
Miczyński, Sebastjan, 22, 24, 25, 27, 29, 31
Mikhoels, Solomon, 230, 240, 241, 245, 246
Ministry of Internal Affairs (Russia), investigation into Jewish ritual murder, 80–83, 87, 89
Minsk, ritual murder allegations in, 68
Mirandola, Gianfrancesco Pico della, 26
Mirele of Brahilov, 49
Miriam (daughter of Boethus), 49–50
misogyny, in witchcraft accusations, 20, 30
Modebdze, Sara Iosifovna, 158
Mogilev province, Jewish population in: ritual murder charges against, 68; Saratov ritual murder case and alleged connections to, 80, 84
Mogilner, Marina, 7, 9
Molotov, Viacheslav, 230, 246
Montefiore, Claude, 93n49
Montefiore, Moshe (Moses), 12, 188
Mortara Affair, 188, 195
Moscow: in early Soviet era, 204–5; Jewish population in, 205, 214; ritual murder accusation in, 13, 187, 204, 208–13, 215
Moscow Jewish Religious Community, 205
Moscow Society for Helping Jews in Need, 205
Moskvin, Ivan Nikolaev, 75–76
Multan human sacrifice case, 133; Beilis trial compared to, 140, 147n7, 159; expert testimony at, 137–39
Murav, Harriet, 9, 147n7, 176
Musiał, Stanisław, 270
mysticism: in Beilis ritual murder trial, 176–77, 178; in Hasidic communities, 68; in late imperial Russia, 173

Nakhamkis, Ovshii, 213
Nash, Manning, 30
Nathan, Paul, 113
nation(s): blood as trope for, 7, 131; life span of, Danilevskii on, 154
nationalism: Jewish, blood libel and, 146; and pogroms against Jews, 95, 102–3; and ritual murder charges against Jews, 6, 130; science and, 146
nationality: Jewish, blood and, 6–7, 143–45; racialized notions of, 152, 156
Naumov, Vladimir, 242
Nazism, and antisemitism, 220, 223–25, 229, 230, 232
neighborhood disputes: and ritual murder charges, 5, 65, 67–68, 139; and witchcraft charges, 67
Neophyte (Noah Belfer), 175
Neo-Primitivists, 161
Ner, Zvi Rav, 270
New Economic Policy (NEP), Soviet, 205, 207; and antisemitic sentiments, 205, 213; ritual murder accusations during early years of, 13, 204
newspapers. *See* press
Nicholas I (Tsar of Russia): ritual murder accusations against Jews and, 5, 87, 99–100; suppression of Uniate Church under, 70n17
Nicholas II (Tsar of Russia): anti-Jewish policies of, Western pressure regarding, 192; assassination of, presented as ritual murder, 226; Beilis trial and, 189, *190*; pogroms during rule of, 222; Revolution of 1905 and, 185; and State Duma, 186
Nider, Johannes, 26, 30
Nirenberg, David, 248–49
Nitkiewicz, Krzysztof, 271
Nora, Pierre, 52, 253, 254
Nordau, Max, 143, 144
Nuremburg city hall, stained glass art in, 22

Obriady zhidovskie (Jewish Rites), 81, 92n27
"Odessa" (Babel), 164, 166
Odorico, Raynaldo, 258
officials: and expulsion of Jews, complicity in, 29; and mob violence following ritual murder accusations, efforts to prevent, 100–101, 102, 117; response to ritual murder charges, 98–99, 105–6; Soviet, stance against antisemitism, 13, 212, 213, 214–15, 221, 227–28, 229–32; views of, and investigation of ritual murder charges, 98–99

Index | 287

Old Multan: Votiaks of, 133. *See also* Multan human sacrifice case
Olfactory and Tactile Relationship of Jews to Blood, The (Rozanov), 161, 166, 177
Operation Vistula, 232
oral culture: and ritual murder accusations, 68, 70n5, 96, 98. *See also* legend(s); rumors
Origins of Languages, The (Renan), 152
Ostling, Michael, 3, 4
otherness: defamatory clichés associated with, 21, 30; of Jews, nationalistic ideology and, 103; of Jews, Nazi brutality and, 224–25; Russian nationalism and, 139, 142
Ottoman Empire: ritual murder charges in, 188 (*see also* Damascus Affair); Russia's war against, Dostoevsky on, 156

Pale of Settlement, 62; conversion as way to escape, 84; pogroms of 1880s in, 96, 104–5
Passover (Easter): anti-Jewish sentiment during, 96; misrepresentation of Jewish rituals at, 40, 86; Prophet Elijah at, 41, 54n11; ritual murder accusations during, 2, 7, 40, 48, 56, 96, 118, 175
Pavlov, Evgenii Vasil'evich, 140
Pavskii, Gerasim Petrovich, 87, 88
peasants, German, attitudes toward Jews, 116
peasants, Lithuanian: attitudes toward Jews, 97, 104; testimonies in ritual murder investigation, 97, 98; vigilante justice threatened by, 100–101, 102, 105–6
peasants, Russian: attitudes toward Jews, 206–7; discourse of ritual murder used by, 139; emancipation of, and relations with Jews, 159; vs. Jews, Dostoevsky on, 157; in Kronstadt rebellion of 1921, 207; Russian identity embodied by, 142; at turn of 20th century, 186, 191
Peretz, I. L., 49
Perovskii, Lev Alekseevich, 81–82; report on Jewish ritual murder, 83–87
Peter of Bern, 26
Petrashevskii circle, 153
Petravičius, Juozapas, 97, 98
Petrycy, Sebastian, 28
philanthropy. *See* transnational intercession
Pietromartino di Anversa, *Simonino da Trento* by, 266, *267*
Pobedonostsev, Konstantin, 159
pogroms against Jews: explanations for, 5–6, 95, 101, 102–6; in imperial Russia, 5–6, 102,

188, 192–93, 221–22; in Pale of Settlement (1880s), 96, 104–5; in Polish-Lithuanian Commonwealth, 50, 55n39, 95, 101, 102; Revolution of 1905 and, 102, 188, 193; ritual murder accusations and, 24, 95, 190; during Russian Civil War, 189, 221; in Soviet Union, 207–8, 232; Western Jews' response to, 192–93; after World War II, 219–20, 230
Polacco, Martino Teofilo, 261
Poland, early modern. *See* Polish-Lithuanian Commonwealth
Poland, post-World War II: anti-Jewish violence in, 36n46, 219–20, 230; culturally homogeneous population of, 255; ritual murder accusations in, 220, 231
Poland, present-day: Catholic-Jewish relations and dialogue in, 269–72; church paintings of Jewish ritual murder in, 4–5, 253, *254*, 261–63, *262*, *263*, 266–69, 270–71; memory about Jews in, 253–55, 256
Poles, and Ukrainians, alliance against Jews, 220, 232, 237n60
Polish-Lithuanian Commonwealth: animosity toward Jews in, 25–26, 27–28; Christian-Jewish interactions in, 19, 31–32, 38n92, 62, 96–97; demonological literature in, 18–19, 26–27; expulsion of Jews from, 4, 19, 21, 24, 29; host-desecration trials in, 19, 23, 24, 32n3; partitions of, 57, 175; pogroms against Jews in, 50, 55n39, 95, 101, 102; restrictions on Jewish residence in, 62, 71n21; ritual murder accusations/trials against Jews in, 1–2, 3, 4, 16n7, 19, 22, 23–24, 31, 175, 253, 261; Simon of Trent's cult and, 4–5, 25, 260–61; tracts on ritual murder in, 24–26, 27–28; witch trials in, 3, 18–20, 22, 23–24, 27, 30, 35n32. *See also* Lithuanian lands; *specific locations*
Polish nationalism, 103, 109n46
politics, and ritual murder charges, 130
Polná, ritual murder trial in, 111, 112, 118, 123–25
Prague: anti-Jewish purges in, 242; expulsion of Jews from, 195; Holocaust survivors in, golem legend among, 45–46
praise legends (*aggadot shevah*), 39, 43
Pranaitis, Justin (Justinas) Bonaventūra, 8, 103, 161, 174–75, 177
Praszka, expulsion of Jews from, 4, 24
press: on Beilis trial, 166, 173, 193–94, 196; Catholic Lithuanian, antisemitic stereotypes in, 104; on Doctors' Plot, 238, 239–41,

press (*cont.*)
243, 244, 245–47; and Jewish transnational intercession, 11, 12; on Kutaisi trial, 158; Lithuanian, and anti-Jewish violence, 101, 108n39; on Moscow trial, 13, 208, 209–10, 212, 213; on Polná trial, 124; and ritual murder accusations, sensationalization of, 2, 12, 28, 111; Russian, as challenge to autocracy, 186; Russian, on "Jewish question," 191; Russian, racialized concepts in, 152; on Šalnaičiai ritual murder accusation, 101, 108n39; Ukrainian, on Nicholas II's assassination, 226; on Votiak sacrificial rituals, 137, 139; Western, on antisemitism in early Soviet Russia, 207; Western, on Beilis trial, 193–94, 196; Western, on Moscow trial, 13, 210, 212; Western, on pogroms in Russia, 193; on Xanten ritual murder trial, 116

Primitive Culture (Tylor), 131–32
primitivism, 161. *See also* savagery
projective inversion: ritual murder accusations against Jews as, 40, 250; in Soviet Union, 250–51
Prokof'eva, Agaf'ia, 56, 57, 59, 63, 64
Prokof'eva, Kharitina, 56, 64
Protocols of the Elders of Zion, 8, 222, 243, 244, 246, 247
Pruszcz, Piotr Hyacinth, 26
Przemyśl (Poland), host-desecration accusation in, 22, 24–25, 32n6
Purim (Jewish holiday), Christian suspicions regarding, 40, 85–86, 93n49

Rabinbach, Anson, 244
race(s): competition of, Social Darwinism on, 141; concept of, biology vs. culture in, 152; Danilevskii on, 154, 155; inferior, as sacrificial scapegoat, 142; and Jewish identity, 6–7, 141, 142–43, 153, 157; types of, Gobineau on, 153; use of term in 19th century, 152, 154
racialist theories: absence in Lithuanian antisemitic ideology, 104; of Jewish ritual murder, 2, 6–7, 140–41; in Russia, 153–55; in Western Europe, 153, 154
Rafes, Moyshe, 213–14
Rawa (Poland), expulsion of Jews from, 4, 24
Reed, Andrew, 4, 9, 173
Reitzes, Hayim and Joshua, 46, 49
Renan, Ernst, 152
resettlement programs, for East European Jews, 188, 189. *See also* immigration

revenge, ritual murder charges as, 65, 67–68
Revolution of 1905 (Russia), 185; and pogroms against Jews, 102, 188, 193, 222
Ricchi, Pietro, 261
Rinkevičius, Nikodemas, 100
ritual murder, Jewish: Beilis trial and confirmation of, 141, 163, 182–83, 186–87, 189; Dostoevsky on, 158–59; doubts regarding, 28–29; fascination with, 131; folklore/legends of, 2, 3, 4, 5, 27, 39–40, 68, 69n5, 111; iconographic vocabulary of, 257; Nicholas II's assassination presented as, 226; Perovskii report on, 83–87; Polish tracts on, 24–26, 27–28; Pope Innocent IV's rejection of, 66, 71n36, 194; popular conceptions of, 111, 122; Rozanov on, 161, 162, 176; Russian Ministry of Internal Affairs report on, 80–83, 87. *See also* images, of Jewish ritual murder
ritual murder accusations against Jews: anti-communist propaganda and, 224–25; antisemitism and, 62, 68, 222; Catholic Church and condemnation of, 66, 71n36, 194, 260; Catholic Church and spread of, 3–4, 5, 40; in Central Asia, 222, 226–28; as collective performative acts, 232; contingency vs. structure in, 125; crises of faith and, 248, 250; cultural trends in Russia and, 151, 161, 162, 163, 176; Doctors' Plot compared to, 238, 240, 248, 249–50; in early modern Europe, 2, 3–4, 6–9, 11–12; economic rivalries and, 62, 68; ethnographic discourse and, 9, 131; evolution of, 173–74; explanations for, 5, 14, 40, 62, 64–65, 67–68, 248, 250; and expulsion of Jews, 4, 19, 21, 24, 31; history of, 2, 175; Jewish blood libel legend in response to, 4, 39, 40, 41–49, 52–53, 120; in medieval Europe, 1–2, 4, 17n19, 175, 249; neighborhood disputes and, 5, 65, 67–68, 139; persistence of, 14, 58; and pogroms against Jews, 24, 95, 190; as projective inversion of Christian ritual, 40, 250; religious and civic authorities discrediting, 66–67; religious roots of, 3–4, 5, 7; rumors and, 5, 11, 14, 57, 59, 64–65, 68, 79, 83, 97–98, 100, 117–18, 120–21; in Russian Empire, 57, 66–67, 68, 73, 89, 175–76; Russia's Great Reforms of 1860s and, 130; scholarship on, 2–3; secularization of, 6, 11–12; small towns and, 3, 6, 70n5, 112–13; Soviet government's response to, 13, 212, 213, 220; in Soviet Union, 13, 187, 204, 208–13, 220, 221, 222–23, 226–28, 248; transnational efforts to

combat, 10–13, 187–90; and violence against Jews, 24, 31, 36n46, 99, 219–20; Votiak sacrificial ritual accusations compared to, 136, 137; before World War I, 111
ritual murder trial(s): appeals to science and medicine at, 2, 6, 7, 8–9, 76, 112, 117–18, 123, 130–31, 173–74, 244; church authorities' intervention in, 23; cultural work accomplished by, 20; decline in Western and Central Europe, 57; defense in, 12; impact on Jewish communities, 4, 24, 31, 141, 182–83, 186–87, 189; legal measures preventing, 66–67, 90n2; medieval, 1–2, 4, 17n19, 175; merger of Eucharist, Passion, and Nativity in, 22; modern, 111–12, 122–23; sensationalization of, 2, 12, 28, 111; suspects in, identifying, 116–18, 125; witch trials compared to, 3, 4, 20–24, 30–31, 67–68. *See also specific trials/locations*
Rogger, Hans, 14, 168n1
Roth, Cecil, 40, 242
Rothberg, Michael, 272
Rothschild, Nathaniel, 193, 194, 195
Rozanov, Vasilii, 8, 159–63; antirationalist stance of, 151–52; and Babel, 165–66, 167; and Dostoevsky, 160; on Jewish ritual murder, 161, 162, 176; *Olfactory and Tactile Relationship of Jews to Blood, The*, 161, 166, 177; "Secret Writing of the Jews, The," 161–62; and trope of bloodthirsty Jew, 9, 162–63, 165–66; on vitality of Jews, 151, 160, 163
Rozanov, Vladimir, 149n38
Rubin, Miri, 31
rumors: and demonization of the other, 21, 30; origins of, 128n27; and ritual murder accusations against Jews, 5, 11, 14, 57, 59, 64–65, 68, 79, 83, 97–98, 100, 117–18, 120–21; of Votiak sacrificial rituals, 137
Russia and Europe (Danilevskii), 153
Russian antisemitic literature: Babel and, 164–67; Dostoevsky and, 9, 156–59; Ministry of Internal Affairs report (1844) and, 81; Rozanov and, 8, 159–63; Saratov ritual murder trial and, 89; trope of bloodthirsty Jew in, 9–10, 158–59
Russian Civil War: anti-Bolshevik propaganda during, 224, 235n23; anti-Jewish pogroms during, 189, 221
Russian Empire: blood libel in, spread of, 175–76; government response to ritual murder charges in, 5, 87, 99–100, 105–6, 173; Great Reforms of 1860s in, 130, 191, 201n16; heterogeneous society of, challenges associated with, 132, 139; infant mortality in, 58–59; Jewish population of, 57; Ministry of Internal Affairs report on Jewish ritual murder in, 80–83, 87; Perovskii report on Jewish ritual murder in, 83–87; pogroms against Jews in, 5–6, 102, 188, 192–93, 221–22; ritual murder accusations in, 5, 57, 66–67, 68, 73, 89, 175–76; ritual murder trials in, legal requirements for, 66–67, 90n2; upheavals at turn of 20th century, 139, 185–86, 190–91; war against Ottoman Empire, Dostoevsky on, 156. *See also specific locations*
Russian identity: ambiguity at turn of 20th century, 139, 141–42; Danilevskii on, 155; fears of Jewish efforts to undermine, 83–84, 89
Russian nation: organicist model of, 156. *See also* peasants, Russian
Russian nationalism, and ritual murder charges against Jews, 130, 139, 141–42
Ryvkin, Miron, 61

Sakharov, Andrei, 236n59
Salmonowicz, Stanisław, 21
Šalnaičiai (Vil'na province): anti-Jewish violence in, 6, 101; ritual murder accusation in, 100–102, 108n30
Samoilov, David, 204
Sandomierz (Poland): church paintings of Jewish ritual murder in, 4–5, 253, *254*, 261–63, *262*, *263*, 266–69, 270–71; evolution of Jewish-Christian relations and, 270–72; ritual murder accusations in, 4, 22, 24, 26, 253, 255, 261, 266–69; witch trial in, 22
Saratov (Russia): history of, 73–74; Jewish population in, 73, 74, 83–84
Saratov ritual murder trial, 4, 9, 73, 74–80; Alexander II on, 88, 89; medical reports used in, 76–78, 173; Perovskii report on, 83–87; and perpetuation of blood libel, 89; special commission on, 87–88, 93n58; State Council on, 88–89; suspects in, 78–80, 84, 88, 90n1; as turning point in anti-Jewish sentiments, 74, 89–90
Sauer, Lorenz, 258
savagery: anthropological perspectives on, 132, 141; in development of races/nations, Danilevskii on, 154; fascination with, transition to modernity and, 139–40; Jews

savagery (cont.)
  associated with, in early modern Europe, 9, 21, 140; as "survival," 141. *See also* human sacrifice
scapegoating: in Beilis trial, 141–42; human sacrifice as, 132–33, 141
Scharf, József, 119–22
Schedel, Hartmann, *History of the World*, 258, *259*
Schiff, Jacob, 192, 196, 202n39
Schramm, Max Helmutt, 225–26
Schudrich, Michael, 270, 271
Schultz, Magdalene, 40
science: Doctors' Plot and, 243, 244; and modern nationalism, 146; in ritual murder trials, 2, 6, 7, 8–9, 76, 112, 117–18, 123, 130–31, 173–74, 244; role in Beilis trial, 8–9, 140–41, 183; vs. superstition, in Beilis trial, 173, 183
Second Vatican Council, 260, 269, 270
"Secret Writing of the Jews, The" (Rozanov), 161–62
Sefer Yezirah (The Book of Creation), 44
Seifullina, Lidia, 205
sexuality, Judaism and, Rozanov on, 160, 163, 166
Shakespeare, William, 247
Sharett, Moshe, 250
Shcheglovitov, Ivan, 209
Shcherbakov, Aleksandr S., 239, 240, 241
Shepilov, Dmitry, 239
Sherstobitov, Efim Grigor'ev, 75
Sherstobitov, Feofan, 74–75, 77, 85
Shimeliovich, Boris, 241, 245
Shklovsky, Viktor, 163
Shlifferman, Mikhel, 78–79, 84, 85, 88
show trials, Soviet, 245
Shtern, Lina, 241
Shternberg, Lev, 145
Shternshis, Anna, 165
Sicher, Efraim, 164, 166
Sidonskii, Fedor Fedorovich, 87, 88
Sikorsky (Sikorskii), Ivan Alekseevich, 9, 140–41, 144, 145, 149n37, 174
Silver Age, in Russia, 159, 176; and Beilis trial, 151, 161, 162, 163, 176
Simon of Trent: authoritative Christian histories on, 258–60; cult of, 4, 257–60, 269; cult of, impact in Poland, 4–5, 25, 260–61; iconography associated with, 4–5, 257, *259*, 261, *264*, 266, *267*, 271, 272; liturgy for, 262; Sandomierz paintings alluding to, *254*, 261–63, *262*, *263*, 266–69; trial for alleged ritual murder of, 21, 172

Sixtus IV, Pope, 257
Sixtus V, Pope, 257, 260
Skarga, Piotr, 25
Slansky, Rudolf, 242
Slavophiles: on Russian identity, 141–42; theories of, 153–54, 155
Śleszkowski, Sebastian, 25, 26, 27, 28
Słupecki, Jerzy, 29, 31
Smirnov, Ivan (judge in Moscow trial), 211, 213
Smirnov, Ivan Nikolaevich, 137–38; expert testimony at Multan case, 137–39
Smolensk pogrom, 207–8
Sochaczew (Poland), host-desecration trial in, 19, 23
Social Darwinism, 141
socialism. *See* communism
social knowledge, and ritual murder accusations, 110–11
Society for the Preservation of the Health of the Jewish Population, 145
Soloviev, Evpl Titovich, 136, 137
Sołtyk, Kajetan, 23
Solymosi, Eszter, 118, 119, 123
Solymosi, Maria, 119, 120, 121
Sovietization, antisemitism in response to, 223
Soviet Union: agitprop trials in, 165; anti-Judaism campaigns in, 222–23; antisemitic sentiments in, 206–7, 223; authorities' stance against antisemitism in, 13, 212, 213, 214–15, 221, 227–28, 229–32; Christian theology and worldview of, 247–48; collapse of, ritual murder accusations after, 226; confiscation of church valuables for famine relief in, 206, 207, 209, 210, 213, 214; "diaspora nationalities" in, persecution of, 248; Doctors' Plot in, 13–14, 238–41; Jews in, creation of Israel and, 248, 249–50; Jews in, prominent role of in early years of, 205, 207, 211, 222; Jews in, Stalin's campaign against, 239, 241–42; judicial system in early years of, 211; Moscow in early years of, 204–5; New Economic Policy (NEP) and social tensions in, 13, 204, 205, 207; pogroms in, 207–8, 232; projective inversion of guilt in, 250–51; purges in, 213; ritual murder accusations in, 13, 187, 204, 208–13, 220, 221, 222–23, 226–28, 248; show trials in, 245; during World War II, 224. *See also specific locations*
Spain: Jewish converts in, suspicion regarding, 244; witch hunts and ritual murder trials in, 21

Stalin, Joseph: death of, 14, 242; and Doctors' Plot, 13–14, 238, 239, 240; Nazi propaganda on, 224; and persecution of "diaspora nationalities," 248; postwar campaign against Jews, 239, 241–42, 245
Staliūnas, Darius, 5, 6
Staszów (Poland), expulsion of Jews from, 4, 24
Steklov, Iurii, 213
Stolypin, Pyotr, 209
St. Petersburg (Russia), Haymarket Square kidnapping in, 81, 82
St. Petersburg Military-Medical Academy, 140
Strakhov, Vasilii Ivanovich, 69
Stukov, Innokentii, 209, 212, 213
St. Vladimir University, Kiev, 9, 174
Suchestow, Gabriel, 47
Surius, Laurentius, 258
"survival(s)": concept of, 132; elimination of, 141; human sacrifice as, 131, 137, 141; in life of contemporary Jews, need to address, 143
Suslova, Apollonaria, 160
Sverdlov, Yankel, 226
Szembek, Krzysztof Antoni, 23
Szymon Kierel, 22
Szyszkowski, Bishop, 19

Taft, William Howard, 192
Talmud: and ritual bloodletting, claims regarding, 7–8, 174–75, 177; women martyrs in, 50
Talmud Unmasked, The (Pranaitis), 103
Taub, Emánuel, 119
Teller, Adam, 19
Tel'shi (Lithuania), ritual murder trial in, 5, 97–100, 102
Teofilowicz, Marcin, 261
Terenteeva, Maria, 57, 59, 60, 63–64, 65, 67, 68, 69
Teter, Magda, 4, 14, 29
"Three Gifts" (Peretz), 49
Timasheff, Nicholas, 249
Timashuk, Lidia, 241
Tiszaeszlár (Austria-Hungary), ritual murder trial in, 111, 112, 118–22, 123, 125
Tokarska-Bakir, Joanna, 21, 27
Tokmak (Kirgizia), antisemitism in, 227
Tolstoy, Leo, 160
Tolz, Vera, 152
torture: barrel as instrument of, 266, *268*, 275n56; elimination in Western and Central European criminal investigations, 57, 112; in medieval ritual murder/witch trials, 1–2, 3, 22; in Soviet Union, 248

transnational intercession, Jewish, 10–13, 188–89; anxieties regarding, 207, 245–47; Beilis trial and, 11, 187–90, 193–99
Trent (Italy): Council of, 257, 258; ritual murder trial in, 4, 26. *See also* Simon of Trent
Troitskii, Ivan Gavrilovich, 90, 102
Trotsky, Leon, 211, 221, 235n23
Tsetlin, Evzik, 59, 61, 64, 65
Tsetlina, Khanna, 61, 62, 64, 65, 67, 68, 69
Tylor, Edward, 131–32, 146; influence on Russian ethnographers, 132, 137, 138, 139, 141, 147n3

Udmurts. *See* Votiaks
Ukraine: famine in (1932–1933), cannibalism during, 230; Nazi occupation of, and legitimation of antisemitism, 220, 223–25, 229; ritual murder accusations in, 13, 228–33; trope of bloodthirsty Jew in, 223. *See also* Kiev; Lviv
Ukrainians, and Poles, alliance against Jews, 220, 232, 237n60
Uniate Church/Uniates: partitions of Poland and, 175; suppression in Russia, 70n17; in Ukraine, 237n60; in Velizh, 61, 62
Union of Russian People, 172–73
Union of the Archangel Michael, 172–73
United States: Beilis's emigration to, 189, *190*, 194, 197, 198–99; commercial treaty with Russia (1911), 192; entry into World War II, 228; human rights abuses in, 192, 275n56; Jewish leaders in, responses to ritual murder accusations in Eastern Europe, 10–13, 194, 196; press coverage of Moscow trial in, 13, 210, 212; Soviet Jews accused of collaborating with, 241, 245, 247. *See also under* American

Val, Rafael Merry del, 194
Veidlinger, Jeffrey, 13
Velizh (Russia), Christian-Jewish relations in, 61, 62
Velizh ritual murder trial, 4, 5, 56–69; accusers/witnesses in, 57, 59, 60, 63–64; archive of, 58; events leading to, 56–57, 59; investigation in, 57, 58–61, 63–66; Jewish community's response to, 65; neighborhood dispute and, 65, 67–68; and perpetuation of blood libel, 87, 89; reopening of, 68–69; role of rumors in, 57, 59, 64–65; sociopolitical context of, 57; suspects in, 64–66; and Tel'shi trial, 99–100; verdicts in, 67

Verein zur Abwehr des Antisemitismus, 111
Verga, Yehuda ibn, 266
Vestman (Saratov chief of police), 76
Viker, Khon, 101, 102, 108n33
Vil'na: attitudes toward Jews in, 97; restrictions on Jewish residence in, 62, 71n21; ritual murder allegations in, 22, 68, 97. *See also* Šalnaičiai
Vincent Ferrer, 21
violence against Jews: ritual murder accusations and, 24, 31, 36n46, 99, 219–20. *See also* pogroms against Jews
Vipper, Oskar, 210
vitalism, 161; organicism and, 152
vitality of Jews, Russian writers on, 151, 160, 163, 166, 167
Vlasik, Nikolai, 241
Voronsky, Alexander, 164
Votiaks (Udmurts), 133–34, 159; human sacrifice practiced by, accusations of, 133–39
Vovsi, Miron, 240, 245

Warsaw (Poland), restrictions on Jewish residence in, 62
Weinberg, Robert, 8, 147n7, 187
Weiner, Amir, 224
Wendroff, Zalman, 205
Western Europe: elimination of torture in criminal investigations in, 57, 112; human rights abuses in, at time of Beilis trial, 192. *See also* medieval Europe; *specific countries*
Western Jews: domestic human rights struggles and, 192; and immigration of East European Jews, ambivalence regarding, 190, 199, 203n59; intercession of behalf of coreligionists, 10–13, 187, 188–89, 191–93; and Mendel Beilis, posttrial interactions with, 197–99, 202n45, 203n50
Westeutsche Rundfunk, 115
White, Luise, 27
William of Norwich, 2
witchcraft: ambiguity in constructs of, 30–31; neighborhood disputes and charges of, 67–68; punishment for, 23–24; writings on, 18–19, 26–27. *See also* witch trials
Witch denounced (anonymous tract), 18–19, 27
witch trials: church authorities' intervention in, 23; decline in early 19th century, 57; and host desecration by Jews, claims regarding, 22,

24–25; in Polish-Lithuanian Commonwealth, 3, 18–20, 22, 23–24, 27, 30, 35n32; ritual murder trials compared to, 3, 4, 20–24, 30–31, 67–68
Wolf, Lucien, 193–94, 195, 198, 202n33
women: ethnographers, 135; in Jewish blood libel legends, 39, 46–52; racialized discourses on, 152; in times of persecution, legends about, 50–52, 53; witch trials of, 20–21, 30
World War I, antisemitism on eve of, 111, 173, 175, 176
World War II: allegations of Jewish cannibalism after, 13, 14, 230–31; anti-Jewish violence following, 219–20, 230; Jewish conspiracy blamed for, 247; Nazi occupation and legitimation of antisemitism during, 220, 223–25, 229, 230; Poland after, 255
World Zionist Organization, 143
Wright, Charles H. H., 120

Xanten (Germany), 112–13; history of anti-Jewish disturbances in, 127n20; ritual murder trial in, 110, 111, 113–18, 123

Yeven metzulah (Abyss of Despair), 50
Yurovski, Yakov, 226

Ząbkowic, Stanisław, 27
Zaidman, Ezdra, 79, 84
Zdoniškė Manor, Tel'shi, 95. *See also* Tel'shi
Zeltser, Arkadi, 204
zemstvo system, in Russia, 191, 201n16
Zhdanov, Andrei, 239, 240, 241, 244
Zhemchuzhina, Polina, 246
Zhitomir (Ukraine), restrictions on Jewish residence in, 71n21
Zionist movement, 189; ritual murder accusations and, 12; in Russia, 143–45
Zohar, 184n6; and ritual bloodletting, popular beliefs regarding, 8; and wound analysis in Beilis trial, 178
Zolotnitskii, Nikolai Ivanovich, 136, 137
Żuchowski, Stefan, 4–5, 19, 25, 26, 27, 29, 261, 265
Žukovskis, Augustinas, 97, 98
Zuskin, Benjamin, 241
Żydokomuna, 222, 224. *See also* Judeo-Bolshevism

www.ingramcontent.com/pod-product-compliance
Lightning Source LLC
Chambersburg PA
CBHW070301240426
43661CB00057B/2614